The Intelligent Layman's

Stained & Art Glass
A Unique History of Glass
Design & Making

Judith Neiswander & Caroline Swash

ISBN 0 947798 65 X

© The Intelligent Layman Publishers Ltd
Thornton House, Thorton Road
London SW19 4NG

Judith Neiswander and Caroline Swash
assert their moral rights to be identified
as the authors of this book.

Designed by 442 Design, Edinburgh
www.442design.com

ISBN 0 947798 65 X

November 2005

Contents

Introduction   i

I.   The Arts & Crafts Movement
       in England and America   1
       British Glass from 1890-1930   9
       The Stained Glass Revival in Ireland   12
       The Arts & Crafts Movement in America   14

II.   Art Nouveau in Europe   20
       Glassmaking in France   24
       Jugendstil in Germany and Austria   32
       Art Nouveau in Britain   36

III.   Art Nouveau Glass in America   38
       Tiffany Stained Glass Windows   44
       Tiffany Blown Glass   53
       Tiffany Lamps   58

IV.   Glass Between the Wars   64
       Art Deco Glass in France   68
       Art Deco in England and America   80
       Architectural Glass   84

V.   Form and Function   88

VI.   Post-Impressionists in Glass   104

VII.   Glass Design in
       Scandinavia and Italy   140
       Scandinavia   144
       Finland   145
       Sweden   148
       Italy   154

VIII. Scandinavian Architectural Glass   160

IX.   Innovation in Germany   198
       The Painter in Glass   225

X.   Coventry and Beyond   234
       The Stained Glass Artists of Coventry Cathedral   248
       The Baptistery Window: John Piper and Patrick Reyntiens   249
       The Nave Windows of Coventry Cathedral:
       Lawrence Lee, Keith New & Geoffrey Clarke   266
       The Engravers Art   286
       The Engraving Revival   292

XI.   Pioneers of Studio Glass:
       The Great Leap Forward   296
       Harvey Littleton   300
       Dominick Labino   304
       Erwin Eisch   305
       Marvin Lipofsky   306
       Sam Herman   308

XII.   The 'Rock Star' of Glass   310
       Chihuly's Students   332

XIII. Architectural and Studio
       Glass in the UK   336
       Glass in the Community   364
       Studio Glass   374
       Engraved Glass   388

XIV.   North American
       Architectural Glass   400
       Divine Geometry   406
       A Passion For Paint   416
       Figures and Stories   428
       Creative Technologies   440

XV.   The Czech Connection   448

XVI.   New Ideas in Australia   462

XVII. Japanese Glass Today   496
       Japanese Cut Glass   509
       The Studio Glass Movement in Japan   510

XVIII. The Way Ahead   518
       Glass in the Built Environment   522
       Collaboration and Support   533

       Glossary   554

       Index   558

       Glass Artists   564

'Glass shows thousands of different characteristics depending on the light. We have taken up the challenge of showing how some 300 artists and other workers in glass throughout the world and across time have used it'

Introduction

Glass is a magical medium, capable of infinite manipulation. When hot it can be blown or moulded, drawn out as thin as a butterfly's wing or cast into shapes of awe-inspiring monumentality. When cold it can be cut into infinite shapes, roughened with sand blasting or eaten away with acid. While still transparent it can be made tough enough to stop bullets, or so delicate it trembles at a touch. Glass has been made for thousands of years, yet we are still just beginning to explore its potential.

A complex silicate of metallic oxides, glass dates at least from ancient Mesopotamia. During succeeding centuries it was formed into objets de luxe for the wealthy few or used to adorn architecture, especially houses of faith, with miraculous windows. In the 19th century, new methods of production brought glass within reach of the general population, but it was still mainly used for such functional applications as tableware and lighting, or for the occasional display piece. Only toward the end of the 19th century did individual artists begin to explore this material as an expressive medium, a fascinating evolution that this book attempts to trace over the last 150 years. Most books on glass focus either on the work of a specific artist or on a particular way of working the material – either 'flat' (stained) glass or 'hot' (studio) glass. In this book we have tried to consider both from the artist's point of view. While the different methods have their own histories, at every step experiments by individuals have produced the hugely expanded range of techniques available to glass artists today.

The 'story' of both architectural and hot glass is very much a tale of personal contacts. We have tried to pursue these and to suggest the moments that really made a difference. At times these were the friendships formed when younger artists sought out older practitioners whose work had been almost completely forgotten. At other points they were the conferences (so few in this world compared to the realms of money and business) and the lectures and workshops that made a sudden difference to people's ideas. Through these relationships new ways of thinking about glass have travelled across the globe, so we have tried to examine art glass from a world perspective. Finally, we have surveyed the recent history of glass from the combined point of view of two different disciplines – one of us is an art historian and the other, a practicing artist and teacher. We hope these viewpoints have reinforced each other to produce a thoughtful assessment; we certainly enjoyed the stimulating process of collaboration.

In researching the background to the material presented, we have uncovered many connections between worlds that have hitherto been treated as separate. Paintings, drawings and prints by an artist who has designed glass for architecture are rarely included in books on stained glass, while his or her windows are excluded from publications dealing with fine art. The prejudices that divide art and craft seem to us both to be unnecessary and often risible. That a magnificent window by Georg Meistermann should be deemed less valuable than his paintings or that John Piper's work in glass should be thought less important than his drawings in line and wash seems bizarre. But so it is. With this in mind, we have included where possible the art work that fired the vision that made the glass. Another area of glass work that we have included is the design and experimental fabrication of industrial glass. We have endeavoured to find the 'art' in this subject since the fascinating world of mass-produced glass ware is beyond the scope of this publication. Writing about the activities of artists over the last century and a half has given us almost too much to understand. Regrettably, many very worthy individuals have had to be left out.

Certainly the current state of art glass is both active and exciting, with a responsive audience keen to be engaged. How different from earlier times when the role of stained glass especially was expected to be exclusively ecclesiastical and generally dignified and traditional in approach. Now both art and glass are expected to SAY much more and even to perform a responsible role in society. Environmental glass art, for example, is expected to enhance the effectiveness of hospitals and schools, while anything purchased by the collector is expected to rise in value. There is also a theatrical aspect to contemporary glass art that is immensely stimulating. In the hands of an artist and impresario such as Dale Chihuly, glass can even be part of the world of popular entertainment.

While all these developments are vitalising and welcome, we both feel that the great skills need fostering. Engraving on glass is an incredibly worthwhile thing to do, glass-blowing skills can take a life time to master, painting stained glass windows well is also exceedingly important. These slowly developed hand skills that also require imaginative and meditative minds have been neglected and need encouragement. Their basic disciplines, drawing and painting, have also been sadly neglected. In our desire for the 'New' we must never be satisfied by the facile or half-hearted. Happily, the contemporary world of glass is well supplied with dedicated, if too often under appreciated, practitioners and has become truly international. Advanced by the efficiencies of the internet, it is supported by voluntary societies, by individual enthusiasm and by intermittent bursts of energy from institutions. All this support is essential for the medium to continue to flourish. For when the work is done, the glass artist must almost always be alone.

———————

The authors would like to thank Gordon Birtles of Intelligent Layman Publishers. This book was his brainchild, he made it possible and his good judgment along the way has improved it at every stage. Its shortcomings are, of course, completely our own. IL's Jeanne Berkeljon has kept a complex project organized and moving ahead and, with help of Meenal Gupta, sourced images from all over the world. Susan Mathews at the Stained Glass Museum was enthusiastic from the beginning and Emma Stouts at Christie's Images has been unflaggingly helpful. Finally, we would like to thank our husbands, William Gleason and Michael Swash, for their patience and flexibility in the face of fraught deadlines, and for their unfailing support.

Judith Neiswander

Caroline Swash

*Emerald Green Ikebana with Stem, Three leaves
and Putti, 1991. Permission granted by the
Chihuly Studio. © Dale Chihuly.
Photograph by Scott M. Leen*

I

The Arts & Crafts Movement in England and America

I

The Arts & Crafts Movement in England and America

Although commercially-made panels of decorative glass had long been a staple of the Victorian interior, the artists of the Arts and Crafts Movement took a fresh look at stained glass as a significant art form. In England William Morris (1834-89), a talented pattern designer who revered the handcrafts of the Middle Ages, was the prime mover of this late 19th century crafts revival. He was fascinated by the Gothic cathedrals he visited on his exploratory trips to Europe, with their rich fittings and windows resplendent with mysterious, glowing colour. But when he married Jane Burden in 1859 the shoddy construction and poor design of the available mass-produced household furnishings appalled him. For the couple's first home, The Red House, designed by the architect Philip Webb, Morris and his friends took matters into their own hands, building chunky settles and wardrobes that were brightly painted with tales from medieval literature and creating tiles and window glass embellished with birds and flowers.

Inspired by their success, the friends founded their own firm in 1861 (later re-organised as Morris & Co.) to produce a wide range of furnishings for public and private buildings, including mural decoration, wallpapers, furniture, carving, metalwork, ecclesiastical embroideries and hand-painted tiles, as well as stained glass. Glass formed the major part of the Firm's output, however, especially in the early years when commissions for windows comprised over two-thirds of the Firm's annual turnover. Most of these commissions were for new Gothic Revival churches in the expanding cities of late-Victorian Britain, but the Firm designed many windows for domestic settings as well. Wealthy industrialists commissioned complete schemes of interior decoration for large town and country houses. Stained glass panels depicting romantic tales of gallant knights and fair maids, drawn from the legends of King Arthur and the Knights of the Round Table or the tragic love story of Tristram and Iseult, were in great demand, especially by prosperous middle-class households with literary tastes.

'David Poeta', a stained glass window by Morris & Co. © Christie's Images Limited

A cartoon of St. Dorothea by Burne-Jones for the East window of All Saints Church in Cambridge, England, 1866. © Christie's Images Limited

Drawing on such early sources as illuminated books of hours, herbals and bestiaries, Morris designed windows with lifelike figures and organic motifs copied directly from nature. In a typical early window such as 'David Poeta', a single figure in richly embroidered drapery is silhouetted against a background of clear, diamond-shaped quarries decorated with repeating patterns of tiny flowers and leaves. Completely self-taught, Morris collaborated with artists like Edward Burne-Jones, Dante Gabriel Rossetti, Ford Madox Brown and the architect Philip Webb to interpret traditional stories in compelling new ways that appeared convincingly natural instead of rigid or abstract. In addition to lifelike figures, lush decorative patterns were a key element in the Firm's stained glass. Morris's greatest talent lay in designing these dense, intricate vegetal patterns that became the signature element of the company style.

Much to Morris's disappointment, the Firm never produced its own coloured glass, but purchased glass from John Powell & Sons of Whitefriars. As early as the 1850s, John Powell had joined up with the amateur historian Charles Winston to create coloured glass using the same chemical compounds as medieval glass. This 'antique glass', mouth blown and handmade, was manufactured in intense, glowing colours previously unavailable to modern glass artists. Morris selected the glass and immersed himself in the entire process of transforming a designer's black and white cartoon into the brilliant materials of the medium. His colour sense was particularly acute, as the architect W. R. Lethaby recalled: 'Morris's colour-work glows from within; something happens to the several items in association, as when bells chime.'

Morris often used himself and his friends as models for figures in his windows, especially in the early years. But Burne-Jones was a master of the pose and by 1875 had become the principal figure designer. His refined elongated forms lent a classical elegance to the Firm's tapestries, embroidered hangings and painted panels, as well as the stained glass windows. For the East window of All Saints Church in Cambridge, England, Burne-Jones drew a cartoon of St. Dorothea. The figure shows the influence of Botticelli, his favourite Renaissance artist.

Morris concentrated on pattern design, often re-using Burne-Jones's figures for different compositions. In many windows, backgrounds consisted of conventional foliage that could be easily adapted to openings of different shapes. In a stained glass window based on a design for St. Martin's Church in Brampton, Cumbria, Burne-Jones's figure of the Virgin Mary is robed in complex folds of drapery inspired by his numerous drawings of classical sculpture in the British Museum. Morris created the background of opulent foliage, fruit and flowers in luminous shades of green and gold. The strips along the sides and the panel at the top were added to fill out the shape of the window opening.

A Morris & Co. stained glass window based on a cartoon drawn by Edward Burne-Jones, 1878. © Christie's Images Limited

*William Morris and Edward Burne-Jones in their
later years. Courtesy of The William Morris Gallery*

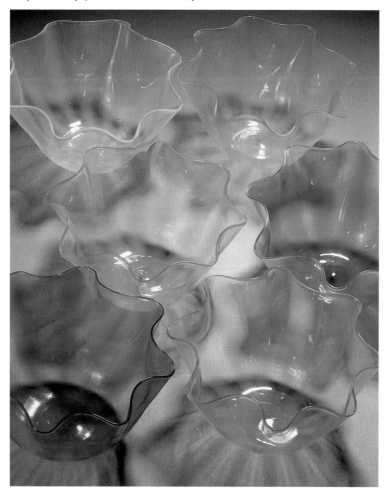

The Firm prospered through the end of the century and beyond. Morris died in 1896 and Burne-Jones two years later. The stained glass department was taken over by John Henry Dearle and continued until 1940, fulfilling numerous commissions from around the world for both ecclesiastical and domestic windows. While many of these windows repeated earlier designs, Morris's innovative spirit inspired generations of glass artists to explore the medium in new and creative ways.

Although the art of blown glass did not attract the attention of the pioneers of the Arts and Crafts movement, important technical advances were made by such commercial firms as Powell and Sons of Whitefriars. In addition to supplying flat glass in special colours to virtually all of the stained glass artists of southern England, Harry Powell, grandson of the company's founder, experimented with blown and moulded vessel glass as well. Powell's produced blown glass tableware designed by Philip Webb, including finger bowls in various colours. Webb's wine glasses, for which drawings survive, were adapted from the glassware made for Morris at The Red House. These were manufactured by Powells exclusively for sale at Morris, Marshall, Faulkner & Co. (later Morris & Co.) from 1862.

Harry Powell also designed iron and glass vessels that were shown at the first Arts and Crafts Exhibition in 1888. Among these were such objects as a moulded 'blue opal' glass vase supported by a wrought-iron tripod stand. About 10 years earlier Powell had introduced 'blue opal' and 'straw opal' glass in milky colours with areas of opalescence. Hand-forged iron fittings for glass became a speciality of the firm, which had its own blacksmith shop.

Powell also partnered with Arts and Crafts metalsmiths to produce glass vessels with intricate handcrafted mounts of silver or pewter, such as a green glass claret jug with pewter fittings by Archibald Knox. Knox's 'Tudric' pewter was inspired by the elaborate interlace patterns found on ancient Celtic and Norse crosses on the Isle of Man, his birthplace. The 'Tudric' line was designed for the London shop Liberty & Co. and introduced around 1900. When his glass display at the Arts and Crafts Exhibition of 1896 was criticised as monotonously colourless, Powell developed a line of coloured, layered glass vessels with silver and gold inclusions. An example is a blue glass inkwell with hand-hammered silver cover, hallmarked 'JP', London 1909. The silver mounts and covers were often designed and made by members of the Guild of Handicrafts, a craft co-operative founded in 1888 by C. R. Ashbee.

*Finger bowls designed by Philip Webb for J. Powell
and Sons, c. 1888. © Christie's Images Limited*

Wine glasses designed by Philip Webb, c. 1862.© Christie's Images Limited

A 'blue opal' glass vase with tripod stand, probably designed by Harry Powell of Powell and Sons, Whitefriars. © Christie's Images Limited

A claret jug with pewter fittings by Archibald Knox and a green glass liner by Powells. © Christie's Images Limited

A glass inkwell by Powells with a silver cover, hallmarked 'JP', London 1909. © Christie's Images Limited

British Glass from 1890-1930

William Morris believed that the beauty of medieval stained glass windows resulted from the craftsman's direct participation in all aspects of production, from the initial design to the final installation, according to his understanding of medieval craft practices. While this model flourished during Morris & Co.'s early years when commissions were few, it was difficult to sustain when demand increased. In the 1890s a younger generation of artists and craft workers emerged who were committed to putting Morris's early ideals into practice. By working independently in small studios instead of large firms, they could be intimately involved in the entire hand-made process. One of these was Christopher Whall (1849-1924), who had a powerful impact as a teacher and writer, as well as a designer and maker of beautiful stained glass. His influential instruction manual, *Stained Glass Work*, published in 1905, is still read by artists today.

Whall's windows in the 15th century Lady Chapel at Gloucester Cathedral, completed 1897, were a triumph, described by the American architect Ralph Adams Cram as 'perfectly medieval and perfectly modern'. The six windows incorporate fragments of medieval glass that had survived in the uppermost tracery. Upon these precious remnants Whall based the proportions of white and coloured glass, the scale of the figures and size of the background quarries for the rest of the windows. Especially effective was his use of white glass to frame the figures as can be seen in his panel of 'St. Chad', a smaller version of one of the Gloucester windows possibly made for display at the Ninth Exhibition of the Arts and Crafts Society in 1910. After close study of late-medieval stained glass windows, he employed subtle tints of grey, brown and blue to modulate the contrast between the delicately leaded whites and the brilliant tonalities of the figures and backgrounds.

'St. Chad', a stained glass panel by Christopher Whall, 1901-10. V&A Images / Victoria and Albert Museum

Whall taught at the new Central School of Art and at the Royal College of Art in London and almost every major stained glass artist of the period was inspired by him in some way. These included, in England, Louis Davis, Mary Lowndes, Henry Payne, Karl Parsons and James Hogan; in Scotland, Douglas and Alex Strachan; in Ireland, Wilhelmina Geddes and Harry Clarke; and in America, Charles Connick. Connick was especially impressed by Whall's mastery of stained glass as an art of light manipulation, not simply pictorial decoration. He was astonished by the 'lovely, low-toned vibration' of light from Whall's windows in the new Church of the Advent in Boston, Massachusetts, installed in 1910.

Christopher Whall's most talented pupil was Karl Parsons (1884-1934), who learned his craft in Whall's studio starting at age fifteen. While still an apprentice he made a preparatory drawing for a cartoon of St. Cecilia playing the organ and subsequently executed the design for St. Oswald's church in Ashbourne, Derbyshire, in 1904-5. The composition is closely related to Dante Gabriel Rossetti's illustration of the same subject for the 1857 Moxon edition of Tennyson's *Poems*. Parson's glass is particularly notable for its fine draughtsmanship, rich colour and lively, spontaneous figure style, as is clearly apparent in a roundel illustrating the comic poem *Hammer and Tongs*. The roundel is made of cullet, discarded fragments too small for normal glazing. Parsons often exhibited at the Arts and Crafts Exhibition Society, the major body through which artists of the movement promoted their work. Like Whall, he also taught at the Central School of Arts and Crafts and succeeded Whall when he retired from The Royal College of Art.

In 1897 the suffragist Mary Lowndes, an early colleague of Whall's, formed a partnership with Alfred Drury and founded the Glass House in custom-built premises on Lettice Street in Fulham. The firm of Lowndes and Drury, Stained Glass Workers, employed a team of cutters, glaziers, kiln-men and others whose services could be hired by any freelance artist who wanted to be involved in all the steps necessary to create a design in stained glass. Karl Parsons rented a studio there for twenty years. The Glass House was especially important for women artists, who, for the first time, could use the facilities to undertake independent commissions on the same professional basis as men.

Women played important roles in a number of Arts and Crafts associations. At Bromsgrove, an ancient market town south of Birmingham, England, Walter Gilbert founded the Bromsgrove Guild in 1895. It attracted many craftspeople from the area, including Mary Newill (1860-1947), a teacher of embroidery and stained glass at the Birmingham School of Art. Newill designed both domestic and ecclesiastical stained glass and won first prize in a competition held in 1897 by *The Studio*, a prestigious international art journal. In a pair of stained glass panels she depicted sailing ships before a castellated medieval town. The panels, which once belonged to Walter Gilbert, were illustrated by Christopher Whall in his book *Stained Glass Work*. The Guild produced an astonishing variety of crafts products in wood, glass, plaster, textiles, metals, enamel, pottery, mosaic, and stone and lasted until 1966, far longer than any of the other idealistic Arts and Crafts ventures.

A drawing for a stained glass window of St. Cecilia by Karl Parsons. © Christie's Images Limited

A pair of stained glass panels by Mary Newill. © *Christie's Images Limited*

The Stained Glass Revival in Ireland

In Ireland, many artists strove to articulate a nationalist vision of a liberated and renewed country. Christopher Whall was invited to create a school of stained glass, but was unable to give time to such an enterprise. Instead, he sent his experienced assistant Alfred E. Child to act as instructor at the Dublin Metropolitan School of Art. In 1903 the painter Sarah Purser, inspired by the example of the Glass House in Fulham, joined with Child to organise a cooperative venture to provide technical support and shared facilities for stained glass artists in Dublin. Calling this studio 'An Tur Gloine', Gaelic for 'The Tower of Glass', she invited dynamic young artists to work there. Among the most renowned were Michael Healy, Wilhelmina Geddes and Evie Hone, all of whose work she actively promoted.

Stricken with polio at an early age, Evie Hone (1894–1955) did not allow her disability to deter her from a career as a painter. Her breakthrough opportunity came when she travelled to France in 1920 with her lifelong friend, the painter Mainie Jellett. There they studied with the most austere of the Cubist masters, Albert Gleizes, who challenged them to create designs using only the basic elements of colour, line and shape. An abstract work in gouache on paper by Hone bears the stamp of the Gleizes studio. This careful approach to colour and composition made Hone a sensitive artist when she came, quite late in her career, to glass. Gleizes's intense involvement in a search for spiritual ideals had resonated strongly with Hone and is reflected in her later compositions. Her faith deeply influenced her work and she converted to Roman Catholicism in 1935. She created her windows at the Tower of Glass, producing an enormous amount of work despite her disability. Her most famous commissions were the windows for Eton College Chapel and the Jesuit Church, Farm Street, London. A small stained glass panel of St. John is characteristic of her abstract style.

An abstract composition in gouache on paper by Evie Hone with the stamp of the Alfred Gleizes studio. © Christie's Images Limited

A stained glass panel depicting St. John by Evie Hone. © Christie's Images Limited

Harry Clarke (1889–1931) was the most eccentric and gifted of the artists working in Ireland. Although influenced by Arts and Crafts principles in the fabrication of stained glass, he was fundamentally a brilliant draughtsman with an exotic and sensual artistic vision. His illustrations for *The Rape of the Lock*, for example, are rivalled only by the voluptuous drawings of Aubrey Beardsley. In 1917 he created nine acided, stained and painted glass panels entitled 'Queens' to illustrate the poem by the Irish playwright J. M. Synge. The poem describes notorious women of the past and Clarke's eccentric imagery is a perfect fit for such stanzas as 'Queens whose finger once did stir men,/Queens were eaten of fleas and vermin/Queens men drew like Monna Lisa/or slew with drugs in Rome and Pisa'. His patron for this quirky invention was Laurence Ambrose Waldron, a barrister, stockbroker and connoisseur known as the 'beloved portly Maecenas of Dublin'.

Clarke's sexual daring, combined with a certain mystical intensity, set him apart from the high-minded socialism of many Arts and Crafts practitioners. Clarke created a number of important windows in both Ireland and England, including those at the Honan Chapel, Cork, and the League of Nations window commissioned by the Irish Free State, now at the Wolfsonian Foundation in Florida. The windows were fabricated in his father's workshop in Dublin, which became the 'Harry Clarke Studios' when he and his brother Walter took them over in 1913.

One of nine panels entitled 'Queens' by Harry Clarke. © *Christie's Images Limited*

The Arts & Crafts Movement in America

In America, the ideas of the Arts and Crafts Movement had a powerful impact, though artists were less concerned with reproducing medieval craft practices or depicting chivalric tales. The writings of Ruskin and Morris were widely read and Arts and Crafts Societies and Handicraft Guilds sprang up across the land. Although based on the same principles, the American movement is characterised by distinct regional variations, many of which differ markedly from the movement's British roots.

On the East Coast artists and designers largely followed English precedents; one example is a leaded glass window by Dard Hunter for the Roycroft Inn, c. 1907. Elbert Hubbard founded the Roycroft Arts and Crafts Community in East Aurora, New York, in 1895. One of the few American ventures that incorporated the model of the medieval guilds as advocated by William Morris, it supported hundreds of craftspeople working primarily in wood, metal and leather. The community became a mecca for those interested in the Arts and Crafts Movement and in 1905 the Roycroft Inn was opened to accommodate the thousands of visitors who journeyed there.

In the Midwest, the Arts and Crafts belief that buildings should reflect the character of the surrounding landscape produced the architecture of the Prairie School. The flat topography and wide skies inspired sprawling designs with low, horizontal roofs and extended ribbon windows. In glass, architects re-thought the relationship between the transparent medium and its solid context, dissolving the boundaries between nature and interior space. At the forefront of this revolution was the extraordinary figure of Frank Lloyd Wright (1867-1959).

From early 1888 until mid-1893, Wright was the chief draughtsman for the Chicago architectural firm of Sullivan and Adler. Louis Sullivan frequently used stained glass to enrich his buildings, as in a leaded glass skylight with burgundy interlace on a pale amber ground for the theatre of the Auditorium Building. But he did not exploit the transparency of glass, approaching the material much as he did his flat stencilled wall decorations. For Wright, glass was the materialisation of light. *'What is this magical material, there but not seen if you are looking through it?'* Wright wrote in 1928. *'You may look at it, too, as a brilliance, catching reflections and giving back limpid light.'* In the same Auditorium Building Wright's influence can be

A skylight by Sullivan and Adler for the theatre of the Auditorium Building, Chicago, Illinois, 1886-90. © Christie's Images Limited

A window by Dard Hunter for the Roycroft Inn, c. 1907. © Christie's Images Limited

felt in another window that reduces the intricate curves of Sullivan's designs to austere geometry. With its coloured, opalescent and textured glass in a geometric pattern of horizontal and vertical lines enlivened with small circles, it is almost certainly an early work by Wright.

Between 1909 and 1913, Wright developed his mature Prairie Style in which the characteristic motif of a building was expressed in the glass. For the B. Harley Bradley House, built in Kankakee, Illinois, in 1900, the stylised geometry of the windows was inspired by American Indian patterns and botanical motifs. For the leaded glass skylight, a stylised Indian design was carried out in white and green glass, tortoise shell and gold, with lead lines of varying thicknesses. Two casements and a transom feature a stylised pendant flower in stained glass. Instead of double-hung windows, Wright preferred the casements used by English Arts and Crafts architects because they opened directly out into nature, facilitating the flow of space between internal and external areas.

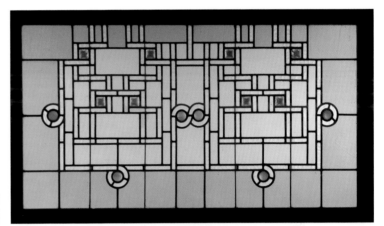

A window for the Auditorium Building attributed to Frank Lloyd Wright.
© Christie's Images Limited

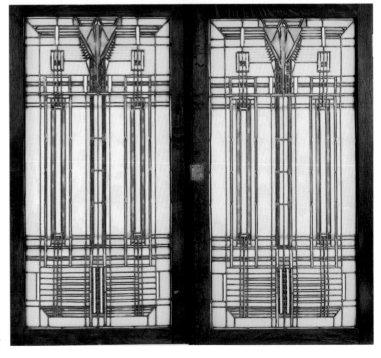

A skylight from the B. Harley Bradley House in Kankakee, Illinois, c. 1900, by Frank Lloyd Wright.
© Christie's Images Limited

Using multiple lead lines and faceted glass, Wright's windows serve as privacy screens that allow light to flood the interior unimpeded by curtains. Glass was also used for internal spatial dividers and skylights; these might repeat motifs from the exterior windows or have a related design in the same colours. A skylight for the Darwin D. Martin House, Buffalo, circa 1903-05, differs in pattern from the windows but is made of the same kinds of glass. The glass for the Martin House, executed by the Linden Glass Company, is considered to be Wright's finest. For the windows of the Avery Coonley playhouse, in Riverside, Illinois, 1912, Wright invented a completely different pattern of randomly placed circles, squares and rectangles in bright primary colours. The playhouse was built as a kindergarten for a private client and the bright colours and simple forms recreate the festive atmosphere of a parade with balloons, confetti and flags.

A skylight from the Darwin D. Martin House, Buffalo, c. 1903-05, designed by Wright and executed by the Linden Glass Company.
© Christie's Images Limited

Two casements and a transom for the Bradley House designed by Wright, c. 1900.
© Christie's Images Limited

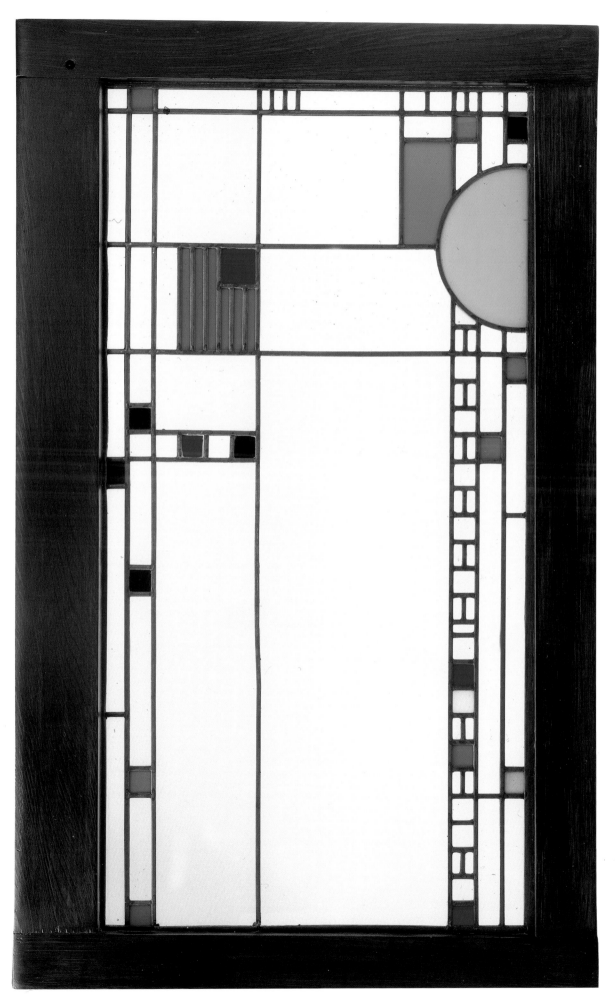

A window from the Avery Coonley playhouse, in Riverside, Illinois, 1912, designed by Wright. © Christie's Images Limited

No detail was too small to escape Wright's vision of the totally designed environment – his protean creativity extended even to lamps and vessel glass. He created a leaded glass and bronze double table lamp for the Susan Lawrence Dana House in Springfield, Illinois, around 1903. This masterpiece among all Wright's table lamps features a sumac motif in the triangular end panels of the green and gold shade, a motif featured throughout the house. For the Glassfactory Leerdam, Amsterdam, in 1929, Wright designed a hexagonal vase in emerald green glass. Because of the complexity of the design it was never put into production, but four samples survive in two sizes.

Other Prairie School architects made equally original use of stained glass. The Midwest firm of William Gray Purcell (1880-1965) and George Grant Elmslie (1869-1952) also evolved out of Sullivan and Adler's Chicago practice. While still a draftsman for Sullivan, Elmslie worked on the country estate of Henry B. Babson, built in Riverside, Illinois in 1907-08. After Purcell and Elmslie set up their own firm, Babson, a wealthy retailer of early Edison phonographs, became their client for further alterations, furnishings and decorations. The windows for this house are a fine example of Elmslie's subtle and elegant style.

They use a simple vocabulary of design elements: circles and rectangles of contrasting transparent and translucent glass in pale shades of blue, yellow and grey connected with lead lines of different widths.

In California, the American Arts and Crafts Movement took on a different guise. Asian influences were strong on the West Coast and were fully expressed in the architectural partnership of the Pasadena brothers Charles Sumner Greene (1868-1957) and Henry Mather Greene (1870-1954). The Adelaide M. Tichenor House, built in 1904-05 in Long Beach, was inspired by the Japanese Imperial Gardens exhibited at the 1904 St. Louis World's Fair that Charles visited at his client's insistence. Facing the ocean, the house was constructed with low, overhanging eaves around an exquisite Japanese garden. Their first domestic commission with a totally integrated design, Greene and Greene created all the interior furnishings, hardware and light fixtures. Their design united the reception, living, and dining rooms into one flowing space, with the dining area raised on a platform in the Japanese manner, two steps above the rest of the room. The tripartite frieze of windows in the dining area featured Japanese cherry trees silhouetted against brilliant, multi-coloured stained glass.

A double table lamp for the Susan Lawrence Dana House, Springfield, Illinois, c. 1903, designed by Wright and executed by the Linden Glass Company.
© Christie's Images Limited

A vase designed by Wright for the Glassfactory Leerdam, Amsterdam, in 1929. © Christie's Images Limited

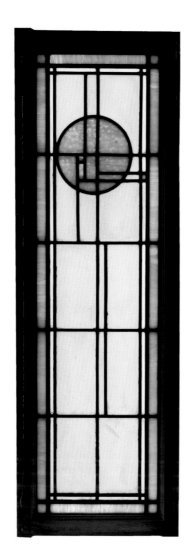

Four windows designed by George Grant Elmslie for the Henry B. Babson House in Riverside, Illinois. © Christie's Images Limited

A window for the Adelaide M. Tichenor House, Long Beach, California, designed by Charles and Henry Greene, c. 1904.

II

Art Nouveau in Europe

Opposite:
A 'Wisteria' lamp, c. 1910, by Emile Gallé.
© Christie's Images Limited

'L'Eternal Debat', c. 1890, by Emile Gallé.
© Christie's Images Limited

Art Nouveau in Europe

Although the ideas of the Arts and Crafts movement found fertile ground in many places in continental Europe, the reaction against historical revivals and the search for a 'modern' style also produced a different hothouse flower – Art Nouveau. More urban, sophisticated and stylised than the Arts and Crafts, the style originated in France at the end of the 19th century, gradually taking root elsewhere on the Continent and in the British Isles. Because of the ductile nature of the material and the lack of a strong formal tradition in glass, Art Nouveau reached its highest and most characteristic expression in the art of the glassmaker.

Glass production flourished in Europe during the 19th century, due to scientific breakthroughs in the chemistry of glass and technological advances resulting in more powerful and stable firing kilns. But it was not until individual artists began to explore the medium that a distinctive Art Nouveau style developed in glass. Like their Arts and Crafts counterparts, artists looked to nature for inspiration, but their choice of subject matter differed markedly. In addition to curvaceous flowers and foliage, artists selected imagery that was darker, more mysterious and, at times, vaguely sinister. Bats, lizards, spiders, pythons, even poisonous jellyfish snaked across flowing surfaces, while female nudes took on a distinctly menacing air.

For some critics, Art Nouveau exudes an aura of decadence, a preoccupation with danger, death and decay that was a manifestation of *fin de siecle* angst. 'L'Eternal Debat', a wheel-carved vase in black glass by Emile Gallé, is a case in point. The decoration of the vase depicts the deadly struggle between good and evil. Evil is represented by a black pterodactyl that menaces the paler, carved pelican overhead thet symbolises goodness. By 1902, such vases had been renamed *vases de tristesse*, because of their sombre subject matter dealing with issues of good and evil, life and death.

Glassmaking
in France

In France, the outstanding interpreter of Art Nouveau was Emile Gallé (1846-1904), born into a family of glassmakers in Nancy. As a young man he studied botany, zoology and the chemistry of glass. While visiting London, he spent hours in the galleries of the Roman, Egyptian and Far Eastern collections in the British Museum and at the Royal Botanic Gardens at Kew. When he took over his father's business in 1874 his earliest vessels were closely based on historical prototypes. An etched, enamelled and applied 'Mamluk' vase of pink and clear glass from 1885 is decorated with scrolling tendrils and enamelled cartouches of warring Saracens on horseback painted in blue, red, white, black and gold. It was inspired by the art of the Mamluk sultanate (1250-1517) in the area that is now Egypt and Syria.

Gallé quickly became fascinated by the protean possibilities of glass and experimented endlessly to discover new forms, colours, techniques and chemical compounds. He drew inspiration from the asymmetries and 'accidents' of Japanese ceramics, the fleeting depictions of light and colour in Impressionist paintings, and the literary works of the Romantic and Symbolist poets. His *verreries parlantes*, introduced in 1884, were inscribed with quotations from such writers as Charles Baudelaire, Victor Hugo, and Robert de Montesquieu. One example, a goblet with an internally decorated stem and frosted orange bowl carved to depict white crocuses and inlaid with orange and purple crocuses, is encircled with the words *Le Safron d'automne/quand les beaux jours font place aux jours amersil/*Victor Hugo.

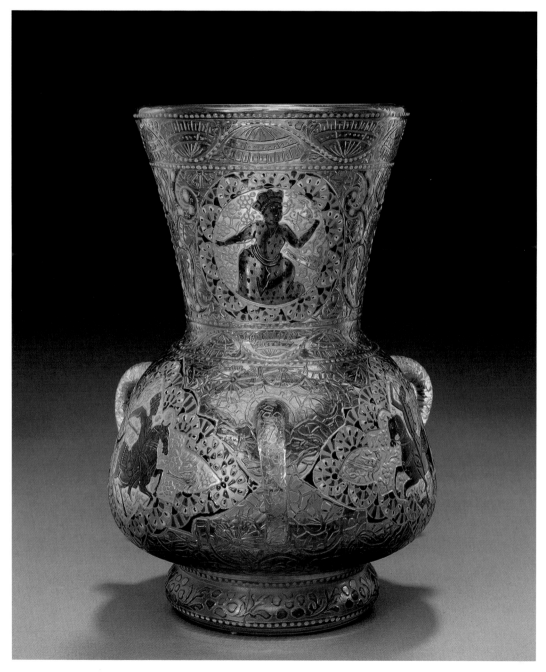

Left:
A 'Mamluk' vase. c. 1885, by Emile Gallé.
© Christie's Images Limited

Opposite:
A verre parlant glass goblet by Emile Gallé
engraved with a quotation from Victor Hugo.
© Christie's Images Limited

Gallé's most significant innovations were cameo glass and *marquetrie de verre*. Cameo glass, or cased glass, was inspired by the Chinese cased glass of the Qian Long period (1736-96), in which two or more fused layers of coloured glass are painted with an acid-resistant solution and dipped in an acid bath. When the unpainted background is corroded away, the decoration appears in low relief that is then refined with carving. In a related technique, a single overlay of several different colours of glass is applied to the same ground before painting and acid-etching.

Gallé's cameo and overlay glass often featured plants and flowers from the Far East or other exotic locales. Peonies had been cultivated in China and Japan for thousands of years and for a dramatic 'Peony' cameo glass table lamp the oriental flower has been depicted with botanical accuracy. A large vase of blue and green glass overlaid onto an amber ground is decorated with desert cactus flowers. The fragrant Wisteria vine, as depicted on a triple-layer cameo glass table lamp, is native to eastern Asia. Lamps made with the cameo technique are particularly effective when lit from within. The pale amber ground of a mould-blown 'Calla-lily' vase has been overlaid with three colours, then acid-etched and carved.

In 1898 Gallé patented the technique for *marquetrie de verre*, in which slivers of hot glass are impressed onto the molten surface of the vessel and lightly carved once the surface has cooled. Some of his most complex and impressive pieces were made using this method. 'La Forêt Javanaise' (or 'Guyanaise'), a glass jug by Gallé, uses the *marquetrie de verre* technique as well as carving, added glass threads and internal decoration with foil inclusions. Applied on the side is a large, realistic stag-beetle, the head and antler-like mandibles of dark amethyst glass. Java and Guyana were European colonies that seemed as dangerous and exotic as they were securely distant. 'La Libellule', a *marquetrie de verre* free-form glass coupe dated 1904, is made of milky white, caramel coloured glass embellished with a dragonfly swooping among a cloud of yellow mayflies. The green body of the dragonfly, one of the most popular motifs in Art Nouveau imagery, has been speckled with inclusions of silver foil. This particular coupe belonged to Mme. Gallé.

For the 'Monnaie du Pape' vase, exhibited at La Société Nationale des Beaux Arts in Paris in 1905, the white seed pods of the Money Plant were each individually applied using the *marquetrie de verre* technique. Because the body of the vase must be cooled and reheated after each application, the process was time consuming and labour intensive. The decoration of some *marquetrie de verre* vessels is so subtle and complex that at first glance it can appear almost completely non-representational. Close inspection of a vase by Gallé dated 1900 reveals lily pads, lotus blossoms, buds and leaves, but the combination of colours and patterns verges on abstraction when seen from a distance.

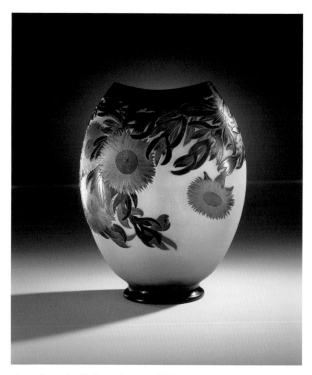

A vase decorated with Cactus flowers, c. 1910, by Emile Gallé. © Christie's Images Limited

A 'Peony' cameo glass table lamp, c. 1910, by Gallé. © Christie's Images Limited

A 'Wisteria' lamp, c. 1910, by Emile Gallé.
© Christie's Images Limited

The 'Calla-lily' vase by Gallé.
© Christie's Images Limited

'La Forêt Javanaise' or 'La Forêt Guyanaise', a glass jug by Gallé.
© Christie's Images Limited

'La Libellule', a marquetrie de verre coupe by Emil Gallé, dated 1904. © Christie's Images Limited

A 'Monnaie du Pape' vase by Gallé, c. 1905.
© Christie's Images Limited

A marquetrie de verre vase by Gallé, dated 1900.
© Christie's Images Limited

Gallé's workshop manufactured three kinds of products: his *pieces uniques*, of which only a few examples were made by himself or his most skilled craftsmen; his limited editions of richly ornamented vessels; and his industrial production of more affordable objects with simpler decoration, which began in 1890. Although this last category included smaller vessels utilising a limited number of decorative techniques, these were designed and finished to the same high standard as his more complicated pieces and were also signed with Gallé's name. Gallé triumphed at the Paris Exposition Universelle of 1900, winning two Grand Prix and the Légion d'Honneur. After his death in 1904 the industrial range accounted for most of the subsequent output of his shop, which closed in 1935.

Gallé's discoveries were quickly imitated by other glassmakers, with greater and lesser degrees of success. Among the best was the glassmaking firm of the brothers Auguste Daum (1853-1909) and Antonin Daum (1864-1931), also located in Nancy. They adapted a variety of decorative techniques – etching, enamelling and casing – for large-scale production, using naturalistic motifs in the Art Nouveau style. They also pioneered simpler techniques for producing cameo effects, such as vitrification, in which powdered glass is rolled or blown onto the hot ground. These vessels were often enriched with applied cabochons carved into three-dimensional insects, gems or teardrops.

A scenic glass vase, c. 1905, by Daum.
© Christie's Images Limited

Martelé glass was given an uneven surface imitating hand-hammered silver to contrast with the smoothness of the cameo design. For an etched cameo vase in white with a transparent *martelé* finish, the ground was carved with a wheel into tiny facets to simulate the surface of hammered metal.

In 1906 the partners began production of *pâte de verre*, in which shapes were formed or moulded in multi-coloured cold glass paste and then fired. This material had first been developed by the sculptor Henri Cros in the early 1880s and further developed by Georges Despret. A small *pâte de verre videpoche* (pocket emptier) surmounted by a lizard is an example of Daum Fréres' work in this medium. It was probably sculpted by Henri Berge, who worked for Daum for 30 years and made most of the models in the *pâte de verre* workshop under the direction of Almaric Walter. After World War I Walter and Berge set up their own independent workshop in Nancy.

With the advent of electricity the Daum brothers capitalised on this exciting new technology by creating striking table lamps with free-form blown shades carved as voluptuous flowers. These remarkable glass flowerheads were fitted onto stems or bases made of bronze, wrought-iron or carved wood, many of which were designed by Louis Majorelle. Majorelle, a childhood friend of Antonin Daum, was the leading Art Nouveau furniture designer of the period.

A vase by Gallé, c. 1890. © Christie's Images Limited

The success of Gallé's striking Art Nouveau imagery as well as his technical achievements were emulated across the French glassmaking industry. In Lunéville, the Muller brothers set up a small glass decorating workshop in 1895 where they made cameo glass in a simplified version of the Gallé manner. A flower form vase is shaped as a slender ruby and white bud with an asymmetrical rim that opens out of a green stem decorated with delicate carved veining. Muller Fréres also experimented with a new technique called *fluogravure*, in which colours in enamel as well as glass were vitrified to a vessel's surface, then acid-etched and carved. Metallic oxides were often added to produce an iridescent sheen.

A cameo vase with martelé finish by Daum.
© Christie's Images Limited

A cameo vase, c. 1900, by Daum,
with applied cabochons carved as
snails. © Christie's Images Limited

A pâte de verre videpoche (pocket emptier) by Daum,
c. 1912. © Christie's Images Limited

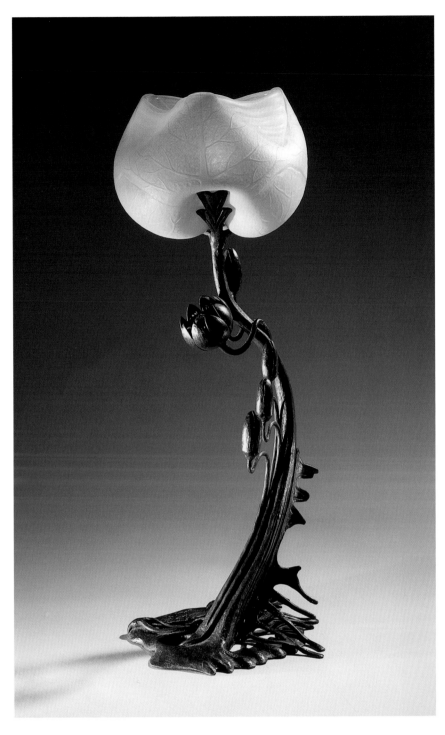

A floriform vase by Muller Fréres.
© Christie's Images Limited

Opposite:
A cameo table lamp by Muller Fréres,
c. 1910, with a Japanese landscape.
© Christie's Images Limited

A selection of Muller Fréres vases and a pitcher in cameo
glass and fluogravure, c. 1910. © Christie's Images Limited

Jugendstil in Germany and Austria

Elsewhere in Europe, Gallé's work was also widely admired and imitated. In Germany, where Art Nouveau was known as *Jugendstil* ('Young Style'), glassmakers quickly adopted the new methods and design vocabulary. Before the annexation of Alsace and Lorraine to Germany following the 1871 Franco-Prussian War, Gallé had worked at the Meisenthal firm of Burgun, Schverer & Cie. There he developed a close friendship with the decorator Désiré Christian (1846-1907). When Gallé moved to Nancy, Christian stayed behind and continued to design in the Gallé style for a number of glass firms in the area. A vase by Christian is made of clear glass cased with coloured layers incorporating swirls of pink, brown, green and white. Three areas of the surface have been carved with flowers and leaves and given a martelé finish.

A glassworks in Darmstadt was established in 1901 under the direction of Josef Emil Schneckendorf (1865-1949). As well as supervising the entire manufacturing process, Schneckendorf provided most of the designs. In one example of his work, metallic oxides have been used to produce a lustrous ceramic-like glaze. In Thuringia, the most restrained *Jugendstil* manner was practiced by the designer Karl Koepping (1848-1914). He created delicate glass vases with stems and leaves of slender glass threads as well as elegant, thin-walled wine glasses embellished only with tiny rings on the stems. These were exhibited and sold at the Paris shop of the entrepreneur and art dealer Siegfried Bing, 'La Maison de l'Art Nouveau', from which the name of the style was derived.

A vase by J. E. Schneckendorf.
© Christie's Images Limited

A vase by Désiré Christian
© Christie's Images Limited

Opposite:
Two liqueur glasses by Karl Koepping,
c. 1898. © Christie's Images Limited

An iridescent vase by Loetz Witwe.
© Christie's Images Limited

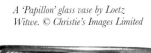

A 'Papillon' glass vase by Loetz
Witwe. © Christie's Images Limited

A selection of deep blue and metallic gold lustre
vases by Loetz Witwe. © Christie's Images Limited

Austrian glass production was dominated by the firm of Glasfabrik Johann Loetz Witwe in Klöstermuhle. After the death of Johann Loetz in 1848 the business was managed by his widow (*witwe*). From the 1890s, under the direction of the founder's grandson, the firm began to specialise in iridescent glass and patented its own metallic lustre technique in 1898. The next year saw the introduction of 'Phenomenon' and 'Papillon' glass, the latter flecked with clusters of shimmering specks like the wing of a butterfly (*papillon*). Loetz also produced vessels inspired by the shapes of Venetian glass and iridescent glass with openwork silver or bronze mounts. An example of the latter type is made of topaz glass decorated with iridescent rainbow swirls and gold 'oil' spots and set into a pierced gilt-metal mount. Louis Comfort Tiffany was deeply impressed by early Loetz glass when he visited the 1889 Paris Exhibition and the company's later iridescent glass was marketed in the United States as a less costly alternative to Tiffany's 'Favrile' products.

A mounted glass vase by Loetz Witwe.
© Christie's Images Limited

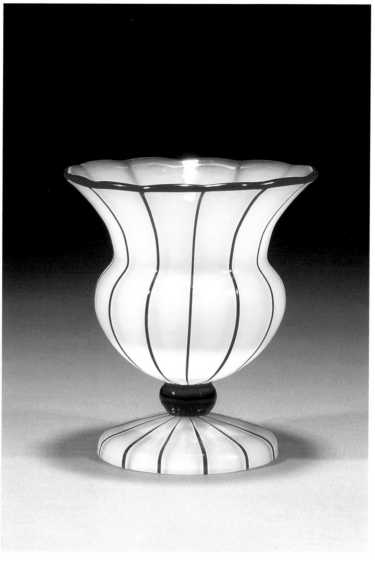

A group of vases designed by Dagobert
Peche and manufactured by Loetz,
c. 1914. © Christie's Images Limited

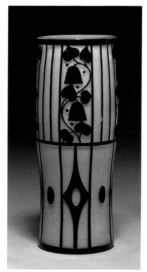

A vase designed by Joseph Hoffman for Loetz.
© Christie's Images Limited

More radically, Loetz commissioned designs from the members of the Wiener Werkstatte (Viennese Workshop), a cooperative of painters, sculptors, architects and decorative artists founded in Vienna in 1903 by the architect Josef Hoffmann and the painter and designer Koloman Moser. Organised along the lines of C. R. Ashbee's Guild of Handicraft in England, these artists rejected the more florid aspects of Art Nouveau in favour of structure and restraint. Hoffman designed a vase for Loetz in cased pink glass with a simplified flat pattern of flowers and foliage painted in black enamel. Michael Powolny and Dagobert Peche, both associated with the Werkstatte, also provided stylish and sophisticated designs for Loetz. Their vessels of plain white or yellow glass were decorated only with narrow stripes or small stylised floral motifs painted in black enamel.

Art Nouveau in Britain

In England, where the principles of the Arts and Crafts Movement were still revered, Art Nouveau met with intense hostility from critics who viewed it as a 'foreign contagion'. 'To persons with healthy bodies and any degree of natural refinement, wrote the editor of The Artist in 1901, "L'Art Nouveau" is repugnant and detestable…' Nonetheless, sinuous ornament became all the rage, although described in such anglicised terms as 'Quaint Style' or 'Liberty Style' after the London shop that carried avant-garde furnishings. In Scotland, however, with its close historic ties with France, Art Nouveau was embraced more enthusiastically, especially in Glasgow. The glassmaking firm of James Couper and Sons employed the designer and botanist Dr. Christopher Dresser (1834-1904) to create their range of 'Clutha' glass – bubbled or streaked glass that was clear or translucent and sometimes embedded with foil or mica but otherwise devoid of ornament. Dresser had travelled

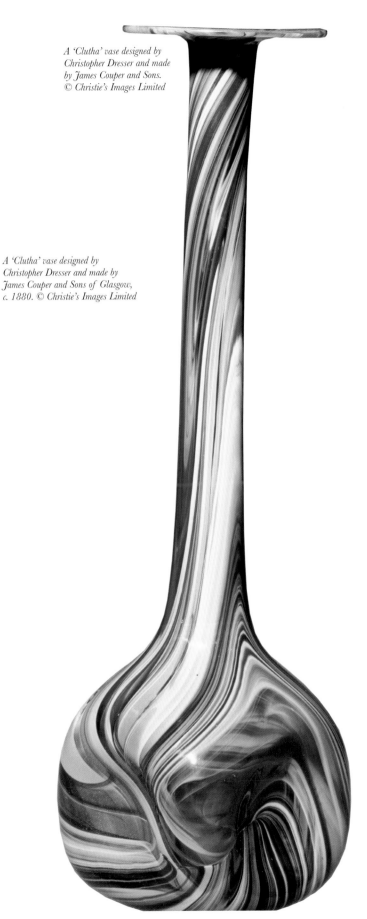

A 'Clutha' vase designed by Christopher Dresser and made by James Couper and Sons. © Christie's Images Limited

A 'Clutha' vase designed by Christopher Dresser and made by James Couper and Sons of Glasgow, c. 1880. © Christie's Images Limited

extensively in Japan and had also studied the pottery and glass of ancient Rome, the Middle East, and even Peru. The elongated, twisted shapes of his graceful vessels were similar to those found in continental Art Nouveau, if less extreme.

The link with the Continent is even more apparent in the work of Charles Rennie Mackintosh (1868-1928), the artist and architect who, along with others of his circle, created 'The Glasgow Style' that was closely related to continental Art Nouveau. When Hoffmann and Moser visited Scotland, they chose Mackintosh and his wife to design a Scottish Room for the Vienna Secessionist exhibition of 1900, which had a profound effect on the design community there. The sweeping curves of Art Nouveau are clearly apparent in the stained glass windows he designed for Miss Cranston's tearooms and for the panels featured in the furniture created for his celebrated Hill House in Helensburgh, Scotland. An ebonised writing cabinet by Mackintosh, with a stained glass panel probably by his wife Margaret MacDonald, was designed for Hill House in 1904. The curvilinear abstract pattern of the panel is ornamented with the 'Glasgow Rose' that frequently appeared in the work of Glasgow artists.

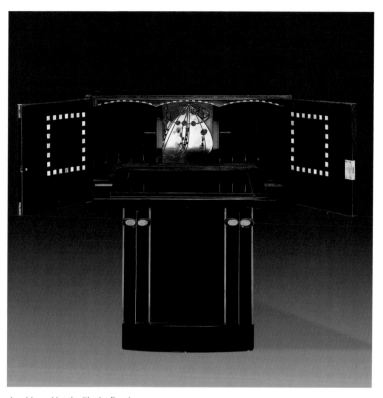

A writing cabinet by Charles Rennie Mackintosh, with a stained-glass panel probably by his wife Margaret MacDonald, designed for Hill House, 1904. © Christie's Images Limited

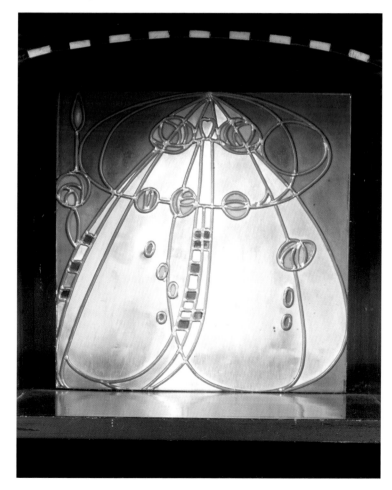

III

Art Nouveau Glass in America

III

Art Nouveau Glass in America

Although Art Nouveau had little impact on American architecture, in the decorative arts it was a different story. The flamboyant style was well suited to a new generation of *arrivistes*, confident, cosmopolitan, and fabulously rich, who demanded a higher level of opulence in their surroundings, both public and private. In glass, lush floral extravaganzas in brilliant colours swirled across the windows of the grandest churches, capitol buildings, and opera houses of the Gilded Age. The dining rooms and conservatories of the wealthiest families boasted elaborate pictorial windows, while the more modest establishments of the house-proud middle class featured simpler glass panels in the front door. Shimmering iridescent vases adorned tables and sideboards, while lamps with glowing, richly hued glass shades held pride of place in front parlor windows. Coloured glass was everywhere and its popularity has never been equalled.

So new was the art of stained glass in America that only two men vied for leadership in the field – John La Farge and Louis Comfort Tiffany. The initial innovator was John La Farge (1835-1910), who grew up in New York City and toured Europe as a young man. In 1859 he moved to Newport, Rhode Island, the playground of the affluent elite, to study painting with William Morris Hunt. He turned to decorative work in the 1870s and his first major commission was to design the interior of H.H. Richardson's Trinity Church in Boston, for which he drew on medieval and Renaissance sources. Widely acclaimed, the scheme was the starting point for the magnificent interiors of the 'American Renaissance'. Stained glass was an important component of the numerous public and domestic commissions that followed.

La Farge traveled extensively in Japan and many of his compositions show the influence of Japanese art. All stained glass windows begin with a coloured design, usually in watercolour. La Farge was a consummate watercolourist and his design of 1890 shows his mastery of the medium to the full. His Japanese print collection, begun as early as 1856, undoubtedly served as a source for this delicate vision of peonies waving in a light breeze. The stained glass window based on this design, 'Peonies in the Wind with Kakemono Border', was made for the Washington, D.C., residence of John Hay, a distinguished statesman in the administration of Abraham Lincoln, and is now in the National Museum of American Art in Washington.

La Farge developed new varieties of glass and new techniques of glass production, several of which can be seen in his leaded glass firescreen. The screen's primary border is composed of opalescent glass and 'confetti' glass containing shreds of contrasting colours, interspersed with flowers made of faceted glass 'jewels'. Around the central panel depicting maple leaf boughs silhouetted against the moon is a border of faux 'pebbles', irregular rounded bits of glass resembling cabochon gems. In addition to fabricating a rich variety of forms of glass, he pioneered the use of copper foil to replace heavier traditional leading. La Farge is credited with being the first to create the lush floral stained glass windows that became a popular feature of 19th-century interior design.

Today, however, La Farge's reputation has been eclipsed by that of Louis Comfort Tiffany, whose name is often considered synonymous with American Art Nouveau. L. C. Tiffany (1848-1933) was the son of Charles Louis Tiffany, the founder of Tiffany & Co., purveyor of exquisite jewellery and silver to the American *nouveau riche*. He travelled extensively in Spain and North Africa before training in Paris as a painter, but in the 1870s he became interested in the decorative arts. His interior decorating firm of Louis C. Tiffany & Associated Artists designed lavishly appointed, eclectic interiors for the White House in Washington, D.C., and the home of Mark Twain in Hartford, Connecticut, among others. After the firm dissolved in 1883, Tiffany headed his own companies under various names, devoted principally to the production of stained glass windows, blown glass, lamps and mosaics. In 1892 he founded the Tiffany Glass and Decorating Co. in Corona, Long Island, New York, where he made his most important discoveries, including 'Favrile' glass.

Both La Farge and Tiffany experimented ceaselessly to master the production of a vast array of tones and textures in coloured glass, which had previously been imported from Europe at great expense. La Farge's most significant technical achievement was the creation in 1879 of opalescent glass, a semi-opaque glass with varying degrees of transparency. Tiffany benefited greatly from his colleague's extensive research, especially in opalescent glass. By adding various compounds of metallic oxides, such as chromium, cobalt, silver, gold and uranium, both La Farge and Tiffany produced glistening iridescent glass that changed colour according to the direction of the light. With the wealth and status of his father's prestigious company behind him, Tiffany quickly achieved a level of near industrial production that La Farge, the multi-talented artist and writer, could not match. By the 1890s the commercial success of Tiffany's Glass and Decorating Company was unsurpassed and the company prospered for nearly 70 years; it closed in 1931.

(Opposite):
Leaded glass firescreen by John La Farge.
© Christie's Images Limited

Tiffany Stained Glass Windows

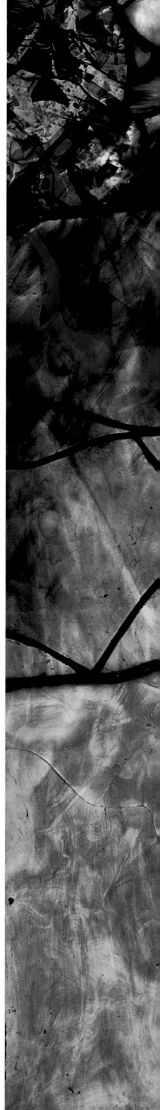

Tiffany's first love was creating gorgeous stained glass windows. Although primarily a designer, he supervised all aspects of glass production. Previous approaches to the medium had relied heavily on painting that blocked the transmission of light. Tiffany's innovation was to design windows as mosaics of coloured glass, with details such as shading created by irregularities in the glass itself. Although true to the spirit of Art Nouveau, Tiffany never abandoned representation completely in the manner of his European contemporaries. The purely abstract whiplash motif never appeared in his work as a design in its own right. His art was always a celebration of nature in recognisably naturalistic forms.

With his firm securely established in the United States by the 1890s, Tiffany sought out prestigious international exhibitions as influential venues for extending his reputation abroad. Initial critical opinion of his work was mixed, however. For his ecclesiastical windows, Tiffany was often constrained by his clients to portray scriptural subjects in a traditional manner that was considered old-fashioned by European art commentators. He therefore showed his most experimental work at foreign exhibitions and at times his floral exhibition pieces dissolve into an impressionistic play of colour that hovers on the edge of abstraction. One example is the 'Snowball' panel exhibited at the Exposition Universelle in Paris in 1900. This interpretation of a branch of a Snowball bush (hydrangea) makes extensive use of fractured or 'confetti' glass, made by embedding bits of coloured glass into glass that was clear or lightly tinted. Plated glass in multiple layers provides depth to the abstract background of mottled purple, blue and amber tones that shade to pale gold. Tiffany's efforts to impress his critics were ultimately successful and his windows won numerous medals in recognition of their outstanding quality.

The 'Snowball' panel by Louis Comfort Tiffany, 1900.
© Christie's Images Limited

A window for The Colonial Club in
New York City, Tiffany Studios, 1896.
© Christie's Images Limited

Figural windows comprise one distinct subset of Tiffany Studios' stained glass production. While religious subjects were usually employed for church windows, many figural windows were made for libraries, state capitols, colleges, railway stations and other public buildings, as well as for domestic settings. These might feature historical or mythological themes, or even portraits. One of Tiffany's favourite models, Gabrielle Drunzer, posed for the central figure of 'Chansons de Printemps' (Songs of Spring). Based on an oil painting by the French academic artist William Bouguereau, this composition features a classically beautiful young woman flanked by two cherubs who whisper into her ears. For the window, made around 1895, the poses of the figures have been copied exactly from the painting, but the vividly coloured, dramatic background was Tiffany's own invention. Tiffany frequently used French sources for his figural compositions. He may have seen Bouguereau's portrait, now lost, at the Exposition Universelle in Paris in 1889, at Tooth & Son Gallery in London, or at Knoedler Gallery in New York where it was subsequently exhibited. A photograph of the painting was also widely available.

Allegorical subjects were selected to fit the purpose of the building for which they were intended. Demurely draped female figures representing Education, Knowledge, or Art and Literature might grace the windows of a library, while a hospital might commission a scene of Aesculapius administering the Hippocratic Oath. Institutions in New England frequently commissioned scenes from American colonial history. For the Colonial Club in New York City, a fine historical window commemorating the original Dutch settlers was designed by Howard Pyle, a popular book illustrator, and made by Tiffany Studios in 1896. While Tiffany prided himself on composing scenes in coloured glass, in figural windows painting could not completely be avoided since the details and shading of hands and faces could only be rendered in opaque enamel.

The purely floral stained glass windows are equally impressive and their brilliant colours and irregular patterns were more suitable to Tiffany's mosaic technique than the depiction of three-dimensional forms. These floral windows are the two-dimensional counterpart to his naturalistic glass lampshades and many kinds of flowers bloomed on both surfaces, including peonies, hydrangeas, trumpet vines, and wisteria, along with grape vines. A leaded glass wisteria triptych window was made for the Albert Mitchell House in Rose Hill, Ohio, around 1908. In three sections, the vines of mottled purple wisteria and the branches of opaque cream-coloured magnolias twine against a blue-green striated sky. The flowers and foliage are supported by a trellis composed of the window's lead lines. The petals of the magnolia are made of drapery glass, which was pulled or twisted into folds while still in a molten state to produce lifelike shadings of colour. Easter lilies and iris are represented most frequently in Tiffany's floral windows, but even vegetables, such as eggplants or gourds, appear occasionally.

One panel of a leaded glass triptych window for the Albert Mitchell House, Rose Hill, Ohio, c. 1908. © Christie's Images Limited

*A window commissioned by Thomas Lynch for his home in
Greensburg, Pennsylvania, 1905.* © *Christie's Images Limited*

The 'Swan Fountain' window, c. 1905.
© *Christie's Images Limited*

His glorious landscape windows won Tiffany his lasting fame and these fully exploited his various technical innovations. Some are depictions of specific vistas, such as the country around a client's home or a location of personal significance. A scenic window depicting a sheep farm in rural Ireland was commissioned in 1905 by Thomas Lynch, the general manager of the Henry Clay Fricke Coke Company, for his new home in Greensburg, Pennsylvania. In the 1850s Lynch's parents had immigrated to western Pennsylvania from Ireland and the sheep farm pictured is that of Thomas's grandfather in Ballyduff, near Dungarvan, in County Waterford. In the window, the rustic thatched-roof cottage with its flowering window boxes has been copied faithfully from an 1896 family photograph, while the surrounding landscape is the creation of Tiffany's imagination. The crimson and fuchsia blooms in the foreground may represent red clover, commonly grown as forage for sheep.

Most compositions, however, were fantasy views of either 'wild' woodland scenes or, more frequently, landscaped gardens. Favourite garden motifs were nearly always classical in style and included fountains, columned pergolas and balustrades draped with vines, sometimes surmounted by parrots or peacocks flaunting their showy plumage. An outstanding example of Tiffany's idyllic vision of 'civilised' nature is the 'Swan Fountain' window. Dark blue-green cypress trees tower in the background, while lush plantings of purple and pink flowers frame a fountain and a rippled pool in which swans glide gracefully. In this tranquil scene mottled or 'fractured' glass has been used for the flowers and foliage and layered, sculpted 'cameo' glass for the flowing water of the fountain. The carefully balanced, classical composition is similar to the 'Garden Landscape and Fountain' mosaic that was once displayed in the Tiffany Studios' showroom and is now in the American Wing of the Metropolitan Museum of Art in New York.

'Wild' scenes often contain waterfalls, reflective pools of still water and distant views across the hills. Birch trees and cypresses provide vertical directional emphasis, balanced by iris or water lilies clustered in the foreground. And everywhere brilliant sunsets streak the skies, reflect off the waters and touch the landscape with multi-hued tints of intense colour. Although Tiffany Studios prided themselves on creating a unique window for every commission, certain compositional devices were repeated numerous times. 'River of Life' windows were often commissioned for mausoleums. This subject was a specialty of the designer Agnes Northrop who worked for Tiffany for nearly 50 years. After his death in 1933 she completed many of his unfinished commissions before retiring in 1939.

A 'River of Life' window with red poppies, pine and cypress trees, and a flowering magnolia.
© Christie's Images Limited

A 'River of Life' window with cypresses, white and rose flowering dogwood branches and clustered purple irises.
© Christie's Images Limited

Even without overt religious symbolism, pictorial subjects were often chosen by clients as memorials for deceased loved ones and given such Biblical inscriptions as "He Leadeth Me beside the Still Waters". The Danner Memorial Window of 1913, one of Tiffany's most spectacular commissions, was created during the period of his greatest achievements between 1910 and 1915. This monumental window, sixteen feet (487.7 cm) tall in seven sections, depicts flowering fruit trees and bears the inscription "Wherefore by their Fruits ye shall know them". It originally graced the east sanctuary of the First Baptist Church of Canton, Ohio, and was commissioned in honour of John and Terressa Danner, who had helped to found the church in 1849.

The Danner Memorial Window, 1913.
© *Christie's Images Limited*

Tiffany Blown Glass

Tiffany visited Paris in 1889, where he was deeply impressed by the magnificent glass of Emile Gallé and the Loetz glassworks displayed at the Paris International Exhibition. Fired with enthusiasm he returned to New York intent on producing smaller, less expensive blown glass objects for a broader audience. With the help of his British-born assistant, Arthur J. Nash, he developed his famous iridescent 'Favrile' glass, which was registered as a trademark name in 1894. Usually blown into very simple vessel shapes, 'Favrile' glass relies on its rich, lustrous surface for dramatic effect. The iridescence was created by spraying the hot surface with metallic salts that were subsequently absorbed into the glass itself. Tiffany's blown glass vessels share the same aesthetic as his stained glass windows in that enamel painting on the surface of the glass was avoided as much as possible.

Tiffany favoured expressive organic forms, such as his 'Floriform' vases that imitate the shapes of stylised blossoms with long fragile stems on domed bases. The edges of these vases were often deftly manipulated with pincers while in the molten state. The 'Goose-neck' vase was inspired by Persian rosewater flasks, which have bulbous bases and curving necks. The 'Jack-in-the-Pulpit' vase is one of Tiffany's most recognisable forms and an icon of American Art Nouveau. The rounded base flows into a narrow stem that expands into a large, flared, flower-like shape. The edges of the iridescent bloom are touched with gold.

Two 'Floriform' vases. © Christie's Images Limited

The 'Jack-in-the-Pulpit' vase.
© Christie's Images Limited

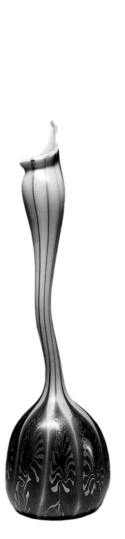

A 'Goose-neck' vase.
© Christie's Images Limited

Opposite Page:
A blue 'Favrile' vase created as
a special order around 1905.
© Christie's Images Limited

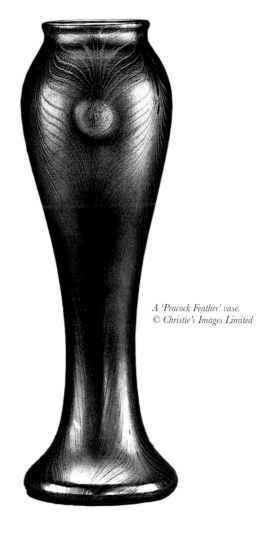

A 'Narcissus' vase made of 'Paperweight' glass.
© Christie's Images Limited

A 'Peacock Feather' vase.
© Christie's Images Limited

Shimmering surfaces were a Tiffany speciality, as seen in the 'Peacock Feather' vase. For the decoration of this vessel the iridescent golden colour in the body has been combed into a feather pattern and inlaid with a piece of dark glass resembling the eye of the peacock feather. Decorative motifs created within the body of the glass itself were highly prized. Tiffany 'Paperweight' Glass was made in many patterns, forms and colours, usually with a floral motif. The 'Narcissus' pattern was created by embedding the glass 'flowers' within an inner layer that was then covered with a layer of clear glass. Other decorative schemes were non-representational, such as those made of multi-coloured strands of glass encased in a transparent outer layer. Examples of Tiffany 'Aquamarine' glass are very rare. The green glass simulates sea water within which images of aquatic plants and marine life are imbedded, the slight depression beneath the neck giving the appearance of a vessel filled with water. The exact technique for 'Cameo' glass is not known, but acid was used to sculpt the surface, allowing the flowers and leaves to stand out in gentle relief. Cameo glass was highly labour-intensive and the simplest form took five to six weeks to complete.

A vase of 'Paperweight' glass with abstract decoration. © Christie's Images Limited

A rare example of Tiffany 'Aquamarine' glass. © Christie's Images Limited

A tiny vase, only 4 inches (11.5 cm) high, made of 'Cameo' glass. © Christie's Images Limited

Art Nouveau Glass in America   55

With continual experimentation Tiffany produced a wide variety of lustrous surfaces, often inspired by ancient glass excavated from archaeological sites in Egypt, Cyprus or regions of the Roman Empire. The 'Tel El Amarna' vase, with its iridescent ground and zigzag pattern at neck and foot, was inspired by vessels found in royal tomb of Amenhotep IV at Tel el Amarna in Egypt, discovered in the late 1880s. 'Cypriote' glass was also inspired by ancient glass that had been corroded by being buried underground for centuries. To create the opaque, pitted, iridescent surface, the body of the heated vessel was rolled in powdered glass, producing a rough texture. 'Lava' glass was fashioned by adding pieces of basalt to the molten glass. The gold iridescence created the effect of flowing lava.

A 'Lava' glass vase, c. 1908. © Christie's Images Limited

A 'Tel El Amarna' vase.
© Christie's Images Limited

A 'Lava' glass vase. © Christie's Images Limited

A 'Cypriote' glass vessel, c. 1919.
© Christie's Images Limited

Tiffany Lamps

Although highly prized today, Tiffany's table lamps, floor lamps and hanging shades were a by-product of his primary focus on decorative windows. Initially, his stained glass shades were pieced together from scraps of coloured glass left over from large pictorial compositions. After the Tiffany Studios Lamp Shop was established in the 1890s the lamps quickly became a commercial success; at the height of production the shop employed nearly 200 artisans. In a 1903 advertisement they were recommended as 'particularly appropriate for holiday and wedding gifts'. The lamps were designed and made on a simple production-line basis, although the artisans were allowed great freedom in the selection of colours and patterns. The pieces of glass are held together by copper foil finished with bronze, a stronger medium than the lead used in stained glass windows, and the shades have impressed metal signature labels. The cast bronze bases were sometimes given a patina of gold or silver or, for the less expensive versions, green or brown.

The decorative lamps fall into six categories that are roughly chronological. The earliest designs, such as the twelve-light 'Lily' lamp, incorporated multiple flower heads with shades of blown 'Favrile' glass. Successful lamp designs such as 'Lily' were produced for many years. 'Geometric' lamps have shades made of coloured glass cut into simple geometric shapes and leaded together. Although sometimes left plain, others are enriched with borders or bands of floral ornament, with 'Favrile' panels or with large iridescent 'turtleback' tiles. The irregular thicknesses of these large iridescent slabs of blown glass produce striking colour variations, sometimes modulating from yellow to green in a single piece. Tiles set into the base could be illuminated from within.

Geometric designs might include Islamic, Renaissance or American Indian motifs. Lamps in the Renaissance Revival style are relatively rare. In one example both the amber shade and the gilt-bronze base are decorated with such Renaissance ornamental motifs as dancing fauns,

A 'Geometric' lamp incorporating 'turtleback' tiles. © Christie's Images Limited

Opposite Page:
A rare example of a Tiffany lamp in the Renaissance Revival style. © Christie's Images Limited

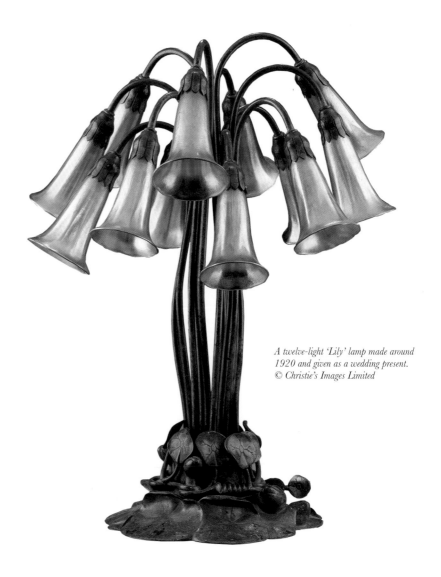

A twelve-light 'Lily' lamp made around 1920 and given as a wedding present. © Christie's Images Limited

medallions and lion's paws. A tiny lamp with a shade only 12 inches in diameter packs a powerful decorative punch. The conical shade features an American Indian basket pattern in shades of ruby red, emerald green and inky black against a yellow brickwork ground. The yellow tiles turn melon-coloured when the lamp is lit and the square column bronze base has a totem face at the top.

'Cone' shades, as described in a Tiffany Studios catalogue of 1906, have straight sides with circular rims. These were easier to produce than shades with curving shapes and more were made of this type. In addition to specific, botanically-identifiable flowers, cone-shaped shades often feature the dragonfly motif so popular in European Art Nouveau designs. In a lamp designed by Clara Driscoll, one of the few women in the design department, this motif has been carried out in tones of blue, green and purple. The 'beanpot' base has been covered with tiny glass mosaic tiles that also reflect the light.

The 'Flowered Globe' group, described as 'domed' in a 1906 catalogue, has a complex arched structure that permits a more naturalistic depiction of floral patterns. A floor lamp 55¼ inches in height is crowned with the rare 'Poppy' shade, of which only two examples are known. At 30½ inches in diameter with exceptionally rich colour and complex design, this is the largest shade produced by Tiffany Studios and represents their finest work. It was once owned by Vito D'Agostino, a legendary early New York collector of Tiffany glass who rescued extraordinary examples from trash bins when they had fallen from fashion during the 1940s and '50s. Shades in this shape usually range in size from 12 inches to 28 inches in diameter.

A 'Dragonfly' lamp designed by Clara Driscoll.
© Christie's Images Limited

A lamp with a shade in an American Indian
basket pattern. © Christie's Images Limited

Detail of floor lamp with the rare 'Poppy' shade. © Christie's Images Limited

Detail of floor lamp with the rare 'Poppy' shade. © Christie's Images Limited

A floor lamp with the rare 'Poppy' shade. © Christie's Images Limited

'Irregular Lower Border' shades have a sinuously curling irregular line along their lower rim instead of a straight metal edge. For the shade of a rare 'Cobweb' lamp, eight spiderweb medallions are interspersed with pink apple blossoms and blue and green foliage on a crackled and textured ground. Brass ribs rise from the base, sprouting branches to support the irregular lower rim of the glass canopy. The baluster-shaped base is set with glass mosaic tiles depicting white narcissi with green and gold leaves. Although now electrified, the base still contains its original fuel canister; the effect of a flickering flame inside this lamp must have been magical.

These shades are particularly effective for the depiction of hanging plants such as laburnum, wisteria and grapes. In the 'Grape' lamp, clusters of grapes are depicted in vivid shades of violet, blue and indigo with leaves in richly mottled green. The clusters hang from a pierced network of vines at the top, beautifully detailed and patinated in green and brown. The final phase of development is represented by shades with both an upper and lower irregular border. In these shades the bronze cap over the top aperture has been replaced by milled bronze openwork of branches or vines that allow the light and heat to disperse upward. An example is the 'Trumpet Creeper' lamp that portrays a vigorous woody vine of luxurious growth with bright orange trumpet-shaped flowers. The shade is constructed with dichroic glass, made of thin layers of a metal oxide, such as chromium, silicon, titanium, aluminium and zirconium depending on the colour wanted, deposited on a base of clear glass. The colour of dichroic glass changes depending on whether light in transmitted through it or reflected by it.

The spectacular 'Lotus' lamp carries the motif of the openwork crown to its ultimate, dazzling finale. The domed glass shade has been reduced to a border of pendant water lilies with thickly-layered full-blown flowers and leaves in rich and varied shades of pink, red, yellow, green and blue. Between the hanging stems round lotus buds of pink 'Favrile' glass can be glimpsed, partially hidden by the openwork of the shade. Their tendrils descend along the shaft of the base, branching at the bottom into a large, spreading lotus leaf with up-turned edges. In December of 1997 this lamp sold for $2,807,500 at Christie's, New York, setting a world auction record not only for any product of Tiffany Studios, but for any example of 20th-century decorative art. Tiffany stained glass lamps represent a pinnacle of American Art Nouveau splendour that has never been equalled.

A 'Cobweb' lamp. © Christie's Images Limited

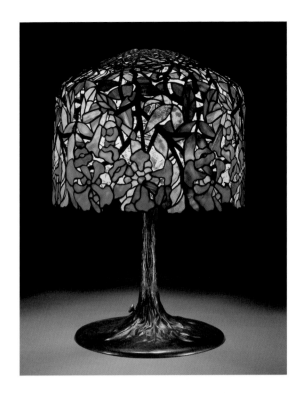

The magnificent 'Lotus' lamp.
© Christie's Images Limited

IV

Glass Between the Wars

Glass Between the Wars

Following the end of the First World War, France was threatened by competition from Germany and Austria and set out to reassert its global pre-eminence in the luxury trades. With government encouragement, artists and designers turned away from elite production to forge a consumer style that celebrated the pleasures of contemporary urban life. Although partially derived from such past national styles as the neoclassicism of Louis XVI, motifs were updated and reinterpreted in an edgy, streamlined idiom. The skyscrapers and jazz clubs of New York, the new archetype of sophistication, were a fresh source of inspiration, while Cubism, Vorticism, Futurism and other European avant-garde movements provided original perspectives of their own. The vogue for 'Modernity' was fused with the 'Exotic', as increasing international trade and travel resulted in surprising discoveries abroad. Motifs borrowed from Mesoamerican sculpture, African tribal art and newly excavated Egyptian artefacts infused 'primitive' vigour into the played-out lassitude of European decorative traditions. Out of this bewildering but glamorous confusion of influences, the Art Deco style was born.

Art Deco Glass in France

Existing glass firms quickly adopted the vocabulary of the new style. After Gallé's death in 1904 the firm continued to operate under his name. One of their most iconic objects – the 'Elephant' vase of 1924 – invokes the allure of the African veldt. The Daum factory was forced to close during The War, but reopened in 1919. Partnering with well-known furniture designers and metalsmiths, they created a series of lamps that incorporated Art Deco motifs from many sources. A bronze and glass table lamp by Daum and Edgar Brandt, the master craftsman of Art Deco metalwork, has an Egyptian theme. The burnished bronze base is in the form of a rearing, open-mouthed cobra, its neck wrapped around a mottled orange and amber glass shade. A glass and wrought-iron table lamp by Daum and Louis Majorelle features mottled pink and violet-flecked glass blown into an open wrought-iron shade with angular Cubist motifs. In the 1930s, Daum produced a number of lamps and vases in clear, transparent or coloured glass with thick walls and deeply etched ribs that resemble stylised versions of a neoclassical fluted column.

The 'Elephant' vase by Emile Gallé, introduced 1924-25. © Christie's Images Limited

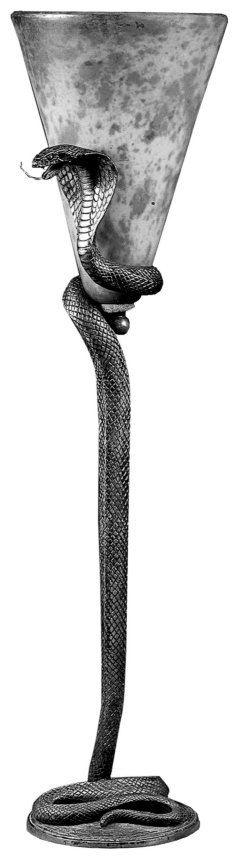

A table lamp by Daum and Edgar Brandt, c. 1925. © Christie's Images Limited

A table lamp by Daum and Louis Majorelle. © Christie's Images Limited

A table lamp by Daum, c. 1930. © Christie's Images Limited

The transition from exclusive manufacture to designing for mass consumption can be seen most clearly in the career of René Lalique (1860-1945). Before the turn of the century Lalique had established a reputation as a celebrated jeweller who provided costly gems in exquisite Art Nouveau settings to the European nobility. He also combined semi-precious stones with such unexpected materials as horn, ivory, enamel and even plastic and glass. Glass fascinated him and in 1902 he rented a small workshop where he created a series of unique vessels using the *cire perdue* (lost wax) process. 'Roses,' a *cire perdue* vase created by René Lalique around 1913, is one example. Since the original model was made of wax and the rough surface of the finished vessel left unpolished, this glass often bears the fingerprints of its maker.

In 1907 Lalique embarked on a new career designing scent bottles and labels for Coty, among other perfume manufacturers. For 'Bouchons Mûres', a scent bottle of clear glass striped with blue enamel, the 'tiara' stopper has been moulded in frosted blue opaque glass as a spray of mulberries. For a bottle created for the perfume 'Le Corail Rouge' (Red Coral) by Forvil, Lalique employed frosted glass and red *patine*, an enamel that coloured the recessed areas of decoration. 'Le Basier du Faune' (Kiss of the Faune) is a scent bottle of clear and frosted glass that Lalique

designed for Molinard. These tiny *flacons* were miniature Art Deco confections, affordable but fittingly associated with luxury fashion, couture and perfume, France's traditional marketing strengths. Demand grew after the First World War when American GIs brought gifts of French perfume for their wives and sweethearts at home. The scent bottles were also sold in American and European department stores, retail outlets that catered to the affluent middle class.

By 1911 Lalique had ceased making precious jewellery altogether. When the war concluded he purchased larger premises where he pioneered press-moulding, a partially mechanised process that enabled his craftsmen to manufacture a vast array of articles in glass – statuettes, clocks, light fixtures, glass jewellery, mirrors, boxes, bowls, carafes, glasses, menu holders, jugs, seals, paperweights, candelabra, bookends, inkwells and ashtrays. 'Suzanne', an opalescent glass sculpture, was made in frosted, opalescent and coloured glass versions; light from the electrified bronze base filters upwards through her diaphanous draperies. The largest and most expensive of Lalique's clocks, 'Le Jour et La Nuit' (Day and Night) made of moulded and frosted glass and bronze, was also available in several different colours. Some of Lalique's designs for perfume bottles were so successful that they were reworked as lighting

'Roses,' a cire perdue vase
by René Lalique, c. 1913.
© Christie's Images Limited

fixtures. For the *veilleuse* or boudoir light 'Deux Paons' (Two Peacocks), a 'tiara' stopper is supported by a frosted and ribbed glass base that is illuminated from within.

By 1925 Lalique was recognised as the leading impresario of the Art Deco style. The pre-eminence of his reputation was confirmed at the 1925 International Exposition des Arts Décoratifs et Industriels in Paris. In addition to having his own pavilion, his work was displayed throughout. He created the exhibition's focal point – a spectacular glass fountain 40 feet high that was illuminated at night – along with frosted-glass panels for the entrance 'Gate of Honour' and, for the Sèvres display, an elegant modernist dining room with a coffered glass ceiling and glass furniture. In the same year Lalique introduced car mascots – automobile bonnet or hood ornaments. Required by the luxurious motor cars of the period as *bouchons de radiateur* (literally, 'radiator stoppers'), these small sculptures could also double as paperweights. More than any other contemporary artefact, the iconic streamlined form of 'Victoire', a tinted and satin finished moulded car mascot, symbolises the exhilarating modern spirit of Art Deco.

'Bouchons Mûres,' a scent bottle and stopper by Lalique, introduced in 1925.
© Christie's Images Limited

'Le Corail Rouge' (Red Coral) by Lalique for Forvil. © Christie's Images Limited

'Le Basier du Faune' (Kiss of the Faun) by Lalique for Molinard, introduced in 1928. © Christie's Images Limited

'Suzanne', a glass sculpture by Lalique, 1922. © Christie's Images Limited

'Victoire', a car mascot by René Lalique,
introduced in 1925. © Christie's Images Limited

'Deux Paons' (Two Peacocks), 1920,
a veilleuse or boudoir light by Lalique.
© Christie's Images Limited

'Le Jour et La Nuit' (Day and Night),
a table clock by Lalique, introduced in
1926. © Christie's Images Limited

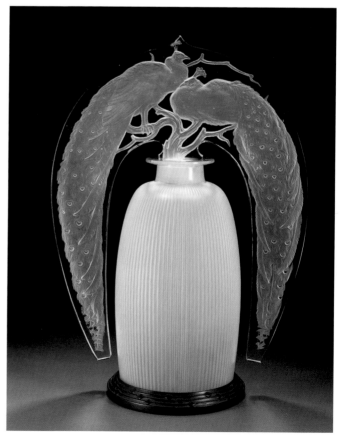

Today, Lalique is perhaps best known for his large, thick-walled vases in clear or coloured transparent glass. These were made in costly precision-cast steel moulds to insure consistent quality and sometimes given a frosted or satin finish. Although not as technically complex as the elaborate Art Nouveau vessels created by the first generation of artistic French glassmakers, the bold forms of Lalique's vases are masterpieces of Art Deco design that have rarely been equalled. His son Marc supervised production from 1922, but René Lalique continued as chief designer during the 1920s and '30s, by which time he was in his 70s. For 'Oranges', a mould-blown clear glass vase, the leaves have been highlighted with black enamel. The model was introduced in 1926 and continued in production until 1947. An emerald green mould-blown vase, 'Languedoc', was first produced in 1929. 'Bacchantes', a blue-stained opalescent glass vase moulded in relief with nude female dancing figures, was one of Lalique's most successful vases. A version of 'Bacchantes' is still made by the firm, which continues today under the Lalique name.

Although undoubtedly the most famous, Lalique was not the only innovative French glassmaker in the Art Deco style. Many of the Art Deco glassmakers built on the technical achievements of their Art Nouveau predecessors; this was especially true for those who worked in *pâte de verre* (vitrified glass paste). The most significant advances in this material were made by the glassmaker Joseph-Gabriel Argy-Rousseau (1885-1953), who created a range of vases, bowls and light fixtures that fully exploited his skill at producing deep, rich colours with subtle gradations. One of his most popular designs, 'Vagues et Poissons' (Waves and Fish), has an intricate pattern of overlapping waves and angelfish. Argy-Rousseau was particularly inspired by historical sources, which he modernised with a light touch. A *pâte de verre* vase called 'Papyrus' was decorated with scrolled Egyptian flower heads in deep blue and green. 'Musiciens Grecs', c. 1928, is in dark purple, pink and white *pâte de verre*, with etched decoration.

In 1928 the sculptor Marcel Bouraine created a number of small female nudes that Argy-Rousseau executed in *pâte de cristal*, a transparent form of *pâte de verre*. One example is 'Papillon' (Butterfly), made around 1928. Other artists, such as Jean Luce, experimented with novel techniques of decoration, including sandblasting Cubist motifs onto black glass. Painting with coloured enamels on glass also enjoyed a revival during the 1920s and 30s. A clear glass vase enamelled with nude female figures and foliage is the work of Marcel Goupy. André Delatte created a clear glass vase acid-etched with irregular ribs, gilt details and painted with flowers. The glass made by the painter Marcel Marinot (1882-1962) was particularly important and influential. One of his enamelled glass vases is painted with geometric ornament and a frieze of female nudes holding garlands. Like Argy-Rousseau, Marinot followed the path of the studio artist instead of pursuing industrial production, creating handcrafted pieces that were one-of-a-kind. After the First World War he began blowing his own glass, fashioning abstract shapes that had a profound impact on later glassmakers. A small glass vase by Marinot of 1927 is of stylised draped form internally decorated in turquoise.

'Oranges', a vase by René Lalique.
© Christie's Images Limited

'Languedoc,' a vase by René Lalique, model introduced in 1929.
© Christie's Images Limited

Opposite Page:
'Vagues et Poissons' (Waves and Fish), a pâte de verre vase by Gabriel Argy-Rousseau, c. 1925. © Christie's Images Limited

'Bacchantes,' a vase by René Lalique, introduced in 1927. © Christie's Images Limited

'Musiciens Grecs,' a vase by Argy-Rousseau, c. 1928. © Christie's Images Limited

'Papyrus,' a pâte de verre vase by Gabriel Argy-Rousseau, c. 1923. © Christie's Images Limited

A vase by Jean Luce, c. 1930.
© Christie's Images Limited

'Papillon' (Butterfly), a pâte de cristal sculpture
by Marcel Bouraine for Argy-Rousseau,
c. 1928. © Christie's Images Limited

A vase by Marcel Goupy.
© Christie's Images Limited

An enamelled vase by Maurice Marinot.
© Christie's Images Limited

A blown-glass vase by Maurice Marinot, 1927.
© Christie's Images Limited

A vase by Andre Delatte, 1920s.
© Christie's Images Limited

Art Deco in England and America

In England, rarely in the forefront of modern design, most glass manufacturers made traditional cut glass between the wars. In an effort to modernise glass and ceramic tableware, Harrods' department store invited 37 contemporary artists, most of whom had no previous experience with these materials, to submit designs. The glass designs were executed by Stuart and Sons of Stourbridge and included a cut and etched glass vase by Eric Ravilious and a similarly embellished glass bowl by Graham Sutherland. Moira and Gordon Forsyth, Paul Nash and Dame Laura Knight also contributed designs. For the resulting display, known as the Harrods' Art and Industry Exhibition of 1934, the wares were produced in signed, limited editions. Although the critics were impressed, the public was less than enthusiastic and 80% of the stock went unsold.

Encouraged by the success of the engraved glass produced in Sweden (see Chapter 6), the Staffordshire glassworks of Stevens and Williams employed the New Zealand architect Keith Murray (1892-1981) to design a line of vases, bowls and decanters. These clear glass vessels with uncomplicated forms and elegant, angular Art Deco engraving were called Brierley Crystal. One Brierley glass bowl designed by Murray has a deeply engraved design of fish amongst seaweed, while another was cut and etched with cacti. The designer W. Clyne Farquharson (1906-1977) also created transparent glass vases with simple shapes and foliate cut decoration for Stevens and Williams as well as for the glassworks of John Walsh Walsh in Birmingham. 'Leaf', a cut and etched glass vase, was designed by Farquharson for Walsh in the 1930s.

A bowl by Graham Sutherland for Stuart Glass, 1934. © Christie's Images Limited

A Brierley bowl by Keith Murray for Stevens and Williams, 1930s. © Christie's Images Limited

A vase by Eric Ravilious for Stuart Glass, 1934. © Christie's Images Limited

A Brierley vase by Keith Murray for Stevens and Williams, 1930s. © Christie's Images Limited

'Leaf,' a vase by Clyne Farquharson for John Walsh Walsh, 1930s. © Christie's Images Limited

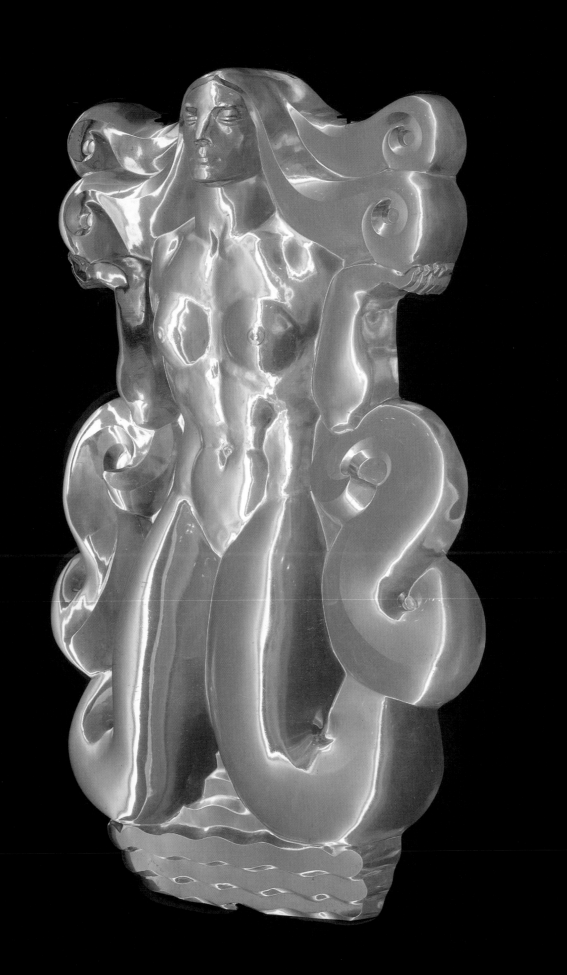

In the United States, Tiffany and Tiffany-style glass continued to dominate the market during the early decades of the 20th century. Among the few manufacturers to break new ground was the Steuben Glass Works, founded in Corning, New York, in 1903 by the English glass designer Frederick Carder in partnership with an American cut-glass maker. In 1918, the company was sold to Corning Glass Works. In the 1930s Steuben was reorganised and production shifted from coloured glass to heavy blown and engraved crystal. The sculptor Sidney Waugh (1904-1963) became the chief designer and his graceful animals and figures in the flattened and stylised Art Deco manner can be seen on the 'Gazelle Bowl' of 1935. He also designed cast and polished glass sculpture such as 'Atlantica', created for the 1939 World's Fair in New York. Over three feet in height, this 300-pound mermaid riding on the waves of the Atlantic Ocean commemorated the start of glassmaking in America by European immigrants. For the less affluent consumer, the Phoenix Glass Company of Monaca, Pennsylvania, introduced 'Ruba Rombic' glass in the late 1920s. Inspired by the Cubist designs on view at the 1925 Paris Exhibition, the coloured glass was moulded into jazzy, irregular shapes.

'Ruba Rombic' fishbowl designed by Thomas McCreary for the Phoenix Glass Company, c. 1928. 32 Courtesy of The Modernism Collection, Minneapolis Institute of Arts

The 'Gazelle' bowl by Sidney Waugh for Steuben Glass, 1935. From the Collection of The Corning Glass Museum, NY, Gift of Mr & Mrs John K. Olsen

Opposite Page:
'Atlantica,' a glass sculpture designed by Sidney Waugh for Steuben Glass, 1938-1939. From the Collection of The Corning Glass Museum, NY, Gift of Mr & Mrs John K. Olsen

Architectural Glass

In architectural glass there was an explosion of creativity as changing requirements and modern technologies provided new opportunities for manipulating the interior environment. Again it was René Lalique who led the way, this time as an interior designer. In an age of luxury transporation, Lalique was in great demand to create stylish surroundings for wealthy travellers on trains and passenger liners, including the liners Paris, the Ile de France and the Normandie. For the last ship, launched in 1932, he designed an enormous first-class dining room, for which 12 illuminated fountains and all the ornamental panels covering the walls and ceiling were fabricated in glass. For the Compagnie Internationale des Wagon-Lits, a French railway, Lalique designed frosted glass panels with moulded designs of bacchantes and grapes.

These panels were used as partitions for the lavish dining cars of the famous Côte d'Azur Pullman Express. He designed similar panels of uncoloured glass for such exclusive shops as the House of Worth and François Coty, for elegant hotels, including Claridge's in London, and even for churches. His most famous ecclesiastical interior is St. Matthew's Church at Millbrook, near St. Helier on the Isle of Jersey, that includes four monumental glass angels and a magnificent glass cross 15 feet high sculpted with Jersey lilies.

In addition to frosted and moulded translucent glass, a wide variety of techniques were used to create striking Art Deco glass panels for fashionable interiors. For a colourful Art Deco panel made in England,

Nine frosted-glass panels for the Compagnie Internationale des Wagon-Lits, c. 1928.
© *Christie's Images Limited*

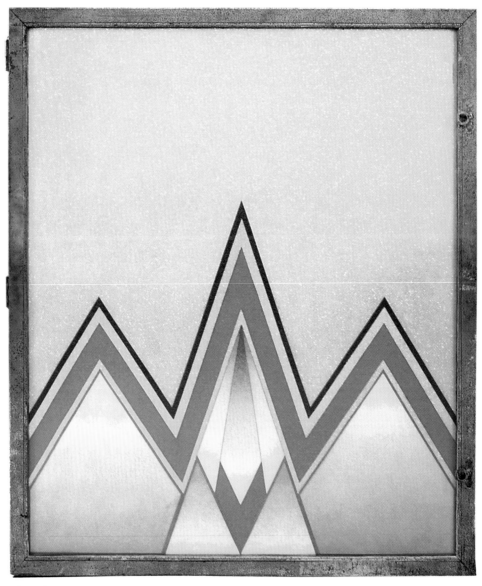

An Art Deco coloured and crushed-glass panel, England, c. 1930. © *Christie's Images Limited*

an Aztec-inspired Ziggurat motif was created from coloured crushed rock crystals sandwiched between two layers of clear glass. Engraved mirrors depicting exotic scenes, often tinted pale silvery-pink or blue, were especially popular. A large painted and engraved *miroir aure boussois* glass panel was designed by Paul Jouve, a well-known sculptor and engraver of animal subjects, and executed by Gaetan Jeannin. Made of nine pink-tinted panels, the mirror was commissioned by Mme. Arlette Dorgere for the dining room of her elegant new town house on Avenue Foch in Paris.

Verre eglomise, the technique of reverse-painted glass, was also used to great effect. A *verre eglomise* panel by Paula and Max Ingrand depicts a pair of doves, butterflies and other flying insects, caterpillars and a lizard. The Ingrands were Parisian designers who created painted, etched and sand-blasted panels for restaurants and private apartments in France, England and America. But in addition to creating decorative panels, it was during the Art Deco period that artists and designers began to fully exploit the dramatic possibilities of illuminating glass with electric light – diffused, reflected and refracted – to create interiors of unsurpassed theatricality, such as Strand Palace Hotel in London by Oliver Bernard. Popularised across the globe by the Hollywood films of the Depression era, the opulent Art Deco interiors of fashionable hotels, theatres, ballrooms and restaurants became the last word in sophisticated glamour.

A verre eglomise panel by Paula and Max Ingrand, 1937.
© Christie's Images Limited

The foyer of the Strand Palace Hotel,
London, 1930-31, by Oliver Bernard.
Courtesy of English Heritage, National
Monuments Record

Opposite Page:

A miroir aure boussois glass panel designed by
Paul Jouve and executed by Gaetan Jeannin,
c. 1930. © Christie's Images Limited

V
Form and Function

V

Form and Function

At the end of World War I, young people returned from the battlefields war-weary, hungry and longing for a new order. With bombastic, feudal old Europe battered into extinction, surely the time had come for a new beginning that would bring hope and comfort for all. Millions had died and the widespread devastation caused by war had rendered millions more homeless; the need for sanitary, functional housing for the masses was urgent. But what should it look like? The replication of past styles, with their pompous ostentation and class-conscious hierarchies was unthinkable and the rhetorical flourishes of 'decadent' Art Nouveau now engendered revulsion. A new purpose had to be found for art and a new style for a new age.

For a fresh start, the first step was a focus on fundamentals. Artists had begun to experiment in this direction before the war. In the 1890s, Paul Cézanne reduced rocks and mountains to the elemental shapes of cylinders, spheres and cones to create a new classicism of firmness and permanence in landscape painting. Picasso and Braque had developed these ideas into the pictorial language known as Cubism. This painting by Georges Braque depicts a still life reordered in an entirely new way. The subject of the picture, a bottle and clarinet, can still be discerned within a web of lines and tones. Instead of a window onto an observed or imaginary world, the canvas or paper sheet has become a flat surface where shapes and lines could be deployed without resort to the old, outmoded rules of verisimilitude.

Other movements besides Cubism added to the excitement of new ideas in art. In Holland, the artist Piet Mondrian (1872-1944) created carefully constructed canvases in which he explored the possibilities of a deliberately limited palette. 'Composition with Red, Blue and Yellow' is a typical example of his mature work. Landscape formed the starting point for these paintings, but reduction and thoughtful arrangement gave Mondrian's shapes a powerful formal balance. His friend, the Dutch painter, designer and critic Theo van Doesburg (1883-1931) collaborated closely with Mondrian in publishing De Stijl (The Style) a hugely influential periodical devoted to the search for new imagery based on mystical and mathematical theories. Although Mondrian restricted his work to paintings, van Doesburg applied his theories to other media including architectural glass. The stained glass window 'Glass composition in Lood' was designed in 1916 but not made until 1956. Note the balanced pattern of geometric shapes and the limited colour range. Van Doesburg felt strongly that the exclusive use of the horizontal and the vertical in art and architecture would create a style that would encourage egalitarian rather than elitist attitudes to life. This austere work can be seen as a precursor to numerous civic and socialist decorative schemes.

However, those that survived the War wanted more than avant-garde aesthetic theories. They yearned for the seamless integration of architecture, the 'fine' arts and the 'useful' arts that would provide a foundation for a new way of life and eventually a new society. Attitudes towards mechanisation had also changed. The tank had been a powerful tool of destruction; could the machine be harnessed for good and help to build a better world for everyone? Where to turn for ideas and training?

At Weimar in northern Germany a pioneering School of Arts and Crafts had already existed before the War, run by the brilliant Belgian architect and designer Henry van de Velde. In 1919 a young architect Walter Gropius succeeded him. Gropius renamed the school the 'Bauhaus' in honour of the 'Bauhutte', the lodges of medieval masons who had built the great cathedrals in which all the arts were united in fervent spiritual expression. Gropius proposed a course of study that would inspire students with similar ideals and equip them to become the builders of the future.

'Let us create a new guild of craftsmen, without class distinctions which raise an arrogant barrier between craftsman and artist. Together let us conceive and create the new building of the future, which will embrace architecture and sculpture and painting in one unity and which will rise one day toward heaven from the hands of a million workers like the crystal symbol of a new faith.'

Lyonel Feininger (1871-1956) made the woodcut to illustrate the Bauhaus Manifesto. It shows a medieval cathedral surmounted by radiant stars against a background of pillared forms expressed in a Cubistic manner. The suggestion of continuity and innovation was exactly the message that Gropius required. Feininger became a 'master' at the Bauhaus, later moving back to America when his work was outlawed by the National Socialists. He helped found the Chicago Bauhaus.

'Composition with Red, Blue and Yellow' by Piet Mondrian, 1930
© Christie's Images Limited

'Glass composition in Lood'
by Theo van Doesburg, 1916
© Christie's Images Limited

'Cathedral'. Woodcut for the Bauhaus
manifesto by Lyonel Feininger, 1919
Courtesy of Bauhaus-Archiv, Berlin

At the Weimar Bauhaus, students were designated 'apprentices', spending a year on a 'Vorkors', a preliminary course during which they would be helped to look afresh at the building blocks of line, shape and colour. Only then were they allowed to enter the workshops to have access to different materials and craft skills as 'journeymen'.

The artist Johannes Itten (1888-1967) was invited by Gropius to run the first Preliminary or Basic Course. He was a Swiss born painter, interested in science, mathematics, theosophy and music. An intense and deeply religious man, he made the course an inspiring experience for his students. Felix Klee, son of the renowned Swiss painter Paul Klee who was also teaching at the Bauhaus recalled his time as a student there. 'Itten… gave lectures three times a week. Once a week there were those marvellous exercises, which especially relaxed the cramped, tense students. Here we also presented the work we had done during the week, both on assignment and on our own. There were studies of materials that we could fool around with in our own studios. These were necessary in order to familiarise us with the materials of any of the Bauhaus workshops, for after the Vorkurs it was mandatory that we learn a handicraft. What magnificent creations were produced by the Bauhaus in 1923! The whole development of modern art – its attempt to create something new at any price – was anticipated by us forty-five years ago, without any particular axe to grind and with a light touch'. Some of the exercises that Felix Klee alludes to would undoubtedly have involved colour theory since this was regarded as fundamental to an understanding of chroma, tone and shade, the tools of the painter and designer. This painting by Johannes Itten was made in 1918 while he was studying the principles of the theory and practice of colour with Adolf Holzel in Stuttgart. The precise arranging of subtle shapes and colours affected every craft practised at the Bauhaus, including weaving and graphic design as well as glass. Itten's own teaching programme was aimed at helping the students 'to rid themselves of all the dead wood of convention and acquire the courage to create their own work'.

Once the Bauhaus student had completed the Preliminary Course, the clay, metal, glass, wood and textile studios were available. Each area had its team of tutors, a master of 'form' and a technical instructor. Although the glass workshop was important in the early Bauhaus years, glass was not continued as part of the curriculum when the school moved to Dessau in 1925.

Gropius' vision of the unity of the arts had derived from the medieval longings of William Morris, yet he did not revere handcraft as an end in itself as Morris had. Instead he believed the most socially constructive role for the artist was as a designer of simple, standardised objects for industrial mass production. In the workshops, students learned to create well-made items for everyday use that were functional as well as beautiful. These included tables, chairs, lamps, drinking vessels, ceramic items, cooking utensils, rugs and wallpaper. However, Gropius did share Morris' enthusiasm for learning through making; thus Bauhaus tutors and students were encouraged to explore the possibilities of combining different media in the search for new ideas.

Within this context glass was valued for its practical characteristics rather than as an expressive medium in itself, an attitude more typical of the engineer than the artist. It was used for architectural decoration, lampshades, containers and other utilitarian objects. German industry gradually warmed to this new approach and many of the products made by tutors and students in the Bauhaus workshops were taken up by German manufacturers and mass-produced. Indeed, several became classics of modern design that are still in production (or imitation) today.

'Ohne Titel' by Johannes Itten, 1918
© Christie's Images Limited

Bauhaus Lamp – Model MT8 by Wilhelm Wagenfeld, 1924
© Christie's Images Limited

Of all the students who struggled to create new objects for the home, Wilhelm Wagenfeld (1900-1990) was among the most commercially successful. He trained at the Weimar Bauhaus between 1923 and 1925 and stayed on as assistant and later head of the metal workshop under Otto Bartning when the Bauhaus moved to Dessau. He later worked for several important German companies, designing new ranges of glassware and appliances. In the iconic table lamp – Model MT8, Wagenfeld has combined circular forms in different materials; contrasting an opal glass sphere with a rounded polished shaft and darker metal base. This prototype, which was made while he was still a student, was exhibited at the Leipzig Fair in 1925 along with several other Bauhaus items. Later the Jena Glassworks put it into production. Copies can be found for sale around the world to this day.

Wagenfeld also designed a wonderfully simple solution to the problem of lighting a room. He used an opaque glass globe in conjunction with a circular nickel-plated reflector for background radiance. This particular light is Model M4 designed in 1927 in the Bauhodishchule Weimar metalworks and intended for industrial production.

Bauhaus Ceiling Light, Model M4 designed by Wilhelm Wagenfeld for the
Bauhodischule Weimar Metalworks, 1927 © Christie's Images Limited

Artists trained at the Bauhaus were fascinated by the problems and possibilities of 'multiples', in particular the standardised items designed for machine production. Wagenfeld created 'Kubus' jars as multipurpose food containers that would be attractive enough to be taken out of the larder or refrigerator and placed directly on the table. He designed different sizes in stackable units for easy storage. Their softened rectangular shapes gave them an attractive sculptural quality. Indeed the creation of tableware for the home was regarded as particularly important. Practicality and beauty were equally relevant. Thus a bowl, plate, glass or jug would be considered afresh in the context of its unique functional characteristics. Harmony between the 'Form' of the object and its 'Function' was the ideal aimed at by the designer. The pressed glass bowls designed in 1938 for Vereinige Lausitzer AG were some of the earliest items to combine qualities we now take for granted. They were visually attractive, easy to clean, durable and inexpensive to make and thus to buy.

Marianne Brandt (1893-1983) was one of the few women who studied and later taught in the metal workshops at the Bauhaus. She designed tableware, cutlery and lamps for manufacture. The ceiling light, Model 657 made in 1929 was designed by her using porcelain and glass. Two lighting companies were particularly interested in her designs and both firms helped the students with practical information on the laws of lighting technique as well as production methods. Brandt was enthusiastic about the role of Laszlo Moholy-Nagy in these projects, describing him as supporting his students with 'stubborn energy' in their pursuit of a good dialogue with industry.

Kubus Containers designed by Wilhelm Wagenfeld, 1938
© Christie's Images Limited

Pressed Glass Bowls designed by Wilhelm Wagenfeld, 1938/39 © Christie's Images Limited

Opposite Page:
Ceiling Light, Model 657 designed by Marianne Brandt, 1929 © Christie's Images Limited

Indeed, the Hungarian artist Laszlo Moholy-Nagy (1895-1946) was one of the liveliest tutors at the Bauhaus. Here he is shown with a group of students in the metal workshop at Weimar. As an avant-garde artist Moholy-Nagy knew van Doesburg and was also acquainted with the Russian Suprematist movement. He joined the staff in 1923 and when the Bauhaus moved to Dessau in 1925 he and Joseph Albers were entrusted by Gropius with the running of the Vorkurs in place of Itten who had returned to Switzerland. T. Lux Feininger, son of the painter Lyonel Feininger who was also a tutor there recalled Moholy-Nagy's 'infectious enthusiasm and delight in experimentation'. Glass was one of Moholy-Nagy's passions amongst which typography, painting, photography, furniture designing and film making should be included. The carefully composed photograph of a 'Light Space Modulator' is an example of Moholy-Nagy's adventurous spirit. Here he has attempted to 'paint with light' using etched, polished and coloured surfaces of different kinds including glass. Moholy-Nagy was also interested in possible architectural applications for his work. The design in gouache painted in 1940 is for a light display mural for a bar. The project was intended to include 'glass tubes, transparencies and filters'. By this time Laszlo Moholy-Nagy had immigrated to the USA and was teaching Bauhaus methods at his own 'Institute of Design' in Chicago. He was also an accomplished painter. This lively picture made in 1943 entitled 'Chicago' is a tribute to the city he made his home. Here ovoid shapes form the letter 'C' with an inner 'C' for the loop railway, while Lake Michigan has been suggested through sparkling notes of blue and white paint. The composition has an underlying geometric construction yet movement is there and a sense of shimmering disintegration.

Laszlo Moholy-Nagy with students at the Bauhaus.
Courtesy of Bauhaus-Archiv, Berlin

Study of the Light Space Modulator. Gelatin Silver print by
Laszlo Moholy-Nagy, 1943 © Christie's Images Limited

Light Display Mural for a Bar
by Laszlo Moholy-Nagy, 1940
© *Christie's Images Limited*

'Chicago' by Laszlo Moholy-Nagy, 1943
© *Christie's Images Limited*

Another important artist working in glass was Joseph Albers (1888-1976). He saw the announcement of the founding of the Bauhaus and immediately decided to leave his teaching job and enrol as a student. Although he had already trained with the renowned stained glass artist Jan Thorn Prikker and constructed several stained glass windows for churches, he decided to abandon this early work and make a fresh start. He later described the move as 'the best step I made in my life'. During his student years at the Bauhaus, he continued to work with glass; indeed, the tutors were so impressed with his work that they reopened the glass workshop for him. Here Albers is discussing sculptural forms with students at the Dessau Bauhaus in 1928.

Albers' earliest 'new' glass was constructed from waste and scrap bound together with wire mesh as well as lead. The formal arrangement of coloured glass crudely held together with lead has been backed by a sheet of fence latticework, which effectively sub-divides the rhythm of the squares. Gradually Albers was finding his own language in this well loved material, linking the ideas imbibed from Bauhaus training with his skills as a glass worker. As his ideas developed, he began to exploit the technique of sandblasting to create new effects. He referred to these panels as 'glass pictures' which would have the status of paintings and not need architectural support. He thought they could be displayed either mounted on a wall or hung in a room. Here Joseph Albers reveals growing confidence in expressing Bauhaus ideas in glass. The composition 'Factory', was made in 1925. Here the red glass has been removed by sandblast to reveal the clear (white) layer beneath. The black shapes have been added with black paint fired for permanence in a kiln. The organisation of the elements that make up the composition is deceptively simple, consisting of pure pattern whose significance is suggested by the title. Albers made the panel 'Upward' in 1926. He used a double-layered blue glass as his 'canvas' and sand blasted the outer colour away with great precision to make the white grid. Black paint has then been applied and fired. This composition has a perceptible visual 'shimmer', not unlike the optical effects explored in the 1960s.

Josef Albers teaching at the Bauhaus, 1928.
Courtesy of The Albers Foundation

'Grid Mounted' glass panel by Josef Albers, 1921.
Courtesy of The Albers Foundation

'Factory', glass picture by Josef Albers, 1925.
Courtesy of The Albers Foundation

'Upward', glass picture by Josef Albers, 1926.
Courtesy of The Albers Foundation

A year later, Albers was still exploring glass. The panel, 'Skyscrapers on Transparent Yellow' is a fascinating tribute to the man made landscape – the ideal city of the future. The brilliant yellow coloured glass must have been especially ordered from the manufacturer indicating a yet more radical departure from Albers' earlier work. Indeed, the simplicity of colour and shape in these glass compositions presage Albers' most famous works in paint and print 'Homage to the Square'.

Josef and Anni Albers were invited to teach at Black Mountain College in North Carolina, a new experimental, multi-disciplinary school for the arts. A photograph shows them on their arrival in New York in 1933. Albers was an enormously gifted teacher, later becoming Director of the College. In 1949 he moved to Yale University to become head of the Department of Design. During this intensely active period, Albers abandoned glass and explored colour through the medium of paint. In over a thousand images he investigated the visual questions posed by the interaction of one colour upon another using the square as his motif. The magnificent sequence of pictures, known as 'Homage to the Square', was widely admired while his 1963 handbook, 'Interaction of Colour', became a useful resource for artists and students alike.

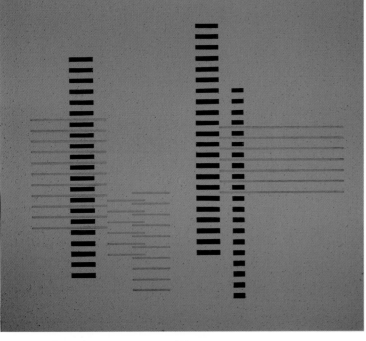

'Skyscapes', glass picture by Josef Albers, 1929.
Courtesy of The Albers Foundation

Photograph of Josef and Anni Albers on
arrival at New York, November 25, 1933.
Copyright Umbo, Otto Umbehr

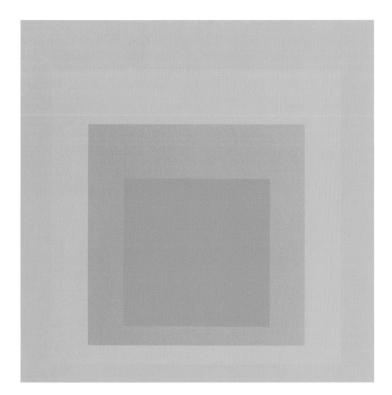

*'Homage to the Square' series of
screen prints by Josef Albers, 1967.*
1 © Christie's Images Limited

VI
Post-Impressionists in Glass

Post-Impressionists in Glass

Air raid damage to French town, 1945,
With permission of The Trustees of
IWM. HU42499

France suffered the trauma of occupation during World War II. The elegant, historic cities with their superb churches and cathedrals were battered almost to obliteration during the final struggle between the Allied and German armies. Once the war ended in 1945 a gradual reconstruction began. Help from America through the Marshal Plan provided aid for housing and essential services. However, at a time of widespread poverty, immediate assistance was also needed to restore the nation's sense of national identity. In 1959 the French government created a new 'Ministry of Culture' with the writer André Malraux in charge. His passion for the arts and his determination to make them accessible to everyone led to the formation of 'Houses of Culture' in every administrative region. This injection of money and state interest encouraged artists to become involved at a local level in the process of healing and rebuilding.

Inevitably many of the aesthetic ideas that had exercised people before the War were looked at afresh. In terms of architectural glass, there had been two important occasions when the work of French artists had been exposed to public view. At the International Exhibition of Decorative and Industrial Arts held in Paris in 1925, the 'Pavilion Vitraux' was filled with stained glass exhibits by French workshops and studios selected by the artist Jacques Gruber. At the same time the painter Maurice Denis had put together an ambitious exhibition of paintings, stained glass, sculpture and metalwork for the specially built church of the 'Village Français' designed by the architect Jacques Droz. These activities brought the possibilities of stained glass to a wide and well-informed audience.

Another event with far reaching consequences was the competition held in 1939 to create new stained glass for the upper windows of the nave of the most important Church in France – Notre Dame de Paris. This competition caused much controversy, particularly as the proposed schemes were on public display at the Petit Palais in Paris. Argument raged around the manner of representing Christian imagery. An updating of the concise story-telling methods of the medieval artists was regarded as one possibility while a complete break with the past through the embrace of abstract art was suggested as another.

These discussions were taken up again in the 1950s during the period of repair and restoration in France. Maurice Denis wrote of the need for a 'living art, deeply felt' that the artists themselves would be proud to develop. Robert Renard implemented this suggestion in 1955. As architect in charge of the historic Cathedral of Metz, he invited the constructivist artist Jacques Villon, and the painters Roger Bissière and Marc Chagall to create new stained glass for the windows in the choir. These commissions were particularly influential since the Cathedral was designated as an historic monument.

The choice of Jacques Villon in particular was surprising. A photograph by Florence Henri shows the artist in characteristic working mode. He was a dedicated painter who had spent most of his life in the village of Puteaux just outside Paris. An aquatint of London made in 1929 reveals something of his early training in graphic art, although the application of colour owes much to the discoveries of 'pointillism' in which a coloured area is broken up into dots to suggest a sparkling or moving surface. In the painting 'Paysage', however, the landscape has been expressed in crisp, clear pen and ink lines similar to the lead lines in the window in Metz. Villon's exquisite use of colour can be appreciated in the 1939 oil painting 'L'Arrivée des Nageurs'. Here the figures of the fishermen have been suggested in black outline and the sea from which they have come represented in blocks of gold and green. The shift from canvas to architecture seems to have inspired Villon to produce stained glass of great splendour. Strong lines and rich colour combine to make a sumptuous window for the historic cathedral of Metz.

'Londres', aquatint by Jacques Villon, 1929. © Christie's Images Limited
© ADAGP, Paris and DACS, London 2005

Portrait of Jacques Villon, 1940.
© Christie's Images Limited

'Paysage', pen and ink drawing by Jacques Villon. © Christie's Images Limited
© ADAGP, Paris and DACS, London 2005

Above:
'L'arrivée des Nageurs', painting by Jacques
Villon, 1939. © Christie's Images Limited
© ADAGP, Paris and DACS, London 2005

Left:
Stained glass windows by Jacques Villon in
Metz, 1955 Cathedral. Photograph by
J. M. Geron & A. Moxhet
© ADAGP, Paris and DACS, London 2005

By far the most influential figure during this period was the dominican monk Father Marie-Alain Couturier (1897-1954). Couturier had trained as a painter and worked as a stained glass artist before entering a Dominican monastery. A lively and courageous writer, he defended the importance of new ideas in ecclesiastical art and architecture through the journal 'L'Art Sacré'. He battled continually with the entrenched conservatism of the Catholic hierarchy and ultimately succeeded in bringing a more enlightened approach to church decoration not only in France but elsewhere in Europe. As a result of his own experience as a glass artist, he was able to facilitate the fabrication of windows by eminent painters inexperienced in glass technique. He materially helped Matisse in the realization of his enchanting windows for the Chapel of the Rosary in Vence.

Couturier was already in America when war broke out and kept in touch with fellow exiles from France, among them Fernand Léger. Through Léger, he met several of the great painters of the Post Impressionist era. On returning to France, Couturier invited many of them to create designs for a new church 'Notre-Dame-de-Toute-Grâce' constructed between 1937 and 1945 among the mountains of the Haute-Savoie at Plateau d'Assy. Léger was invited to make mosaics for the exterior, while Rouault and Chagall among others, were commissioned to design the stained glass windows. All the windows were made at the studio of Paul Bony with whom Couturier himself had previously worked.

Father Marie-Alain Couturier with Jacques Maritain and Marc Chagall, circa 1945.
Source: http://homepage.univie.ac.at/Hartwig.
Bischof/Wissenschaft/Cout_Begegnung.htm

*Exterior of the church of Notre-Dame-de-Toute-Grâce
at Plateau d'Assy, 1937-45, showing murals by
Fernand Léger. © Allan Soedring
© ADAGP, Paris and DACS, London 2005*

*Exterior of the church of Notre-Dame-de-
Toute-Grâce at Plateau d'Assy, 1937-45,
showing window openings. © Allan Soedring*

It is fascinating to observe the way in which those who had never worked in glass before responded to the new medium. The artist Georges Rouault (1871-1958) had been apprenticed to a glazier at an early age and his engravings and paintings had the strength and structure characteristic of a leaded glass panel. His most memorable works are the powerful and deeply spiritual series entitled 'Miserere' which was followed by 'Clowns', 'Girls', 'Judges' and 'Workers'. The print of an equestrienne on her high stepping horse is entitled 'Amazon' in the Circus series. Rouault explored the figure of Christ in a number of pictures and prints. The design for the Assy window was based on one of these and fabricated by Paul Bony between 1958-59.

'Amazon', print by Georges Rouault, 1930.
© Christie's Images Limited
© ADAGP, Paris and DACS, London 2005

Christ Aux Outrages, designed by Georges Rouault and executed by Paul Bony, 1958-59. Church of Notre-Dame-de Toute Grace in Assy. Source www.fabrice.blanc.cc
© ADAGP, Paris and DACS, London 2005

'Christ', print by Georges Rouault. © Christie's Images Limited
© ADAGP, Paris and DACS, London 2005

49/75   G Braque

While the Assy project was underway, Georges Braque (1882-1963) was working on his 'Oiseau' pictures in which he used different colour combinations to explore the shape of a bird in flight. An exquisite series of inexpensive prints exist of these birds, besides the fine window that Braque made with the dove as its theme. The window entitled 'L' Oiseau sur fond violet' was designed by Braque and made at the studios of Charles Marq for the chapel of the Maeght Foundation at St-Paul-de-Vence in 1962.

Fernand Léger (1881-1955) who had befriended Father Couturier in New York, remains one of the best-loved artists of the era. Léger studied architecture at Caen and came to Paris in 1900 as an architectural designer. While serving at the front in the First World War he became fascinated by machinery stating that 'The machine gun or the breach of a 75 are more worth painting than four apples at a table'. He repeatedly painted mechanical objects, searching for a style that would be both new and accessible to ordinary people. He wanted to use colour 'like traffic lights' for its own sake. In the 1952 painting 'Nature-morte au parapluie', each object has been outlined in solid black paint and its shape filled in with a primary colour. The translation of this visual language into mosaic or glass would be entirely appropriate.

Fig 14:
'Nature- morte au parapluie' by
Fernand Léger, 1952.
© Christie's Images Limited
© ADAGP, Paris
* and DACS, London 2005*

Stained Glass Audincourt, France (1950-52)
by Fernand Léger, Audincourt Church,
Besancon, France.
Supplied by The Bridgeman Art Library
© ADAGP, Paris and DACS, London 2005

Indeed, Léger was deeply interested in the possibilities of using art in architecture and was influenced by the ideas of the renowned Finnish architect Alvo Aalto concerning the use of colour to improve people's working lives. For the church of the Sacred Heart at Audincourt, Léger created a wall of brilliantly coloured symbols using thick blocks of glass set into concrete. Known as 'dalle de verre', the technique perfectly suited his trenchant style. More examples of his glass can be seen at Courfaivre in Switzerland (1954) and the University of Caracas in Venezuela (1954). In 1960 his wife Nadia founded a museum in his name at Biot.

For some of the artists encouraged by Couturier, stained glass proved a life long inspiration. This was especially true of the abstract expressionists, Jean Bazaine and Alfred Manessier. Both had distinguished careers as painters, which prepared them for the design of superb windows. Alfred Manessier (1911-1993) had trained as an architect before becoming a painter. He had exhibited widely, winning prizes at the Biennale in Sao Paolo in 1953, the Carnegie Institute, Pittsburg in 1955 and the 1962 Biennale in Venice. The painting 'Le Port', completed in 1945, is a transitional work between landscape and the pure abstraction that Manessier later achieved. Four years later, the artist is composing pictures of real authority using balanced and interlocking shapes, as in 'La Passion'. 'Les champs du bord de mer' was completed while Manessier was beginning to work on cartoons for stained glass. The outlined shapes and dynamic use of colour reveal the suitability of his style for the new medium.

'Le Port 1945' painting by Alfred Manessier, 1945.
© Christie's Images Limited
© ADAGP, Paris and DACS, London 2005

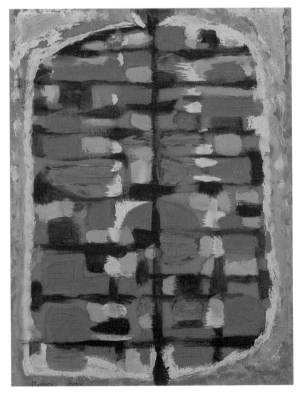

'Le Champs du bord de Mer'
painting by Alfred Manessir, 1951.
© Christie's Images Limited
© ADAGP, Paris and DACS, London 2005

'Le Passion' painting by Alfred Manessier, 1949.
© Christie's Images Limited
© ADAGP, Paris and DACS, London 2005

Manessier created a series of windows for the ancient church of Les Bréseux near Besançon, between 1948–50. The windows are abstract in composition and yet references to figures can be found within the interlocking leads and beautifully orchestrated colours of the glass. Thirty years later Manessier's architectural glass continued to reflect his ideas as a painter. Evidence of his control of harmonious areas of colour can be seen in his designs for the church of St Sépulchre at Abbeville. He worked on windows for this church intermittently from 1982 to 1985. At the age of 73 he began designing a cycle of colourful windows for the Cathedral of St Nicholas in Fribourg, Switzerland which were completed in 1988. Almost all Manessier's windows were fabricated at the Lorin Studio at Chartres.

Jean Bazaine (1904-2004) was a friend and contemporary of Alfred Manessier. He turned to painting in his twenties and became particularly interested in reconciling the figurative and formal aspects of French art; summarizing his ideas in 1948 in a book 'Notes on Painting Today'. In the painting 'La gâre maritime' completed the same year, the depiction of a specific locale is subservient to formal considerations of pattern and design, with a sense of the presence of the railway station and more than a hint of the sea.

One of a series of six windows by Alfred Manessier for the Parish Church of Les Bréseux et Bapteme, Doubs between 1948-50. Supplied by Caroline Swash © ADAGP, Paris and DACS, London 2005

Above:
Tracery detail of 'Pentecost', one of the windows designed by Alfred Manessier for the Church of St Sépulchre, Abbeville between 1982-85. Supplied by Caroline Swash © ADAGP, Paris and DACS, London 2005

Left:
One of a series of windows by Alfred Manessier for the Cathedral of St Nicholas in Fribourg, Switzerland between 1984-88. Supplied by Caroline Swash © ADAGP, Paris and DACS, London 2005

Jean Bazaine checking the colour of
one of his windows. Photograph by
Jean-Marie Geron
© ADAGP, Paris and DACS, London 2005

'La gâre maritime' by Jean Bazaine,
1948. © Christie's Images Limited
© ADAGP, Paris and DACS, London 2005

Like Manessier, Bazaine frequently worked in concrete and glass. At Audincourt in the early 1950s he created a dramatic Baptistery by setting gold, purple and yellow blocks of colour into a sculpturally coherent design. An untitled painting of 1964 indicates how far Bazaine's method of working had moved away from the solid shapes of his post cubist period towards a more expressive and emotionally suggestive style.

In the course of this year Bazaine was awarded the 'Grand Prix National des Arts'. In 1976 he co-founded 'L'Association pour la défense des vitraux de France' (L'ADVF) with Alfred Manessier. He was made a 'Commandeur des Arts et Lettres' in 1980 and continued to paint and work in glass with undiminished vigour. At the age of 87 he produced this elegant and energetic pcture 'Finistère'.

Baptistery at Audincourt by Jean Bazaine,
1954. Supplied by Caroline Swash
© ADAGP, Paris and DACS, London 2005

One of the most underrated artists working in glass at this time is the Belgian Raoul Ubac (1910-1985). He came to Paris in 1930 where he joined the surrealist movement. From 1946 he made prints and engravings, exhibiting these at the Gallery Maeght. The gouache painting entitled 'La Lampe' shows his strong sense of design and passion for intense low-key colour. In addition to paintings he made a number of ardoise, slate stone reliefs inspired by poems. These led on to his later work featuring motifs derived from the natural world including the rhythms of the human body. A retrospective of his work was held in 1968 at Charleroi in Brussels and at the Museum of Modern Art in Paris. Ubac was invited to create new glass for several windows in the romanesque Cathedral of Nevers. Here, in old age and inspired by the austere style of the Cistercians, Ubac formulated a quiet but very satisfactory solution, an enfolded sequence of rhythmic shapes within the simple enclosure of each romanesque arch.

'La lampe' gouache by Raoul Ubac, 1951.
© Christie's Images Limited
© ADAGP, Paris and DACS, London 2005

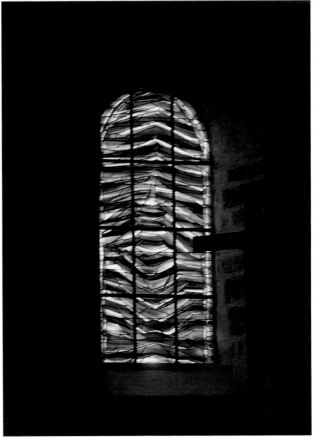

The artist who really captured the imagination of the general public in stained glass was Marc Chagall shown here with his wife Bella in 1934. Although he is renowned principally as a painter, Chagall's work in glass has been highly influential, encouraging other artists to take the medium seriously. The exquisite ruby red window inspired by Psalm 150 which gives authority to the north aisle of Chichester Cathedral contains details of animals, birds and people that can be seen in so many of his painted compositions – participating in mystical adventures. He also made a moving memorial window to Sarah d'Avidgor-Goldsmith for the east window in the small church of Tudeley in Kent.

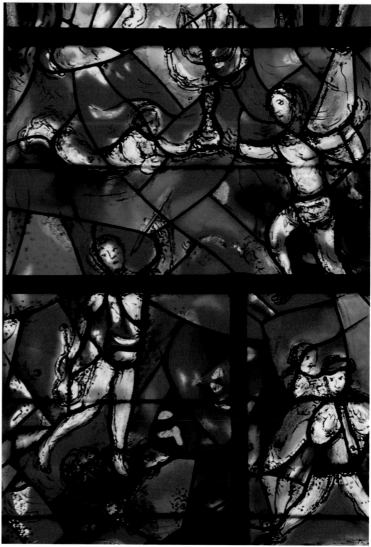

Above:
Marc Chagall with his wife Bella, 1934.
Photographer Roger Viollet. Supplied by Rex Features
© ADAGP, Paris and DACS, London 2005

Top-Right:
Stained glass window for Chichester Cathedral
'Psalm 150' by Marc Chagall, 1978.
Supplied by Caroline Swash
© ADAGP, Paris and DACS, London 2005

Bottom-Right:
Detail of the stained glass window for
Chichester Cathedral by Marc Chagall,
1978. Supplied by Caroline Swash
© ADAGP, Paris and DACS, London 2005

*Detail of stained glass window of
Mother and Child by Marc Chagall
for Tudeley Church in Kent, 1967.
Supplied by Caroline Swash
© ADAGP, Paris and DACS, London 2005*

*Detail of stained glass window of
Crucifixion by Marc Chagall for
Tudeley Church in Kent, 1967.
Supplied by Caroline Swash
© ADAGP, Paris and DACS, London 2005*

*Detail of stained glass window of
Horse and Rider by Marc Chagall
for Tudeley Church in Kent, 1967.
Supplied by Caroline Swash
© ADAGP, Paris and DACS, London 2005*

Marc Chagall (1887-1985) grew up in the village of Vitebsk in Bylorussia, where his Hassidic upbringing furnished him with the evocative imagery from which all his art developed. When he moved to Paris in 1910 he immersed himself in the theoretical discussions and discoveries of the time and became so much part of the French scene that he exhibited with the 'Salon des Independents' from 1912-14. At the time of the Bolshevik revolution, Chagall returned to Russia where he ran a school for workers' children and acquired the title of Commissar for the Arts of Vitebsk. However, he was ousted from this job by the Suprematist artist Kasimir Malevich and returned to Paris. At the outbreak of World War II he was briefly imprisoned by the Vichy government before fleeing to America. There he established his reputation with a series of exhibitions of his paintings. He returned to France in 1947 and settled in the lovely countryside near St Paul de Vence.

Besides producing an astonishing body of work, Chagall became increasingly involved in the designing and painting of stained glass windows. His deeply felt response to the epic tales and dramas of the Bible had already found expression in numerous paintings and in a wonderful series of etchings. In the visionary picture entitled 'David and the angel', for example, a newly wedded couple embrace to the tune of an earthly piper outside a cluster of small dwellings. King David plays his harp for their delight and an angel descends to listen. At the edge of the painting a young mother holds up her baby for our attention. Although the painting was completed in 1977, Chagall's artistic language is so consistent that it appears as if time ceased to be of any importance to him. Indeed, when Chagall designed for stained glass, he simply extended his own pictorial language into the new medium.

Father Couturier thought highly of Chagall's work and invited him to contribute two windows to the pioneering church in Assy. These were made at the glass studio of Paul Bony. Then in 1959, Chagall was asked to create 12 windows for the Cathedral of Metz. These were fabricated at a different studio, the remarkable Simon Atelier near Rheims run by Brigitte Simon and her husband Charles Marq, talented artists in their own right. The 'Empty Tomb', for example, by Brigitte Simon is one of many windows that she made for the Cathedrals of Rheims and Nantes between 1968 and 1980.

'Daive Et L'Ange' by Marc Chagall, 1977.
© Christie's Images Limited
© ADAGP, Paris and DACS, London 2005

Window by Brigitte Simon 'The Empty Tomb'.
Supplied by The Bridgeman Art Library
© DACS 2005

In 1960 Chagall was entrusted with the most demanding task of all, a series of large stained glass windows for the Synagogue of the Hadassah Medical Centre in Jerusalem. Each window represented one of the twelve tribes of Israel, the sons of Jacob, arranged in groups of three on four sides around the tabernacle. As the human figure could not be shown in the synagogue, Chagall created an entire world of his own to suggest the identity of each tribe.

Chagall took the process of constructing the design for his windows very seriously. He began on paper with the fragmentary suggestion of a story, indicating the position of the images he had selected from the rich poetic references clustering around the twelve names of Reuben, Simeon, Levi, Judah, Zebulun, Issachar, Dan, Gad, Asher, Naphtali, Joseph and Benjamin. Such was Chagall's confidence in the ability of Charles Marq that he allowed the windows to be set out from paintings of quite modest proportion, roughly one eighth of the full size. In the completed windows, Marq can be seen to have arranged the lead lines in a straightforward way that would allow the viewer the maximum amount of enjoyment of Chagall's glass and although Marq cut the

glass and prepared the tonal changes, Chagall came to the studio and worked on the windows, strengthening some of the paintwork and adding details which he thought appropriate.

Before the windows were shipped to Jerusalem, they were exhibited in Paris in June 1961, along with the preparatory drawings and gouaches and later that year at the Museum of Modern Art in New York. This exposure not only raised the status of stained glass as an important medium in the hands of artists but fired the imagination of architects, churchmen and students alike. For Chagall himself, demand for his glass continued apace and he received commissions for windows in the USA, Switzerland, England, Germany and France. For the Fraumünster Church in Zurich, Switzerland, Chagall made a superb three light east window in bands of colour which he filled with fascinating detail.

Detail of window showing King David playing his harp in the Fraumünster Church in Zurich, Switzerland – one of Chagall's favourite images.
Supplied by Caroline Swash
© ADAGP, Paris and DACS, London 2005

East window for the Fraumünster Church in Zurich, Switzerland by Marc Chagall.
Supplied by Caroline Swash
© ADAGP, Paris and DACS, London 2005

Undoubtedly the most fascinating of all the projects worked upon by an important French painter is the tiny Chapel of the Rosary at Vence, which contains both mural paintings and stained glass by Matisse. Henri Matisse (1869-1954) trained first as a lawyer and began to paint during his early years as an articled clerk. He studied at the Academy Julian and attended evening classes at the School of Decorative Arts. Like Rouault, he joined Gustave Moreau's studio and spent many hours making copies of paintings in the Louvre. His early work was quite Impressionistic in style and he had a brief flirtation with Divisionism. He also studied sculpture with Eugène Carrière. By combining the formal discoveries of Cubism with new ways of handling colour, Matisse eventually discovered his own way of expressing the 'poetry of forms.' In this early composition, 'Still life with fruit' of 1897, Matisse is already flattening and formalizing the oranges and apples depicted in the still life. These homely objects would continue to provide inspiration for his many adventures in colour and line.

Matisse moved to the south of France in 1917 where he continued to draw and paint, concentrating on a limited range of figural and domestic themes and meditating upon them in line and colour. This method of application produced a remarkable refinement in his work. The 1938 picture 'La Danse' shows how daring Matisse had become in his exploration of recognizable forms flattened to create pattern. When in old age and under the duress of illness Matisse became less able to work fluently with paint, he turned to new techniques: paper cut-outs and collage. Paper shapes were painted to his requirements by his studio assistant Lydia Delectorskaya, providing him with a miraculous entrance to all kinds of pictorial possibilities including design for stained glass. The collage, 'Composition la croix rouge', completed in 1947, includes many of the cut-out shapes that Matisse made his own by a constant process of refinement. Here an unusual balance has been established between the white algae-like forms and the blue, yellow and gold plant shapes placed upon a deep red and blue background. Matisse apparently cut the paper with open scissors rather than by snipping round the shapes. He described this process as 'drawing directly in colour'. Having cut the shapes, Matisse would then arrange and rearrange them until the desired effect was achieved.

Henri Matisse working on designs for the Chapel of the Rosary, Vence.

'Still Life with Fruit', painting by Henri Matisse, 1897.
Photo: © Christie's Images Limited.
© Succession H Matisse/DACS 2005

Detail from the exterior of the chapel, 1947-51 by
Henri Matisse, Chapelle du Rosaire, Vence, France.
Supplied by The Bridgeman Art Library.
© Succession H Matisse/DACS 2005

'La Danse' painting by Henri Matisse, 1938.
Photo: © Christie's Images Limited.
© Succession H Matisse/DACS 2005

In 1942 Matisse moved to Vence to distance himself from a possible invasion of southern France by Mussolini's army. He had endured an operation on his intestine a year earlier and been nursed with great sympathy by Monique Bourgeois who subsequently became a dominican nun. As Sister Jacques-Marie she continued to visit Matisse and when she shared with him her hopes for a new chapel for her order, he offered to help. In 1947 plans for the Rosary Chapel were outlined by a Dominican, the lively Brother Rayssiguier and the whole project supported by Father Marie-Alain Couturier.

Matisse gradually became engrossed in every aspect of this small devotional building. He designed the tiles, wall decorations and the robes for festival occasions. He also started to make collage designs for a series of stained glass windows. The subject chosen was the 'River of Life'. Matisse envisaged this as a 'sweeping decoration' behind the nun's stalls with a vibrant colour scheme suggesting dancing light upon water. However, when Matisse found that the window openings were likely to be altered, he abandoned this subject. Years later when a new school was built in 1955 near his home town of Cateau – Cambrésis, these designs were fabricated in glass by Paul Bony and used to decorate the children's indoor play area. The series of vivid windows became known as 'The Bees'.

Returning to the problem of the design of the Vence stained glass, Matisse decided upon a new symbolic approach and began to explore the idea of a garden enclosed behind a colonnade. This idea evolved into the subject of 'The Tree of Life'. His much observed cactus plant gave Matisse the inspiration for the shapes that would imply growth within the two east windows. In the full sized collage, the yellow frame encloses golden flowers upon a leafy ground arranged as if a heavenly curtain had been let down beyond the altar. The range of windows along the wall behind the nuns' stalls required a different solution. Matisse felt that a more austere and steady rhythm was required. He considered flames or flowers, enigmatically suggesting that the solution might be discovered only after the windows had been constructed.

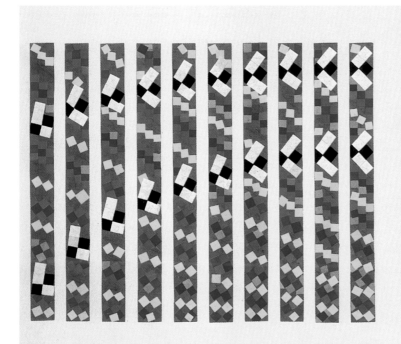

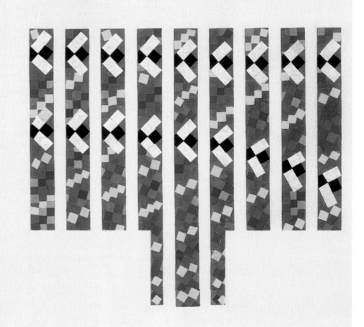

Above:
Collage design in gouache entitled 'River of Life'
by Henri Matisse, 1948. Photograph by Rene
Percheron / Citadelles & Mazenod, Paris.
© Succession H Matisse / DACS 2005

Left:
Interior of the nursery school at Le Cateau showing the series
of windows made in 1955 from the designs 'River of Life'.
Photograph by Rene Percheron / Citadelles & Mazenod, Paris.
© Succession H Matisse / DACS 2005

*Detail of the altar from the interior of the chapel, 1947-51 by
Henri Matisse, Chapelle du Rosaire, Vence, France. Supplied by
The Bridgeman Art Library, © Succession H. Matisse/DACS.*

Indeed glass colour gave Matisse tremendous problems. Blue and green were available but the yellow glass worried him terribly. He became fascinated by the possibilities of the projection of colour upon the white tiled floor surface, and wanted to see an intense 'buttercup' rather than an orange or yellow shade. And when seen against the light, he felt that the yellow should be translucent not transparent. Many trials were made and samples sent for Matisse to look at. He wanted a colour sufficiently saturated to stand on its own next to blue and green and yet have its own 'energy'. He wondered whether a 'plated' (two layered) glass would be best and complained that the sample sent by Bony has 'not enough lemon, not enough of the oboe in it'. Eventually Couturier came to the rescue and managed to find glass of which Matisse approved. The stained glass was finally completed in October 1950 and is considered a masterpiece of 20th century architectural glass.

Roughly 400 churches were either restored or newly built in France during the postwar period. Inevitably many were quite conventional but a few broke new ground in concept and construction, especially in the use of concrete as a building material. As early as 1923, the architect Auguste Perret had built a church on the outskirts of Paris called Notre-Dame de Raincy, entirely in reinforced concrete. Stained glass by Maurice Denis decorated some of the windows but the finest glass was by Marguerite Huré, one of Denis' students. Through her imaginative intervention, the window openings disappeared, seemingly replaced by a wall of coloured light. The sense of unity achieved in this way had an authority that inspired many architects to make concrete the material of choice. An added advantage was thought to be the element of security provided by the unbreakable blocks of glass.

Above:
Interior of the chapel, 1947-51 by Henri Matisse, Chapelle du Rosaire, Vence, France. Supplied by The Bridgeman Art Library, © Succession H. Matisse/DACS 2005

Opposite:
Stained glass Art Deco wall by Maurice Denis, Church of Notre-Dame, Le Raincy, Ile de France, France. Supplied by Caroline Swash
© ADAGP, Paris and DACS, London 2005

Perhaps the most famous of all these buildings is the church at Haut Ronchamp in the south of France. Father Couturier was responsible for recommending the Swiss architect Charles-Edouard Jeanneret (Le Corbusier) as the right person to rebuild this small pilgrim church. Besides his architectural practise, Corbusier was a talented painter and enthusiastic colourist. These two prints, both made in 1955 reveal Corbusier's lively understanding of shape, colour and proportion.

Exterior of Chapel Notre Dame de Haut Ronchamp, 1955, designed by Le Corbusier. Photograph by Simon Glynn, source www.galinsky.com © FLC/ADAGP, Paris and DACS, London 2005

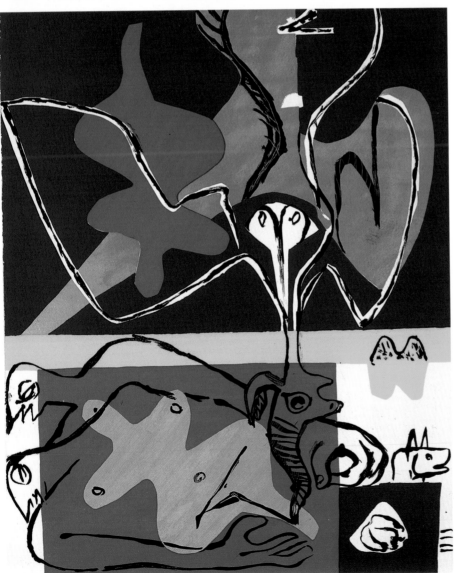

Left and Opposite Page:
'Poémes de L'Angle droit', lithographs by Le Corbusier, 1955.
© Christie's Images Limited
© FLC/ADAGP, Paris and DACS, London 2005

At Ronchamp, Le Corbusier redefined the concept of the glass wall that had inspired the imagination of the medieval builders. He designed deep recesses in the wall of the building to hold small panels of glass whose colour would change with daylight to create a very special atmosphere for worship and prayer.

The impetus to provide exciting new work in glass for France's magnificent churches has not diminished with time. In 2000, for example, a series of experimental windows were designed by internationally renowned artists for the 13th century cathedral of Nevers. Projects of this kind keep the medium of architectural stained glass alive.

Interior of Notre-Dame de Haut Ronchamp
by Le Corbusier. Photograph by Jeffery Howe
© FLC/ADAGP, Paris and DACS, London 2005

VII
Glass Design in
Scandinavia and Italy

Glass Design in Scandinavia & Italy

After the disruption of World War II, a number of European countries devised national strategies to revitalise their depleted economies. Among these, Italy and Scandinavia stand out for promoting design as a fashionable 'added value' to their products. 'Artist-designers' were invited into the factory to create imaginative prototypes for mass production and home furnishings that combined beauty with utility were emphasised. Marketing efforts focused on showcasing these objects in high-status venues. Large travelling exhibitions, often supported by state and corporate funding, presented stylish domestic wares to sophisticated international audiences. In 1932, the Museum of Modern Art in New York created the first permanent collection of industrially made products that exemplified 'Good Design' and other museums soon followed.

Scandinavia

In Scandinavia, designers fused the sleek lines and minimal ornament of Functionalism with natural materials and national handicraft traditions to create a new style of elegant furnishings. This style became known as 'Swedish Modern' or 'Danish Modern,' often without regard to the actual country of origin. Teak furniture, rough textured wall-hangings, inventive light fixtures and even simply-cut, brightly-patterned clothing radiated an aura of warmth, comfort, progressive values and high-style refinement that became a standard of good taste during the 1950s and 60s. In glass, exquisite objects for display were favoured by interior designers. Their production drew on craft traditions already established before the war, especially in Finland and Sweden.

The 'Savoy' vase, designed by Alvar Aalto in
1936 and made at the Karhula Glassworks.
© Christie's Images Limited

Finland

A vibrant culture of glass was well developed in Finland by the early decades of the 20th century. The Finnish architect Alvar Aalto (1898-1976) was a consummate designer of glass as well as other interior furnishings. His early influences included the National Romantic movement in architecture as well as Art Nouveau, both of which instilled in him a love of organic forms. In 1929 he became friendly with Walter Gropius and became a convert to Modernism as it had evolved at the Bauhaus in Germany. Aalto humanised the strict geometry of this austere style by introducing curving shapes as well as warmer materials, such as wood. In his iconic 'Savoy' vase of 1936, his undulating forms are lyrically expressed in transparent, mould-blown glass. Named after a luxury restaurant in Helsinki and made at the Karhula Glassworks, this design classic has been in production in several colours for over 65 years. The vase is a beautiful organic form on its own and displays flowers and plant material in an informal, natural arrangement.

After the war Finland's international reputation for outstanding domestic design was burnished by the creative ingenuity of Tapio Wirkkala (1915-1985) and Timo Sarpaneva (b.1926). At the Milan Triennial exhibition in 1951, Finland was awarded six Grand Prix prizes, four honourable mentions, seven gold medals and eight silver medals, primarily for the glass by these two men. Considered the 'father figure' of Finnish design, Tapio Wirkkala created prototypes for a wealth of industrially-produced products in ceramic, metal and wood, as well as glass. He designed lighting fixtures, furniture, appliances, graphics and exhibitions. Drawing on the materials and processes of Finnish handicraft as well as naturalistic forms, his work expresses a recognisable sense of national identity.

Wirkkala became a glass designer for Iittala in 1947 and artistic director of the Central School of Industrial Arts in Helsinki from 1951 to 1954. His glass first achieved international recognition in the late 1940s and 1950s with the introduction of his 'Kantarelli' (Chanterelle) vases in 1946; the series was produced until 1960. In clear, paper-thin glass this vase imitates the natural structure and surface of the frail ribboned mushroom after which the series is named. Wirkkala's simple and elegant form captures the spirit of organic growth in its swelling shape and the vertical lines of its cut decoration. He also designed for other European glass manufacturers, including the Italian firm Venini.

The 'Kantarelli' (Chanterelle) vase, designed by Tapio Wirkkala and manufactured by Iittala Glassworks.
© Christie's Images Limited

Timo Sarpaneva began working in glass at the Iittala factory in 1950 and opened his own firm in 1962. Owing to the close ties between Finnish art and industry, Sarpaneva has also designed ceramics, metalware, textiles, graphics and interiors, although he is best known for his utilitarian and sculptural glass. In his words, 'glass is the material of space, it is best suited as a material to be given to light'. His 'Orkidea' (Orchid) vase was designed in 1953 and produced in steam-blown clear glass by Iittala Glassworks. In 1954 a vase from the 'Orchid' series was chosen as the 'most beautiful object of the year' by the American magazine House Beautiful.

In the 1960s Sarpaneva discovered a group of discarded wooden moulds once used for blown glass; partially burned, these were charred on the inside. He re-used the moulds to create vases with richly naturalistic surfaces that he named 'Finlandia'. Celebrated designs from the 1980s and 90s include his 'Archipelago' series and his 'Marcel' vases. Incorporating random bubbles and irregularly incised horizontal lines and stress marks, the 'Archipelago' candleholders resemble cracked ice or the trunks of birch trees.

An 'Orkidea' (Orchid) vase, designed by Timo Sarpaneva and produced by Iittala Glassworks. © Christie's Images Limited

'Archipelago' candleholders, designed by Sarpaneva in 1981. © Christie's Images Limited

Sweden

At the end of the 19th century, a number of small glass factories were established in the densely forested region of Småland, on the southeast coast of Sweden. Orrefors Glasbruk was founded in 1898 and initially produced utilitarian vessels and art glass in a derivative Art Nouveau style. In the hope of developing a fresh identity, in 1916 the fledgling firm hired the painter and graphic designer Simon Gate (1883-1945). A year later he was joined by the artist Edward Hald (1883-1980), who had studied briefly with Matisse in Paris. As Sweden had no previous tradition of glass engraving, the two men set out to master this craft. By the 1920s, with the help of experienced engravers brought from Czechoslovakia, Orrefors was producing engraved glass of extraordinary quality. Gates's designs were often in an elaborate neo-

classical style, especially for exhibition pieces such as the 'Bacchus' bowl, designed for the Paris Exhibition of 1925 and engraved by Gustaf Abels. Edward Hald, an ardent modernist, designed the 'Fireworks' bowl in a lighter and more playful narrative style. Although vessel glass was his major focus, Hald also designed glass panels with this technique. A large etched and engraved glass panel designed by Hald depicts a voyage to an exotic island and may have been part of a decorative scheme for an ocean liner. This level of excellence continued with the Art Deco designs of Vicke Lindstrand (1904-1983), who joined the firm in 1928. In 'Shark Killer', an engraved glass cylinder by Lindstrand, the undulating surface of the glass heightens the dynamic movement of the underwater drama.

The 'Bacchus' bowl, designed by Simon Gate for the Paris
Exhibition of 1925 and engraved by Gustaf Abels, Orrefors.
Photograph by Per Larsson

Above:

The 'Fireworks' bowl, by Edward Hald,
1921. Photograph: Orrefors Arkiv

Above-Right:

An etched and engraved glass panel,
designed by Edward Hald for Orrefors,
c.1948. © Christie's Images Limited

'Shark Killer', an engraved glass cylinder by
Vicke Lindstrand, early 1930s, for Orrefors.
© Christie's Images Limited

During the same period Gate and Hald developed the 'Graal' technique, in which a layer of decorated glass is encased between two layers of clear glass. This technique was developed further by Edvin Öhrström (1906-1994) in 'Ariel' glass, in which tiny bubbles are captured in heavy-walled crystal. He used this technique for his 'Red Panther' vase of 1938, made of clear glass internally decorated with flowers and animals embellished with air bubbles. A third variation is 'Ravenna', which was created in 1948 by Sven Palmquist (1906-1984) to capture the rich glowing tones of the 17th century stained glass he had seen in Ravenna, Italy. The 1950s and 60s was the golden age of Swedish glass: Ingeborg Lundin (b.1921) created a sensation at the 1957 Triennial with the pure form of his 'Apple' vase that highlighted the clarity of the green crystal. Gunnar Cyrén (b.1931) added a light-hearted note to the craft of painting on glass, using imagery from Swedish folk art to decorate vessels such as his 'Cycle Touring' bowl of 1969.

Many of these traditional techniques are still in use at Orrefors today, as in the work of the contemporary artist Martii Rytkönen (b.1960). In more recent years, Orrefors has drawn on the talents of artists who trained in the studio rather than in industry. Per B. Sundberg (b.1964) began as a ceramist before joining the company in 1994 and his work often invokes the malleable character of that material, as in his 'Vase Black/White'.

A series of mergers in the 1990s amalgamated a number of smaller glass factories in Småland, some of which dated from the 18th century. Among them was Kosta Boda, where the Art Nouveau style had been introduced by the artist Gunnar Wennerberg in 1900. The company retains an independent identity and today produces the work of Bertil Vallien and his wife, Ulrica Hydman-Vallien, among others. Vallien (b.1938), who also trained in ceramics, mastered the technique of sandcasting; his long cuts of glass with symbolic boat-like forms are represented in museums around the world.

'Red Panther' vase in 'Ariel' technique, designed by Edvin Öhrström, 1938, for Orrefors. Photograph: Orrefors Arkiv

'Fish Graal' vase designed by Edward Hald, 1938, for Orrefors. Photograph: Orrefors Arkiv

Bowl in 'Ravenna' technique, designed by Sven Palmquist, 1961, for Orrefors. Photograph by Per Larsson

The 'Apple' vase, designed by Ingeborg Lundin for Orrefors, 1957. Photograph by Per Larsson

Bowl in the 'Ravenna' technique, designed by Martti Rytkönen, 2001, for Orrefors. Photograph by Rolf Lind

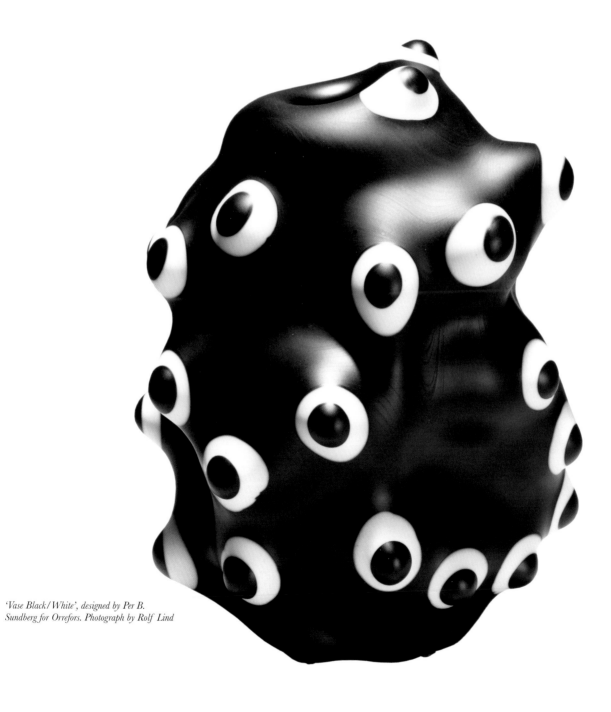

'Vase Black/White', designed by Per B. Sundberg for Orrefors. Photograph by Rolf Lind

Italy

In Italy, innovative modern design, often supplied by architects rather than artists as in Scandinavia, fused with the long tradition of high-quality craftsmanship among the master glassblowers of Venice. In 1921 Paolo Venini (1905-59), a lawyer from Milan, established a new factory at Murano and required his glassblowers to abandon the ornamental Venetian style in favour of the clean lines and sculptural shapes of contemporary abstract art. Among his early designers was the architect and painter Tomaso Buzzi, who in 1932 designed a large 'Coppa delle Mani' (Cupped Hands) chalice. The shallow bowl of pink glass with gold foil inclusions is supported by a paired of moulded hands, each with an applied glass bracelet and ring.

Buzzi was followed in 1934 by the young architect Carlo Scarpa. Scarpa's internal filigree vase, made of deep amethyst threads encased in clear glass, incorporates a traditional Venetian technique recast in a modern form. His 'Macchie' (Stained) bowl is internally decorated with geometric motifs in amethyst and blue. Produced under difficult wartime conditions during the early 1940s, the decoration of this bowl reflects Scarpa's interest in Japanese art.

A 'Coppa delle Mani' (Cupped Hands) chalice, designed by Tomaso Buzzi for Venini in 1932.
© Christie's Images Limited

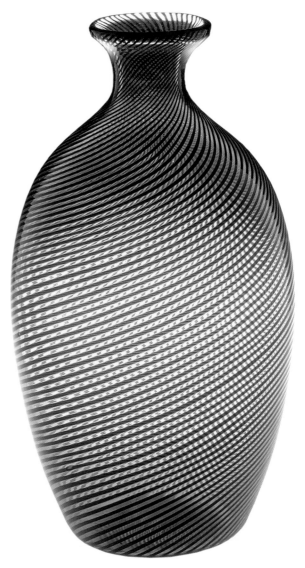

An internal filigree vase designed by Carlo Scarpa for Venini, c. 1932-36.
© Christie's Images Limited

Around the same time, Ercole Barovier (1889-1974) from an old Muranese family of glassblowers, experimented to find new techniques for blowing coloured glass, inspired in part by the thick-walled vessels of Maurice Marinot in France (see Chapter 4). The body of Barovier's 'Mosaic' glass vase, designed for Vetreria Artistica Barovier & Co., is composed of irregularly shaped glass tesserae of amber outline and decorated with four large stylised roses composed of crimson, emerald green and eggplant tesserae. Barovier sliced rods of glass into discs, arranged them in a mosaic pattern and then blew them, an extraordinarily difficult technique.

The 1950s witnessed an explosion of creativity in Italian glass. Among the most inventive was Dino Martens (1894-1879), the head designer for hollow glass for the firm Aureliano Toso. The bold colours of his asymmetrical forms resemble the rough, gestural brushstrokes of Abstract Expressionist painting. The 'Oriente' patchwork vase designed by Martens in the 1950s features a pear-shaped body with foil inclusions and an applied handle pulled up at the rim into two points. The brightly coloured patches were created by powders, granules and sections of glass rod. Martens' originality was more than matched by Fulvio Bianconi (1915-1996), a freelance designer for Venini who worked closely with the master glassblower Arturo Biasutto. In 1949-50 Bianconi and Venini developed the celebrated 'Fazzoletto' bowl that resembles a delicate floating handkerchief. Although the striped effect produced by closely spaced blue, white and colourless cane is a traditional Venetian technique, the whimsical form is pure inventiveness. This was followed by the brilliantly coloured 'Pezzato' vases in which the patterns formed by the fused panels of red, blue, green and clear glass shift in three dimensions as the vase is turned. His whimsical 'Scozzese' vases of interlacing threads of coloured glass cane are elegant but playful variations on Scotch plaids.

Although these extraordinary investigations into the artistic potential of blown glass proceeded separately in Italy and Scandinavia, there was also a great deal of mutual admiration and influence. This can be seen most clearly in the work of Flavio Poli (1900-1984), the head designer and partner in the Murano firm of Seguso Vitre d'Arte. In Poli's 'Corroso' vase, the layers of turquoise and amber glass have been cased in clear glass and the surface treated with hydrofluoric acid. The interplay between the interior and external forms of his vessels relates closely to the thick-walled crystal of Timo Sarpaneva.

The death of Paolo Venini in 1959 marked the end of an era of exuberant creativity. The 1960s were characterised by simpler, more monumental forms and the demand for older designs hampered innovation. Experiments continued with 'murrine' glass, which incorporates glass 'jewels' or slices of rods, themselves fashioned of layers of coloured glass. Anzolo Fuga, a freelance designer who also worked in stained glass, designed a large 'Murrine' vase by for Arte Vettraria Muranese (A.VE.M) in 1960. At the Venini firm the founder was succeeded briefly by the American Thomas Sterns (b.1936). Sterns' 'Facciate di Venezia' (Façade of Venice), a free-blown, applied and iridised glass sculpture, is the last of ten versions of this work that represent the fluctuations and reflections of the surface of the Venice Lagoon. Six of the ten were awarded a gold medal at the Venice Biennale of 1962, only to be retracted when the judges learned that they were not designed by an Italian. Nevertheless, the openness of the Murano workshops to Americans, most especially Dale Chihuly, had an immeasurable impact on the American studio glass movement. The Venini firm is still in operation today.

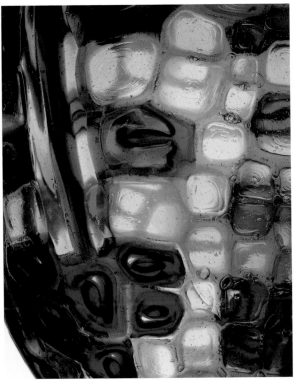

A 'Mosaic' glass vase designed by Ercole Barovier for Vetreria Artistica Barovier & Co., c.1924. © Christie's Images Limited

Opposite Page:
A 'Fazzoletto' (handkerchief) bowl designed by Fulvio Bianconi and Paulo Venini, 1949-50. © Christie's Images Limited

*An 'Oriente' patchwork vase designed by
Dino Martens for Aureliano Toso, 1950s.
© Christie's Images Limited*

*Two 'Pezzato' (Spotted) vases designed
by Fulvio Bianconi for Venini, 1951.
© Christie's Images Limited*

*A 'Scozzese' (Scotch) vase designed
by Fulvio Bianconi for Venini, 1954.
© Christie's Images Limited*

*A 'Corroso' vase by Flavio Poli
for Seguso Vetre d'Arte, c. 1957.
© Christie's Images Limited*

Left and Right:
*'Facciate di Venezia' (Façade of Venice), a glass
sculpture by Thomas Sterns for Venini, 1962.
© Christie's Images Limited*

*A 'Murrine' vase designed by Anzolo Fuga for
Arte Vetraria Muranese (A.VE.M), 1960.
© Christie's Images Limited*

VIII
Scandinavian Architectural Glass

Below:
Exterior of Tromsdalen Church
(The Arctic Cathedral) in Tromsø Norway.
With permission of the photgrapher

Bottom:
Dalle de verre window for Tromsdalen Church
(The Arctic Cathedral) by Victor Spaare.
With permission of the photgrapher

Scandinavian Architectural Glass

In the decades following the end of World War II, the artistry of Scandinavian vessel glass was internationally recognized and acclaimed. The achievements of the region's artists in stained glass are, however, less well known. The hunger for new forms of expression during the post war period led to a number of innovative experiments in this medium. The questions that all artists ask themselves – questions of subject, form, colour and purpose continued to be considered in the context of the achievements of the established giants – Picasso, Matisse and Braque and a host of important sculptors and painters whose work could still be seen in the public and commercial galleries in Paris. Indeed, during this period Paris played host to a number of excited young foreigners determined to create new art out of the ashes of a war-torn world.

In Norway, for example, a competition was organized in 1955 to make new glass for Stavangar Cathedral. This attracted 45 entries. The winner was Victor Sparre and runners up were Atle Ardel and Jorgen Skaare. Skaare traveled to France where he learnt how to work in dalle de verre in which chunks of coloured glass are embedded in cement to make a veritable wall of glass. On returning to Norway he passed on the technique to the G A Larsen workshop where most of Norway's stained glass windows were made. A number of exciting architectural schemes followed including the vast triangular wall of glass made for Tromsdalen Church (The Arctic Cathedral) at Tromsø in the far north of the country. Here, Victor Sparre has created one of the largest dalle de verre windows in the world. The glass covers an area of 140 square metres. The subject accords with Sparre's own aim which was to bring the proclamation of Christ into the actual fabric of the building. His Christ is a radiant presence set in a gold nimbus against a sky blue background, while apostles and holy women stand small and human below.

In Sweden, artists were expected to work in a range of contexts and media. Distinguished painters such as Lennart Rodhe, Sven Erixson, Einar Forseth and Bo Beskow were able to respond with enthusiasm to a wide variety of architectural projects. Most followed the example of the great French glass designers by continuing to exhibit their paintings and drawings while intermittently working on architectural commissions.

Lennart Rodhe (1916-2005) trained in painting at the Art Academy in Stockholm. His work was highly regarded in Paris where he was included in the 1947 'Realités Nouvelles' exhibition. Six years later his work was shown at the prestigious Gallerie Denise René. After a period of working in a semi abstract manner, Rodhe began to explore pattern with increasing confidence. He was particularly interested in the creation of a sense of illusion in which a flat surface could be made to appear to recede and bend through the arrangement of colour and shape. Between

Above:
Detail of 'Skogen' (Woodland) painted by
Lennart Rodhe between 1977-88.
© Tord Lund/Moderna Museet, Stockholm

Left:
Lennart Rodhe in his studio, 1986.
With permission of the artist.

1948 and 1953 Rodhe worked on two important murals. One for the Post office in Östersund and another for an Elementary School at Ängby. The rhythmic pattern of the interlocking shapes that he evolved for these projects were taken further in the superb window 'Fruit garden' which he designed for the Swedish Merchant Bank in Stockholm in 1957. Here the metal construction required for the wall has been designed to form a coherent part of the overall scheme, while Rodhe's interest in pattern and colour has been given a new dimension glass. Rodhe returned to painting with increased confidence, producing a series of unforgettable images, some of which were adapted with great success as repeating patterns for textiles. These included 'Skogen', a richly coloured and complex picture inspired by forest and woodland forms which he worked on between 1977 and 1979. The vivid painting entitled 'Duomo' with its interlaced arches was completed in 1980.

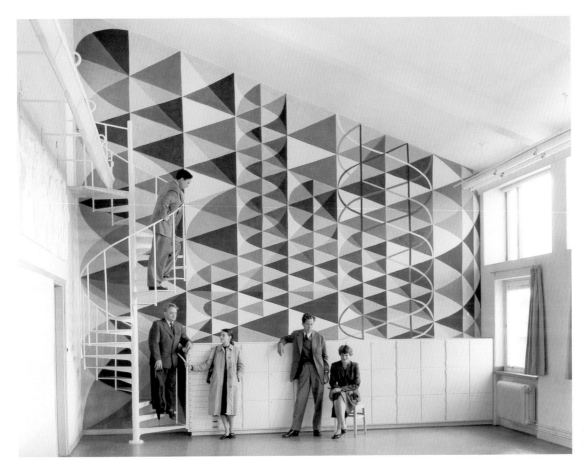

Mural at the Elementary School at Ängby by Lennart Rodhe. With permission of the artist, Lennart Rodhe. © Bertil Höder / Pressfototjänst.

Einar Forseth (1892-1988) was taught by his father, a draughtsman and lithographer before going to Art School in Gothenburg and the Academy of Art in Stockholm. There he worked as assistant to the renowned church decorator, Olle Hjortzberg. His fame was established at an early age by the glass mosaics he designed for the banqueting hall of the Stockholm Town Hall. Ragnar Östberg, its architect intended to make the hall particularly splendid and luxurious. In imitation of the glory of Venice and Byzantium, he decided that the walls should be entirely covered in gold. This apparently extravagant scheme was supported by a donation from the NK department store of Sweden and also by the German Government, whose imperial mosaic workshops were offered at a reduced rate since customers were in short supply following the devastation of the First World War. Ostberg invited Forseth simply to design the motifs for the Banqueting Hall after admiring his lively decorations for the ceiling of the nearby Cellar Restaurant.

However, Forseth had no intention of merely designing the decorations, insisting on supervising the entire project himself. Between 1921 and 1923, he traveled between Stockholm and Berlin where the German and Italian craftsmen were at work setting gold leaf between squares of clear and coloured glass. Without diminishing his personal style, Forseth made the Banqueting Room a space to rival the splendour of the ancient world. However, when the Stockholm Town Hall was opened to public view, Forseth's figure of 'Queen of the Mälaren' gave great offence. Her elongated body and staring eyes, snakelike hair and powerful arms were considered ugly and grotesque. Alteration was mooted, but Forseth stood his ground and refused to respond to the suggestion that the figure should be changed in any way

'Queen of the Mälaren' designed by Einar Forseth in 1920, for the mosaic decoration of the Banqueting Hall of Stockholm Town Hall completed in 1923. The figure is 'Queen of Mälaren' surrounded by figures representing northern and southern Sweden.
© Crown Copyright. UK Government Art Collection
© DACS 2005

Forseth made his first window for the church of Frövi near Örebro. This commission was followed by a number of others including this fine window for the church of Halmstad. Here Forseth's lively mind and expressive method of painting can be seen to advantage. In this panoramic composition he has included a number of scenes of everyday life treated in a humorous yet sympathetic way. His windows were fabricated in the well equipped Stockholm studio of the experienced master glassmaker Gustav Ringström. There Forseth was able to work on the glass himself, experimenting with different colours and adding detail to the surface of the glass through engraving and painting. Work on each window included a coloured design as well as full size drawings in pencil and charcoal. Sometimes Forseth would explore the colour further through scaled up paintings before selecting the glass. He was self critical about his own work, describing his windows as 'naturalistic picture type with the colour arranged independently'.

Designs by Einar Forseth displayed in his studio, 1985. Supplied by Caroline Swash

Window for Halmstad Church by Einar Forseth. Supplied by Caroline Swash

Detail of Halmstad Church window by Einar Forseth, Supplied by Caroline Swash

Forseth enjoyed the stimulus of new ideas. He made several richly coloured concrete and glass windows including those for the Columbarium at Engelbrekts Kyrka, Stockholm. When he heard of the rebuilding of Coventry Cathedral he was determined to take part in the project. Forseth not only designed a mosaic for the Chapel of Unity but also created five windows, his own personal gift. Basil Spence, architect of Coventry described his encounter with the artist.

'However, one day a dynamic character blazed into the Cathedral orbit: the famous Swedish artist, Einar Forseth, who designed and carried out the gold mosaic in the Golden Hall of the world-famous Stockholm Radhuset. Like a comet with a trail of fire he came into my house in Canonbury, said he had visited the Cathedral and wanted to do something for it. The Swedes would pay, he said. The cultural attaché from the Swedish Embassy and others were present. They were cautious and reticent, but nothing could restrain Einar. He would do an inlaid marble floor for the chapel.

A month later he appeared with a design and some full-size drawings which filled my entrance hall. A subscription had been started by Mr Torsten Landby, a Swedish business man resident in London, with support from the highest in Sweden.

The floor is not enough for Einar, however, and he is making five stained glass windows to be set at the top of the stair from the undercroft. These are his personal gifts to the Cathedral, their subject the bringing of the Gospel to Sweden from these islands.' (from 'Phoenix at Coventry' by Basil Spence).

Glass and concrete window by Einar Forseth for the Columbarium at Engelbrekts Kyrka, Stockholm. Supplied by Caroline Swash

Glass and concrete window by Einar Forseth for the Columbarium at Engelbrekts Kyrka, Stockholm. Supplied by Caroline Swash

Glass and concrete window by Einar Forseth for the Columbarium at Engelbrekts Kyrka, Stockholm. Supplied by Caroline Swash

Like most Swedish painters, Bo Beskow (1906-1989) trained at the Art Academy in Stockholm. His first exhibition in 1929 was well received and he began a successful career as a portrait painter. He disliked the limitations of this profession, however, and left Sweden at the age of 23 to discover what he described as his 'personal syntax'. He travelled to Rome, Paris and Portugal and spent a few years in the United States where he met and became friends with the author John Steinbeck. He then returned to Sweden and in 1938 painted his first fresco for the crematorium chapel in his native town of Djursholm. Mural painting led Beskow to consider the possibilities of glass and in 1945 he began work on a series of windows for the newly restored Cathedral at Skara, one of Sweden's oldest cities.

These windows occupied Beskow for 30 years, constituting an intermittent dialogue with glass within the context of a busy life as a painter and writer. During his travels he had studied the great windows of the Gothic Cathedrals in France and England and the small churches of Swedish Gotland, an island in the Baltic Sea. He admired the colour quality and irregularities of early glass an example of which can be seen in the Stained Glass Museum at Ely, England. In 1958, writing for 'Stained Glass' by E. Liddell Armitage, he observed that 'the story told by windows is of secondary importance' adding that the 'blue space between the figures' makes the wonderful windows at Chartres live and sparkle. Beskow also pointed out that the famous 'Five Sisters' windows in York Minster have 'no story but the story of the beautiful pieces of glass put together by a good craftsman'.

Bo Beskow in his studio, 1985. Supplied by Caroline Swash

Detail of medieval glass of the kind admired by Bo Beskow in the collection of the Ely Stained Glass Museum, UK. Courtesy of the Stained Glass Museum, Ely, England

At first Beskow attempted to build his windows with commercial glass, painting, firing and even melting the sheets in order to get the 'life' he wanted. Eventually with the help of a Danish craftsman he set about trying 'to find the way back to the primitive glass' by taking the molte silica directly from the furnace and rolling it out on a board into small manageable sheets. In this way Beskow gradually built up a stock of glass 'where every piece is individually full of all the small blemishes and irregularities that make glass interesting, make it sparkle and break the light' adding that 'the range of colours is partly built on pieces of medieval glass, collected through the years. This glass is my palette, I can work directly with it'.

Between 1945 and 1949 Beskow worked on Old Testament subjects for the north side of the Cathedral under three titles 'The Creation, The Patr‸ ‸, The Prophet'. In composing these windows, Beskow gave ‸ ‸ ancient stories by selecting the scenes that he wanted ‸ ‸ them together in a satisfactory composition. ‸ ‸ series, it would seem that Beskow's ‸ ‸ ‸ s well as glass. Noah and his animals, the ark an‸ ‸nd olive branch fill a considerable part of this w‸ ‸ subject suggested material for Beskow's enchanting ‸ 'n which the Ark's human and animal inhabitants live a ‸ 's before the waters subside.

Left:
Bo Beskow making his own glass, circa 1940. Supplied by Caroline Swash

Below:
Glass made by Bo Beskow placed against the window in his studio, 1985. Supplied by Caroline Swash

The 'Creation' Window in Skara Cathedral designed and made by Bo Beskow, 1945. Supplied by Caroline Swash

Detail showing Noah and his Ark with animals and birds in Skara Cathedral designed and made by Bo Beskow, circa 1947. Supplied by Caroline Swash

From 1950-1952 Beskow worked on the three New Testament windows for the south side of the Cathedral entitled 'The Nativity, The Gospel, The Passion'. He composed these windows in the same updated medieval format as the others, using clearly defined stories framed with bands of colour allowing the viewer the double pleasure of seeing the entire window 'shining like a jewel set in the wall' as well as following the story line arranged by the artist. The section of the window depicting Mary holding Christ's body shows how powerful Beskow's updated medieval format could be.

Beskow's masterpiece, however, is the great east window. Here the orchestration of colour is entirely original. Grey blues, greenish blacks and marvelous marbled whites have been used to express the Apocalyptic vision described in the Book of Revelations. In this magnificent window, Beskow has cast aside his admiration for medieval glass and created an entirely new idiom of his own.

Detail of the 'Passion' window designed and made by Bo Beskow, 1950-52. Supplied by Caroline Swash

Opposite Page:
The 'Apocalypse', window in Skara Cathedral, designed and made by Bo Beskow, 1960s. Supplied by Caroline Swash

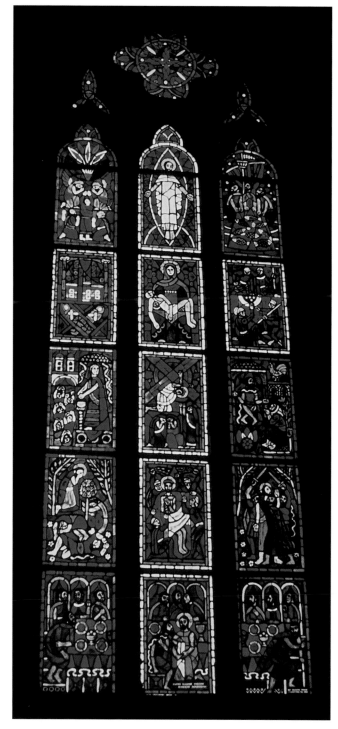

The 'Passion' window in Skara Cathedral designed and made by Bo Beskow, 1950-52. Supplied by Caroline Swash

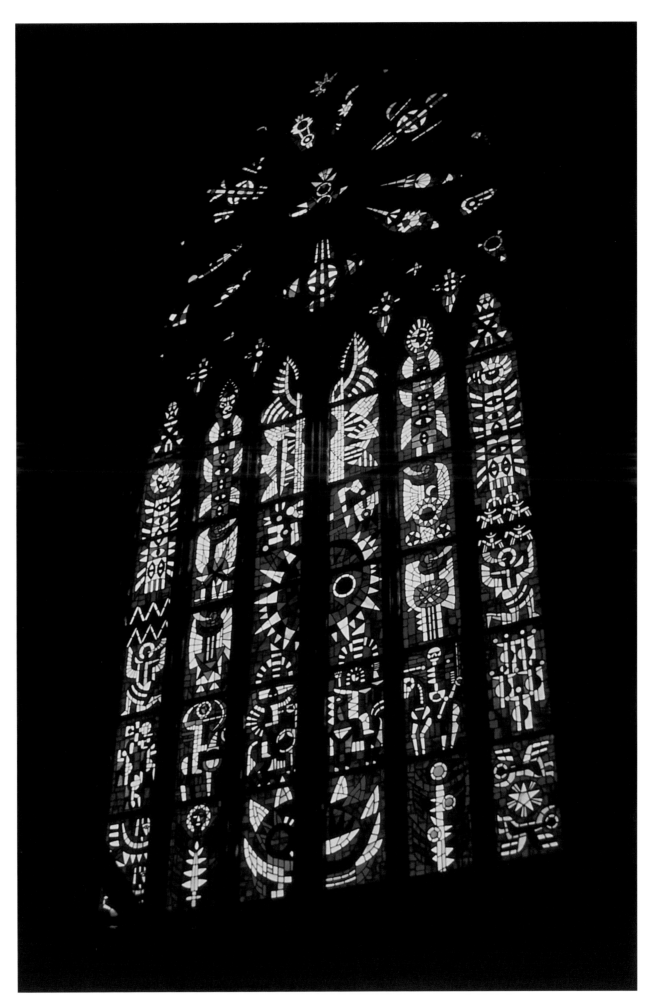

Detail of 'Death' in the Apocalypse window in Skara Cathedral, designed and made by Bo Beskow, 1960s. Supplied by Caroline Swash

Detail of 'Horseman' in the Apocalypse window in Skara Cathedral, designed and made by Bo Beskow, 1960s. Supplied by Caroline Swash

Opposite Page:

Detail from the Apocalypse window in Skara Cathedral illustrating Matthew 25 1-3 (the parable of the wise and foolish virgins) showing the foolish virgins without their lamps, designed and made by Bo Beskow, circa 1960s. Supplied by Caroline Swash

Besides this epic task, Beskow continued to paint and draw with energy and skill. His pictures continued a life long dialogue with colour, shape and rhythm. The mythological figure of the Minotaur, part man, part bull formed the subject of a series of powerful oil paintings. Music remained an inspiration. Players and their instruments provided him with material for compositions in many media. Beskow was sympathetic to adornment in art and his paintings project an impressive and very satisfactory feeling of balance. Indeed, his description of Noah's son's wife in 'Two by Two', conveys a sense of how he thought about the structure of the human body. 'She was a beautiful sight, with her straight back stretching up from the ample curves of her hips. She had gathered her wide skirt so that it fell in soft folds, and the lower part of her body formed a spherical base from which her trunk rose like a pillar, supporting her high, firm bosom. Flat and curved surfaces moved in rhythmic harmony, shifting slightly around the vertical axis of her body. As if to give further emphasis to the line, her newly washed hair hung straight down her back as far as her waist.'

Bo Beskow in his studio with designs and cartoons pinned to the wall. Caroline Swash in the background, 1982. Supplied by Caroline Swash

Left:
One of the 'Musicians' series of paintings by Bo Beskow, in progress 1984. Supplied by Caroline Swash

Bottom:
'Minotaur' painting by Bo Beskow, in progress 1984. Supplied by Caroline Swash

Below:
'Minotaur' painting by Bo Beskow, in progress 1984. Supplied by Caroline Swash

In Iceland the lure of the sophisticated art scene in Paris was especially strong. The young Icelandic artist Gerdur Helgadóttir (1928-1975) made her name there as a sculptor before turning to glass. After a brief period of training in Reykjavik and Florence, Helgadóttir moved to Paris where she studied with the émigré Russian artist Ossip Zadkine, learning the new approach to carving and modelling that had evolved from Cubism. Along with Alexander Calder, Shinkichi Tashiri, Robert Jacobsen, Auguste Herbin and Antoine Pevsner, Gerdur quickly established herself as one of a group of artists exhibiting radically new sculpture at the Galerie Denise René and the Galerie Arnaud in Paris. The theories behind their new work were best expressed by Victor Vasarely in his introduction to the catalogue of the Le Mouvement exhibition held at the gallery in April 1955. According to Vasarely, pure composition should consist of abstract elements used either to indicate a sense of space or the illusion of movement. Colour was expected to achieve a new role either as coloured light or as coloured form. Together these elements were intended to create a new form of beauty.

Above:
Solo Exhibition of Gerdur Helgadóttir's work at the Gallerie Arnaud, Paris Feb-March 1952. With permission of the artist, Gerdur Helgadottir

Opposite Page:
Gerdur Helgadóttir at work in her studio in Rue Daguerre, Paris, 1951-52. With permission of the artist, Gerdur Helgadottir

Despite critical success, the postwar years were financially lean and with few sales from her Paris exhibitions, Helgadóttir looked about for another source of income. The sculpture entitled 'Firmament' made in 1956 shows how skillfully she was already using glass in combination with metal. Helgadóttir wondered whether money could be earned from making stained glass windows for the new churches being built in Iceland and elsewhere in post-war Europe.

After learning the craft in the Paris studio of Jean Barillet, she submitted designs in 1958 for a competition to create new windows for the newly refurbished church of Skalholt in Iceland. She won the competition and the Skalholt series were a resounding success bringing this austere building to life with a sequence of radiant geometric constructions in glass and lead. Helgadóttir had made these windows with the Oidtmann Studios in Linnich. The brothers, Ludovikus and Fritz who ran the studio, recognized her talent and arranged for her to submit designs for several new projects in Germany. These included complete schemes for new churches in Essen (1964) and Herkenrath (1962). One of her most dramatic glass compositions was made for the new church of Kópavogur in Iceland. Here Helgadóttir's complete scheme reveals her background as a sculptor. The entwined lead lines form the armature for a complex glass composition bringing coloured light into the structure of the interior.

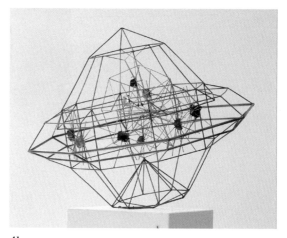

Above:
Iron and glass sculpture 'Firmament' by Gerdur Helgadóttir, 1956. With permission of the artist, Gerdur Helgadóttir

Designs for windows in Skalholt Church, Iceland by Gerdur Helgadóttir, 1958. With permission of the artist, Gerdur Helgadóttir

Windows in Skalholt Church by Gerdur Helgadóttir, 1959. With permission of the artist, Gerdur Helgadóttir

(L-R) Ludovikus Oidtmann, Gerdur Helgadóttir and Friedrich Oidtmann working on the Skalholt windows at the Oidtmann Studio in Linnich, Germany, 1950. With permission of the artist, Gerdur Helgadóttir

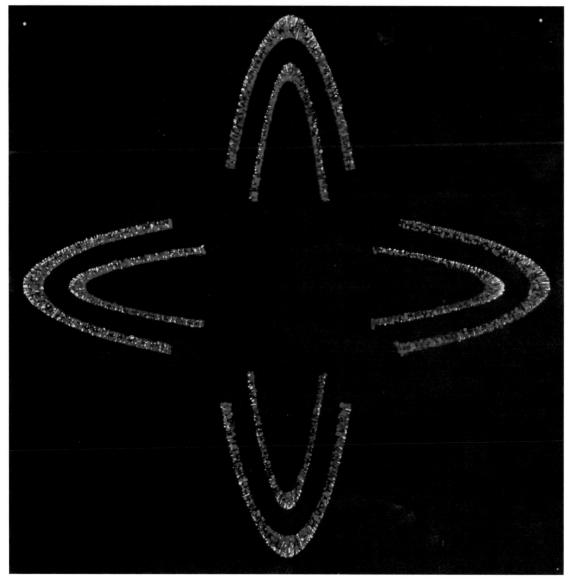

Design for the windows in Kópavogur Church, 1962. With permission of the artist, Gerdur Helgadóttir

Helgadóttir continued to build sculpture as well as design glass for the duration of her short life. Some of her most exciting works were made combining both media. Following a trip to Egypt, she returned to France and was inspired to create a series of magnificent standing sculptures in which cast concrete and glass inserts were combined in an entirely original way. After her death at the age of 47 her cartoons, tools, drawings and sculpture were gathered together and brought from her studio in Paris back to Iceland. In Kópavogur, a superb art museum was commissioned from the architect Benjamin Magnússon to house her archive.

Opposite Page:
'Untitled' stained glass panel by Gerdur Helgadóttir in the collection of the Gerdasafn (Kópavogur Art Museum), 1970. With permission of the artist, Gerdur Helgadóttir

Above-Left:
'Composition' stained glass panel by Gerdur Helgadóttir in the collection of the Gerdasafn (Kópavogur Art Museum), 1970. With permission of the artist, Gerdur Helgadóttir

Left:
'Untitled' stained glass panel by Gerdur Helgadóttir in the collection of the Gerdasafn (Kópavogur art Museum), 1969. With permission of the artist, Gerdur Helgadóttir

'Meeting 1' concrete and glass sculpture by Gerdur Helgadóttir in the collection of the Gerdasafn (Kópavogur art Museum), 1969. With permission of the artist, Gerdur Helgadóttir

Above:
View of the 2005 Exhibition of glass,
cartoons and sculpture by Gerdur Helgadóttir at
the Kópavogur Art Museum. With permission
of the artist, Gerdur Helgadóttir

Left:
The Gerdasafn, Kópavogur Art Museum
with Kópavogur Church in the distance. With
permission of the artist, Gerdur Helgadóttir

Among the younger generation currently working in Scandinavia, the most consistently creative artist is the Icelander Leifur Breidfjord (b.1945). He achieved international recognition through winning the competition to design the 'Robert Burns' window in St Giles Cathedral, Edinburgh one of the most prestigious commissions of the 1980s. Breidfjord trained in architecture and design at Edinburgh under the lively and eccentric Sax Shaw. He then worked and studied with Patrick Reyntiens at Burleighfield House, meeting the liveliest and brightest young artists gathered there for summer courses from all over the world. Returning to Iceland he set up his own studio and rapidly established a reputation as an artist of practicality as well as originality. Breidfjord's understanding of architectural fitness made him the obvious choice for the decoration of the ceiling of the new Keflavik Airport. Entitled 'Yearning for flight' the kite shaped composition softens the angular construction of the building and warms the interior with golden light.

Leifur Breidfjord in his studio, 1970.
With permission of the artist, Leifur Breidfjord

The Robert Burns memorial window designed by Leifur Breidfjord for St Giles Cathedral, Edinburgh, 1982-85. With permission of the artist, Leifur Breidfjord

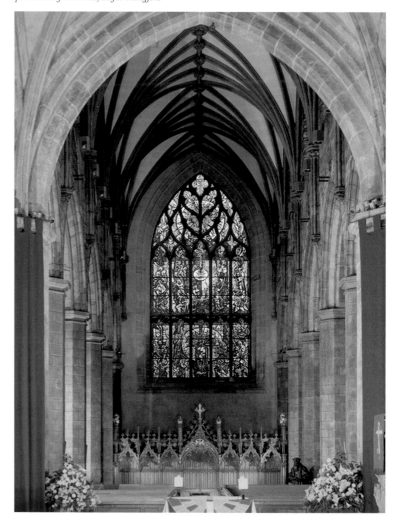

Daytime view of 'Yearning for flight', glass sculpture for Keflavik Airport, Iceland, 1987. With permission of the artist, Leifur Breidfjord

Nightime view of 'Yearning for flight', glass sculpture for Keflavik Airport, Iceland, 1987. With permission of the artist, Leifur Breidfjord

The source of the imagery in Breidfjord's architectural schemes comes from his continuing practice as a fine artist. He draws from life every week to refresh his vocabulary of lines and tones and for the sheer fun of drawing. Indeed, Breidfjord's paintings have a mischievousness that gives even his monumental work an approachable quality. His glass composition above the stairwell of the National Library in Reykjavik suggests the theme of 'Learning through the Ages.' The medieval past is represented as a mysterious dark profile shot through with brilliant episodes of poetic revelation. The present is coloured in shades of gold inscribed with computer lettering and a sentence from the romantic poet Jonas Hallgrimsson. The third profile is constructed of transparent glass, the yet unwritten texts of the future.

Life drawings by Leifur Breidfjord. With permission of the artist, Leifur Breidfjord

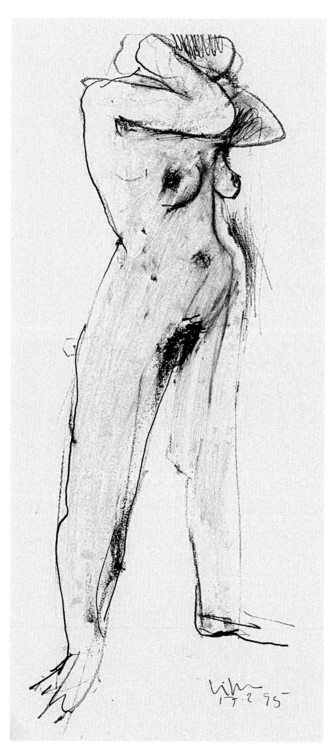

Iceland's increased prosperity has allowed the restoration and enrichment of several historic buildings, among them Reykjavik's best known landmark, the dramatic Hallgrims Church. Here Breidfjord has designed and constructed a brilliantly coloured window for the east tower that dominates the old fishing port. The imagery has been drawn from the Book of Revelations whose fantastic subject matter accords well with the 'word pictures' of the Icelandic Sagas. Breidfjord has set the scenes within the time honoured quatrefoil shape so beloved of medieval architects. In this way the window is cleverly integrated into the building which, designed in 1937, is itself an up-dated interpretation of High Gothic architecture. As Breidfjord has remarked 'A stained glass window must always constitute a balanced counterpoint to the building and its surroundings. Although a window is designed according to a certain architectural pattern and forms an integral part of the building, I always look upon it as an independent work of art.'

Window by Leifur Breidfjord for The National Library of Reykjavik, 1994. With permission of the artist, Leifur Breidfjord

Every space is different and Breidfjord has responded imaginatively to each. In 1996 he created a glass ceiling for The Supreme Court Building of Iceland. This required very careful planning since the glass had to curve over and across the end wall. For a potentially uninspiring bank reception area, Breidfjord used three layers of colour and texture to make a fascinating and constantly changing pictorial effect

Breidfjord's most impressive achievements have been the colour orchestration of complete interiors. With his wife, Sigridur Johansdóttir, a talented seamstress and weaver, he has been able to offer more adventurous churches in Iceland the opportunity to acquire interesting vestments. For festival occasions, Johansdóttir has designd dramatic charubles for the clergy that complement the stained glass, filling these otherwise austere spaces with brilliant colours and patterns.

Right:
Detail of the interior of the Supreme Court of Iceland with glass designed by Leifur Breidfjord, 1996. With permission of the artist, Leifur Breidfjord

Below:
Interior of the Supreme Court of Iceland with glass designed by Leifur Breidfjord, 1996. With permission of the artist, Leifur Breidfjord

Glass walls for the Engineering Savings Bank by Leifur Breidfjord, 1996. With permission of the artist, Leifur Breidfjord

One of the two glass walls for the Engineering Savings Bank by Leifur Breidfjord, 1996. With permission of the artist, Leifur Breidfjord

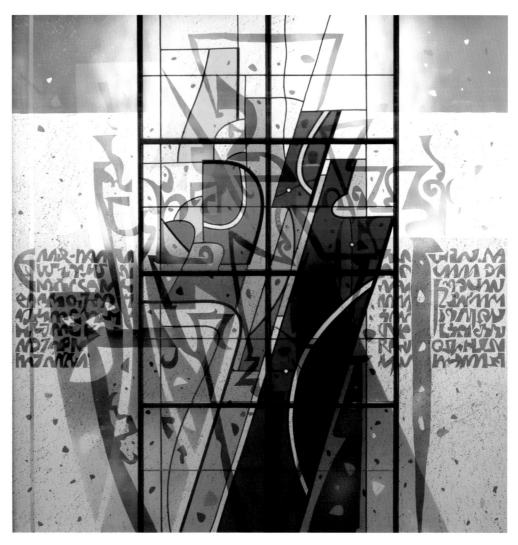

Overview of the interior of Fetla and Hola Church,
1997-98, Stained Glass by Leifur Breidfjord.
With permission of the artist, Leifur Breidfjord

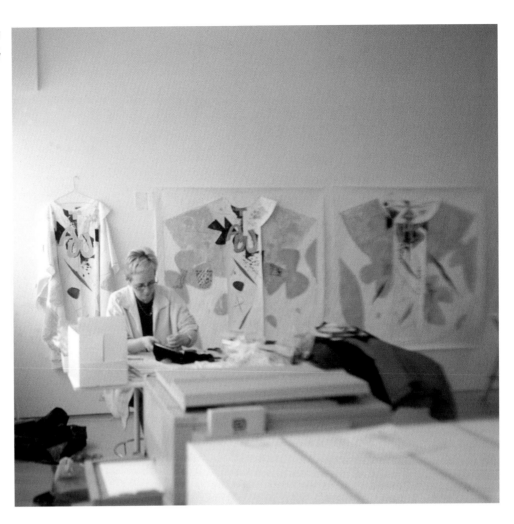

Sigridur Johansdottir wife of Leifur Breidfjord, working on vestments from Breidfjord's designs, 1997. With permission of the artist, Leifur Breidfjord

Cartoons and colour designs for vestments for Fetla and Hola Church in the studio, Leifur Breidfjord, 1996. With permission of the artist, Leifur Breidfjord

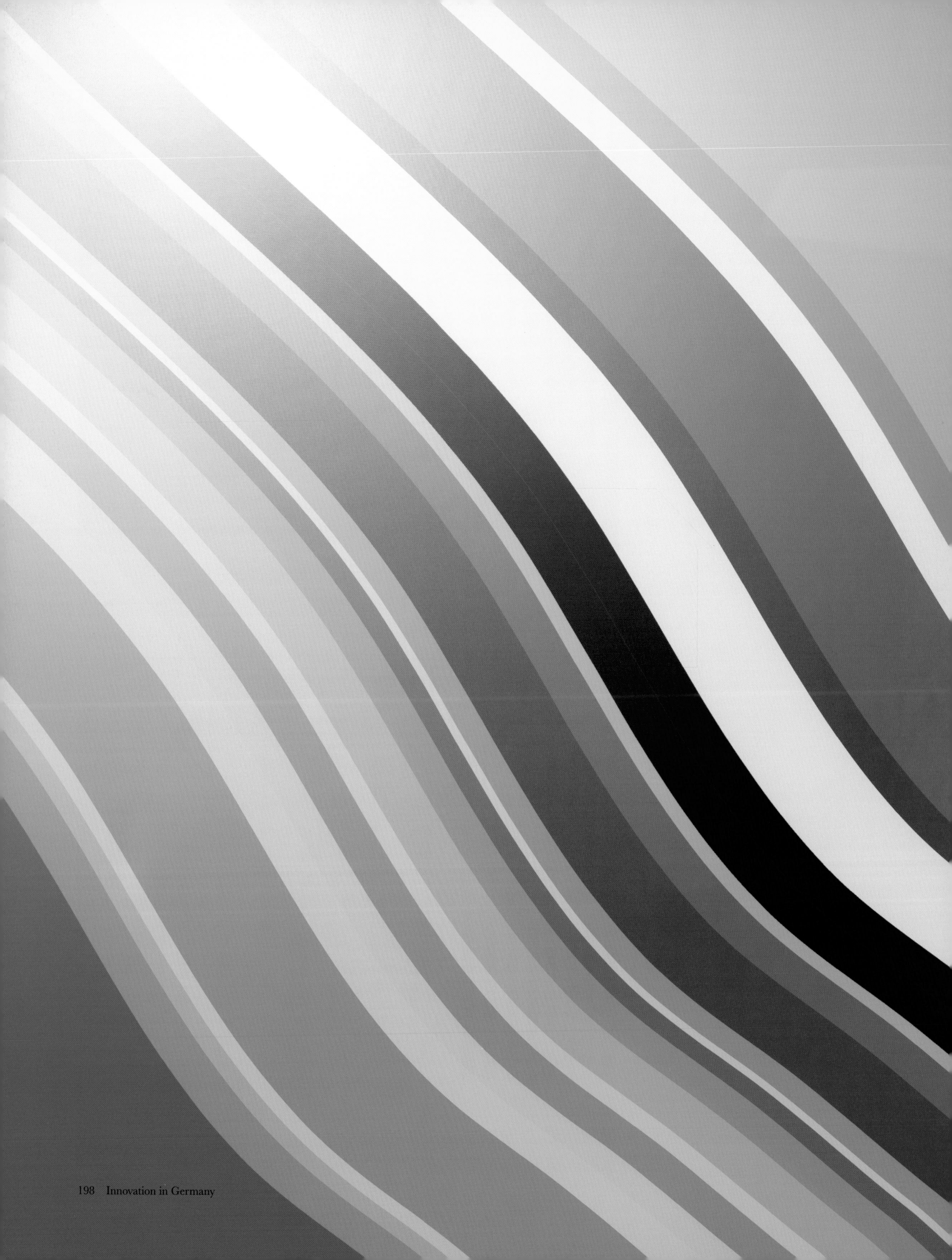

IX

Innovation in Germany

An aerial photograph taken from an RAF De Havilland
Mosquito showing badly damaged buildings in the area
between Friedrich Hain and Lichtenberg, Berlin.
Supplied by Caroline Swash

Innovation in Germany

Germany in 1945 was a shattered and defeated nation. 5.5 million of its citizens had perished, 4.6 million were wounded and many of its buildings had been destroyed. The country itself was divided, with the west falling to the Allies and the eastern part with its historic towns and cities under the control of Russia. Total collapse was prevented by the generosity of American aid through the Marshall Plan. In West Germany (The German Federal Republic), recovery was astonishingly swift and by the mid 1950s, the phrase 'Economic Miracle' was already being used to describe the speed of the rebuilding programme.

Public buildings, such as churches and town halls, were singled out for special attention during reconstruction. For many Germans, struggling to make sense of what had happened to their country, these buildings represented the positive, fruitful side of German culture and history that had been corrupted by the Third Reich. Many were restored to a simulacrum of their former glory to resume their role as the centres of religious and civic life for rebuilt towns and villages. Although evidence of exterior construction remained, the interior furnishings, including the stained glass windows, had generally been destroyed. The funding to replace these treasures was supplied through church taxes. Almost all West Germans at that time contributed a percentage of their income to either the Lutheran or Catholic Church. This tithe was collected by the state and disbursed to churches to enable them to run schools, hospices and outreach services as well as to beautify places of worship.

The question of a suitable visual language for the post-war era was a matter of deep concern. As in France, the possibilities included a revived medievalism that would reconnect the present to the past, or a search for new forms of art that would suggest spiritual regeneration. An interesting example of an attempt to recreate a 'medieval' style can be seen in Walther Benner's 'Madonna and Child' made for the Stiftskirche at Herdecke between 1949 and 1951. However, an entirely new way of presenting time honoured Christian imagery had already been explored during the difficult years between the wars by several artists influenced by the ideas of De Stijl and the Bauhaus

(see Chapter 5). Jan Thorn-Prikker (1868-1932) designed and made stained glass windows in this new way. During the years of domination by the National Socialists, abstract art had been reviled as degenerate while figurative art was highly praised. To distance themselves from the horrors of the Nazi regime, many church leaders looked to adventurous artists, particularly those whose work had been suppressed, to create the redemptive images of the future. This attitude led to the encouragement of new and expressive ways of using the medium, effectively transforming the status of stained glass in Germany from a craft to a significant art form.

Details of windows by Jan Thorn-Prikker. Source: Tim Lewis

Between 1960 and 1990, the great period of German reconstruction, most of the artists commissioned to design stained glass windows were not trained in the techniques needed to make architectural glass. Like their French colleagues, they depended upon the managerial and technical skills of family firms, many of which had been founded in the heyday of enthusiasm for the revival of Gothic art in the late 19th-century. The most active of these studios during the post-war period belonged to the Oidtmann family at Linnich, the Derix family at four locations in Taunusstein, Kevelaer, Wiesbaden and Rottweil and the Mayer family in Munich. These studios provided the skilled labour and new equipment necessary to fulfil the requirements of the artists. They also acted as agents for architects requiring sympathetic designs for their buildings. Commissions tended to be handled on a regional basis. The area around Aachen, for example, fell to the Oidtmann Studios, while the Derix Studios at Taunusstein handled the orders from further south.

Working on windows at Derix studio, Taunusstein with Johannes Schreiter in the background, 1990.
Supplied by Caroline Swash

Exterior of Derix Studio, Taunusstein, 1990.
Supplied by Caroline Swash

Some of the first windows to be designed after the war were the uncompromisingly geometric series made for the Choir of Aachen Cathedral between 1949 and 1951 by Anton Wendling (1891-1965). These windows show how effectively Wendling used the discoveries he made when he explored ideas in pure form and colour. The design of this vast undertaking has a deceptive simplicity. At the heart of the repeating pattern is the idea of the Radiant Cross – a cruciform shape enclosed by a circle, symbol of eternity. This simple emblem has been repeated throughout the window with variations of colour and tone. Red, blue and gold link the colours of this wall of glass to the hues of the medieval windows nearby, while derivative or imitative iconography has been avoided through the use of the universal symbol.

Ludwig Schaffrath (b.1924) trained with Anton Wendling for several years after the War. During the 1960s, he designed a groundbreaking series of windows for the cloister of the canon's cemetery in Aachen Cathedral. Essentially, this was a plain glazing scheme elevated to high art by the artist's ingenuity and skill. Taking the idea of the 'epitaph' as his starting point, Schaffrath constructed a series of elegant windows on the theme of mortality in uncoloured glass and lead. His method of using lead created enormous interest, since the thick and thin lines interact with the support bars of the window in a fresh and convincing way. Examples of this radical approach can be seen in Schaffrath's windows for St Michael's Church, Schweinfurt designed in 1967 and in the later wall of glass for the Hessisches Landesmuseum, Darmstadt. The careful analysis of the fundamentals of his craft has made Schaffrath such an influential artist.

Stained glass scheme by Anton Wendling for the Choir of Aachen Cathedral, 1949-1951.
Source: www.glasmalerei-oidtmann.de

Right:
Windows from the cloister series at Aachen Cathedral by Ludwig Schaffrath, 1962-65.
Source: Rodney Bender

Detail of window for St Michael's Church, Schweinfurt by Ludwig Schaffrath, 1967. Source: Tim Lewis

Window for the ground floor of the Hessisches Landesmuseum in Darmstadt. Supplied by Caroline Swash

Schaffrath specialises in the use of glass that has been manufactured with a lightly textured surface. The tone or pattern he requires is always selected from the sheet and never applied afterwards. Thus, the varied 'glassy' qualities of the material are allowed to interact with other materials selected by the architect for the exterior or interior surfaces of the building. For the Liobas School at Bad Neuheim, Schaffrath has enhanced the window area with a lively pattern of blue and clear glass. The 'Labyrinth' window at St Joseph's Church, Aachen made in 1975, was inspired by lines written by the 17th century poet Daniel Caspar von Lohenstein which refer to life itself as a labyrinth in which only the wise man will not lose his way. Like Wendling, Schaffrath uses symbols to suggest ideas, integrating the selected image within a graphic composition. In 1976, he made a superb series of windows for St Antonius Hospital in Eschweiler. These included references to life and growth within a strong semi-abstract design.

Labyrinth window for St Joseph's church, Aachen by Ludwig Schaffrath, 1975.
Source: Rodney Bender

Below:
Windows by Ludwig Schaffrath for St Antonius Hospital. Supplied by The Bridgeman Art Library

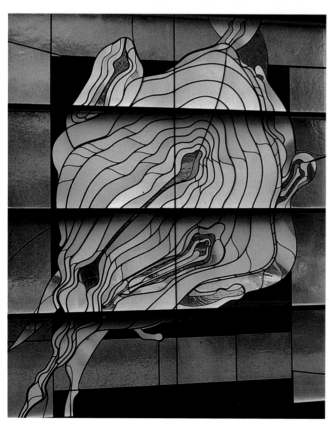

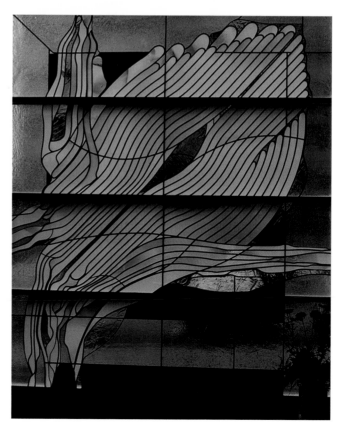

Exterior view of the glass designed by Ludwig Schaffrath for the swimming Pool at Ubach-Palenberg, 1973. Source Tim Lewis

Interior view in winter of the glass designed by Ludwig Schaffrath for the swimming Pool at Ubach-Palenberg, 1973. Source Tim Lewis

Windows designed by Ludwig Schaffrath for the Priest's Training Centre at Aachen, 1982. Source: Rodney Bender

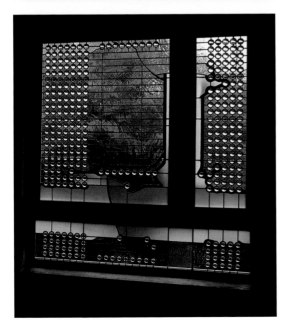

Schaffrath's glass has also been used to give importance to municipal buildings. The swimming pool at Ubach-Palenberg (1973) has been enlivened by rippling forms in clear and opal glass that hold the interior light, while a strong blue tone links the glass wall to the pool. In this composition, Schaffrath has used lenses to establish glittering lines within the areas of lightly textured glass. He also uses lenses to make walls of sparkling light. At the Training Centre for Priests in Aachen, Schaffrath has combined subtly modulated pink opaque glass with hundreds of lenses in the creation of a shimmering surface.

Schaffrath's influence on the international development of architectural glass has been considerable. From his studio in Aachen he has produced the drawings, paintings and cartoons for the superb windows and mosaics for which he is renowned. During the 1970s he was a guest of Patrick Reyntiens at Burleighfield House in the UK and was subsequently appointed artist-in-residence at Swansea College of Art. He also taught in Australia and the United States, passing on the ideals of an exacting approach to line and colour to the next generation of artists and designers.

Ludwig Schaffrath in his studio. Source: Tim Lewis

Johannes Schreiter sitting between Rodney Bender (L) and Tim Lewis
(R) surrounded by students at the Master Class in Swansea, 1989.
Source: Tim Lewis

Johannes Schreiter (b.1930) has been equally influential in the world of contemporary architectural glass. Not only has he lectured worldwide at seminars and master classes, but also publications in English have brought his ideas to a considerable public. Schreiter studied drawing and painting first at Münster, then Mainz and Berlin. Between 1960 and 1963 he taught at the Bremen Academy of Art before becoming Professor at the School of Decorative Arts in Frankfurt, where he taught until 1988. He won numerous prizes for his work in painting and engraving and had established a reputation as a major graphic artist before designing glass for architecture.

Schreiter's pictures were the source for his earliest works in glass. During the 1960s, he produced a collage series that included the use of smoke in the creation of new shapes and tones. The subtlety of these works influenced the way in which he came to perceive the possibilities of colour in architecture. The same sombre colour, torn edges and fractured sense of movement can be observed in the glass composition made for the church of St Margaret, Bürgstadt.

In 1966 Schreiter created an enormously influential window for the Chapel of the Brotherhood of Saint John in Leutesdorf/Rhein. The design reveals an entirely blue composition enfolding three sides of the Chapel. Blue was deliberately chosen to create an atmosphere of tranquillity, an aid to contemplation. Schreiter's innovative use of lead was also immensely important. Here every lead line has been integrated in such a way that it cannot be interpreted anywhere as a 'service' lead with a supportive task. Almost all lines crossing others shortly afterwards end freely in the glass, unattached to the frame. 'I often recall the wonderful vault of St. Anne's Church at Annaberg in the Erzgebirge', wrote Schreiter. 'Every time I entered that church as a child, I particularly marvelled at the vaulting ribs of the New Vestry breaking off abruptly. We all know how impressive childhood experiences can be. Perhaps this is the starting point for my passion towards destabilisation.'

Collage 'Bagatelle 5' by Johannes Schreiter 1965. Source: Johannes Schreiter

South gable of St Margaret's Church at Bürgstadt/Main, 1959. Source: Johannes Schreiter

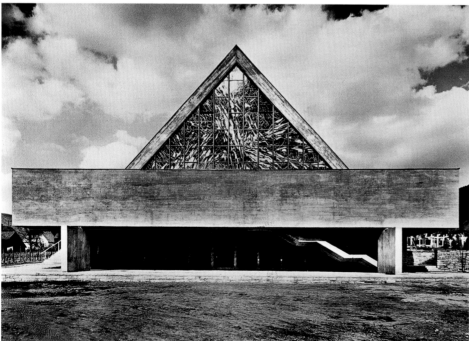

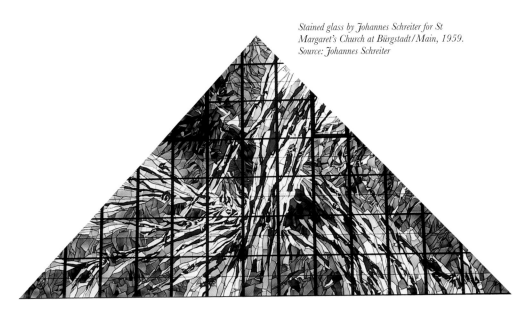

Stained glass by Johannes Schreiter for St Margaret's Church at Bürgstadt/Main, 1959. Source: Johannes Schreiter

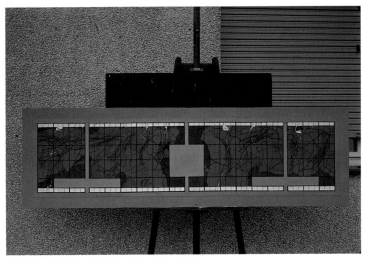

Left:

Exterior of the Chapel of the Exerzitienhaus Johannesbund at Leutesdorf. Source: Johannes Schreiter

Above:

Design for the Leutesdorf Chapel by Johannes Schreiter, 1965. Supplied by Caroline Swash

Innovation in Germany   211

The concept of the lead line as a vibrant 'graphic' line was not unknown, but Schreiter took its use much further through his enthusiasm for drawing which he feels enlarges his graphic repertoire. Indeed, his windows are miracles of construction. The lead itself must be shaved to the correct thickness in accordance with the cartoon – the full size drawing for each window. The glass is always specially ordered and carefully tempered to enable the cutting of the requisite shapes.

Glass walls by Johannes Schreiter
for the Leutesdorf Chapel, 1965.
Supplied by Caroline Swash

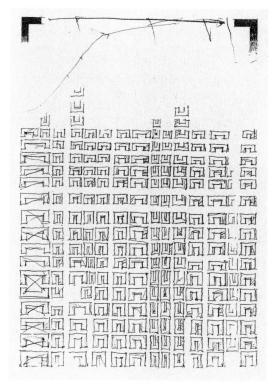

*Drawing (Fazit 24/1986) by Johannes
Schreiter. Source: Johannes Schreiter*

*Detail of the cartoon drawing by Johannes Schreiter
for the east window in the choir of St Nicholas,
Lüneburg, 1985. Supplied by Caroline Swash*

*Interior of Johannes Schreiter's
studio at Langen, Germany*

The fame of the Leutesdorf project brought many commissions during the 1970s and 1980s. These included the series of windows for St John's Church, Troisdorf, Sieglar that occupied Schreiter from 1979-1985. The idea for the design arose from the desire of the church community to retain the existing diamond panes. Schreiter took the rhomboid shape and fashioned it into a subtle composition that gently alluded to the image of a fishing net, as well as the more sombre reference to a torn veil. This theme was explored by Schreiter in other windows, including those made in 1981 for St Mary's Church, Lübeck. A related image comes from the scrolls that appear either at the base of medieval windows or around the figures depicted. Schreiter sometimes uses these ribbons to suggest the unravelling of the grave cloth to indicate Christ's Resurrection, as in the window designed for Limburg Cathedral in 1976, while an important example of wood carving in the Hessisches Landesmuseum at Darmstadt, has been enhanced by three windows which use the binding cloth as a reference to the empty tomb and focus attention on the medieval masterpiece below.

Designs for St John's Church, Troisdorf, Sieglar by Johannes Schreiter, 1978. Source: Johannes Schreiter

Windows by Johannes Schreiter for the Letter Chapel at St Mary's Church, Lübeck, 1981. Source: Johannes Schreiter

Windows by Johannes Schreiter for the Chapel of the Hessisches Landesmuseum Darmstadt, 1980. Source: Johannes Schreiter

Window by Johannes Schreiter for the Tomb Chapel in Limburg Cathedral, 1976. Source: Johannes Schreiter

More than any other artist of the Post-war period, Schreiter has directly confronted the challenge of the past and has attempted to suggest ways of healing. His appeal for the importance of quiet, for the need to find meaning in life is expressed in the rationale of the work itself. For windows in the Juvenile Centre at Schifferstadt, he chose a simple linear design and calming colours. Schreiter has always been fascinated by the effect of colour on an interior, suggesting that those who experience the space become emotionally altered, for better or worse, through the influence of 'coloured air'. For this reason he reduced the colour range in the Meditation Room of the EKD in Berlin to a quiet monochrome, preventing the intrusion of the busy, brightly coloured world outside. In the Franciscan Church at Rothenburg, Schreiter has filled all the openings with soothing colours in opaque glass.

The project that brought Schreiter to the attention of thoughtful artists all over the world was the series of designs for the Church of the Holy Ghost at Heidelberg. In honour of the famous collection of books, the 'Biblioteca Palatina' once housed in the church, Schreiter took as his theme nothing less than the entire scope of Western civilisation. Some of the subjects selected for the series, such as Music, Literature and Philosophy, were to be expected; but others were unusual and some entirely new including the subjects Chemistry, Biology, Medicine, Physics, Economics, Media and Traffic. For the first time in contemporary stained glass design, maps, graphs, newspaper and television images were used as source material. Regrettably, the designs were too radical for the church authorities and the scheme was rejected in favour of an open competition, won by the artist Hella Santarossa.

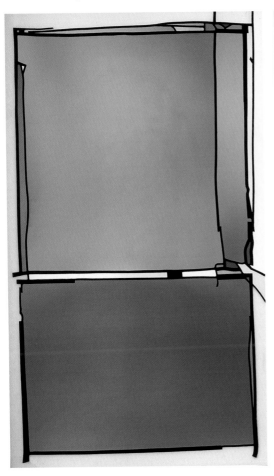

Window by Johannes Schreiter for the Juvenile Centre at Schifferstadt, 1990. Supplied by Caroline Swash

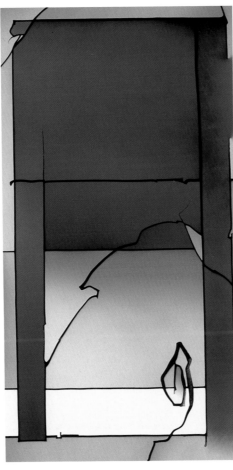

Window by Johannes Schreiter for the Meditation Room at the EKD in Berlin, 1999. Supplied by Caroline Swash

Choir windows by Johannes Schreiter for the Franciscan Church at Rothenburg, 1996. Source: Johannes Schreiter

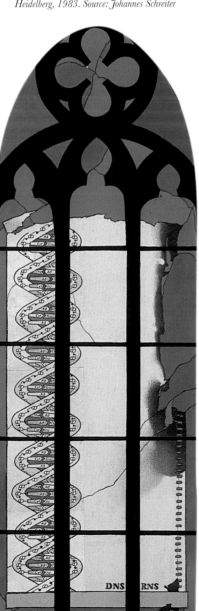

Design for the 'Biology' window by Johannes Schreiter for the Church of the Holy Ghost, Heidelberg, 1983. Source: Johannes Schreiter

Design for the 'Traffic' window by Johannes Schreiter for the Church of the Holy Ghost, Heidelberg, 1983. Source: Johannes Schreiter

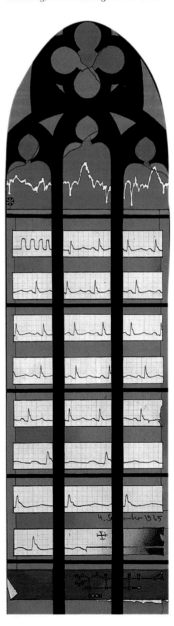

Design for the 'Medecine' window by Johannes Schreiter for the Church of the Holy Ghost, Heidelberg, 1983. Source: Johannes Schreiter

One important commission did emerge from this groundbreaking scheme – a series of windows on scientific themes for the Library of the Medical Colleges of St. Bartholomew and the Royal London Hospitals at Whitechapel, London. Here, subtle pink glass warms the interior while the designs for the windows address important subjects in medical education. The 'AIDS' window contains a diagram that shows the spread of the disease from Zaire in 1959 to different parts of the world. Schreiter suggests the healing process through the image of a red arrow halting the continuum of infection. The broken chain of brackets indicates the destructive power of AIDS and the resulting dislocation of young lives. The 'Molecular Biology' window contains three diagrams that suggest genetic varieties. Diagrams A and B, which shimmer on a dark red background, refer to combinations of genes that produce abnormality, while Diagram C shows the normal recombinant. Schreiter has placed these against a white background supported by a purple column to indicate calm and stability. These information-bearing areas of colour are linked to each other with playful graphic lines that form a linear dialogue with the kite-shaped traceries of the window itself.

The challenge of architectural integration also fascinated Jochem Poensgen (b.1931). He took the idea of interior harmony within the building a step further by suggesting that stained glass should reach people through subconscious means. He coined the phrase 'civil inattention' to describe the reaction he wanted. In 1983, Poensgen won the competition to design a foyer window for the Police Academy at Münster-Hiltrup. This is a bright transparent window whose elegant pattern effectively conceals the service area beyond. Using gold glass to warm the interior space of a small chapel in a Senior Citizen Complex at Heiden in Borken, Poensgen shows how effectively coloured glass can 'support the special character of the room'. Poensgen was among the first to include time-honoured images by revered artists in his church windows. His 1985 window for the Church of St. Martin at Bad-Orb, for example, makes effective use of Rembrandt's fine etching of the subject of Adam and Eve. The enlarged, screen-printed version of the engraving somehow connects the powerful image with our own time.

Jochem Poensgen standing beside one of his cartoons, 1985.
Source: Tim Lewis

'AIDS' window by Johannes Schreiter for the Library of the Medical Colleges of St. Bartholomew and the Royal London Hospitals at Whitechapel, London, 2000. Supplied by Caroline Swash

'Molecular Biology' window by Johannes Schreiter for the Library of the Medical Colleges of St. Bartholomew and the Royal London Hospitals at Whitechapel, London, 1998. Supplied by Caroline Swash

Window by Jochem Poensgen in the lobby of the Police Academy
at Münster-Hiltrup, 1983. Photograph © Jochem Poensgen

Detail of the lobby windows at the Police Academy at Münster-Hiltrup by Jochem Poensgen, 1983. Photograph © Jochem Poensgen

Window by Jochem Poensgen for
St Martin's Church, Bad-Orb, 1985.
Photograph © Jochem Poensgen

Another artist to use glass in an exceptionally sensitive way is Joachim Klos (b.1931). A master of line, he usually works on a background of clear glass. His originality and imagination can be seen displayed in the lively and entertaining details of the windows he made for the church of St's Kosmos and Damian at Bienen. His sense of the importance of decoration can be deduced from the beautiful 'Mystical Rose' panel made for the 'Glass Masters' exhibition held at The Glynn Vivian Gallery in Swansea, Wales in 1980. Klos continues to explore the dynamics of black line and clear colour in architecture. One of his recent works, an impressive glass entrance to the Telecom Regional Headquarters at Osnabrück made in 1992, shows how these preferences have been successfully adapted to new techniques of bonding colour onto large sheets of float glass.

Joachim Klos standing beside the completed windows at the Mid Glamorgan Crematorium at Bridgend, Wales. Source: Tim Lewis

Joachim Klos in his studio working on cartoons for the windows in the Mid Glamorgan Crematorium at Bridgend, Wales. Source: Tim Lewis

Detail of a window by Joachim Klos for the Church of St's Kosmos and Damian at Bienen. Source: Rodney Bender

Below:
Details from windows by Joachim Klos for the Church of
St's Kosmos and Damian at Bienen. Source: Rodney Bender

'Mystical Rose' by Jochem Klos at the Deutsches Glasmalerei
Museum, Linnich. Supplied by Caroline Swash

The Painter in Glass

During the Post-war period, many German artists approached architectural glass as graphic designers; theirs has been the art of the line. Schaffrath's new walls of glass are essentially scaled-up drawings with colour used to infill the spaces between. For Schreiter, line has always expressed a range of intellectual and emotional possibilities, while colour influenced the physical impact of the enclosed space. Poensgen and Klos have both used line in their dialogue with light, decorating a number of buildings in a sensitive and effective manner. However, the art of painting, as opposed to drawing, also holds an important place in post-war German glass design, particularly among those artists who were responsive to the achievements of their French colleagues.

The work of Wilhelm Buschulte (b.1923) is particularly interesting in this context. Buschulte was drafted into the army immediately after leaving school. He was wounded and allowed to return to civilian life, studying art in Munich. Between 1943 and 1950, with many interruptions, he explored engraving and printmaking as well as oil, watercolour, tempera and pastel. He returned to his hometown Unna, where a studio was found for him in the tower of St Katherine's Church.

An early window made in 1957 for The Protestant Church, Worms, shows Buschulte's predilection for soft shapes, light spaces and a strong design. Two windows – the Easter window and the Whitsun window – made for the Chapel of St. Katherine's Hospital, Unna in 1968 are essentially the work of a painter. Both show Buschulte's command of colour and his personal, inventive approach to the story. The Easter window, for example, uses the 'empty tomb' as the focus for the composition, while the Whitsun window takes the 'tongues of fire' as the

Wilhelm Buschulte in his studio in 1985. Source: Tim Lewis

Below-Left:
Window by Wilhelm Buschulte for The Protestant Church, Worms, 1957. Source: www.glasmalerei-oidtmann.de

Below-Centre:
Design by Wilhelm Buschulte for the Chapel of St Katherine's Church, Unna. Source: Tim Lewis

Below-Right:
Window by Wilhelm Buschulte for the Chapel of St Katherine's Church, Unna, Source: Tim Lewis

starting point. The relationship between Buschulte's manner of painting and his work in glass can be seen in the transition between sketch design and finished window for a three-light window in St Katherine's Church, Unna. Besides these colourful compositions, Buschulte designed windows of the utmost austerity, using subtle patterns in glass and lead to trap the light against the sky. These windows relate to the Cistercian tradition of grisaille (painted glass without colour), typified by the so-called 'Five Sisters' windows in York Minster, England. Such harmonies in black and white inevitably imply the centrality of grief in the post-war experience. In a very different spirit, the dramatic coloured glass in the Treasure House of St Peter's Church, Aachen made in 1977, presents the mystical subject of the woman defeating the seven headed dragon to be found in the Book of Revelations. This window has been described as bringing 'strong jewelled colours to the small dark chapel'.

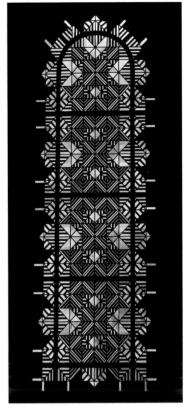

Black and white windows by Wilhelm Buschulte for St Katherine's Church, Unna. Source: Tim Lewis

Black and white windows by Wilhelm Buschulte for St Katherine's Church, Unna. Source: Tim Lewis

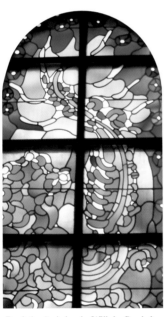
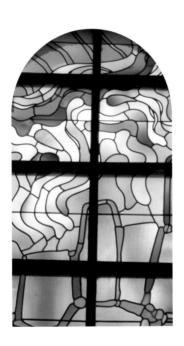

Revelations' window by Wilhelm Buschulte for St Peter's Church, Aachen, 1977. Source: www.glasmalerei-oidtmann.de

In the painterly, as opposed to the graphic, approach to architectural glass, no one explored the opportunities provided by architecture more thoroughly than Georg Meistermann (1911-1990). Before the war, between 1930 and 1933, Meistermann studied at the Art Academy at Düsseldorf, but was prevented from continuing his education by the rise of National Socialism. Paintings such as his 'Komposition 111' of 1952 have links with Miró and other French artists of the late Surrealist movement. Certainly the tension between balance and activity owes more to the verve of the avant-garde in Paris than to the austere disciplines of the Bauhaus. When invited to make a glass wall for the exterior of the Broadcasting House in Köln, Meistermann adapted his style to architecture, creating an entertaining composition in bright colours and black shapes to interact with the metalwork of the open stairway.

Portrait of Georg Meistermann. Source: Meistermann website

Painting 'Komposition III' by Georg Meistermann, 1952.
© Christie's Images Limited

Glass wall by Georg Meisterman for West German Broadcasting House in Köln, 1952. Supplied by Caroline Swash

Detail of the Glass wall by Georg Meisterman for the West German Broadcasting House in Köln, 1952. Source: Rodney Bender

Glass wall by Georg Meisterman for West German Broadcasting House in Köln, 1952. Source: Rodney Bender

Meistermann also brought recognisable imagery into his windows. The crisply painted figures of the Horsemen of the Apocalypse and the semi-abstract pattern windows made in the 1950s for the Old Town Hall in Wittlich show how impressive his method could be when applied to a familiar image. However, his designs for church windows grew from another aspect of his work. During the 1950s, Meistermann had developed a technique that involved the use of delicate washes of colour in gradated layers. He adapted this method of layering to his designs for glass, building up a coherent structure of colours and tones to establish the desired emotional impact for each work. The figures in the windows for the Church of St. Mary at Köln-Kalk designed in 1957 float convincingly above the earth and sea. Meistermann achieved this otherworldly effect through interlocking layers of glass and the judicious use of colour. The imagery is sufficiently precise to permit recognition, yet varied enough to impart a sense of dreamy contemplation. It has

been suggested that in works of this period, Meistermann was influenced by the French artist Alfred Manessier's use of fluttering abstract shapes (see Chapter 6). Among the masterpieces of the Post-war period are the windows by Meistermann for the cupola of the Church of St. Gereon at Köln. No photograph can do justice to the variety and invention of this marvellous scheme. Each window opening has its own integrity, both in terms of subject and orchestration of colour.

Meistermann had considerable influence on those who travelled to Germany to see his work. Unlike Schaffrath, Schreiter and Poensgen, he rarely taught outside Germany. His prestige as a painter largely outweighed his reputation as a glass artist. From 1967 to 1972 he was President of the German Artists Federation. In addition to winning numerous prizes for both painting and glass design, he was awarded the Order of Merit by the Federal Republic of Germany in 1990.

Coloured cartoon by Georg Meistermann for one of the Four Horsemen of the Apocalypse, 1955. Source: Tim Lewis

'Horseman' window by Georg Meistermann for the Old Town Hall, Wittlich, 1955. Source: Tim Lewis

Detail of 'Horseman' window by Georg Meistermann for the Old Town Hall, Wittlich, 1955. Source: Tim Lewis

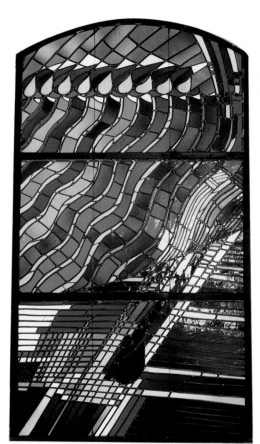

Window by Georg Meistermann in the Old Town Hall, Wittlich 1956. Supplied by Caroline Swash

'Rosa Mystica', Exhibition panel by Georg Meistermann. Supplied by Caroline Swash

Detail of 'Pentecost' window by Georg Meistermann at St Mary's Church, Köln-Kalk, 1965. Source: Tim Lewis

'Pentecost' window at St Mary's Church, Köln-Kalk, 1965. Source: Tim Lewis

Another painter to work in glass was Hans Gottfried von Stockhausen (b.1920). After imprisonment in Egypt by the British during the war, he studied glass and mosaic at the State Academy of Fine Art in Stuttgart. In addition to working as an independent painter and glass artist, he returned to the Stuttgart Academy to teach drawing and art fundamentals before becoming Professor of Stained Glass from 1970 until 1980. Since his retirement he has taught at Pilchuck in the United States and in Edinburgh and his influence on young artists in Germany and elsewhere has been enormous. Besides encouraging a highly personal approach to glass he has helped to reawaken interest in the craft side of the art. By stressing the importance of the artist's own hand in the actual fabrication of the work, he has reconnected current practice to earlier traditions. His focus on the 'glass picture' as an entity in itself, free from architectural constraints, has helped a number of young artists develop their own ideas in interesting ways.

Hans Gottfried von Stockhausen's architectural glass repays attentive examination. His windows are filled with incident, both profound and humourous. Those created for the Liebfrauen Church at Koblenz (1990-91) are a magnificent example of his work. Here genuinely new imagery has been comfortably fitted into the rhythm of the ancient building. An earlier work, the Tree of Jesse window made in 1970 for the Church of St. Maria zur Wiese in Soest shows Stockhausen entirely at ease with the challenge of integrating his own ideas with surviving medieval glass.

Portrait of Hans Gottfried von Stockhausen. With permission of the artist. Supplied by Hessisches Landesmuseum Darmstadt

Stained glass window in the Liebfrauen Church at Koblenz by Hans Gottfried von Stockhausen, 1990-91

In this window the Gothic fragments from 1500 that were damaged during the war have been reset and a new decorative version of the Tree of Jesse added to complete the scheme. The foliage has a rough, almost spiky appearance, suggesting that the Tree itself has been terribly damaged but not destroyed.

During the 1960s, Stockhausen experimented with abstract forms, using them in a symbolic way within independent glass panels. By the 1970's he was already perfecting the lively brushwork and evocative choice of colour that make his panels so satisfying. Like other visionary artists, he allows the ancient tales of the Classical and Christian worlds to speak to us in new and kindly ways.

'Lovers' glass panel by Hans Gottfried von Stockhausen. With permission of the artist. Supplied by Hessisches Landesmuseum Darmstadt

'Burning Bush', glass panel by Hans Gottfried von Stockhausen. With permission of the artist. Supplied by Hessisches Landesmuseum Darmstadt

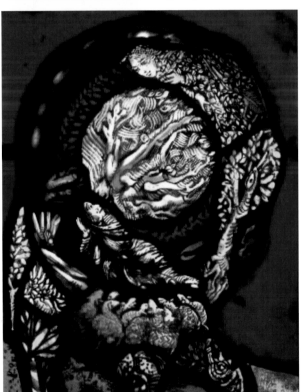

'Daphne' glass panel by Hans Gottfried von Stockhausen, 1984. With permission of the artist. Supplied by Hessisches Landesmuseum Darmstadt

'Shepherd's Dream', glass panel by Hans Gottfried von Stockhausen, 1979. With permission of the artist. Supplied by Hessisches Landesmuseum Darmstadt

Coventry and Beyond

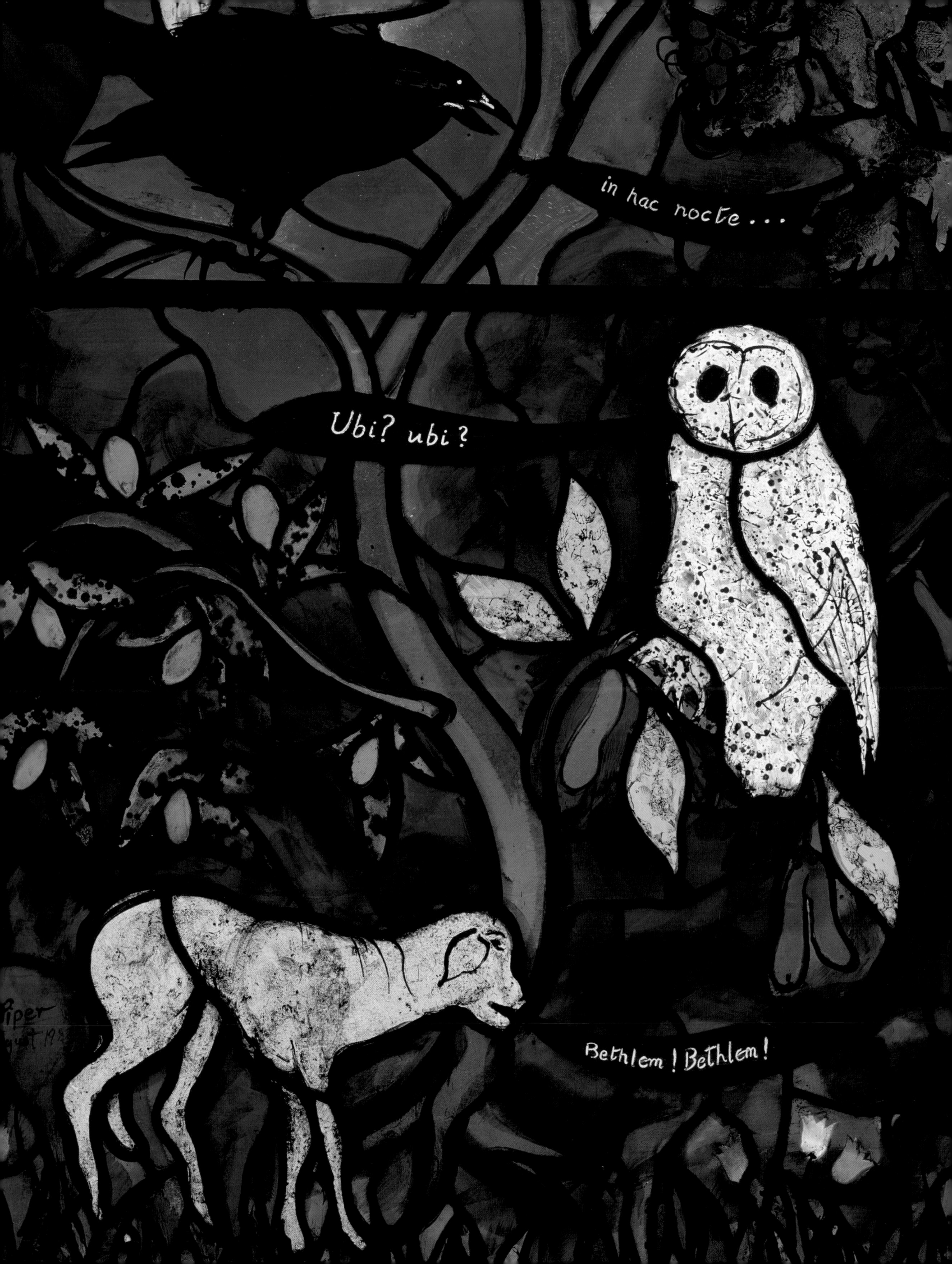
in hac nocte . . .
Ubi? ubi?
Bethlem! Bethlem!

X

Coventry and Beyond

O n the night of November 14, 1940, the city of Coventry was shattered by aerial bombardment and its ancient Cathedral, a fine medieval building was, in large part, damaged beyond repair. When the war ended, the Harlech Commission, set up to consider the future of the ruins, recommended that a new Cathedral be built on the site of the old. The architect was chosen in 1951 by an open competition and the winner was Basil Spence. His simple and dignified design depended for its effect on a rich interior, which would include sculpture, tapestry and mosaic as well as beautiful stained and engraved glass. For Spence, the contribution of contemporary British artists was crucial to a building that would, in the words of the competition brief, 'speak to us and to generations to come of the Majesty, the Eternity and the Glory of God.'

Following his selection, Spence traveled to France to visit the recently completed churches at Audincourt and Vence (see Chapter 6). He particularly admired Matisse's glass for the Chapel of the Rosary, noting the effect of colour projected onto the white tiled walls and floor, 'a shimmering overlay of blue and gold as one moves slowly around'. Spence came home determined that his own cathedral would have glass of outstanding artistic value executed in a range of contemporary styles and techniques.

Spence was deeply impressed by the recently completed windows for the Chapel of Oundle School near Peterborough by the artist John Piper and his collaborator Patrick Reyntiens. Spence thought them 'most beautiful' and commissioned Piper to design the huge Baptistery window near the west end of the Cathedral. For the ten floor-to-ceiling windows he planned for the nave, he searched for artists working in a modern style that reflected the 'true English tradition – virile and strong'. At the 1952 degree show at the Royal College of Art, London, he discovered what he wanted in the work of students Geoffrey Clarke and Keith New. They and their tutor, Lawrence Lee, were invited to construct the nave windows using RCA facilities. Intrigued by the concrete and glass technique (dalle de verre) used by Fernand Léger, Spence entrusted these windows to talented artist Margaret Traherne. The challenging commission to make an engraved glass screen to divide the new Cathedral from the remains of the old was given to Spence's colleague, the New Zealander, John Hutton. Having found the right artists for each space, Spence exhorted them all to do their utmost to make 'singing, breathing windows'.

Spence's firm support for contemporary styles and techniques was at variance with the way glass was viewed elsewhere in England in the post war years. Most of Britain's major industrial cities had been affected by the wartime bombing. Much of the destroyed stained glass had been made during the 19th century. It was dark in tone and rich in colour, designed to give churches the 'dim religious light' fashionable at the time. On the whole, congregations were rather relieved to be rid of these gloomy windows. Furthermore, government subventions for financial compensation for war damage were low and tended to be available for minimal replacement rather than innovation. Another factor discouraged change, having won the war, the British people felt that the values of the past should be retained as pointers to an even better future.

When new windows were commissioned, certain themes were felt to be particularly appropriate. These included the triumph of good over evil and the commemoration of loss and sacrifice. For example, the Church of St Mary-le-Bow in London, was rebuilt by the architect Lawrence King with stained glass by John Hayward (b.1925). Hayward's 1963 window shows St Mary cradling the new building against a patterned background of spires of London churches damaged in the Blitz. Hayward's image of victory in the church of St Michael Paternoster Royal shows the archangel Michael triumphing over the rebel angel who lies bound and engulfed in flames.

'St Mary' stained glass window by John Hayward at the east end of St Mary-le-Bow church, City of London, 1963. Supplied by Caroline Swash

*Detail of 'St Mary'
stained glass window by
John Hayward in St
Mary-le-Bow Church,
City of London, 1963.
Supplied by Caroline
Swash*

*Stained glass windows by John Hayward
in the church of St Michael, Paternoster
Royal, City of London, 1963.
Supplied by Caroline Swash*

*'Archangel Michael in triumph over the
devil', stained glass window by John
Hayward for the church of St Michael,
Paternoster Royal, City of London, 1968.
Supplied by Caroline Swash*

Detail of 'Archangel Michael in triumph over the devil', stained glass window by John Hayward for the church of St Michael, Paternoster Royal, City of London, 1968. Supplied by Caroline Swash

In the church of St Lawrence, Jewry, windows designed by Christopher Webb (1886-1966) include a grieving angel holding the fire-damaged church and a joyful angel presenting the rebuilt church. Webb worked with the influential architect Ninian Comper and shared his views on the importance of light glass, clear colour and elegant draughtsmanship. This attractive style enabled Webb to include a wide variety of subject matter within a generally light window. The rebuilding of St Lawrence, Jewry, for example, was commemorated with portraits of workmen, contractors and committee members set into the decorative border of the window dedicated to Sir Christopher Wren. In 1954, a competition was held to create a new Shakespeare memorial window for Southwark Cathedral. A fine marble sculpture of the poet, carved in 1912 by Henry McCarthy, had survived bombardment, but the window above honouring the dramatist was destroyed. Webb won the competition and included references to all the well known Shakespeare plays in the windows. The comedies were placed in the left hand light and the tragedies in the right while the base of the window features a frieze of figures – the seven ages of man.

Detail with a sad angel holding the damaged church. Scenes of the London Blitz in the background by Christopher Webb in the church of St Lawrence Jewry, City of London. Supplied by Caroline Swash

Detail with a happy angel holding the restored church by Christopher Webb in the church of St Lawrence Jewry, City of London. Supplied by Caroline Swash

Detail showing a carpenter at work in the west window by Christopher Webb in the church of St Lawrence Jewry, City of London. Supplied by Caroline Swash

Detail showing a stained glass artist drawing a cartoon and a stone mason in the west window by Christopher Webb in the church of St Lawrence Jewry, City of London. Supplied by Caroline Swash

Detail showing portraits of the architect and vicar in the west window by Christopher Webb in the church of St Lawrence Jewry, City of London. Supplied by Caroline Swash

Detail showing 'Bottom and Puck' from Shakespeare's play 'A Midsummer Night's dream' designed by Christopher Webb for the Shakespeare Memorial in Southwark Cathedral, 1954. Supplied by Caroline Swash

Detail showing Hamlet and Lady Macbeth from Shakespeare's tragedies 'Hamlet' and 'Macbeth' designed by Christopher Webb for the Shakespeare Memorial in Southwark Cathedral, 1954. Supplied by Caroline Swash

Detail showing the battle scene in Shakespeare's tragedy 'Richard III' designed by Christopher Webb for the Shakespeare Memorial in Southwark Cathedral, 1954. Supplied by Caroline Swash

In damaged buildings, replacement glass was usually designed in a style that would harmonise with the original historic context. Architects who admired the work of Sir Christopher Wren in the City of London were encouraged to rebuild in a similar style. The scholarly painter Brian Thomas (1912-1990) was an invaluable help in the creation of appropriate stained glass for these remodeled churches. His passion for the Baroque style in art and architecture enabled him to respond with wit and sensitivity to the requirements of architects such as Seeley and Paget, W. Godfrey Allen and Stephen Dykes Bower. Windows by Thomas combine imaginative detail with glowing colour entirely appropriate to their setting.

Although these windows were well made and carefully researched, they did not suggest a new direction for glass. In Germany and France, artists were struggling both to make sense of their recovering world and to find a visual language that broke with the past. In England, however, only in Coventry Cathedral, a completely new structure of enormous patriotic and religious significance, could a hint of a different future be discerned.

Brian Thomas in his studio, 1975.
Supplied by Caroline Swash

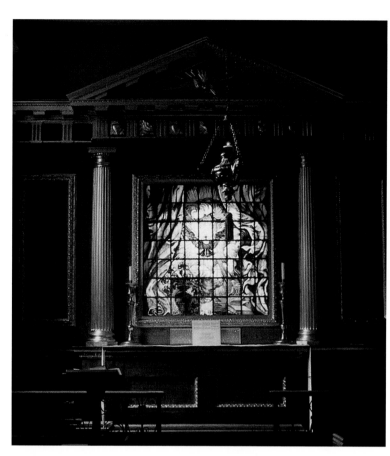

Stained glass window by Brian Thomas for the chapel of St Andrew's church, Holborn. Supplied by Caroline Swash

Detail of the Dove (Holy Ghost) by Brian Thomas for the chapel of St Andrew's church, Holborn. Supplied by Caroline Swash

*Detail showing Queen Clothilde by Brian Thomas in
the west window of St Vedast church, City of London.
Supplied by Caroline Swash*

The Stained Glass Artists of Coventry Cathedral

*Detail of the Baptistery window by John Piper and
Patrick Reyntiens in Coventry Cathedral, 1959-62.
Supplied by Caroline Swash*

Baptistery window by John Piper and Patrick Reyntiens in Coventry Cathedral, 1959-62. Supplied by Caroline Swash

The Baptistery Window:
John Piper and Patrick Reyntiens

John Piper (1903-1992) who was commissioned to design the Baptistery window, had studied first at the Slade School of Art and then at the Royal College. As a young man visiting France, he met with artists of the 'avant garde' and his early work reflected their enthusiasms. During the war, Piper was made an official war artist and his unforgettable paintings of London's ruined buildings remain the most impressive of their kind. As an artist, Piper is best known for his attractive atmospheric landscapes. A painting of Dalham, Suffolk is typical of his style which included cleverly gradated washes of colour combined with incisive drawing. After the war, he was closely involved in the 1951 'Festival of Britain', a celebration of contemporary British science, art and design. Termed a 'tonic for the nation', the Festival was arranged by the Labour government to bring a sense of hope and fun into the lives of the British people.

Above:
*John Piper in his studio.
© estate of Bob Collins/
National Portrait Gallery,
London*

Above-Right:
*Painting, 'Dalham, Suffolk'
by John Piper, 1972.
© Christie's Images Limited*

Right:
*Painting, 'Venice Fantasy' by
John Piper, based on his stage
designs for the Opera 'Death in
Venice' by Benjamin Britten with
libretto by Myfanwy Piper, 1974.
© Christie's Images Limited*

Piper also created sets and costumes for the theatre. These included the design for the Opera 'Death in Venice' by Benjamin Britten based on the novella by Thomas Mann. The libretto was written by Myfanwy Piper, the artist's second wife and first performed in 1973. With the poet, John Betjeman, he worked on a pioneering series of architectural guide books that were published in the late 1940s by John Murray. Comprised of text and photographs that were equally lyrical, they aimed to encourage the appreciation of English architecture and landscape. Through Betjeman he was introduced to Patrick Reyntiens as an artist with the skill and sensitivity to help make the windows for Oundle Chapel. Their partnership was an immediate success.

Piper's language in stained glass grew from his interest in the dynamics of colour, which he explored through watercolour, crayon and collage in such compositions as 'Abstract'. His studies of medieval carvings and stained glass were another source of inspiration. The black ink drawing of the Tympanum at Donzy-le-Pré in France, made in 1970, is typical of the work that occupied him throughout his life, providing him with source material for so many of his ideas in architectural glass.

Watercolour, crayon and collage
'Abstract' by John Piper.
© *Christie's Images Limited*

Black ink painting 'Donzy- Le -Pré
Tympanum' by John Piper, 1970.
© *Christie's Images Limited*

Piper's method of designing for new windows involved the exploration of scale and colour as well as figural content. In the drawing of a row of Kings for the Oundle Chapel windows, the static frieze of figures has been enlivened by variations in stance and gesture while crowns denote their status. Colour sketches followed preparatory drawings. Studies for the window in the King George VI Memorial Chapel at St George's, Windsor completed in 1969, shows Piper arranging the disposition of colour across the mullions, breaking up the dominant blue tones with notes of red and establishing outer borders of a lighter hue. Piper enjoyed reworking certain themes and his design for the East Window at Nettlebed Church, Oxfordshire, painted in 1970 includes several of his favourites. The Tree of Life became the subject of several exceptional windows while the iconic forms of fish, birds and plants are seen repeatedly in his prints and paintings as well as glass.

Colour study by John Piper for the stained glass window in the King George VI Memorial Chapel, St George's Chapel, Windsor, 1969. © Christie's Images Limited

Study for the east window of St Bartholomew's Church, Nettlebed, Oxon by John Piper, 1970. © Christie's Images Limited

Opposite:
Three Figures of Christ, 1956, stained glass by John Piper, & Patrick Reyntiens for the Oundle School Chapel, Northamptonshire, UK, in copyright

'The Nativity', stained glass window by John Piper & Patrick Reyntiens for the Iffley Church, Oxfordshire. In copyright until 2063, Patrick Reyntiens Archive

Benjamin Britten memorial window depicting 'The Prodigal Son, Curlew River, and the Burning Fiery Furnace', 1979 by John Piper & Patrick Reyntiens for the Aldeburgh Church, Suffolk. In copyright until 2063

One of the recurring images in Piper's work from 1953 onwards is that of the 'Foliate Head', sometimes called the 'Green Man'. This pre-Christian image of a man peering through leaves with vegetation sprouting from his mouth remains one of the mysterious figures of English folk lore. Besides making numerous paintings in crayon and watercolour of this subject, Piper used some of the drawings as the basis for tapestry designs and lithographs. A particularly attractive version was made in glass for the British Glass Exhibition held in 1977 at the Centre International de Vitrail in Chartres, France.

Patrick Reyntiens (b.1925) who took on the challenging task of translating Piper's designs into stained glass, had spent four years in the Army followed by five years training in painting and architecture at Marylebone School of Art and Edinburgh College of Art. He learnt the craft skills needed for building windows at the studio of Joseph E. Nuttgens (1892-1982) who specialised in the complex work of interpreting other artists' designs as well as making his own windows. Nuttgens was a true follower of the Arts and Crafts tradition and handled every stage of the process himself, a philosophy he imparted to Reyntiens.

Watercolour, crayon and black ink painting
'Foliate Heads' by John Piper, 1953.
© Christie's Images Limited

Lithograph 'Foliate Heads 1' with added
colour by John Piper, part of an edition of
70 published by John Erskine, 1953.
© Christie's Images Limited

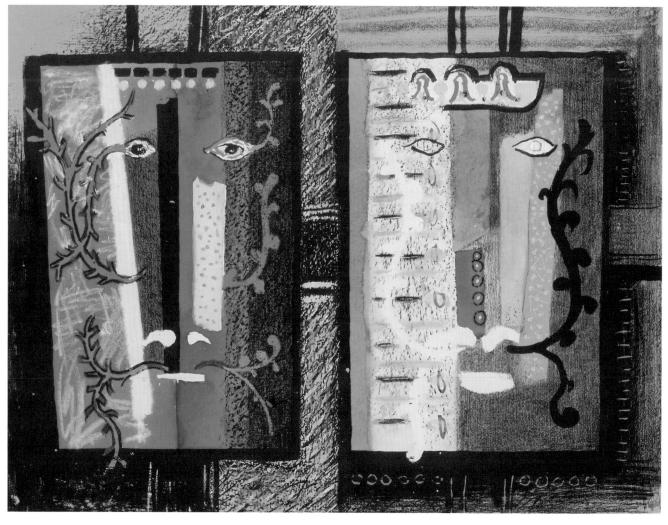

Stained glass panel 'Four Seasons' by John Piper, 1977. Supplied by Caroline Swash

Below:
Patrick Reyntiens in his studio.
Supplied by Caroline Swash

In order to make the Baptistery window for Coventry Cathedral, Reyntiens enlarged a substantial coach house to make a studio at Burleighfield near his home at Flackwell Heath near High Wycombe. He continued to work there when the Coventry commission was completed, making new windows with Piper for the Liverpool Metropolitan Cathedral (1965-66), St Margaret's Westminster (1967-68) and St George's Chapel, Windsor (1969) and many others. Piper's windows for St Margaret's, entitled 'Spring in London' depend for their effect on Reyntiens' skill in transforming the dense textures of the design into lively glass. Reyntiens was equally perceptive in the fabrication of Piper's later work, such as the glass wall featuring abstract flowers made for Sanderson's showrooms in central London and the harmonious green glass wall for the Chapel of Robinson College, Cambridge. Besides running the studio for the fabrication of Piper's windows, Reyntiens developed his own language in glass. Throughout the 1970s, he explored the possibilities of wavy, soft-edged shapes, so different from the crisp linear formalities of the contemporary German school.

Indeed, Reyntien's architectural work continued to reflect his interest in the tension between the personal vision and the formal requirements of the building. He wrote about this predicament in 1990 in 'The Beauty of Stained Glass'. "On the one hand 'art' is the triumph of the individual, the prophetic side of man – the liberation of people's aspirations. It is the guarantee of individuality and personal worth. On the other, 'design' is the expression of the sinews of society, of those activities that hold the whole of the fabric of society together. As architecture lies uneasily between the two categories, inclining more to the impersonal than to the personal, it is easy to see that the antipathy between a personalised art, such as painting is, and stained glass, in certain circumstances should be, and the machine finished milieu of architecture today poses very profound problems."

*Interior of the Burleighfield Studio with
a window in process of construction.
Supplied by Caroline Swash*

*View of the south wall with stained glass
windows by John Piper and Patrick Reyntiens in
St Margaret's Church, Westminster, 1967-68.
Supplied by Caroline Swash*

Reyntiens' solution to this dilemma was to search for fresh ways of presenting time-honoured themes. His cool, evocative window made in 1992 for the Sisters of Mercy in Whitechapel, London veils the curved glass wall of the nuns chapel, while the lively brushwork for which Reyntiens is renowned brings subtle shifts of light and colour to the composition.

During the 1980s and 90s, Reyntiens turned his attention to the glass picture. He drew inspiration from the classical world, particularly the poem 'Metamorphosis' written in the 1st century BC by the Roman poet Ovid. From Ovid's tales, he produced a series of vivid images that he described as 'the fresh shoots of a humanising spring' for exhibition in the United Kingdom, United States and Canada. The tales of Apollo and Daphne, Europa and the Bull and Danae and the Shower of Gold were reinterpreted through the medium of stained glass. In 1992, Reyntiens began work on a new series of 'Commedia del Arte' panels, featuring clowns and columbines. Another series were related to figures in contemporary entertainment such as the character of Dame Edna Everage created by Barry Humphries. Reyntiens suggested that these panels should be enjoyed in the same way as a poem or a piece of music; a matter of private taste.

Reyntiens' interest in the aesthetics of glass in the widest sense made him an inspirational teacher. From 1968 he and his artist wife, Anne Bruce, set up an educational centre at Burleighfield where students from all over the world could work together in an atmosphere that stimulated new ideas. Reyntiens later became Head of Fine Art at Central Saint Martins College of Art in London from 1976-1986 and thereafter continued to run master classes overseas. The most important work of his later years was the west window for Southwell Minster made at the studio of Keith Barley. His subtle and attractive 'Angels in Heaven' window shows how far Reyntiens had developed his own method of interpreting the past using his considerable powers in the bravura handling of paint.

East window by Patrick Reyntiens with Bernard Becker for The Sacred Heart Nunnery, Whitechapel, 1992. Supplied by Caroline Swash

Detail of the east window by Patrick Reyntiens with Bernard Becker for The Sacred Heart Nunnery, Whitechapel, 1992. Supplied by Caroline Swash

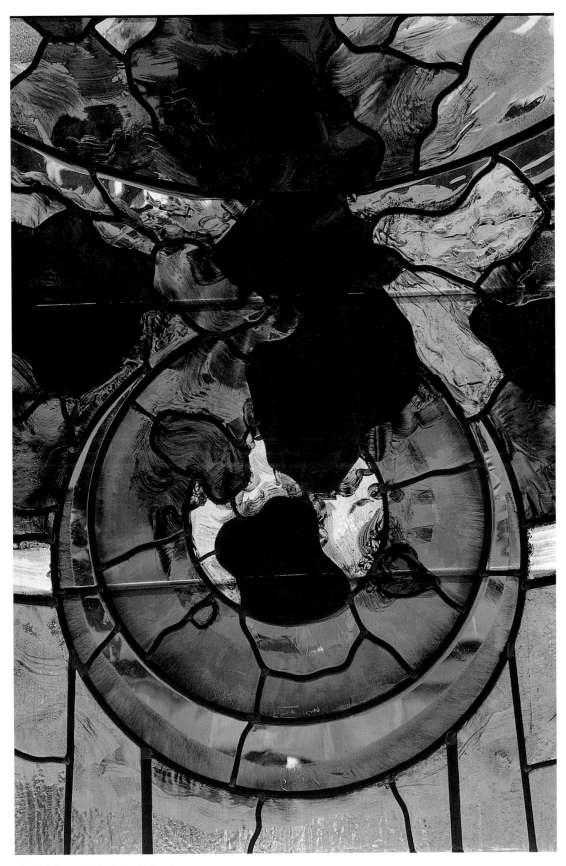

Detail of the east window by Patrick Reyntiens
with Bernard Becker for The Sacred Heart
Nunnery, Whitechapel, 1992.
Supplied by Caroline Swash

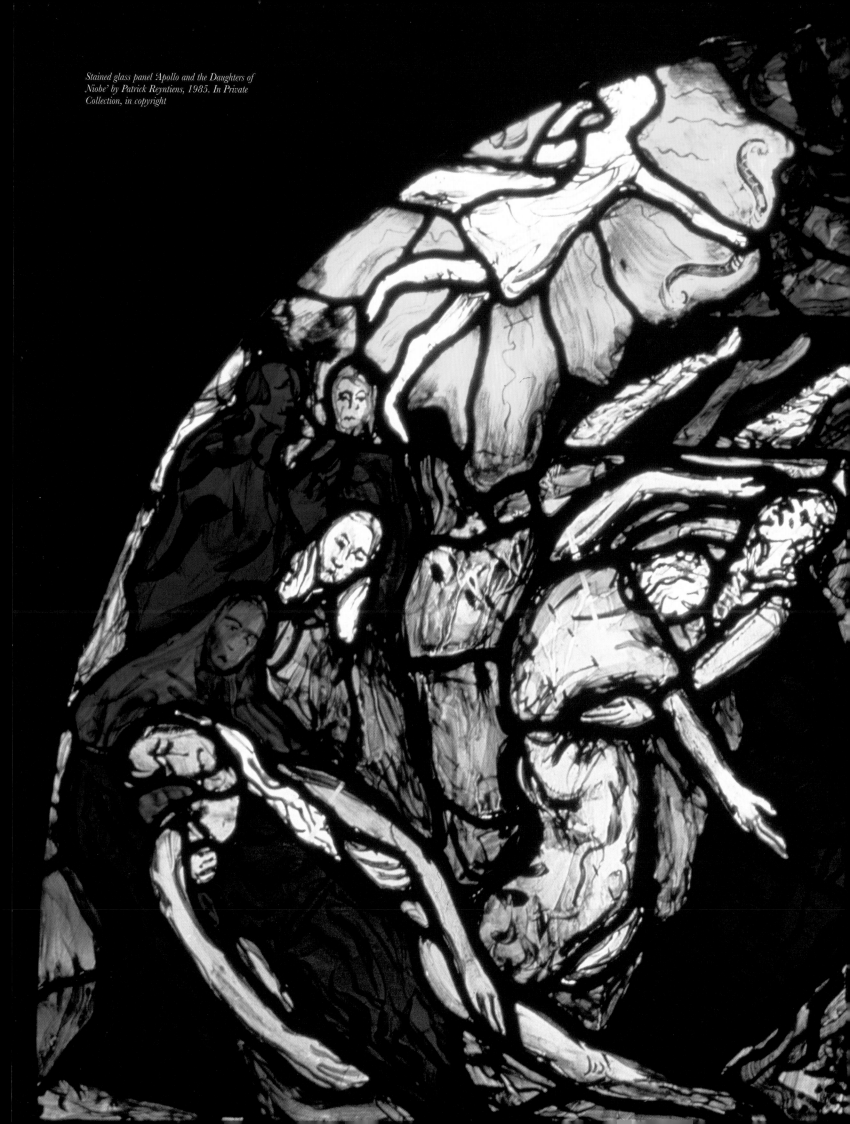

Stained glass panel 'Apollo and the Daughters of Niobe' by Patrick Reyntiens, 1985. In Private Collection, in copyright

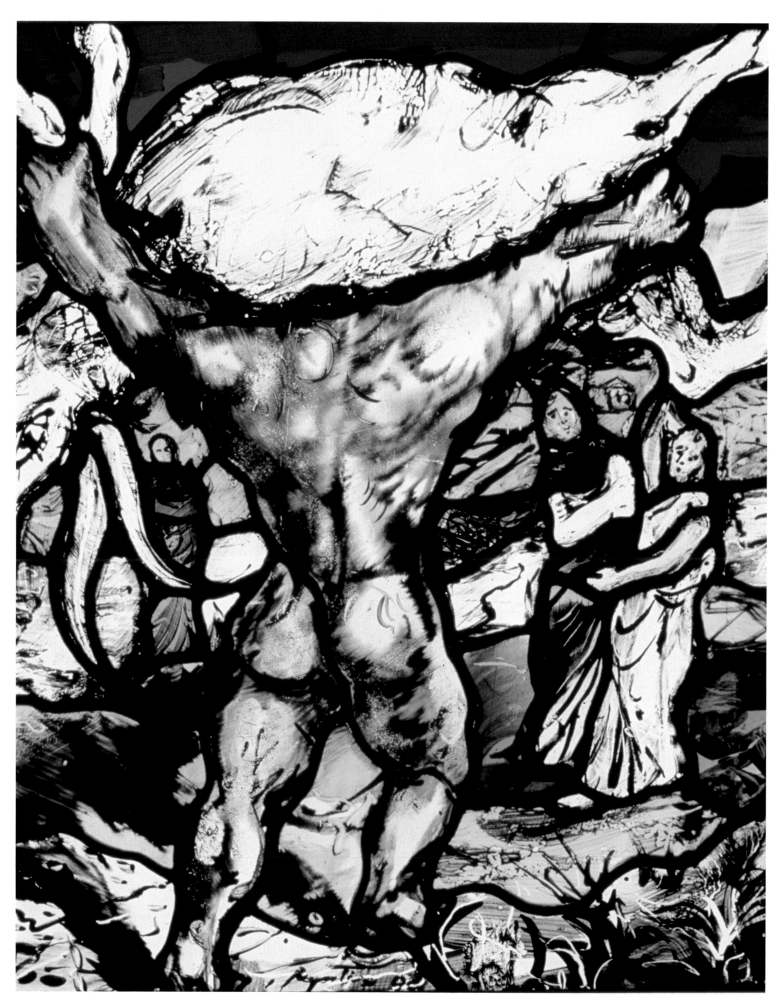

*Stained glass panel 'Commedia del Arte'
series by Patrick Reyntiens, 1990.
Supplied by Caroline Swash*

*Stained glass panel 'Dame Edna
Everidge' by Patrick Reyntiens, 1994.
Supplied by Caroline Swash*

The Nave Windows of Coventry Cathedral:
Lawrence Lee, Keith New & Geoffrey Clarke

At the Royal College of Art, space was set aside for the Coventry commission in the mural decoration studios. Spence had established a 'God' side (south) and a 'Man' side (north) for the five sets of windows in the nave of the Cathedral, assigning each pair a colour scheme. These were chosen to typify the five stages of human life from childhood (green) through youth (red), middle age (red and gold), the maturity of old age (purple) and the afterlife (white) and were to be filled with appropriate symbols. Lawrence Lee described the need to treat the stone fenestration as a 'forest of artificial trunks and branches' which should be used 'as a trellis'. The daunting task of creating these enormous windows (9' wide and 75' high) was divided equally. Students assisted in various ways, gaining invaluable insight which served them well in the future.

Lawrence Lee, who was in charge of the commission, was head of the Department of Stained Glass at the Royal College of Art from 1948-1968. Besides his teaching schedule he ran his own studio at Penshurst in Kent. His glass work revealed his keen interest in research for the background 'story' of the window combined with enthusiasm for finding new ways of working glass and paint together. Vignettes from his Tradescant window made in 1987 for St Mary's Church, Lambeth, show Lee's ability to use telling details in an imaginative way. The church building had recently been adapted to house The Museum of Garden History, so Lee's windows featured gardening themes, such as the first gardeners, Adam and Eve, two young lovers in a Persian garden and the Elizabethan horticulturalists, John Tradescant (father and son), homeward bound from America with their botanical specimens.

Stained glass windows by Lawrence Lee, Keith New and Geoffrey Clarke for the nave of Coventry Cathedral. Supplied by Caroline Swash

Above:
Detail by Lawrence Lee showing the first gardeners
'Adam and Eve' in the Tradescant window,
St Mary at Lambeth (The Museum of Garden
History), 1972. Supplied by Caroline Swash

Top-Right:
Detail by Lawrence Lee showing young lovers in
a Persian Garden in the Tradescant window,
St Mary at Lambeth (The Museum of Garden
History), 1972. Supplied by Caroline Swash

Right:
Detail by Lawrence Lee showing the botanical
explorers John Tradescant (father and son),
St Mary at Lambeth (The Museum of Garden
History), 1972. Supplied by Caroline Swash

In describing the effects of light through glass he observed that 'The persistent lines of lead can only be extended, complemented, by something which is itself linear: a form of drawing moving from dense and immobile black lines into the energy and eroding power of light.' Lee's personal style combined textures as well as clearly painted passages. He described himself as one of the 'last of the Pre-Raphaelites', a statement that refers both to his observant inclusion of plants and flowers as well as to the romantic element in his work. These qualities can be seen in the window made in 1971 for the church of St Mary the Virgin, Cuddington.

When orders for new windows began to arrive following the Coventry commission, Lee left the Royal College to devote more time to these commissions at his Penshurst Studio. He was joined there by former students and young artists, establishing something of a craft community in the quiet Kentish village. Alan Younger (1930-2004) worked with Lee for six years after studying at the Central School of Art and working as assistant to Carl Edwards. Younger often spoke fondly of his time at Penshurst, recalling the pleasant atmosphere of the studio, the kindliness of Lee and the discussions that ebbed and flowed around the task of building windows. The home and studio that Younger and his actress wife Zoë later created in South London retained many of the qualities that he had so admired.

Although Younger's work retained the imprint of his years with Lee, he rapidly developed his own style and his stained glass is instantly recognisable. This is mainly due to the care that he lavished on each piece of glass. His methods included softening away the colour with hydrofluoric acid, applying paint to the surface in various ways then firing the glass to fix it before painting again. Silver stain would be added to warm the lines and give the glass a wonderfully rich glow. In 1989 he completed an impressive Rose for the west end of St Alban's Cathedral. The entire window had been cut and painted, etched and stained in Younger's studio at Crystal Palace. This monumental achievement was matched some years later by stained glass for the Henry VII Chapel in Westminster Abbey. Of this he wrote 'I would like the new window to appear to be of its time in its tendency to move towards abstraction and deliberate ambiguity, with details not completely resolved, leaving scope for individual interpretation.'

Detail of the youthful St Mary by Lawrence Lee in the Church of St Mary the Virgin, Cuddington, Surrey, 1971.
Supplied by Caroline Swash

Stained glass window by Lawrence Lee in the Church of St Mary the Virgin, Cuddington, Surrey, 1971. Supplied by Caroline Swash

Left:
Alan Younger in his south London studio.
Supplied by Caroline Swash

Below-Left:
Rose window (1989) in the north transept
of St. Albans Cathedral, Hertfordshire.
Photo courtesy of Zöe Younger

Below:
The Arms of Lord Harris, detail of the
clerestory East window (2000) in Henry
VII's Chapel, Wesminster Abbey.
Photograph by Peter Cormack

Following the completion of Coventry Cathedral, Geoffrey Clarke (b.1924) took over the teaching at the Royal College, shifting the direction of the glass department away from stained glass towards a more varied approach to the material that has continued to this day. His own work in glass had a roughness and energy evident in the panel in the collection of the Victoria and Albert Museum. Having designed a powerful altar cross as well as the three windows for Coventry Cathedral, Clarke received many orders for three dimensional works ranging from exquisite medallions to substantial free-standing pieces in bronze and other metals.

Detail of stained glass panel by Geoffrey Clarke in the collection of the Victoria and Albert Museum. Supplied by Caroline Swash

High Altar Cross by Geoffrey Clarke, 1962

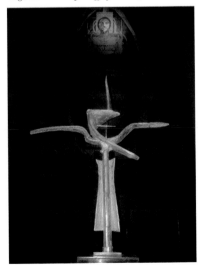

Once the Coventry commission was finished, Keith New (b1926) established a studio next to his house in Wimbledon. Here he built windows of great boldness and originality. His background in graphic design (studied at Cheam Art School), gave him an unusually direct attitude to subject matter. He once described stained glass as 'colour and form, a bit like a poster advertising God'. Although his most exciting windows have a verve and richness unrivalled by any other artist at this time, painting remained his chief interest. Even at the height of his post-Coventry success he felt that 'designing and making windows was very much a giving out process. With my paintings I could make personal discoveries and take creative chances that fed back into my glass'. Painting gradually took over from his glass work. The formal qualities of his landscapes relate to his years designing for architecture, while the scale and texture of his brushwork reflect his experience in glass painting.

Window by Keith New for Highgate School Chapel in North London, 1967. Supplied by the artist.

Left:
*Detail of window by Keith New for
Highgate School Chapel in North
London, 1967. Supplied by the artist*

*Stained glass window by Keith New for
St John's Church, Ermine, Lincoln, 1966.
Supplied by the artist*

Top Left:
*Painting 'Line-up. The Gardens, Penshurst' by
Keith New exhibited at the Llewellyn Alexander
Gallery, London, 1999. Supplied by the artist*

Above:
*Detail of window by Keith New for
St John's Church, Ermine, Lincoln,
1966. Supplied by the artist*

Top Right:
*Keith New in his studio
with his daughter Clarissa.
Supplied by the artist*

The years following the Coventry commission were a period of experimentation in the technical aspects of glass as well as imagery.

Almost all innovations came from France, the most popular being the 'dalle de verre' technique that used thick pieces of glass set into concrete blocks. Artists also experimented with the technique of 'Glass appliqué,' in which pieces of glass are bonded onto a clear glass sheet to create a collage of brilliant colours. In 1960, New was asked to create portraits in glass for the entrance area of the new Commonwealth Institute in Holland Park. He successfully combined printed images with a richly coloured glass collage. His assistant on this project was the Indian artist Amal Ghosh (b. 1933) who had studied painting first in India and then with the artist Cecil Collins at the Central School of Art. Ghosh later ran the glass course at Central Saint Martins, teaching enamel and transparent imagery. His work in mosaic can be seen at the Eastman Dental Institute in London while his glass designs have been used in many new buildings in India. His glass and paintings have brought him a world wide audience and his example has encouraged young Indian artists to study glass, including Sisir Sahana in Hyderabad and Tandra Chanda in Calcutta.

Detail of glass appliqué windows by Keith New for the Foyer of the Commonwealth Institute, 1960. Supplied by the artist

Glass appliqué panel by Endré Hevezi for the Scout Centre, South Kensington, 1963. Supplied by the artist

Painting 'Flight' by Amal Ghosh, 1989.
Supplied by the artist

Glass appliqué windows by Keith New for the
Foyer of the Commonwealth Institute, 1960.
Supplied by the artist

Margaret Traherne was invited by Basil Spence to make the glass for the Chapel of Unity at Coventry Cathedral. Traherne trained in painting, embroidery and dress design before studying with Lawrence Lee at the Royal College. She continued to work out her ideas in different media, creating machine-embroidered pictures some of which were included in the Leicestershire Education Authority's 'Pictures for Schools' scheme. In 1953 she spent a year studying glass with Tom Fairs and John Baker at the Central School of Art and began to build windows. Her stained glass memorial window for St Peter's Church, Wootton Wawen reveals an original and sensitive approach to colour and design. Traherne encountered concrete glass on a study tour of France in the 1950s, returning to make her own experimental panels which were seen and admired by Basil Spence. After the success of Coventry, Traherne received several commisions. Examples of her architectural glass can be seen in Manchester and Liverpool Cathedrals.

Stained glass window by Margaret Traherne for Wootton Wawen church, Warwickshire, 1959.
Supplied by Caroline Swash

Critical approval of the concrete glass in the Chapel of Unity encouraged architects to commission dalle de verre and other kinds of slab glass for new public buildings where security was important and brilliant colour desirable. Whitefriars Studio in Wealdstone, Hertfordshire was one of the most adventurous commercial firms involved in glass at this time. Alfred Fisher started as a trainee with the company, rising rapidly to become one of their chief designers. He developed fused glass from an experimental stage to a practical architectural application so that new colours could be used within a concrete or other support system. Later Fisher established his own Chapel Studio in Hertfordshire where he built up a fine conservation workshop while continuing to design and make stained glass windows. Besides encouraging this research, Whitefriars invited Pierre Fourmaintraux from Metz to set up a department for fabrication of dalle de verre. The windows he made in 1961 for the Church of Latter Day Saints in London show how well this technique was suited to contemporary architecture. Outside, the organic appearance of the concrete panels complement the gold spire marking this plain functional building as a church. Inside, brilliant colour enlivens the stairwell. Another fine example of concrete glass was designed and made by Tom Fairs for the entrance hall of the Holborn College of Law, Language and Commerce in Red Lion Square, London. Fairs had assisted Geoffrey Clarke on the Coventry project at the RCA and went on to teach stained glass at the Central School of Art.

Detail of stained glass window by Margaret Traherne for Wootton Wawen church, Warwickshire, 1959. Supplied by Caroline Swash

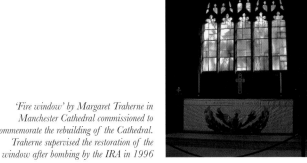

'Fire window' by Margaret Traherne in Manchester Cathedral commissioned to commemorate the rebuilding of the Cathedral. Traherne supervised the restoration of the window after bombing by the IRA in 1996

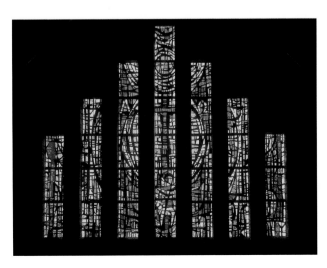

Above

Dalle de verre window by Pierre Fourmaintraux for the Church of Latter Day Saints, Kensington, London, 1961. Supplied by Caroline Swash

Far Left:

Window by Alfred Fisher for Whittington College Chapel, Felbridge, Sussex, 1988. Supplied by Alfred Fisher

Left:

Window in glass and concrete by Alfred Fisher for St.Cuthbert's Hospital, Hurworth Place, Darlington, 1972. Supplied by Alfred Fisher

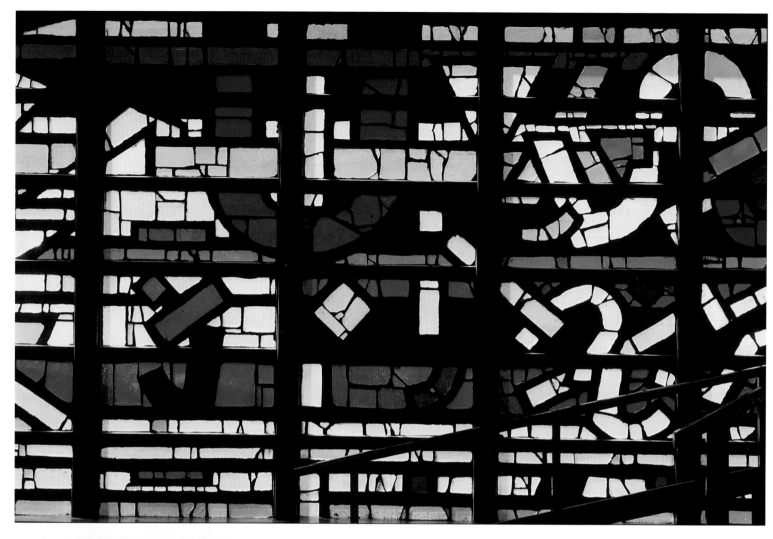

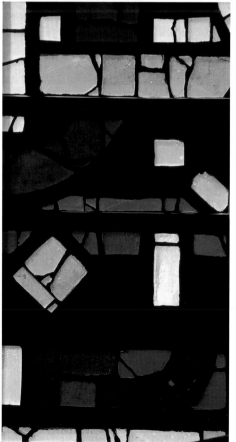

Above:

Dalle de verre window by Tom Fairs at the Holborn College of Law, Language and Commerce, Red Lion Square, Holborn. Supplied by Caroline Swash

Left:

Detail of the dalle de verre window by Tom Fairs at the Holborn College of Law, Language and Commerce, Red Lion Square, Holborn. Supplied by Caroline Swash

Anthony Hollaway (1928-2000) collaborated with Keith New on the Coventry windows. After graduating from the Royal College he joined the architect's division of the Greater London Council to create glass and ceramic murals for schools and hospitals. In 1971 he began work on the five windows for Manchester Cathedral that would occupy him for the next twenty years. For the west window, Hollaway took the Magnificat (the Song of Mary) and rearranged the words to make a rich pattern of colour and shape at the base of the composition.

Exterior view of the dalle de verre window by Tom Fairs at the Holborn College of Law, Language and Commerce, Red Lion Square, Holborn. Supplied by Caroline Swash

Top-Right:
Detail of the 'St Mary' window by Anthony Hollaway in Manchester Cathedral, 1982. Supplied by Caroline Swash

Stained glass window by Anthony Holloway in St Mary's Church, Mablethorpe. Lincolnshire. Supplied by Caroline Swash

The capacity to design glass for many different contexts is shared by Ray Bradley (b.1938). After graduating from the Royal College in 1962, Bradley set up his own studio in west London and made superb architectural glass for the new hotels and restaurants of the growing hospitality industry. Glass dividers made for the reception area of the Post House Hotel in Hampstead feature a swirling design suggested by the circuits of the Vanwall Racing Car Works which had previously occupied the Hotel site. Bradley was one of the first artists to successfully use the appliqué technique in a commercial interior.

Another innovation was the use of etched and sandblasted glass in ecclesiastical settings where security was a concern. From the 1980s onwards, Bradley designed several screens and windows to enhance areas of public and private access. These included the fine Baptistery glass for Bar Hill Shared Church, Cambridge; windows for the entrance of the Hartley Library, Southampton University and new doors for the Upper Perrin Gallery at Leighton House Museum and Art Gallery, London.

Ray Bradley in his west London studio selecting glass for the Orpington church commission. Supplied by the artist

Foyer glass by Ray Bradley for the Post House Hotel, Hampstead, 1965. Supplied by the artist

Sandblasted screen and stained glass window by Ray Bradley for Bar Hill Shared Church, Cambridge, 1972-74. Supplied by the artist

'DNA…and'. Window for the entrance foyer of the Hartley Library, Southampton University by Ray Bradley, 1989. Supplied by the artist

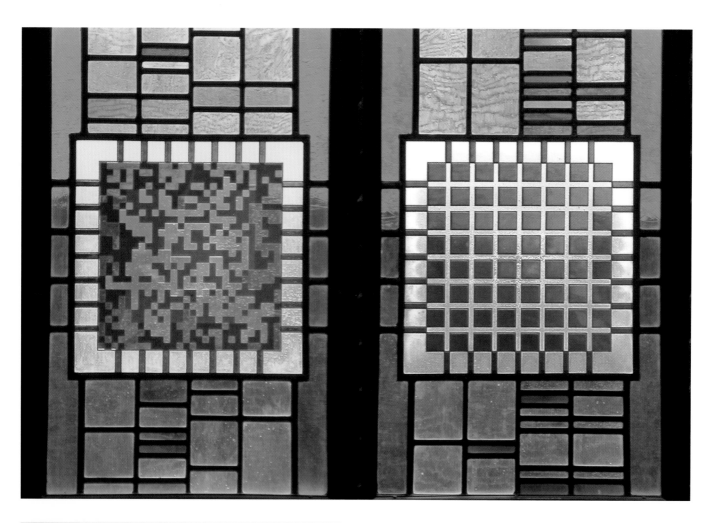

Detail of 'DNA...and' by Ray Bradley featuring a Nucleotide Sequence of the DNA code of a growth hormone from the University's Biology Department research programme, 1989. Supplied by the artist

Double doors to the Upper Perrin Gallery, Leighton House Museum and Art Gallery, London by Ray Bradley, 1994. Supplied by the artist

Detail of the Leighton House doors by
Ray Bradley showing the layers of screen
printed glass, 1994. Supplied by the artist

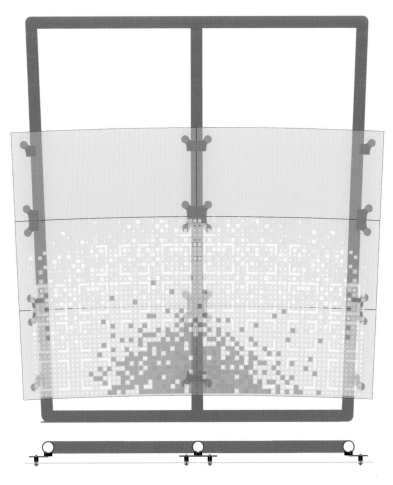

Suspended glass canopy over the entrance of an 'RIBA
Selected' residential property in Kent. Joint proposal by
Ray Bradley and the Italian artist Denise Basso, 2005.
Supplied by the artist

The Engravers Art

In designing the Cathedral, Basil Spence had wanted to connect the new building to the remains of its ruined predecessor. He decided to solve this problem with a monumental wall of transparent glass engraved with angels and prophets. Such was the publicity surrounding the Cathedral that this ingenious solution established a precedent for architects and designers all over the world to follow. The artist who made the engraved window was John Hutton (1906-1978). Born in New Zealand, he spent his early years studying law in order to make a living. However, his enthusiasm for drawing and painting led to his first commission, a mural painting of figures representing the Zodiac for a cinema in Christchurch.

In 1934 he sailed to London with his artist wife Nell Blair and there he painted murals for ships of the Orient Line. During the war Hutton worked as a camouflage officer in the Middle East, helping to disguise the presence of airfields. Returning to Europe in 1943, he was placed in charge of the 21st Army Group Camouflage Pool in France where he met Basil Spence. Upon returning to London, he painted a number of murals for projects designed by Spence, such as the 1946 'Britain Can Make it' Exhibition held at the Victoria and Albert Museum and the 'Sea and Ships Pavilion' for the 1951 Festival of Britain. Hutton's first glass commission grew from the 'Enterprise Scotland Exhibition' at the Royal Scottish Museum, Edinburgh for which Spence required figures of Scottish entrepreneurs to decorate a glass screen at the entrance. Hutton used the firm of London Sand Blast Ltd, to execute subsequent designs including the 'Angel' lunettes for Guildford Cathedral and the Commonwealth Air Forces memorial at Runnymede.

Opposite:
Engraved Glass Wall by John
Hutton for Coventry Cathedral.
Supplied by Caroline Swash

Hutton was disappointed when he saw how little impact the completed windows at Runnymede made in natural light and realized that he needed to control the engraved line himself. Once the designs for the glass screen at Coventry Cathedral were approved, Hutton turned to the glass department at the Royal College of Art for help with their execution. One of the College's technicians suggested that Hutton experiment with a grindstone fixed to the handpiece of a flexible drive ie an old fashioned dentists drill. This method was successful, allowing Hutton to create his own 'line' on the glass. However, the creation of different tones and textures required further research before work on the glass wall of angels, prophets, saints and martyrs could commence.

Preparation also took the form of exploring the 'personality' of each figure to be represented, followed by careful drawings from life with Marigold Dodson (later Hutton's second wife) as model. Full size drawings in white chalk on black paper preceded work on the glass itself. A silhouette of each figure was prepared by London Sand Blast and then engraved directly by Hutton in the studio. The final touches were added on site. When the wall of angels, saint and prophets was in position, Spence became concerned that the figures were too white, too opaque. Hutton climbed onto the scaffold and reduced the tone, rubbing the glass with emery paper to return transparency to the surface.

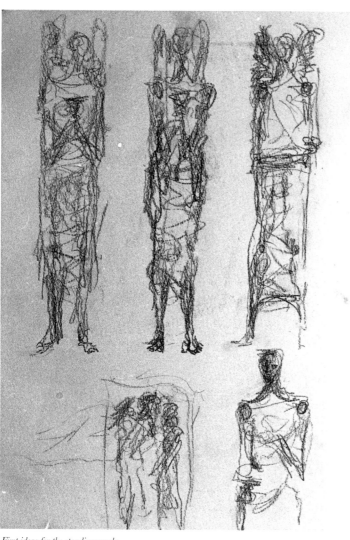

*First ideas for the standing angels –
page from a sketch book, 1955.
Supplied by Caroline Swash*

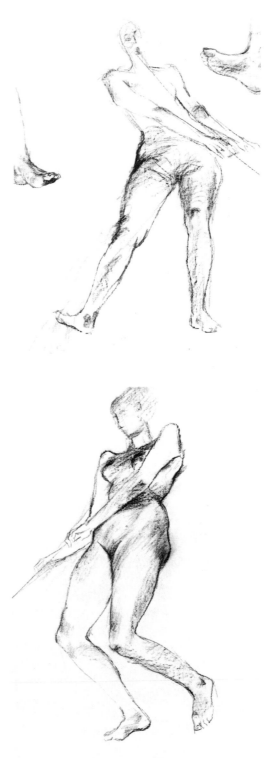

*Life drawing for flying angels, 1955.
Supplied by Caroline Swash*

'King Lear' by John Hutton. Detail of engraved glass for the Shakespeare Centre, Stratford upon Avon, 1963. Supplied by Caroline Swash

The Coventry window brought Hutton fame and more commissions. In 1957 he made the fine Dunkirk War Memorial. He engraved glass screens for Mercury House, London, Plymouth Civic Centre (1957 and 1962), panels for New Zealand House (1963) and windows for the Shakespeare Centre at Stratford on Avon (1964). Besides glass engraving, Hutton taught at Goldsmiths College and continued to paint and draw. His art revolved around the human figure which he described as 'the most absorbing and limitless subject in all art. Its association with history and mythology and its infinite ways of being represented make it an everlasting source of inspiration'

'Ophelia' oil painting by John Hutton, 1963. Supplied by Caroline Swash

The Engraving Revival

John Hutton's achievements inspired others. David Peace (1915-2003) trained as an architect but shifted his attention to glass engraving through his interest in text. Sally Scott collaborated with Peace in the creation of several schemes including the decoration of glass walls for a chapel within the church of St Botolph, Aldgate, London Peace designed the inscriptions for the entrance and Scott made an evocative glass wall whose imagery included an Ark, Burning Bush and Dove. Here the glass has been sandblasted, etched and engraved in a way that gives privacy yet keeps the interior light. Letter forms fascinated Peace and he embellished many different kinds of glass vessels with carefully chosen texts and poems. Scott's background as a painter influenced her treatment of the decoration of glass. The spun glass roundels 'Images of Rajasthan' and 'Icarus' show the range of effects obtainable through a combination of sandblast, engraving and rubbed colour. Her work in an architectural setting includes screens for the Royal Albert Hall, the Victoria and Albert Museum and numerous Hotels as well as memorial windows for churches where the light transmitting qualities of sandblasted and engraved glass are much appreciated. In 1999 she worked with the renowned engraver Laurence Whistler in the creation of a Millenium window for the Church of the Ascension, Burghclere.

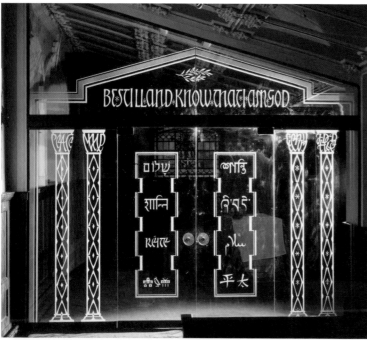

Doors designed by David Peace for the chapel of St Botolph's Church, Aldgate, London. 'Peace' has been inscribed in eleven languages on the pilasters and doors. Supplied by the artist

Reredos screen for St Botolph's Church, Aldgate by Sally Scott fitted into an existing wooden screen, 1988. Supplied by the artist

Engraved glass 'Obelisk with Six Latin Mottoes' by David Peace. Supplied by the artist

Sally Scott at work in her studio. Supplied by the artist

'Images of Rajasthan' by Sally Scott, 1997. The spun crystal disc is by Neil Wilkin. Supplied by the artist

Detail of 'Images of Rajasthan' by Sally Scott. Supplied by the artist

Memorial window by 'Peace and Scott' in St Mary's Church, Newick, Sussex. Supplied by the artist

Memorial window for Burghclere Church designed by Laurence Whistler and sandblasted and engraved by Sally Scott, 2004. Supplied by the artist

The Galaxy Window (One of Twelve), St Nicholas Church,
Moreton, Dorset. Designed/Engraved by Laurence Whistler,
1984. Photograph by Graham Herbert

Laurence Whistler (1912-2000) engraved many remarkable windows himself. His most impressive creation in this field is undoubtedly the series of windows made over a thirty year period for the church of St Nicholas, Moreton, in Dorset. The spectacular west window depicts a spiral galaxy with other invented galaxies in the distance. Whistler is known all over the world for his engraved bowls. His work involves the precise and delicate use of a diamond point drill with which he works (sometimes on both sides of a vessel) building up carefully chosen details to create an illusion of perspective in a mesmerizing miniature world.

Diamond point engraving on glass vessels has been practised in England since the 16th century and enjoyed a revival from the 1930s onwards. Such was the renewed enthusiasm for the technique and for glass engraving generally during the postwar years that 'The Guild of Glass Engravers' was formed in 1975 with Laurence Whistler as its first president and John Hutton its Vice-President. The art of engraving on vessels and the use of engraving and sandblasting for buildings continues to interest architects and designers wherever light and art are required.

Bowl illustrating a story in Come Hither by Walter de la Mare. Engraved by Laurence Whistler, 1973. Owner: On loan to the Birmingham Museum and Art Gallery. Photograph by Graham Herbert.

'The Grass Cathedral' Grasses turning into architecture. Goblet engraved by Laurence Whistler, 1972. Owner: St Hugh's College, Oxford. Photograph by Graham Herbert.

XI

Pioneers of Studio Glass:
The Great Leap Forward

Suomi-Finland Series, 1970, by Marvin Lipofsky,
blown at the Nuutajarui Factory, Finland
with help from Jaakko Niemi.
In private collection. Photography by M. Lee Fatherree

Pioneers of Studio Glass:
The Great Leap Forward

With a number of practitioners in various locations internationally, artistic evolution in stained glass proceeded at a more or less steady pace. For artists in hot glass, however, the rate of progress was much more uneven and the early 1960s marked a dramatic turning point. Prior to this time artists in vessel glass like Gallé and Tiffany had worked within a factory setting. Although they might control the entire process of creation, they depended on the skill of the craftsmen to execute their designs. Despite the experiments of a few pioneers such as Maurice Marinot in France, hot glass was thought to require too many separate steps and too much expensive equipment to be practical for the individual artist working on his own. Sidney Waugh, the head designer at Steuben, summed up this position in his 1947 book *The Making of Fine Glass*:

'It must be emphasized that glass blowing, as described on these pages, is not within the scope of the amateur or even the most talented artist or craftsman working alone. In the making of fine glass a multiplicity of tools and equipment is required. Furthermore, even such comparatively simple pieces as are here illustrated could not be produced without a number of artisans working together as a team.'

Isolated attempts at glass blowing had been made by individuals, most notably by Jean Sala in Paris, but around 1952 he closed his workshop, leaving no direct disciples of the craft. For ten years there were no recorded glass-blowers working on their own. Seeking to remedy this situation, the American ceramic artist Harvey K. Littleton set out to make hot glass a creative medium for the individual artist. His efforts succeeded beyond his wildest dreams, resulting in what is now known as the international Studio Glass Movement.

Harvey Littleton

It is striking how many disparate strands of 20th century glass history are woven into the life of Harvey Littleton (b. 1926). The son of a physicist employed as Director of Research at the Corning Glass Works, Littleton grew up surrounded with glass. After studying at the University of Michigan he began his career as a potter and, from 1949 until 1951, worked as a ceramics instructor at the School of Design of the Toledo Museum of Art in Toledo, Ohio. He received a Master of Fine Arts degree from the Cranbrook Academy of Art in Bloomfield Hills, Michigan, in 1951 and was appointed to the faculty of the University of Wisconsin the same year. The Louis Comfort Tiffany Foundation provided research funding to expand his role as an artist and educator.

Although he was an accomplished ceramic artist by his early 30s, Littleton always knew that his first love was glass and he refused to accept that the medium was too difficult for the individual practitioner. In 1957 he visited glass factories and technical schools in Europe to learn what he could about glass techniques and technology. In Paris he called on Jean Sala and received valuable advice, although by this time Sala no longer blew glass himself. In a literal gesture of passing the torch of glass blowing, Sala gave his personal blowing pipe to the younger man.

After Littleton returned to America he continued his research. From his days as a ceramics instructor, he knew Otto Wittmann, the director of the Toledo Museum, who invited him to lead a seminar on glassblowing in a garden shed on the museum grounds. Held from March 23 to April 1, 1962, the workshop enrolled seven students, ranging from a new potter to a university art professor. Other curious participants included Dominick Labino, vice-president and director of research at the Johns-Manville Fiber Glass Corporation in Toledo, and Harvey Leafgreen, a retired blower from the Libbey Division of Owens-Illinois in Toledo, who had read about the event in the local paper.

The group's initial efforts were not promising. Attempts to melt the material were unsuccessful until Labino contributed glass marbles used for making fiberglass, which were easy to handle and had a low melting temperature. No one in the group, including Littleton, had any idea of how to blow glass until Leafgreen was persuaded to demonstrate blowing techniques. The resulting objects were clumsy in the extreme and quickly dubbed 'garage art', but the immediacy of the process and its potent but unexplored possibilities aroused the passionate interest of a new generation of artists.

Additional seminars followed and in the next decade a growing number of glass artists struggled to master the most basic skills through a process of trial and error. In his own work Littleton stressed creative expression rather than sophisticated, exacting techniques. His early vessels, 'Prunted, Imploded and Exploded Forms', challenged the symmetry and unblemished perfection of traditional blown glass. Inflated and collapsed, lopsided, dissolving, his vessels were the solidified forms of 'a man breathing his desire into the molten glass,' according to Littleton.

'Four Seasons', 1977, by Harvey Littleton. Washington DC, Smithsonian American Museum, Washington DC. Copyright 2005

Opposite:

Harvey Littleton and Erwin Eisch, originally photographed by Herbert Wolf in April of 1974. Image is courtesy of the Harvey K. Littleton papers, 1946-1975 in the Archives of American Art, Smithsonian Institution

By the end of the 1960s Littleton abandoned the vessel concept altogether to blow glass into shapes that were purely sculptural. Some of these he cut and polished into simple geometric shapes, often combining them in ways that explored the interpenetration of colour, transparency and light. In 'Four Seasons' of 1977, the glass has been blown, cut and polished into multiple half-spheres. Nested together, these are perceived as concentric rings of shifting colour. Using the same minimalist approach he created tubes or columns of layered colours encased in clear glass. While still warm these were allowed to slump, creating dramatic shapes. Some were sliced at various points to focus attention to the flow of space around the work and between the parts. In 'Red-Blue Sliced Descending Form' of 1984, the hot glass sculpture is internally decorated with orange, fuchsia and purple stripes and cut into two sections.

The integration of the space around and between separate pieces was developed further in his segmental 'Crown' series, such as 'Opalescent Red Crown'. These multipartite works were intended to enlist the imagination of the owner to arrange as desired. With the larger pieces turned outward into a crownlike form and the smaller pieces placed between, the grouping commands the space around and within it. In the 1970s Littleton began experimenting with glass intaglio printing, called vitreography. He stopped blowing hot glass in 1990, but continues his work in printmaking.

'Rose Opal Combination C Form',
1983, by Harvey Littleton.
© Christie's Images Limited

'Red-Blue Sliced Descending Form',
1984, by Harvey Littleton. © 2005.
Photo: Smithsonian American Art
Museum/Art Resource/Scala, Florence

Opposite Page:
'Opalescent Red Crown', 1983, by Harvey
Littleton. Washington DC, Smithsonian American
Museum, Washington DC. Copyright 2005

Dominick Labino

The involvement of Dominick Labino (1910-1987) was critical to the success of the Toledo experiment. In addition to technical assistance he provided essential equipment, materials and funding. Labino had spent his professional career developing glass fibre for the American space program and had invented a type of glass marble (known as the #475 fibreglass marble) that was easy to handle and to melt. For subsequent trials he designed and constructed a tank furnace that melted glass more efficiently in small batches. With his interest piqued by the artistic potential of blown glass, Labino took early retirement to begin a new career as a glass artist and built a studio with extensive research facilities on a farm outside Toledo. He was particularly concerned with finding the optimal balance between art and technology, between glass as personal expression and glass as a skilfully-handled material. He was also fascinated by the formulation of unusual colours in glass. Works from his 'Emergence' series are made of hot-tooled glass with entrapped air bubbles and veils of dichroic glass that change in colour with the light.

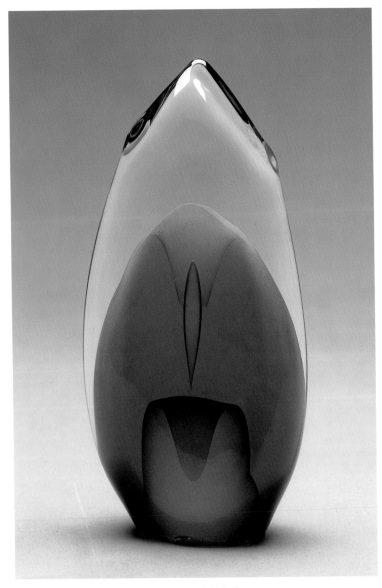

Sculpture from the 'Emergence' series, 1984, by Dominick Labino.
© 2005 Photo: Smithsonian American Art Museum / Art Resource / Scala, Florence

Erwin Eisch

Hot glass enthusiasts quickly found each other across the Atlantic. During Littleton's travels in Europe he encountered the work of Erwin Eisch (b.1927) in a showroom in Frauenau, Germany. He was astounded by its originality and immediately sought out the artist. In an interview conducted by the Archives of American Art in 2001, Littleton remarked, 'Erwin Eisch was absolutely unique. And he wanted to be an artist. He had no limitations . . . I saw his work and I realized that he was doing what I wanted to do – play with the glass, to make forms that had no other reason for being than that he wanted to make them.' The two became friends for life.

Eisch was born into a family that had worked in glass for nearly 300 years. In 1949 he completed a seven-year program at the school for glassmaking in Zweisel, but was dissatisfied with the abstract, impersonal Bauhaus aesthetic of the period. For Eisch, imagery that is muddled, incomplete and suggestive has far greater vitality. He actively subverts the special characteristics of glass. Instead of celebrating its vibrant colour and light-conducting optical potential, he coats it with gold and silver paints or coloured flock, scribbling the thick surface with symbols, metaphors or philosophical texts until the material is solidly opaque and no longer recognisable as glass.

Eisch's work is always figurative and he often creates multiple variations on the same image. His most well known series are of idiosyncratic 'portrait' heads of himself or of friends such as Littleton. Others are of Thomas Buechner, the writer and former director of the Corning Museum, as well as the Buddha, his father and Picasso, the giant of 20th-century art. These are blown into clay moulds that are broken off while the glass is still soft; the glass is then manipulated, annealed, painted and engraved.

Eisch also makes sculptures of everyday objects, such as telephones, shoes or books. His images appear melted or deformed in the manner of German Expressionist painting or the 'soft sculptures' of Claes Oldenburg. Beauty and functionality are of no interest to Eisch. Instead, according to the artist, 'It is my endeavour to guide glass from the so-called circle of good form, and to release it again and to consider it as an element with might harbour a whole world of poetical possibilities.' According to Littleton, Eisch treats glass with the 'contempt and freedom' of a fellow artist.

The first generation of American studio glass artists had their greatest impact as teachers. Following the success of the Toledo seminars, creative glass-blowing was gradually introduced into the curricula of art schools and art departments of colleges and universities in the United States during the 1960s. The first academic course was taught in 1963 by Harvey Littleton at the University of Wisconsin at Madison, where he was on the faculty. Erwin Eisch made many visits to Madison as a guest instructor. Many of Littleton's students went on to become teachers elsewhere, including Marvin Lipofsky at the University of California, Berkeley, Robert Fritz at San Jose State University and Tom McGlauchlin at the University of Iowa in Iowa City. In 1965 Norman Schulman, a staff member at the Toledo seminars, established a programme at the Rhode Island School of Design and was soon joined by Dale Chihuly, another Littleton student. Dominick Labino continued to offer workshops through the Toledo Museum of Art School of Design.

'Picasso Head, Nature', 1990, by Erwin Eisch.
Photo courtesy of Barry Friedman Ltd.,
New York. Photograph by Spencer Tsai

Marvin Lipofsky

One of Littleton's first students at Madison was Marvin Lipofsky (b.1938). After graduating from the University of Wisconsin with a Master of Fine Arts degree in sculpture, Lipofsky went on to establish the second college-level studio glass programme in the country at the University of California at Berkeley in 1964. Three years later he became the founder and head of the glass department at the California College of Arts and Crafts in Oakland. Because of his role as an inspired teacher, the San Francisco Bay area became a lively centre for studio glass enthusiasts.

Unlike artists who experiment with a number of different forms over the years, Lipofsky has spent his entire career exploring the distorted bubble with exquisite subtlety and refinement. Paradoxically, his work is both profoundly organic as well as abstract. His blown forms, either broken open or wholly enclosed, seem to resemble internal organs, engorged micro-organisms or globules of living matter. His 'California Loop' series makes extensive use of plating, fuming and rayon flocking to differentiate the surfaces of his whimsical, creature-like forms. At the same time Lipofsky's work is closely related to the Abstract Expressionist movement in painting of the 1960s, echoing in three dimensions the colourful stained canvases of Morris Lewis or the rippling contours of Helen Frankenthaler's colour fields.

Lipofsky is a tireless ambassador for the studio glass movement. In cooperation with the world's finest artists and craftsmen he blows glass at factories across the globe, shipping work back to Berkeley where he finishes it by cutting, grinding, plating, acid etching, sandblasting, flocking and other cold techniques. His 'Suomi Series,' of transparent, lightly tinted forms was mould-blown at the Nuutajärvi, the oldest glass factory in Finland. The 'Soviet Series' of 1989 was blown at the Experimental Ceramic Sculpture Factory in L'vov, Ukraine, USSR, with glassmaster Ivan Karolevich Shumanski and his team. The colourful, billowing shapes were first blown into moulds, then cut and acid polished. Their organic, visceral effect is heightened by the contrast between the matte surface of the exterior 'skin' and the fire-polished interior, which appears 'wet.' The 'Four Seasons (I Quattro Stagioni) – Summer, Autumn, Winter, Spring' was blown at the Fratelli Toso Glass Factory in 1976 with help from Gianni Toso and finished in the artist's studio in 1998. One of the four pieces has been covered with gold leaf, another blown from narrow canes of different colours.

Marvin Lipofsky holding a glass violin.
www.goodwin.ee/erikik/est/mt/mt1-4.html

California Loop Series #30, 1970, by
Marvin Lipofsky. Collection of the artist.
Photograph by M. Lee Fatherree

'Soviet Series,' 1989, by Marvin Lipofsky, blown at the Experimental Ceramic Sculpture Factory L'vov, Ukraine, USSR, with glassmaster Ivan Karolevich Shumanski and team. Collection of the artist. Photograph by M. Lee Fatherree

The 'Four Seasons (I Quattro Stagioni) – Summer, Autumn, Winter, Spring', by Marvin Lipofsky, blown at the Fratelli Toso Glass Factory, 1976, finished in the artist's studio, 1998. Collection of the artist. Photograph by M. Lee Fatherree

Sam Herman

amuel J. Herman (b.1936) was another of Harvey Littleton's students who spread the word about the revolution in glass. After receiving a Master's degree from the University of Wisconsin, Herman was awarded a Fulbright scholarship to attend the Edinburgh School of Art, followed by a Research Fellowship at the Royal College of Art in London. There he constructed a small furnace and, in 1967, taught the school's first course in glassmaking. Although he occasionally used drawings or watercolours to develop his ideas, Herman preferred the direct experience of creating with the blow pipe. Herman's approach to glass was a revelation to his British students. In the brash and irreverent spirit of the 60s, Herman encouraged them to abandon any preconceived ideas about the final appearance of the object.

'Once the initial choice of glass is made, instinct and experience lead onward. As the form alters, it is necessary to be alert to this so that the piece may be developed through the plastic changes that occur during creation. In effect it is to be hoped that the glass itself will initiate its own final form.'

Herman remained at the RCA as tutor in charge of the glass department until 1974 and trained most of the glass artists working in Britain today. After graduation, many of his students faced the challenge of buying their own equipment, a costly proposition for young artists working on their own. In 1969 Herman established the Glasshouse in Islington where students could rent space and facilities at nominal cost. The Glasshouse lasted until 1999, providing support and community for independent glassworkers. From 1974 until 1980, he moved to Australia to teach and founded the studio glass movement there. In Adelaide he established the Glass Workshop in an old jam factory (later re-named the Jam Factory Workshops, Inc.) for the South Australian Craft Authority.

Herman's own work is noteworthy for capturing the moving, liquid appearance of glass in its molten state. Examples include vessels of cased glass embedded with multi-coloured whorls and streaks. Herman's attitude toward form and function is irreverently capricious. This is apparent in his glass and metal lamp of 1971. Constructed of shaped glass blocks held aloft by attenuated chromed wires, the spindly table lamp looks as delicate as a spider.

Vase, 1977, by Sam Herman.
© *Christie's Images Limited*

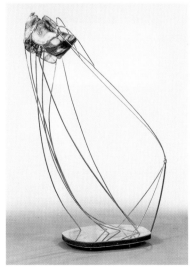

XII
The 'Rock-Star' of Glass

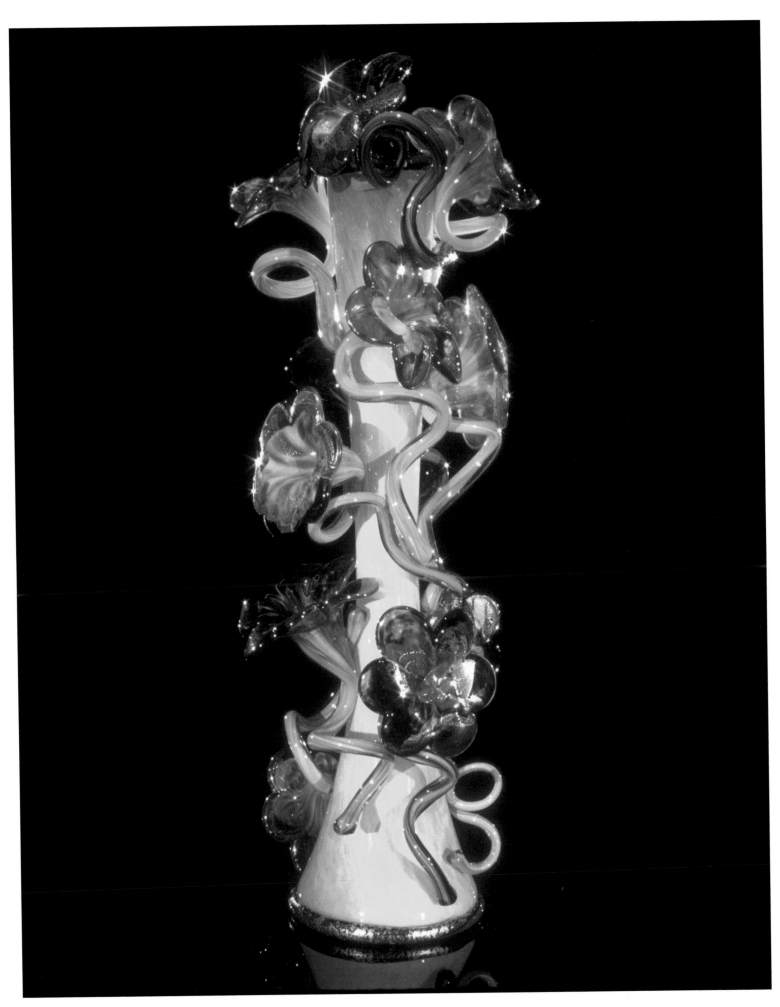

The 'Rock-Star' of Glass

*Dale Chihuly with Niijima Floats, 1991, Honolulu,
Hawaii. Permission granted by the Chihuly Studio.
© Dale Chihuly. Photograph by Russell Johnson*

Harvey Littleton's most famous student is undoubtedly Dale Chihuly (b.1941). Chihuly has expanded the art of glass blowing to a level of extravagant opulence never previously imagined. Unlike Erwin Eisch and others who defy the seductive physical properties of glass by hiding its surface or otherwise subverting its nature, Chihuly revels unashamedly in the 'glassiness of glass'. Sumptuous in the extreme, his exhibitions and installations are theatrical events in which the material's liquid transparency, ravishing colour and inexhaustible variety of form are brilliantly, and fully, exploited. Dubbed the 'Rock Star of Glass', he has become the most famous glass artist the world has ever known. Because of his enthusiastic following and the enormous demand for his work, his production has evolved into something of an industry, one that is unique in the history of artistic glass.

Nothing about Chihuly's background suggests the artistic phenomenon he would become. He was born in Tacoma, Washington, south of Seattle, where his father was a coal miner, a butcher, and later a union organizer. After studying interior design at the University of Washington, he moved to Madison to learn glass-blowing from Harvey Littleton at the University of Wisconsin. The time was the 1960s, a period that celebrated liberation from constraints of all kinds. With his characteristic bold exuberance, Chihuly saw in glass a chance to explore a form of expression that was unhindered by previous assumptions. After graduating with a Master's degree in sculpture he continued his studies at the Rhode Island School of Design in Providence, Rhode Island (RISD). He visited Murano in 1968 in order to learn the demanding, time-honoured techniques of Italian glass-blowing first hand and was welcomed at the Venini factory. When he returned to Providence a year later, he established the glass department at RISD, where he taught for next 15 years.

Chihuly thrives on the vigorously improvisational, collaborative process of blowing glass with a team of 8 to 10 glassworkers. He has surrounded himself with a group of talented craftspeople, all of whom contribute to the creation of the final result. Since 1970 this group effort has been essential. Due to an automobile accident he lost the sight of one eye and can no longer blow glass himself. Instead he scribbles vigorously with coloured pencils and crayons to give his team the concept he is striving for. While his finished creations may seem 'over the top' to some, they are always firmly grounded in his respect for historical traditions in glass.

He began by blowing a series of small cylinders in the mid-1970s. Familiar with textiles from his training in interior design, he decorated these with patterns derived from traditional woven Navajo Blankets. Chihuly usually executes his ideas in a series. These are roughly sequential, although years later he has revisited earlier forms with a fresh eye. This is the case with the 'Navajo Blanket' series, to which he returned in the 1990s to produce additional examples with more complex designs.

In the late 1970s he came upon a group of Native American baskets in the storage area of the Washington State Historical Society. These were nested inside each other, their sides slumped downwards with the passage of time and the force of gravity. Recognising immediately that these forms could be reproduced in blown glass, he created the 'Basket' series. These were blown in muted earth tones of terracotta, maize yellow and sky blue, and often feature the rhythmic pattern of fibres woven into the glass.

'Crimson Lake Venetian', 1989, by Dale Chihuly
with the original pastel on paper design.
© Christie's Images Limited

Chihuly working on a Blanket Cylinder, 1975. Permission granted by the Chihuly Studio. © Dale Chihuly

Early Navajo Blanket Cylinders, 1975. Permission granted by the Chihuly Studio. © Dale Chihuly.

Early Cylinder with Horse Drawing, 1976.
Permission granted by the Chihuly Studio.
© Dale Chihuly. Photograph by Ira Garber

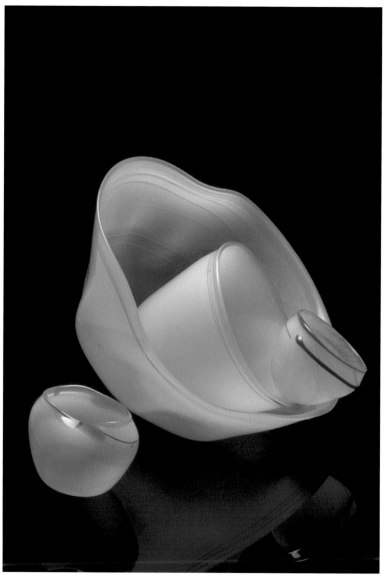

Pink Basket Set with Blue Lip Wraps, 1978.
Permission granted by the Chihuly Studio.
© Dale Chihuly. Photograph by Scott M. Leen

Opposite Page:
Tabac Basket with Oxblood Spots, 1977.
Permission granted by the Chihuly Studio.
© Dale Chihuly. Photograph by Terry Rishel

While experimenting with blowing glass into ribbed moulds to increase the strength and durability of his 'Baskets', Chihuly noted that the resulting shapes resembled sea shells or spiny aquatic creatures washed up by the tides or floating in the ocean. The resulting series is called 'Sea Forms', some of which resemble giant clams, round spiky sea urchins, waving jellyfish or giant sea anemones. Various forms nestle together, barely touching, as if deposited by the waves and buoyed up by the watery milieu. Some are ribbed with contrasting colours in straight or spiralling lines, while in others brightly hued glass threads trail across ridged contours. Instead of the applied motifs of the 'Navajo Baskets', form and decoration merge into an integrated whole. 'I love to walk along the beach and go to the ocean,' says Chihuly, 'and glass itself, of course, is so much like water. If you let it go on its own, it almost ends up looking like something that came from the sea.'

From nominally representative imagery, Chihuly moved in the direction of greater abstraction. In 1981 he began the 'Macchia' series (named after the Italian word meaning both 'spotted' and 'patina') as an exercise in the infinite permutations of intense colour combinations. 'I was always looking at all these 300 different colour rods that make up our palette', wrote Chihuly in 1992. 'I think it was in 1981 that I woke up one morning and said, 'I'm going to use all 300 colours in as many possible variations and combinations as I can.' I began making a series of pieces with one colour inside and another colour outside, and I discovered a way to put opaque white 'clouds' between the two layers to clarify the colours, to keep the colours separate.' When brightly lit, these distended, vaguely vessel-like forms look like large drops or dollops of luminous molten liquid captured in the process of transformation.

Opposite:
Pale Orange Sea Form Set, 1980.
Permission granted by the Chihuly Studio.
© Dale Chihuly. Photograph by Scott M. Leen

Above-Left:
Translucent Seaform Set with Brown Stripes,
1982. Permission granted by the Chihuly Studio.
© Dale Chihuly. Photograph by Scott M. Leen

Above-Right:
Light Blue Seaform with Yellow Lip Wrap,
1995. Permission granted by the Chihuly Studio.
© Dale Chihuly. Photograph by Claire Garoutte

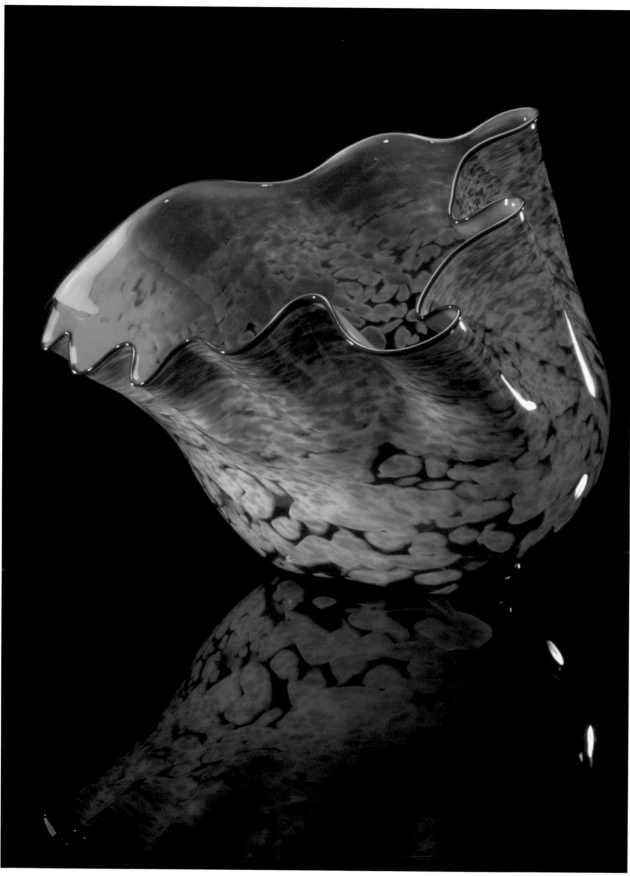

Tangerine Macchia with Imperial Blue Lip Wrap,
1985. Permission granted by the Chihuly Studio.
© Dale Chihuly. Photograph by Scott M. Leen

For the 'Soft Cylinders' series, begun in 1984, a great deal of preparation is required before the act of blowing can take place. A highly complex glass 'drawing' is prepared, made of hundreds of glass threads. This is laid onto on a hot surface and when the final gather of glass has been dipped from the furnace, the gaffer rolls the molten glass over the woven threads, fusing the design to the exterior. The resulting form, slumped and puckered, is covered with patterning, as if the whole surface had been energetically doodled with colour. Two years later Chihuly began the series called 'Persians' that invoke associations with the romantic and mysterious ancient Near East. Elements of these often composite works are derived from plates and vessels surviving from past civilisations that are brought to light in archaeological excavations.

In 1971 Chihuly started a summer course in glass blowing at an isolated wooded location near the Cascade Mountains outside Seattle. He and his 16 students constructed all their own equipment, including two furnaces. Under the artist's charismatic leadership this small, experimental programme has grown into the renowned Pilchuck Glass School, the largest centre for glass education in the world. Nearly every important glass artist from across the globe has spent time at Pilchuck, either as a teacher or artist in residence. In the mid-1980s Chihuly took up permanent residence at Pilchuck and his presence has attracted a large community of glass artists to the Seattle area – around 500 live there today where 30 years ago there were none.

Topaz and Oxblood Persian with Blue Lip Wrap, 1986. Permission granted by the Chihuly Studio. © Dale Chihuly. Photograph by Scott M. Leen

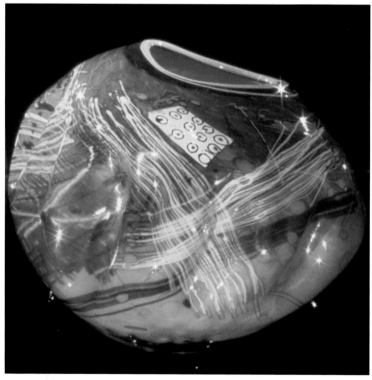

Cadmiuim Red Soft Cylinder with Green Lip Wrap, 1989. Permission granted by the Chihuly Studio. © Dale Chihuly. Photograph by Claire Garoutte

Oxblood Persian with Red Lip Wrap, 1986. Permission granted by the Chihuly Studio. © Dale Chihuly. Photograph by Scott M. Leen

The Venetian glass artist Lino Tagliapietra (b.1934), probably the most highly skilled technical glassblower in the world, has been a frequent visitor at Pilchuck over the years. At first, the restrained elegance of Tagliapietra's classical style seemed antithetical to Chihuly's expressive bravado, but in 1988 the two men decided to work together. Chihuly designed a series of inflated, almost cartoon-like imitations of Venetian glass in the Art Deco manner, challenging Tagliapietra to blow glass into increasingly complex and difficult forms. With their deliberate exaggeration, the resulting objects are a delightful parody of the playful style of the 1920s. Rather than variations on a theme, as is the case with other Chihuly series, each of his 'Venetians' has a separate and distinct personality. Tagliapietra's closest follower is the American Dante Marioni (b.1964), whose stylised vessels have an exaggerated, Post-Modern feel.

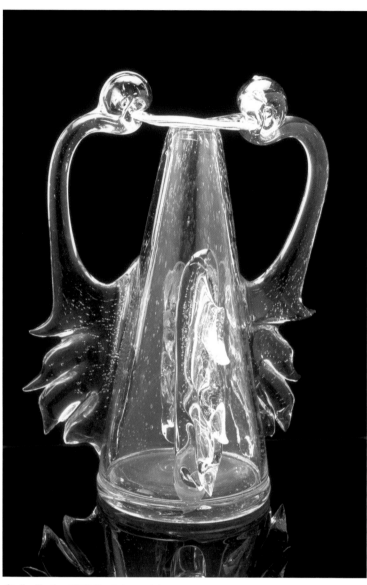

Opaline Venetion, 1988. Permission granted by the Chihuly Studio.
© Dale Chihuly. Photograph by Scott M. Leen

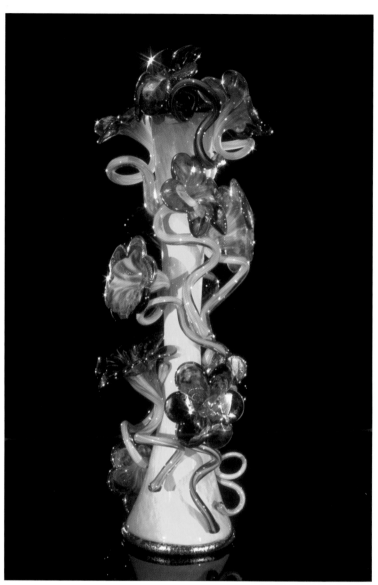

Cadmium Yellow Venetian with Flowers, 1990. Permission granted by the Chihuly Studio.
© Dale Chihuly. Photograph by Claire Garoutte

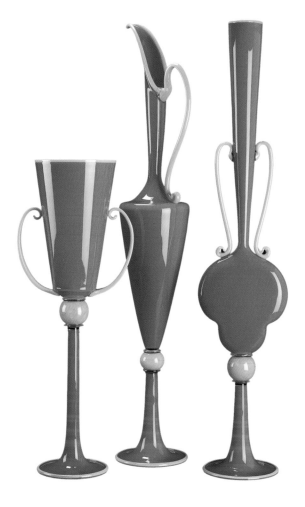

'Red Trio with Yellow', 2000, by Dante Marioni.
Supplied by the Dante Marioni Studio, with
permission of the artist

'Coloured Vessel Display', 2003, by Dante
Marioni. Supplied by the Dante Marioni Studio,
with permission of the artist

Works in Chihuly's 'Ikebana' series are likewise clearly differentiated one from another. Inspired by the Japanese art of flower arranging, the artist began making these in 1989. In Japan, flower arranging can be an intensely spiritual pursuit imbued with both aesthetic nuances and symbolic significance. In keeping with this philosophy, the placement of each attenuated stem and blossom is a well-thought out decision for Chihuly. Some 'Ikebana' combine elements of his 'Venetian' series – in one work a pair of golden putti clamber over a yellow glass flower that has been carefully placed in an aubergine-coloured vase. The putti were created by the famous Venetian glass artist Pino Signoretto, whose specialty is making hot-formed glass sculpture.

Since the early 1990s, Chihuly has become increasingly interested in creating monumental public installations of his work, which he describes as his favourite form of art because so many people can enjoy them. His museum exhibitions often include room installations that feature a clear glass ceiling abundantly heaped with layers of glass elements that reflect patterns of coloured light on the walls below. The first of his celebrated 'Chandeliers' was made in 1992 for Seattle Art Museum. Today, these have become signature pieces in the grand entry halls of museums and other public buildings all over the world. They are assembled from multiple free-blown parts, usually in a single colour range, hung on a central core of metal rods. Some look like an explosion of fireworks overhead, while others resemble pendent clusters of succulent berries.

The culmination of his 'Chandelier' series was 'Chihuly over Venice' of 1996. As a tribute to the city's rich glassblowing tradition, he created fourteen 'Chandeliers' at glass factories across the globe – in Mexico, Ireland, Finland, the United States, and Venice – and installed them in various locations during the Venezia Aperto Vetro. Visitors wandered throughout the city, surprised and delighted by bursts of colour and light in unexpected locations. In 1999 he devised installations of glass spears and ice sculptures inside the stone walls of the ancient Citadel in the Old City of Jerusalem.

Emerald Green Ikebana with Stem, Three leaves and Putti, 1991. Permission granted by the Chihuly Studio. © Dale Chihuly. Photograph by Scott M. Leen

Plum Ikebana with Single Stem, 1991. Permission granted by the Chihuly Studio. © Dale Chihuly. Photograph by Claire Garoutte

Room Installation, 'Persian Ceiling', 2001, Victoria and Albert Museum. Permission granted by the Chihuly Studio. © Dale Chihuly. Photograph by Terry Rishel

Cobalt Blue Chandelier, 1995, Nuutajärvi, Finland. Permission granted by the Chihuly Studio. © Dale Chihuly. Photograph by Russell Johnson

Chihuly's site-specific installations inside the greenhouses of botanical gardens, such as his impressive displays at the Garfield Park Conservatory in Chicago in 2001 and at Kew Gardens in London in 2005, have been particularly effective. These are composed of multiple separate pieces that appear to sprout among the exotic plants, climb in their branches, or float in artificial pools. Included in these are his latest series, the 'Niijima Floats', begun in 1991 and named after the glass floats of Japanese fishing-nets. These giant glass orbs are his most challenging series to produce because of the large size of the unbroken bubbles or globes. 'I want my work to look like it just happened, as if it was made by nature,' says Chihuly. 'Glass is so spontaneous, so immediate, that it inspires almost anyone to work with it, the sense of accomplishment, and the danger, and the excitement. It's all one package.'

View of Palm House installation. Dark Gold Ikebana with Red Flower, 2001, Chicago. Permission granted by the Chihuly Studio. © Dale Chihuly. Photograph by Terry Rishel

Chihuly's Students

There is no such thing as the 'Chihuly style'. His work is so distinctive that no individual can follow in his footsteps. But Dale's enthusiasm for glass and his eagerness to share his passion has spawned a large pool of talented glass artists who, having worked with him either in Rhode Island or at Pilchuck, have gone on to become the most famous names in contemporary glass. The diversity of their styles is a tribute to the freedom and encouragement they have received from their mentor. Each of them has evolved their own identity in glass and made the medium their own.

Among the most widely known is Howard Ben Tré (b.1949). Ben Tré studied with Chihuly at RISD, graduating in 1980. He has pioneered and refined two ground-breaking processes in glass – large-scale glass casting and patinating glass with a layer of metal, using a technique similar to electro-plating. Studying 3000-year-old Chinese casts of bronze ceremonial temple vessels, he became intrigued by the ways in which objects can project a mystical spirituality. His iconic sculptural forms, often *tours de force* of large-scale casting, are made with greenish industrial glass. They are sometimes patinated with copper, bronze and gold and rubbed with pigmented waxes or metallic dust. Metal inserts are sometimes used to capture and deflect light deep within the interior of the work, creating an aura of incandescence. Many of Ben Tré's works are commissioned for specific sites, often outdoors where they must withstand the rigors of the natural environment.

Dan Dailey (b.1947) was one of Chihuly's first students, graduating from RISD in 1972. His idiom could not be more different from his teacher's. Like Chihuly, he spent a year in Venice at the Venini factory before moving to Boston, where he started the glass department at the Massachusetts College of Art in 1979. For Dailey, every object tells a story, a story related with wit, humour and flair. He is most famous for his light-hearted wall pieces that are really three-dimensional jigsaw puzzles fit together with carefully shaped pieces of plate glass or Vitrolite, a shiny, hard-edged material available in a wide range of colours. These are attached to a metal armature with polished, precision-turned screws or rivets. His craftsmanship is both complex and exquisite; he has mastered all the techniques of glass plating, blowing, engraving and sandblasting, but never exploits material effects for their own sake. Technique is always subservient to narrative. In 'Anguish', a wall sculpture of cut and polished Vitrolite and plated brass, a sober-suited collector (wearing argyle socks) wails in despair over a broken glass masterpiece. For the last 30 years he has worked as an independent designer for the Daum Factory in France, creating *pâte de verre* sculpture with Art Deco panache. Dailey now has a large workshop and is in great demand for commissioned work, including lighting fixtures for Modernist landmarks such as Rockefeller Center in New York City. His recent quirky table lamps with blown glass shades on figural bases are eccentric and delightful whimsies.

'First Vase', 1989, by Howard Ben Tré. Washington DC, Smithsonian American Museum, Washington DC.

Right:
'Anguish', 1984, by Dan Dailey. Supplied by the Dan Dailey Studio, with permission from the artist. Photo by Susie Cushner.

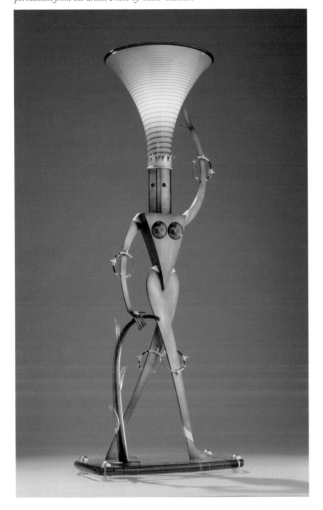

*'Statuesque', a bronze lamp by Dan Dailey.
Supplied by the Dan Dailey Studio, with
permission from the artist. Photo by Susie Cushner.*

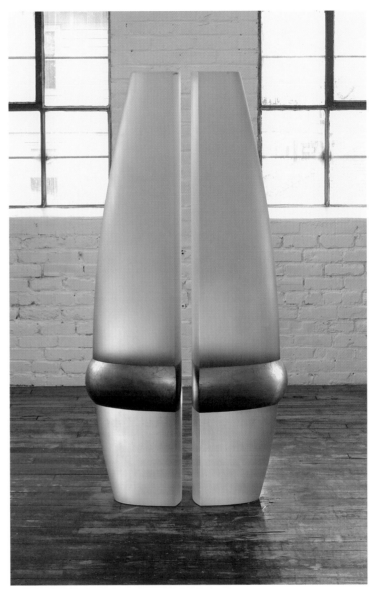

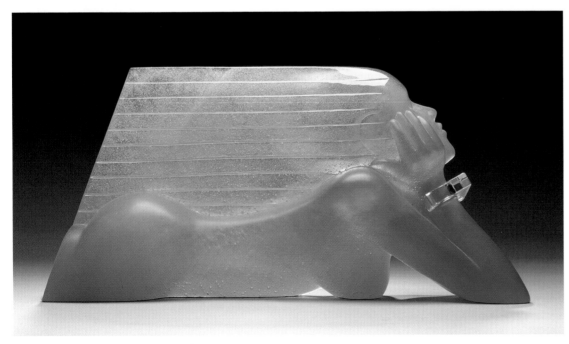

*'Le Vent' (The Wind), 1986, a pâte de verre sculpture
by Dan Dailey for Daum. © Christie's Images Limited*

Michael Glancy (b.1950) discovered glass blowing in his early twenties and, like other hot-glass enthusiasts, moved to Providence to study with Chihuly. While caught up in the excitement of this experimental technique, he also began to explore the possibilities of cold-worked glass. At RISD he came across a book about the early pioneer of studio glass in France, Maurice Marinot (see Chapter 4). Marinot was among the first to blow his own glass and his thick-walled vessels with deeply engraved geometric patterns were a revelation to Glancy. At first he hacked his glass with saws, then attacked the surface with acid, finally settling on sandblasting as the technique that allowed him the greatest control. Glancy had studied jewellery at RISD and his glass resembles precious ornaments with multiple facets encased in copper, silver and sometimes gold. His vessels are often covered with chequered patterns of raised squares, circles or triangles in spiralling diagonals. The glass sculpture 'Beta Pictoris', consists of two parts – a cylindrical vessel form of magenta blown glass, the exterior coated with electroformed copper, and a plate glass base, also electroformed with copper. 'Arete-the-Virtue' is made of blown glass with copper, brass, silver and gold, and rests on a base of black African granite.

For ten years William Morris (b.1957) was Dale Chihuly's favourite master glassblower. His ongoing fascination with glass began in 1978 when he was hired as a truck driver at Pilchuck Summer School. His imagery explores the relics of prehistoric cultures, including burial finds, 'primitive' tools and hunting weapons. As a hunter who has shot game with a bow and arrow, the cave drawings of wild animals at Lascaux have been especially meaningful. 'Sumatran Sambar' echoes the shape of ancient drinking horns, while the recent 'Crocodile Mask' reflects his interest in Inuit ceremonial dance masks. Although he makes no attempt to imitate surviving artefacts, Morris is absorbed by the challenge of representing the mystical relationship between man and nature.

Mary Ann (Toots) Zynsky (b.1951), on the other hand, explores a more abstract aesthetic. She carries on the vessel tradition in her work, but creates her colourful 'containers' from an innovative material – fused glass threads. Called *fillet de verre*, these thin fibres are pulled from hot glass cane and then fused into a fabric-like material that is not only luminous but tactilely rich. 'Bushfire', from her Tierra del Fuego series, is a fused fibre bowl with a wavy rim in vibrant orange, red, blue, black and shades of green. Zynsky has lived in Europe for most of her career, first in Amsterdam and then Paris, but has recently returned to the United States. Another of Dale Chihuly's students from RISD, she is one of the original founders of the Pilchuck Glass School.

Beta Pictoris', 1984, a glass sculpture by
Michael Glancy. © Christie's Images Limited

'Arete-the-Virtue', 1991, a glass sculpture by
Michael Glancy. © Christie's Images Limited

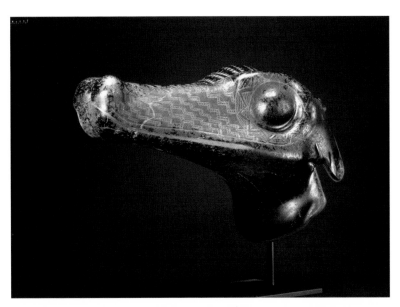

XIII
Architectural and Studio Glass in the UK

Glass vessel by Peter Layton.
Supplied by the artist

Architectural
and Studio Glass
in the UK

Architectural Glass

In the United Kingdom, the 1960's saw the beginning of real prosperity after the war. Rationing was a bad memory, the rubble had disappeared under new housing estates and the class system was splitting open to the songs of the Beatles and the Rolling Stones. For glass, however, the 1960s was a transitional period. Once the major building restoration work was completed, many stained glass firms shut down. Those that survived did so only by looking overseas for orders. In the oil-rich states of the Middle East, new palaces, hotels, airports and mosques were being constructed to a scale and standard unimagined in Europe since the 19th century. Since colour and pattern in architecture were deeply embedded in their cultural history, the Arab peoples commissioned decorative work of the highest standard to enrich their new buildings in a manner both sumptuous and traditional.

Fortunately for the London glass firm of Goddard and Gibbs, their Managing Director Charles Clarke and his successor Neil Maurer were salesmen of considerable vision. Through their efforts the firm succeeded in obtaining orders for new stained glass in the Middle East. The preferred style tended to be an updated version of time-honoured decoration to be found in wall and dome mosaics and in the design of carpets. Geometric patterns for new stained glass were approved as well as designs based on formalized flowers and plants. The beauty of these ancient forms had long been admired in the west. Indeed, the carpets for sale in London's shops and photographs of mosaics in travel books provided a rich source of imagery for these projects.

John Lawson and Harry Cardross, resident designers for Goddard and Gibbs, succeeded in creating many fine schemes on these terms. Domes designed by the firm for villas in the 1980s show how well suited this 'Divine Geometry' could be in filtering out the desert sun from the rooms below with a soothing glass veil. One of the most impressive of these schemes was designed by Alan Younger (see chapter 10) who brought a personal sensitivity to the subtle arrangement of shape and colour to the Laylayty Wedding Hall in Jeddah.

John Lawson in Shoreditch Studio of Goddard & Gibbs, 1995. Supplied by Goddard & Gibbs Photo Archive

Harry Cardross on site in the Middle-East, 2004. Supplied by the artist

Opposite Page:
Dome for the United Arab Emirates Chancery, Washington, DC designed by John Lawson, 1978. Supplied by Goddard & Gibbs Photo Archive

Dome for a private villa in the Gulf designed by Harry Cardross, 1980s. Supplied by Goddard & Gibbs Photo Archive

Exterior of the Laylayty Marriage Hall, Jeddah designed by Alan Younger. Supplied by Goddard & Gibbs Photo Archive

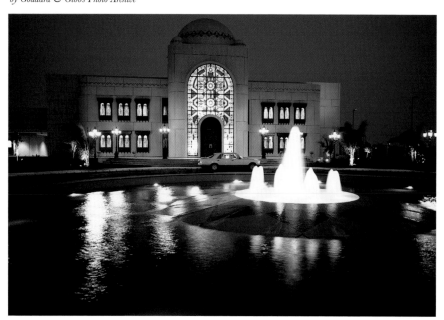

Entrance to the Laylayty Marriage Hall, Jeddah designed by Alan Younger, 1993. Supplied by Goddard & Gibbs Photo Archive

Not all new structures in the Middle East were traditional in form. Many architects pushed the local building types to new limits, an approach which required equal innovation. The floor to ceiling windows in the Ramada Hotel, Dubai in the United Arab Emirates shows how effectively the 'carpet' design could be translated into coloured glass. The scale of the building was such, that the window was documented in the Guinness Book of Records as the tallest made at that time. Another impressive scheme was the decorated glass wall at the Grand Hyatt Regency Hotel in Muscat, Oman designed by Harry Cardross. The composition includes imagery from Muscat's warlike past presented in

a breathtakingly contemporary manner by expert engraver Mike Welch. Some of the ornamental motifs were worked into clear glass to which gold and silver foil were added, while multi layered coloured glass was used to form the mosaic surround.

The technology for creating architectural glass on a grand scale had existed for some time in the building industry. However, durable transparent adhesives were needed, derived from space-age bonding materials before decorative work could be produced on this scale. Once the safety aspect of these materials had been approved, all kinds of possibilities were open for exploration.

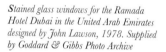

Stained glass windows for the Ramada Hotel Dubai in the United Arab Emirates designed by John Lawson, 1978. Supplied by Goddard & Gibbs Photo Archive

Exterior view of the Grand Hyatt Regency Hotel in Muscat with glass designed by Harry Cardross and fabricated under the supervision of Mick Welch. Supplied by Goddard & Gibbs Photo Archive

Detail of the Grand Hyatt Regency Hotel in Muscat with glass designed by Harry Cardross and fabricated under the supervision of Mick Welch. Supplied by Goddard & Gibbs Photo Archive

One of the first artists to respond imaginatively to these new developments was Alex Beleschenko (b. 1951). Trained in painting and printmaking at Norwich and the Slade Schools of Art, he studied glass at Swansea College of Art where he encountered the Minimalist work of the German masters. His own refined understanding of colour and surface has always been fired by a determination to push the boundaries as far as possible. In 1998 Beleschenko was invited by Arap Associates to create glass screens for a new atrium at St John's College, Oxford. By setting squares of glass between two sheets of toughened clear glass, Beleschenko provided the viewer with a delicately enhanced sense of the translucency as well as the transparency of the glass.

Above:
Photograph of Alex Beleschenko. Supplied and used with permission of the artist

Opposite Page:
Part of the glass screen for the Atrium in St John's College, Oxford by Alex Beleschenko, 1998. Supplied and used with permission of the artist. Photograph by Alex Beleschenko

Right:
Detail showing the cut glass set between toughened float glass sheets for the the Atrium in St John's College, Oxford by Alex Beleschenko, 1998. Supplied and used with permission of the artist. Photograph by Alex Beleschenko

Following the success of this project, Beleschenko became involved with the architect Richard McCormack in the decoration of one of the stations on the new Jubilee Line. With the opening of Tate Modern in 2000, Southwark Station had become an important stop. Beleschenko designed a complex webbed wall of coloured glass incised with a sophisticated repeating pattern of stripes to greet the passenger emerging from the Underground into daylight. Being glass, the luminous blue of the wall changes colour as the light shifts through the day. Blue has remained an inspirational colour for the artist. For The Lighthouse in Glasgow, a newly restored historic building designed by Charles Rennie Mackintosh in 1895, Beleschenko broke with tradition again by using computer-manipulated images of the ginkgo leaf as the subject of a blue glass wall.

His most impressive work to date has been the glass decoration of the astonishing Herz-Jesu church in Munich, Germany, completed in 2000. Building on his experience in the use of computer-generated images, Beleschenko constructed an alphabet of nails in which he wrote extracts from the Gospel of St John. These enigmatic letters that suggest the suffering of Christ were screen printed with blue enamel paint onto float glass to create a wonderfully soothing and elegant environment for worship. Beleschenko makes his windows with the large studio of Franz Mayer in Munich. Many British artists have their work fabricated in Germany because of the technical expertise available there. In addition, these studios do not have resident designers, as do the British workshops.

Left:
Blue glass wall for Southwark Underground Station designed by Alex Beleschenko, 2000. Supplied and used with permission of the artist

Below:
Detail showing the patterning of the glass wall for Southwark Underground Station designed by Alex Beleschenko, 2000. Supplied and used with permission of the artist

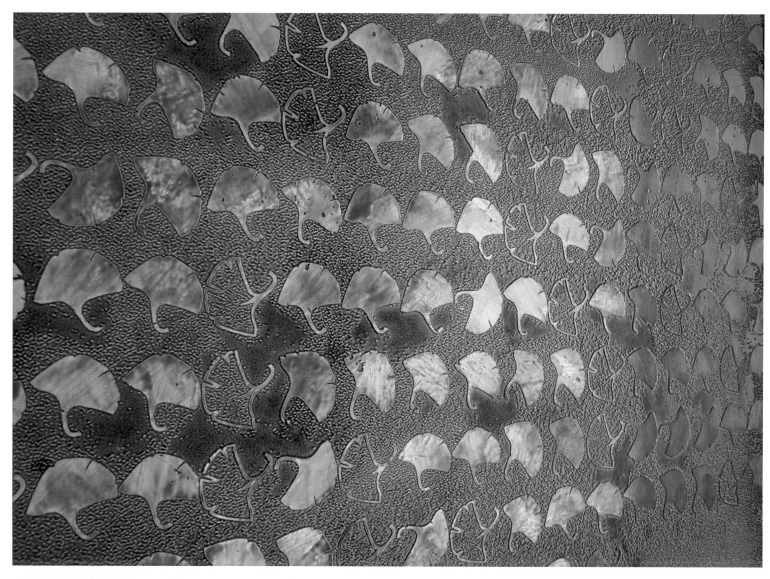

Above:
Detail of the blue glass wall with screen printed Ginkgo leaf imagery designed by Alex Beleschenko for The Lighthouse, Glasgow. Supplied and used with permission of the artist

Left:
Glass doors and walls at the Herz-Jesu church in Munich, Germany designed by Alex Beleschenko, 2000. Supplied and used with permission of the artist

Opposite:
Detail showing the computer generated Gospel of Nails designed by Alex Beleschenko for the Herz-Jesu Church in Munich, Germany. Supplied and used with permission of the artist

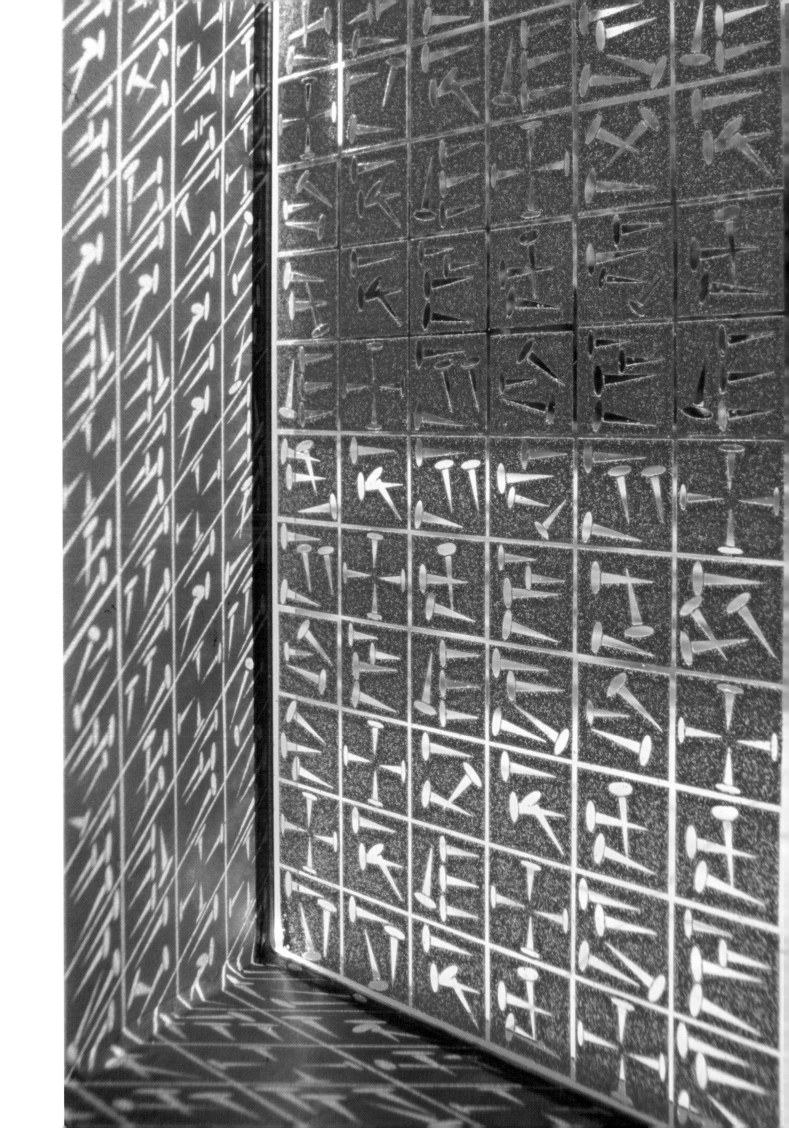

The pioneer in this move to mainland Europe was Brian Clarke (b.1953). A miner's son from Oldham in Lancashire, Clarke began his studies in glass at an early age at North Devon College. His perception of the architectural possibilities of glass was awakened through the opportunity of a Winston Churchill Traveling Scholarship that enabled him to see the magnificent post-war windows in Germany and to visit the artists who had made them, particularly Schaffrath and Schreiter (see Chapter 9). Returning to the UK, Clarke quickly made a name for himself as a radical designer and witty newcomer to the stained glass scene. Clarke also knew how important it was to develop his ideas in paint. His energetic exploration of form and colour has always underpinned his superb glass works for architecture. 'It is through painting that I understand architecture... without painting it would be very difficult for me to design stained glass. It would be difficult for me to have any sense of scale or sense of development of narrative. And you know, when I am designing a stained glass window, I am painting... when I am making the cartoon for a tapestry I am painting'.

Brian Clarke working at the Derix studio,
Taunusstein, 1990s. © Brian Clarke 2005

*Brian Clarke at work on his paintings in his studio
in north London, 1990s. © Brian Clarke 2005*

At Stansted Airport in Essex, Clarke's diapered glass tower formed a link between the architect Norman Foster's tent like roof and the busy floor of the terminal building. Clarke also created a series of brilliant glass 'pictures' to make a stylish wall for the airport food hall. The daringly vivid glass ceiling that has revitalized Victoria Quarter, a dowdy Victorian arcade in Leeds, displays Clarke's abilities as a colourist and his understanding of architecture. In London, he used ribbons of bright colour in conjunction with his favoured pattern of squares to highlight the entrance hall of a recent building by Peter Shaw of Renton, Howard, Wood, Levin at 100 New Bridge Street. During the drab months of winter the impact of Clarke's glass is particularly effective. Indeed, the fame of his windows has encouraged other UK developers to use coloured glass to bring style and status to their buildings.

Above:

Glass tower at Stansted Airport designed by Brian Clarke and fabricated at Derix Studios, Taunusstein, 1991. Image supplied by Caroline Swash

Left:

The series of glass 'pictures' for the restaurant at Stansted Airport by Brian Clarke, 1991. Image supplied by Caroline Swash

Opposite:

The Prudential group commissioned Brian Clarke to design a 125 metre long stained glass roof to span Queen Victoria Street, Leeds. The architects for the renovation were Derek Latham and Company, 1990. © Brian Clarke 2005

Design by Brian Clarke for the stained glass
entrance screen for 100 New Bridge Street,
architects Renton, Howard, Wood, Levin, 1991.
© Brian Clarke 2005

Detail of Window at 100 New
Bridge Street by Brian Clarke,
1991. © Brian Clarke 2005

Exterior views of 100 New Bridge Street with glass
by Brian Clarke, 1991. © Brian Clarke 2005

Clarke has become an artist of international reputation and has enhanced the status of architectural glass worldwide. Although based in London, he too has his projects fabricated at the Mayer Studios in Munich, although earlier stained glass windows were made at the Derix Studios in Taunusstein. Among his works are The New Synagogue, Darmstadt, Germany, the Lake Sagami Country Club, Yuzurihara, Yamanashi, Japan and the circular wall of bold, brightly coloured shapes made in 1996 for the auditorium of the Valentino Village in Bari. In June 2005, Clarke showed his recent ideas in glass at the Gagosian Gallery, London. Here screens of toughened float glass had been decorated with printed images of oak leaves to entice the viewer into a carefully structured urban forest.

View of Lake Sagami Country Club, Yuzurihara, Yamanashi, Japan built by architect Arata Isozaki Associates, 1989. © Brian Clarke 2005

Stained glass for the lantern and skylight windows designed by Brian Clarke for Lake Sagami Country Club, Yuzurihara, Yamanashi, Japan built by architect Arata Isozaki Associates, 1989. © Brian Clarke 2005

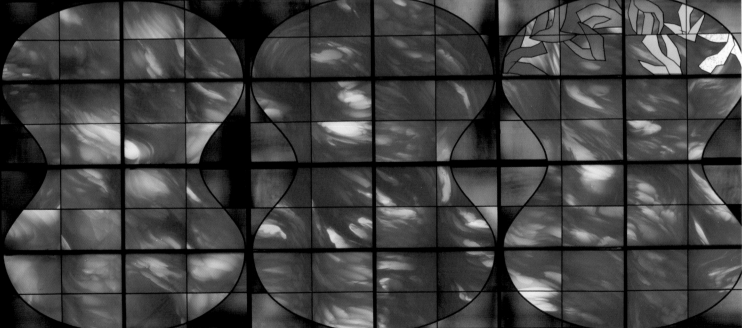

*Curved stained glass wall and detail designed by Brian Clarke
for the main auditorium of the conference and leisure centre,
Valentino Village, Bari, Italy, 1996. © Brian Clarke 2005*

Lamina (2005) interior view. Courtesy of Gagosian Gallery. © Brian Clarke. Photography © Richard Davies

Lamina (2005) exterior view. Courtesy of Gagosian Gallery. © Brian Clarke. Photography © Richard Davies

Graham Jones (b.1958) trained at Swansea College of Art and was particularly influenced by the work of Johannes Schreiter, artist-in-residence during his time as a student. He has also been impressed by the romantic sensitivity to texture and colour apparent in the work of John Piper and Patrick Reyntiens (see Chapter 10). This is particularly evident in the 'Poet's Corner' window he designed and made in 1994 For Westminster Abbey. Here, he decorated two tall lancet windows with wreaths of flowers leaving space for the names of future Poets. Despite the dominance of the Abbey's historic architecture, Jones managed to create a window that pays tribute to the Gothic style while being entirely contemporary in idiom.

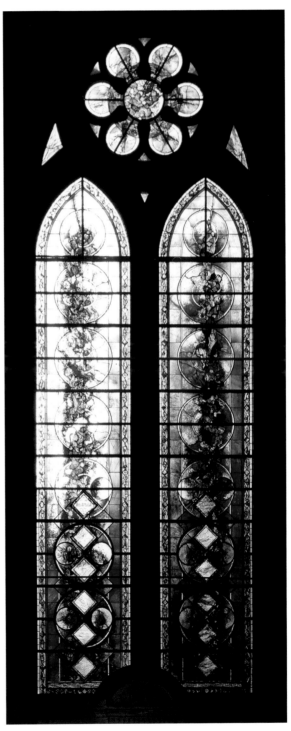

Graham Jones as a student with Tim Lewis at Swansea College of Art. Supplied by the Gagosian Gallery

Poets memorial window by Graham Jones with assistance from John Reyntiens for Westminster Abbey, Poets Corner, 1995. Supplied by the Artist

However, Jones's real gift is for the decorative contrast of colour and texture. A circular feature window made in 1998 brightens the plain glass foyer of No. 3 Minster Court in the City of London. In one section of the window, references to the history of the area have been made on white glass set against varied and lively colour. Indeed, Jones has frequently been involved in projects in which glass is needed to bring a sense of animation and drama to staid surroundings. For each project, he prepares the glass himself, covering the surface with protective bitumen before immersing the sheets in dilute hydrofluoric acid. In this way he says 'he can bring the surface of the glass alive'. Jones' sensitivity to the requirements of the architectural setting can be seen in his recent work for two new churches in Germany. He has used light gold, pink and blue glass to complement the pure white surfaces of the walls of the interior of Friedberg Church. While the floor to ceiling windows in the Melancthon Church, Dortmund have been filled with shafts of colour enhanced with elegant dancing shapes to give a sense of light and life to this austere interior.

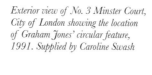

Exterior view of No. 3 Minster Court, City of London showing the location of Graham Jones' circular feature, 1991. Supplied by Caroline Swash

Detail of the Circular feature for the foyer of No. 3 Minster Court, City of London by Graham Jones, 1991. Supplied by Caroline Swash

Detail of the coloured and textured glass in Friedberg church designed by Graham Jones, 2004. Supplied by the artist

View of the interior of Friedberg church, Germany with glass designed by Graham Jones, 2004. Supplied by the artist

Circular feature for the foyer of No. 3 Minster
Court, City of London by Graham Jones, 1991.
Supplied by Caroline Swash

Above:
Interior of Melancthon Church, Dortmund
with glass by Graham Jones, 2000-2005.
Supplied by the artist

Top-Right:
Three windows in Melancthon Church
by Graham Jones. Supplied by the artist

Detail of the glass in Melancthon Church
by Graham Jones, Supplied by the artist

Glass and the Community

From the 1980s onwards, UK government at both national and local level began to regard art and craft in the community as serving a useful social function. Policies were developed to encourage artists and crafts people to contribute their skills and even their presence in locations that had suffered from the collapse of traditional industries. The organization of the Coin Street Cooperative on London's South bank, for example, has set a precedent. Here rents have been kept low in order that makers can work in studio accommodation that would, at times, be open to the public. With unusual items for sale and a range of annual activities, many organised for children, this craft cooperative

has been enormously successful. Other London cooperatives include the Clerkenwell Workshops founded by Michael Murray in the 1970s and the more recent Cockpit Studios in Holborn and Deptford where several talented glassworkers share kilns and studio expences.

Taking their cue from business practice, the Arts Council, local government agencies and charities have encouraged the commissioning of site-specific public art that confers prestige on its surroundings while illuminating local historical connections. For example, for the City Library and Arts Centre in Sunderland a series of stained glass windows

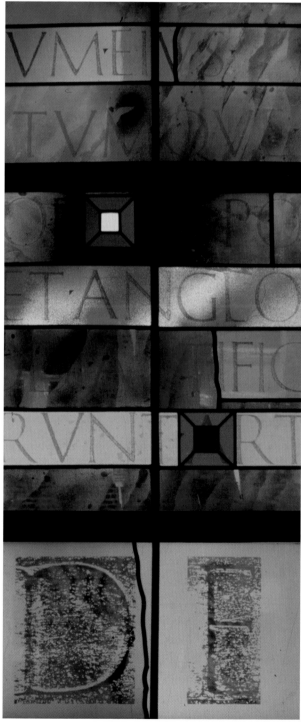

Detail of City Library and Arts Centre window by Catrin Jones in Sunderland, 1995. Supplied and used with permission of the artist

were commissioned in 1995 from the Welsh artist Catrin Jones. In a fragmentary form that viewers can quietly unravel, these tell a complex story. The design is based on formal Roman lettering, taken from Trajan's Column in Rome. The Latin text is taken from 'Gifts for the Monastery' by the Venerable Bede and reads across the windows, commencing on the first floor and continuing on the second. Much of her work is rooted in her passion for the flora and fauna of the Welsh coast. Jones was trained at Swansea College of Art and has her studio in the town. She specialises in composite sandblasted and kiln-fired work of great delicacy, such as the exhibition piece entitled 'The wind that blows me is called light'.

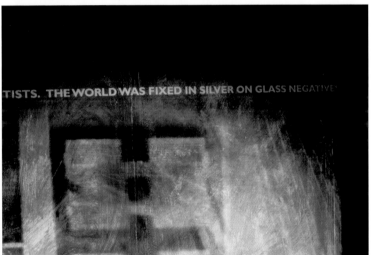

Details of the exhibition piece 'The wind that blows me is called light' by Catrin Jones. Supplied and used with permission of the artist

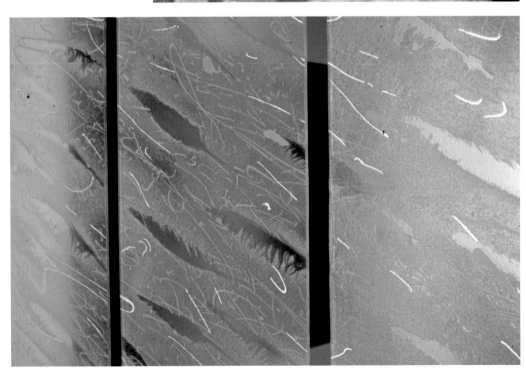

'The Laboratory of the Spirit' by Catrin Jones. Supplied and used with permission of the artist

Amber Hiscott also trained at Swansea College of Art and studied with Ludwig Schaffrath before setting up her own studio in Swansea with husband, David Pearl. The glass panel that she created for the Great Western Hospital in Cardiff makes a colourful focal point for the reception area. The dramatic free-flowing improvisation designed for the Wales Millennium Centre, reflects Hiscott's enthusiasm for painting and her daring use of digitally-printed glass.

Another architectural glass artist who has won commissions for Public Art is Martin Donlin. In 1998 he made a glowing wall of glass called 'Urban Splash' for the Tibb Street Bridge Link in Manchester. Donlin's growing enthusiasm for changing light effects influenced the glass he designed for The Oracle Centre, a new shopping mall in Reading.

Amber Hiscott with Ludwig Schaffrath in Germany. Supplied by Tim Lewis

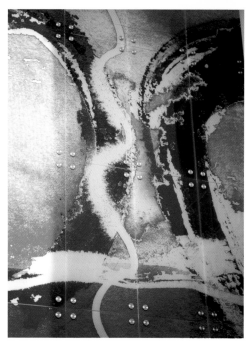

Detail of Glass composition by Amber Hiscott for the Centre for Visual Arts, Cardiff, 1999. Supplied and used with permission of the artist

Glass composition by Amber Hiscott for the Centre for Visual Arts, Cardiff, 1999. Supplied and used with permission of the artist

Glass composition by Amber Hiscott for the Wales Millenium Centre in Cardiff, 2004. Supplied and used with permission of the artist

Detail of the Glass composition by Amber Hiscott for the Wales Millenium Centre in Cardiff, 2004. Supplied and used with permission of the artist

The Oracle Centre, Reading with glass by Martin Donlin, 1999. Architects: Haskoll & Company. Photograph by Paul Highnam

Amber Hiscott, Catrin Jones, Martin Donlin, Alex Beleschenko, Mark Angus, Rodney Bender, Graham Jones, Debora Coombs, Shelley Jurs, Yanos Boujoucos, Paul Lucky, Susan Bradbury, Keith Gale, Lydia Marouf, Kuni Kajiwara, Sachiko Yamamoto, Sarah Hall and many others studied glass at Swansea College of Art during the late 1970s to 1980s. They owe their good training to the tough-minded leadership of the Welshman Tim Lewis. Lewis trained under Lawrence Lee at the Royal College of Art and returned to Swansea to set up his own studio and to assist Howard Martin in the running of the glass course. After Martin's death in 1972, Lewis initiated the programme of master-classes with German artists Shaffrath, Schreiter, Klos, Meistermann and Poensgen (see Chapter 9) with the aim of enriching the course. These artists not only gave lectures and tutorials but worked with the students in the fabrication of windows for the Mid Glamorgan Crematorium in Bridgend, a project that lasted for almost 20 years. This combination of intellectual and practical contact had an inspiring effect on the ideas and expectations of the students fortunate enough to be educated in Swansea at that time.

Tim Lewis with students working on coloured cartoons at Swansea College of Art, 1979. Supplied by Tim Lewis

Stained glass memorial by Tim Lewis to the lifeboat men who lost their lives in the Samtampa disaster at All Saints Church, Oystermouth, Swansea, 1977. Supplied by Tim Lewis

Above:
Stained glass window with lenses by Tim Lewis for All Saints Church, Rhiwbina, Cardiff, 1990. Supplied by Tim Lewis

Left:
Detail of the stained glass memorial by Tim Lewis to the lifeboat men who lost their lives in the Samtampa disaster, All Saints Church, Oystermouth, Swansea, 1977. Supplied by Tim Lewis

Photograph taken in 1989 after the judging of the Hetley Hartley Wood Competition held at Swansea College of Art. The event was sponsored by the British Society of Master Glass Painters. L-R Tim Lewis, Glenys Cour (painter and tutor), Caroline Swash (Hon Sec, British Society of Master Glass Painters), Edith Schreiter-Diedrichs, Colwyn Morris (tutor in traditional processes), Janet Lewis, Professor Johannes Schreiter, John Edwards (tutor in design and glass painting), Rodney Bender (Head of school since 1990). Supplied by Tim Lewis

While the course at Swansea concentrated on updating the traditional techniques including those less frequently taught such as sandblast and acid etch, students trained at the Royal College were exploring the possibilities of kiln formed glass for architecture. Ann Smyth was commissioned to design the tiled floor and decorate the glass walls for the entrance area of the Public Record Office when it moved to Kew in 1995. For this prestigious site she made a number of lightly coloured sculptured glass panels. She feels strongly that people should have 'pleasant and uplifting things around them'. Smyth has developed her own way of creating coloured kiln-formed panels in low relief. Details from the entrance window of the Michael Tippett Centre, Bath Spa University College made in 1998, show the refinement of surface achievable by these means. According to the artist, 'I wanted the glass to create a watery dream-like quality and to have the vibrancy and energy found within Tippett's music'. While making the window I listened to his music hoping that its energy and passion would be captured within the glass. Sometimes the music was flowing and lyrical, sometimes angular and hard listening'.

In all these architectural schemes for public spaces, glass is being used in new ways made possible by modern technologies. Although the traditional use of lead came has faded somewhat, glass itself is still valued for its intrinsic qualities – colour and transparency. Whatever their subject and intention, these glass creations are part of the building in which they are installed. The design has been chosen for stylistic suitability and the colour and mode of expression selected to facilitate integration into the architecture.

Opportunities to reach a wider audience are facilitated by individual art colleges and voluntary organisations. The Royal College of Art held a three-day conference on architectural glass in 1996; this was followed in 1998 by 'The Search for Meaning' conference held at the Victoria and Albert Museum. The City Livery Company, the Worshipful Company of Glaziers based at Glaziers Hall near London Bridge, maintains a library and runs an annual programme of events including a competition for students and emerging designers in glass. The British Society of Master Glass Painters is the most active organisation in this field. Founded in 1921 to promote the practice and scholarly study of stained glass, the Society has members worldwide who are involved in its history, conservation and technical development.

Detail showing the coloured and textured surface of glass by Anne Smyth for the Entrance window to the Michael Tippett Centre, Bath Spa University, 1998. Supplied and used with permission of the artist

Exterior of the Public Record Office at Kew showing glass by Anne Smyth, 1995. Supplied and used with permission of the artist

Opposite Page:
Detail of glass at the Public Record Office at Kew by Anne Smyth, 1993. Supplied and used with permission of the artist

Studio Glass

The studio glass movement in the United Kingdom began when the glass artist Sam Herman arrived from America in 1969, first as a Fulbright Scholar in Edinburgh and then as a part time member of staff in the Department of Glass and Ceramics at the Royal College of Art. Herman was an inspiration. He had trained with Harvey Littleton and brought the sense of adventure to London that had characterised the movement of studio glass in the United States (see Chapter 11). Many of his pupils have since become leaders in the field and tutors for the next generation. In 1976 John Cook, a student of Herman's and by then head of Ceramics and Glass at Leicester Polytechnic, persuaded the newly formed Crafts Council to arrange a conference at the Royal College entitled 'Working with Hot Glass'. This was an event of seminal importance. Besides a series of stimulating lectures, the contribution of the great Czech glass artist, Stanislav Libenský, made delegates aware of the drama and beauty possible in kiln-formed glass (see Chapter 15).

This Page:
Four bowls by Pauline Solven. Supplied by the artist

Before he left for Australia in 1974, Herman helped set up The Glasshouse in Neal Street near Covent Garden. Herman hoped that graduates would be able to continue to develop their work and find a buying public. Over the years The Glasshouse provided studio facilities and a convivial context for many of Britain's glass blowers. Jane Bruce, one of the most influential people in glass today worked there in the early 1970s. Other renowned artists involved in the cooperative were Pauline Solven, Annette Meech, Christopher Williams, Fleur Tookey, Stephen Newell and David Taylor. From Neal Street, The Glasshouse moved to Long Acre and then to Islington before closing in 1999. By then many of the artists who had worked there had already set up studios of their own. Annette Meech and Christopher Williams moved to Burgundy. Pauline Solven and her husband Harry Cowdy went to North Gloucesterhire where they ran a glass blowing workshop as well as their famous Cowdy Gallery.

Gourd Vase-Bulbes Rayes, by Annette Meech. © 2005 Glasshouse de Sivignon

Glasswork by Fleur Tookey, Supplied by the artist

Peanuts, by Christopher Williams. © 2005 Glasshouse de Sivignon

Design from the Courtesan Series, 2005, by Steven Newell. In the collection of the National Museums for Scotland, Edinburgh. Photograph by Chris Scott

Devil's Conspire, 2005, by Steven Newell from his solo exhibition and catalogue, The Scottish Gallery, April 2005 – Reflections from a Floating World. Photograph by Chris Scott

My Omi's, 2005, by Steven Newell from his solo exhibition and catalogue, The Scottish Gallery, April 2005 – Reflections from a Floating World. Photograph by Chris Scott

The Thing that He Desires, 2004, by Steven Newell from his solo exhibition and catalogue, The Scottish Gallery, April 2005 – Reflections from a Floating World. Photograph by Chris Scott

Interior of Cowdy Gallery. Photograph by Harry Cowdy

The Hero and the Fish Monster, 2005, by Steven Newell from his solo exhibition and catalogue, The Scottish Gallery, April 2005 – Reflections from a Floating World. Photograph by Chris Scott

Moon Dance, 2005, by Steven Newell from his solo exhibition and catalogue, The Scottish Gallery, April 2005 – Reflections from a Floating World. Photograph by Chris Scott

The 'Working with Hot Glass' conference in 1976 also inspired the formation of an important society. British Artists in Glass (BAG) was set up after the conference by John Cook, Karlin Rushbrooke, Dillon Clarke, George Elliott, Charles Bray, Alison McConachie and Peter Layton with the aim of bringing contemporary glass to the attention of the public. Later members included Keith Brocklehurst, Tessa Clegg, Rachael Woodman, Deborah Fladgate, Colin Reid and Diana Hobson. British

Artists in Glass ran annual exhibitions of work and held conferences which undoubtedly helped to raise critical interest in glass as a new art form. Since several practitioners were involved in writing and teaching, their ideas soon spread to a wide audience of students, makers and collectors. From the early 1980s, enthusiasm for glass encouraged the establishment of several courses throughout the country. Sam Herman returned from Australia and taught at High Wycombe with Deborah

Handscape 2005. Sandcast, flameworked, engraved glass by Keith Brocklehurst.
© 2005 Keith Brocklehurst.
Photograph by Simon Bruntnell

Inquisition 2004. Sandcast, jetcut, engraved glass by Keith Brocklehurst.
© 2005 Keith Brocklehurst.
Photograph by Simon Bruntnell

Fladgate; Colin Webster developed a glass course at Farnham in Surrey; Liz Swinburne worked at Stoke-on-Trent before moving to the Royal College of Art in London. Stuart Garfoot, Chris Bird-Jones and Professor Keith Cummings expanded the glass course at the University of Wolverhampton. In 1990, Dr. Ray Flavell took over the glass and architectural glass course at Edinburgh. Seminal books on studio methods and practise were written by Peter Layton, Keith Cummings,

Charles Bray and Ray Flavell. The writer Dan Klein has been particularly important in the process of communication, bringing thoughtful assessment, lucid prose and beautiful images to the reading public. Quickened enthusiasm for glass suggested the formation of a new and inclusive glass organization to replace BAG, thus The Contemporary Glass Society (CGS) was born.

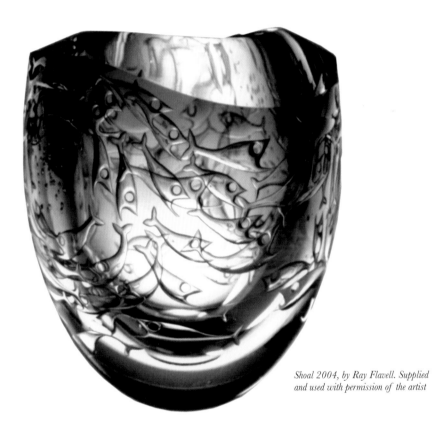

Shoal 2004, by Ray Flavell. Supplied and used with permission of the artist

Greenpiece 1990, by Ray Flavell. In the V&A Collection. Supplied and used with permission of the artist

Interface 2004, by Ray Flavell. Supplied and used with permission of the artist

Glass by Karlin Rushbrooke.
Photograph by Harry Cowdy

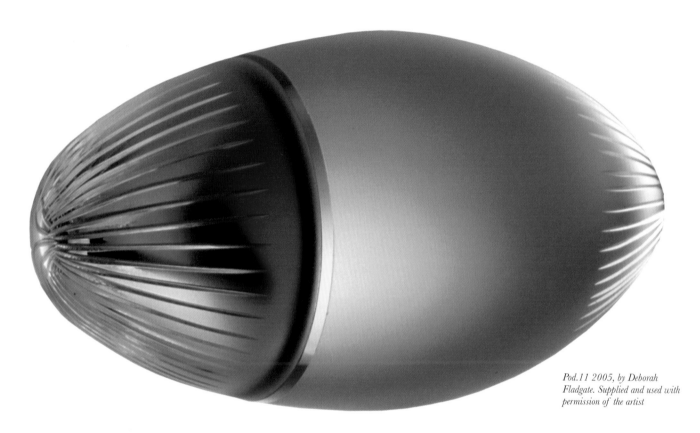

Pod.11 2005, by Deborah
Fladgate. Supplied and used with
permission of the artist

Module.04 2005, by Deborah
Fladgate. Supplied and used
with permission of the artist

Module.04 2005, detail, by
Deborah Fladgate. Supplied and
used with permission of the artist

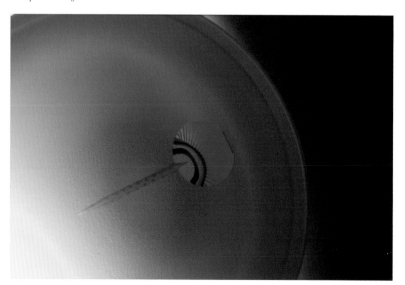

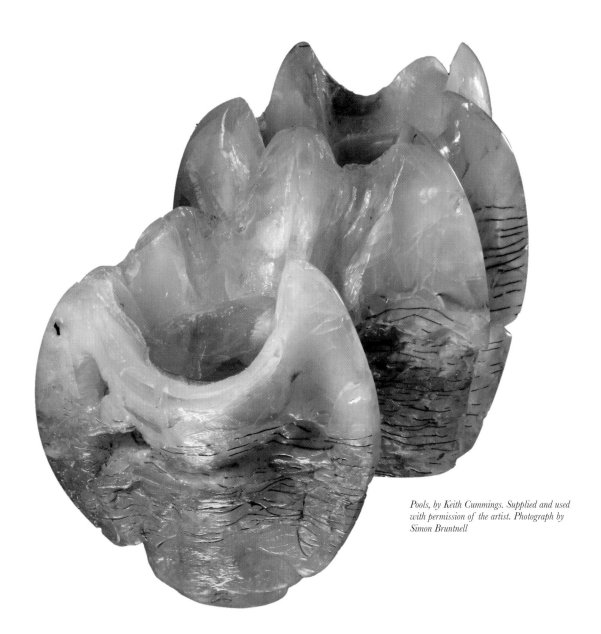

Pools, by Keith Cummings. Supplied and used with permission of the artist. Photograph by Simon Bruntnell

Lilac Time, by Keith Cummings. Supplied and used with permission of the artist. Photograph by Simon Bruntnell

Peter Layton (b.1937) has been of enormous importance in the process of energizing the glass movement in Britain. He was involved in building the first kilns for The Glasshouse and became a founding member of British Artists in Glass and its successor The Contemporary Glass Society. He was trained originally as a ceramicist and happened to be teaching at the University of Iowa in the United States just after the famous Toledo Seminar of 1962. Enrolling on a glass summer school course in 1966, he discovered that he thoroughly enjoyed what he called the 'immediacy' of the process of glass blowing. On returning to the UK he continued working in clay but gradually began to develop his ideas in the new medium. He opened his own workshop in Rotherhithe in 1970 and in 1994 moved to the Old Leathermarket near London Bridge in Bermondsey. Here at the London Glass Blowing Workshop there is space to work, exhibit and teach.

Layton has retained a potter's sense of form and his glass has a sculptural verve, which few British artists can emulate. Colour is vitally important to him and he uses an adventurously sumptuous palette for his major works. He also produces household items such as wine glasses and tumblers with a strong streak of fantasy. Besides his blown vessels, Layton designs and makes large scale works that interact with their environment, from the plantings in a garden to the interior of a Cruise Liner. Layton has been enormously important in the United Kingdom's studio glass movement. His workshop has been a useful starting point for new designers and his short courses have inspired a number of artists to consider glass as a career.

Photograph of Peter Layton in his studio.
Photograph supplied by London Glassblowing

Interior of the Leathermarket exhibition
space. Photograph by Ester Segarra

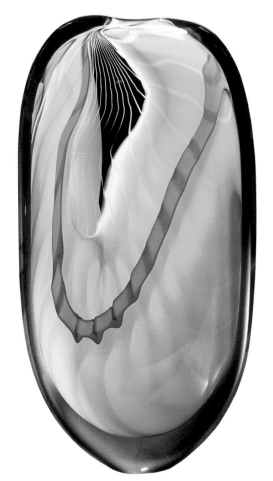

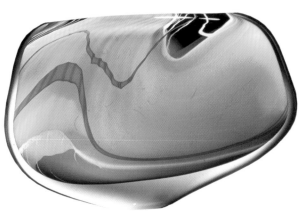

This Page & Next:
Series of glass vessels by Peter Layton.
Supplied by the artist

Glass sculpture, The Office Park Leatherhead,
by Peter Layton in collaboration with Simon Moss.
© 2000 Simon Moss/Peter Layton

Danny Lane (b.1955) is an immensely lively American who moved to the UK in 1975. He studied with the visionary artist Cecil Collins at Central Saint Martins and spent time with Patrick Reyntiens at Burleighfield before setting up his own peripatetic practice in London. Lane uses horizontally stacked pieces of glass for their inherent qualities of sharpness, solidity and transparency while exploiting the viewer's awareness of the potential threat of these jagged shapes. A sculpture of a chair made in 1988 shows the idiosyncrasy of Lane's vision. To imagine sitting on this chair evokes a surreal sense of discomfort, yet the piece is solid and well made, properly secured and stable. A dangerous looking stairway, which is entirely safe, was an inspired commission by the Victoria and Albert Museum for their recently opened Glass Gallery. One of the endearing aspects of Lane's work is the game he plays with our perceptions. His glass figural constructions are entirely unforgettable, solid yet see-through, glinting and dangerous, yet related in some curious way to our own ancestral past.

Balustrade glass by Danny Lane,
Victoria and Albert Museum, London.
Photograph by Ken Jackson

Danny Lane at his Hythe Road Studio, 2005.
Photograph by Peter Wood

Etruscan Chair by Danny Lane, 1992. New York,
Corning Museum of Glass. Photograph: Corning Museum

Clifford Rainey (b.1948) is another visionary sculptor in glass, He grew up in Northern Ireland and worked as an apprentice linen designer with the Belfast firm of William Ewart and Son Ltd. He came to London to study at Hornsey College of Art and the Royal College of Art and improved the technical side of his craft with stints at the Kastrup and Holmegaards Glassworks in Denmark and the Ittal Glassworks in Finland. In 1984 he set up a studio in New York while maintaining a studio in London. He now lives in the United States and is chair of the glass programme at the California College of Arts and Crafts, Oakland, California. Since 1973, Rainey has exhibited yearly either in group or solo shows in the UK, Europe, Japan, the United States and Mexico. He has also built some very substantial architectural pieces including a glass wall for Lime Street Station, Liverpool, in 1984. Through public art projects his ideas have reached a wide audience. His main contribution to the glass world, however, has been a fearless approach to his subject and a fascinating mix of media fabricated to the highest standards. His sculpture often combines metal and wood as well as glass worked in different ways.

Balustrade glass by Danny Lane, 1994, Victoria and Albert Museum, London. Photograph by Ken Jackson

Parting of the Waves, glass by Danny Lane at Canary Wharf, London. Photograph by Peter Wood

Miss Wiggle, glass by Danny Lane, 2000, Exhibited: 'Lawn Sushi and Toblerone' at Henley Festival 2000. Photograph by Peter Wood

Engraved Glass

The tradition of glass engraving gained considerable impetus from the charm of the vessels and architectural decoration made by Laurence and Simon Whistler as well as the contribution of John Hutton, David Peace and Sally Scott (see Chapter 10). The Guild of Glass Engravers, founded in 1975, steadfastly continues to hold exhibitions and promote the work of their members. These include such contemporary practitioners as Chris Ainslie, Peter Dreiser, Josephine Harris, James Denison-Pender, Audrey Leckie, Peter David and Madeleine Dinkel.

'Save the Trees' Engraved bowl by
Josephine Harris. Supplied by the artist

'Let Joy be Unconfined' Engraved
roundel by Josephine Harris.
Supplied by the artist

'Einstein' Engraved
bowl by Tony Gilliam.
Supplied by the artist

'Ancestral Seats' Engraved
roundel by Tracey Shephard.
Supplied by the artist

Engraved goblet by Audrey Leckie.
Supplied by the artist

'Hot Beat', Engraved vessel by Chris Ainslie.
Supplied by the artist

'Bird Fancier' Engraved vessel by
Chris Ainslie. Supplied by the artist

'Vanity' Engraved vessel by Chris Ainslie.
Supplied by the artist

Simon Whistler (1940-2005) was both a musician and an engraver. He played the viola with several distinguished string ensembles including the English Chamber Orchestra and The Orchestra of the Age of Enlightenment. He learnt the craft of engraving from his father but his own work has an unmistakable authority. His method of orchestrating the geometry of architecture within and around the vessel is particularly impressive. He shares with his father a sense of the vision within and beyond the landscape. This quality is particularly apparent in the series of Welsh views inspired by Turner and the landscapes relating to North Devon – works of extraordinary refinement and finesse.

'The Midnight Owl', Llanthony Priory, 1989, engraved goblet by Simon Whistler. Held in private collection. Photograph by John Pasmore.

'River Path' depicting the Torridge River in North Devon, engraved by Simon Whistler, 1984. Held in private collection. Photograph by John Pasmore.

Opposite Page:
The Stowe Bowl, Templa Quam Dilecta, 1990. Engraved by Simon Weissler. Bowl designed by Laurence Whistler. In the collection of Stowe School, Buckingham. Photograph by John Pasmore.

Peter Dreiser trained a number of artists at Morley College in London. After a lifetime of engraving he has turned his attention to the ecological issues of the day expressing his disquiet through a series of memorably complex bowls. His book 'The Techniques of Glass Engraving' written with Jonathan Matcham remains the standard text for the aspiring craftsman.

One of his most distinguished pupils, Katharine Coleman, uses traditional techniques of wheel engraving to create dramatic designs which enhance the glass surface in different ways. Coleman fell in love with engraving after seeing an exhibition of work by Alison Kinnaird and Peter Dreiser in a Cork Street Gallery. She found her own language in glass after many years of practice. Her coloured vessels (blown to her design by Neil Wilkin) invite the viewer into a shifting world of patterns and shapes. Like many engravers, her work often has a poignant or powerful message imbedded within the delicate fabric of the glass. Her short listed piece for the Jerwood Prize of 2003 'Oranges and Lemons' is an outstanding example of glass used in a completely sculptural way while her latest work shows every sign of developing in an even more interesting fashion.

'Sueños de la Alhambra' Engraved form by Peter Dreiser. Supplied by the artist

'A Watchful Eye' Engraved Whitefriars paperweight by Peter Dreiser, 1986. Supplied by the artist

'Noah 11' Engraved roundel by Peter Dreiser. Supplied by the artist

'The Drowning of the Innocents' Engraved roundel by Peter Dreiser. Supplied by the artist

'Barley 11', by Katharine Coleman. Supplied and used with permission of the artist

'City of Glass', by Katharine Coleman. Supplied and used with permission of the artist

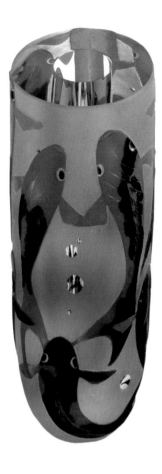

'Koi 111', by Katharine Coleman. Supplied and used with permission of the artist

'Synchronised Swimmers', by Katharine Coleman. Supplied and used with permission of the artist

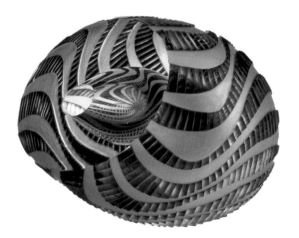

Blue Nautilus, by Katharine Coleman. Supplied by the artist

Alison Kinnaird MBE (b.1949) is a talented Celtic harpist as well as a superb glass engraver. She cuts into the glass from the reverse, gently exploring the inner surface of the material to create compositions in line and low relief. The viewer becomes caught up in her story, a tale about humanity, disconcerting yet resolutely perfect. Her graceful work 'Psalmsong', was made in 2004 for the new Scottish Parliament building in Edinburgh. Inspired by Gaelic psalms, it is 3.1 metres long and comprises 24 panels of glass engraved with figurative images shot through with light and colour.

Ronald Pennell (b.1935) uses the technique of engraving in a very different spirit. He has adapted to glass the skills he acquired as a gem and metal engraver in Birmingham and Germany. His bowls and goblets tell marvelously entertaining stories whose subversive message points out the paradoxes and confusions of everyday life. Writing about his art in 'Modern Myths. The Art of Ronald Pennell' he observed that 'Life is a story. Reality is a confusion of memory and images and the only difference between narrative and actuality is perception'. In 1997 Pennell tried out glass casting and continues to build his own world in this new method in his own inimitable way. His work is highly prized and in 1993 he was made Honorary Professor at the Academy of Arts in Prague and in 2001, Honorary Professor at the University of Wolverhampton.

'Europa-the past is not enough', green overcased glass vessel by Ronald Pennell. Supplied by the artist

'Psalmsong' by Alison Kinnaird for the Scottish Parliament in Edinburgh, 2004. Supplied by and used with permission of the artist

Streetwise I 2004, by Alison Kinnaird MBE. Located at Tutsek Foundation, Munich. Supplied by and used with permission of the artist

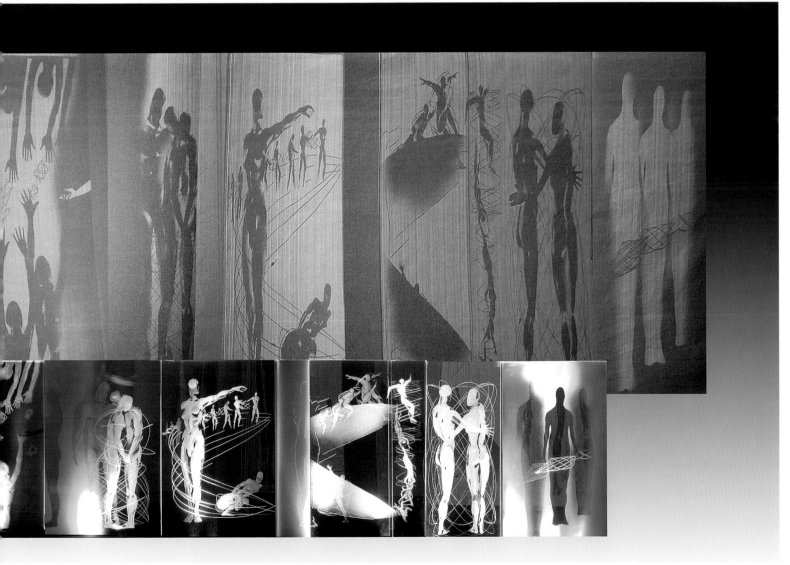

David Reekie (b.1947) learned glass casting at Stourbridge College of Art, later teaching at North Staffodshire Polytechnic. Like Pennell and Kinnaird, his imagry revolves around the human body. His figures are entirely his own, combative and determined, grumpily involved in awkward but important activities. There is a refreshing lack of pretension in his choice of subject. As his audience, we feel drawn towards these difficult men who are not unknown in daily life.

The lengthy and complex art of kiln forming continues to interest British artists. Colin Reid (b.1953) trained first as a chemical glass blower, learning to make retorts on a government training scheme. He then studied with Keith Cummings where he learnt the complicated techniques involved in casting and kiln forming from one of the country's experts. He moved to the Cotswolds in 1981, setting up his own Glass Studio in one of the restored mills on the river Frome near Stroud in Gloucestershire. Reid's methods produce structures of great authority. He is a master at creating textural contrasts in glass, setting off his polished surfaces with crystalline areas of coruscated form.

Different Hats II, 2005, by David Reekie. Supplied by the artist.

Photo of Colin Reid at his studios, New Mills. Supplied and used with permission of the artist

Untitled cast book form #R1283, by Colin Reid, 2005. In private collection. Supplied by the artist

Untitled spiral form #R226,
by Colin Reid, 1987. In private
collection. Supplied by the artist

Bamboo Scroll, glass by Colin Reid, Shanghai Public Library, 1999. Supplied and used with permission of the artist

Although no collector's market exists in the United Kingdom as it does in the United States, there is growing enthusiasm among the general public for studio glass generated mainly by the determination of Museums to acquire beautiful pieces for their collection and show them to advantage. The completion of the Victoria and Albert Museum's Glass Gallery in 1999 gave status to this art form while the opening of Broadfield House near Stourbridge with its engraved glass window by David Prytherch has helped to focus attention on the underestimated skills of the glass blowers of the West Midlands. In Sunderland the International Glass Centre which was completed in 2000 hosts conferences and exhibitions of architectural and studio glass, keeping alive a tradition of glass making which began in that area in the 12th century. The most recent centre for glass studies, North Lands Creative Glass, was set up near the town of Leibster in the far north of Scotland. Every year the centre hosts a number of study days run by artists of international renown.

'One Who Disappeared', stipple engraved goblet by James Denison-Pender, 2005. Supplied by the artist

'Epstein Bronze at Glenkiln', stipple engraved goblet by James Denison-Pender, 2005. Supplied by the artist

'The Old Church', stipple engraved goblet by James Denison-Pender, 2005. Supplied by the artist

XIV

North American Architectural Glass

'America Windows', 1977, by Marc Chagall
in collaboration with Charles Marc.
© The Art Institute of Chicago

XIV

North American Architectural Glass

By the time Tiffany Studios closed in 1931, secular stained glass had largely fallen from favour. Grand architectural gestures, opulently embellished with historical motifs, no longer seemed appropriate for a new century that sought to distance itself from the past. During the Great Depression of the 1930s and early 1940s, the construction of such ornate buildings was no longer feasible. 'Ornament is crime' declared Adolf Loos, one of the pioneer architects of the Modern Movement that swept North America during the 1950s. In the 'less is more' philosophy of Modernism, glass was reserved for form-defining curtain walls of complete transparency.

Stained glass continued being made for churches by professional firms that produced windows in traditional styles. Even so, by mid-century figural representation was gradually supplanted by more symbolic abstract designs. *Dalle de verre* windows of chunky coloured glass set in concrete or epoxy, a technique developed in France in the 1920s, were first introduced in North America in 1939 at Sainte Anne de Beaupré, near Québec City. In 1955, the vivid dalle de verre windows by the French artist Gabriel Loire at the First Presbyterian Church of Stamford, Connecticut, were widely acclaimed and inspired numerous imitations. High-profile installations by European artists, such as Marc Chagall's 1964 memorial to Dag Hammarskjöld at the United Nations building in New York, set important precedents for stained glass in prestigious, non-ecclesiastical settings. A few years later, the Art Institute of Chicago commissioned Chagall to create 'America Windows' to celebrate the nation's Bicentennial.

By the 1970s, however, there was a marked renewal of enthusiasm for stained glass as a secular artistic medium, due to several factors. The counterculture of the 1960s celebrated the handmade object as an authentic medium of self-expression and with the revival of interest in the crafts, adult education centres began to provide instruction in stained glass. A number of small independent studios were set up, although few progressed beyond the level of hobbyists making suncatchers. For those that did, further instruction could be found at university, as the excitement generated by the revolution in blown glass stimulated interest in flat glass as well, resulting in the establishment of graduate-level curricula. Growing awareness of the importance of historic preservation resulted in the rediscovery of earlier stained glass windows, often covered over for decades. In just one example, during the recent restoration of the 1916 Pantages Theater in Minneapolis a stained glass skylight was discovered painted grey behind a false ceiling. Windows and panels of 'antique' stained glass were restored, admired and widely collected, becoming so valuable that they sometimes pilfered from vacant houses or poorly guarded mausoleums.

Finally, 'Percent for Art' programmes brought large-scale commissions for glass in civic buildings as well as public recognition and visibility for stained glass artists. These programmes, instituted from the 1970s onward at city, county or state levels, required that a set percentage (usually 1%) of the construction budget for new or restored government buildings be dedicated to public art. According to the Oregon Arts Commission, for example, the 'Percent for Art Program remains dedicated to the enhancement of public environments and improvement of the character and quality of State buildings in order to create an accessible, publicly owned legacy which is uplifting, enduring and available to all'. Percent for Art projects are usually site-specific and may involve a variety of media – painting, mosaic, glass, textiles, sculpture, and other works that are integrated into infrastructure or architecture. Artworks are usually commissioned or selected by a committee made up of citizens, users of the proposed building (i.e., government employees), architects and design professionals. Durability, security, low maintenance and wide appeal are frequent issues with public art, and glass, when properly designed and installed, easily meets all these criteria.

A small group of inspirational artists and teachers in the 1960s and 1970s were powerful catalysts in the revival of stained glass. Among these, Robert Sowers and Albinas Elskus stand out as particularly influential. After studying in Florida and New York City, Sowers (1923-1990) was awarded a Fulbright Fellowship in 1950 to travel in Europe, where he was deeply impressed by the progressive stained glass in churches and

Stained glass ceiling, 1916, Pantages Theater, Minneapolis. Photograph by George Heinrich

other buildings restored or constructed after the war. One of his major commissions after his return to New York was the 317-foot-long abstract stained glass façade for the American Airlines Terminal constructed at Kennedy airport in 1960. Sowers was widely respected for his seminal publications on stained glass, including *The Lost Art* (1963) and *Stained Glass, an Architectural Art* (1965), and is credited with bringing the work of such Post-war German masters as Ludwig Schaffrath and Johannes Schreiter to the attention of American artists. The influence of the German school can be seen in the subtle modulations of colour and expressive lead lines of Sowers' window for the Stephen Wise Free Synagogue, New York City, of 1975.

Born in Lithuania in 1926, Albinas Elskus studied first in his native land and subsequently in Germany and France before immigrating to the United States in 1949. He taught at the Parson's School of Design in New York and at Pilchuck, and is the author of *The Art of Painting on Glass* (1980), considered by many to be the standard source on glass painting techniques. His work combines exquisite painting with a strong commitment to architectural structure. Although he had many commissions for ecclesiastical glass, he also created autonomous panels meant to be displayed like paintings. In 'Metamorphosis' of 1979, an illusion of three-dimensionality is assembled when the panel is 'read'

from top to bottom. 'Homage to Pontormo' reproduces a portrait by a Renaissance master in a photo-realist style while paying tribute to the underlying geometry of figural representation. In his small exhibition panel 'Eve and the Apple', the undulating contours of the delicately rendered torso contrasts with the pure geometry of the lead lines and areas of silver stain.

Today, spectacular architectural glass can be found in many places across North America – in hospitals, transit stations, libraries, shopping centres, playgrounds, corporate offices, concert halls, schools and many other locations. Suppliers, retailers and professional organisations, including the Stained Glass Association of America and Artists in Stained Glass in Canada, are plentiful. While fewer artists now use the traditional method of assembling pieces of coloured glass with lead came, new techniques have multiplied exponentially. New varieties of thin-filmed reflective or mirror glass, as well as innovative techniques for edge-bonding toughened glass and bolt-fixing it to structural supports, have transformed the technology of architectural glass, allowing creative applications previously unimagined.

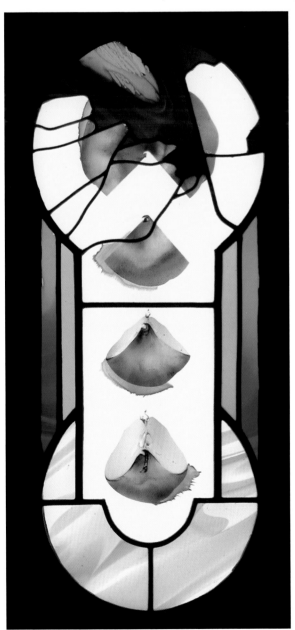

'Metamorphosis', 1979, by Albinas Elskus. Courtesy of the Stained Glass Museum, Ely, England.

Divine Geometry

Stylistic approaches to architectural glass are equally diverse. A number of glass artists working today have extended the geometric tradition pioneered in America by Frank Lloyd Wright. Using innovative fabrication techniques, many of these artists create site-specific three-dimensional works as well as flat glass for windows. The work of Ed Carpenter (b.1946) is exemplary in this regard. Born in Los Angeles, he was educated at the University of California, Berkeley. In the 1970s, after first studying stained glass design and technique with Patrick Reyntiens in Buckinghamshire, England, Carpenter apprenticed himself to Ludwig Schaffrath. The impress of his German mentor is apparent in a comparison between a small leaded-glass panel by Schaffrath and Carpenter's 30 foot arched window for the lobby of the Portland Justice Center, executed in 1983. In both works, light plays across a geometric grid, with pyramidal cast or bevelled pieces adding texture and sparkle. The entry lobby of the Justice Center incorporates a dramatic barrel vault, the western end of which is fully glazed. It frames a park of tall trees touched by changing effects of light, especially at dusk and sunset. Rather than coloured glass, Carpenter prefers to use a variety of clear glass – leaded, handblown, plate and fused – to modulate light, taking colour from the sky, from reflections of objects outside and from the changes of weather and the seasons.

Leaded glass panel, 1968, by Ludwig Schaffrath From the Collection of The Corning Glass Museum, NY. Bequest of Robert Sowers in memory of Theresa Obermayr Sowers

Opposite Page:
West lobby window, Justice Center, Portland, Oregon, 1983, by Ed Carpenter. Photographed by Ed Carpenter

In 1990, the central tower of New York City's Rockefeller Center, a national historic landmark, was purchased by a new owner. As part of the restoration of the grand lobbies Carpenter was commissioned to create a series of seven foot high, 400 foot long leaded glass transoms capping the ground floor windows and focusing on the four entries. The jagged geometry of Carpenter's solution integrates seamlessly with the streamlined Art Deco skyscraper, while the interpenetration of leaded, rolled and hand-blown glass conveys a sophisticated contemporary aesthetic at the same time. In 'Skygrass' at West Valley City Community College in Salt Lake City, Utah, Carpenter uses glass in a sculptural manner to project changing light effects across the interior and exterior surfaces of a building. Created collaboratively with Michael McCulloch and John Rogers, the sculpture's large 'V' shaped panels of laminated dichroic coated glass, rising to the full height of the building, reach out to capture and dramatically redirect the brilliant Utah sunlight. As the sun travels in its daily and seasonal paths, a series of enormous stripes of coloured light play off the building, moving across its geometry and creating a complex kinetic solar diagram.

Lobby Transom Windows, 1251 Rockefeller Center, New York City, 1992, by Ed Carpenter. Photographed by Paul Warchol

Lobby Transom Window (detail), 1251 Rockefeller Center, New York City, 1992, by Ed Carpenter. Photographed by Paul Warchol

'Skygrass', the Science and Industry Building, West Valley City Community College, Salt Lake City, Utah, 1994, by Ed Carpenter, Michael McCulloch and John Rogers. Photographed by Ed Carpenter

In 'Lightstream', 2003, glass integrates light and colour into architecture from the inside. Designed to enliven an extremely long space in the expanded Dallas Convention Center, dichroic glass, stainless steel cables and hardware, aluminum extrusions and computerized lighting unite to create a river of glowing light overhead. Streams of soft color pulse in slow waves of illumination, while myriad floating lines suggest surface and depth. Tinted skies roll with swells of luminescence and ever changing patterns of soft, cool color dissolve into one another. Installations that actively manipulate light are described by the artist as 'a game of layering and texturing, obscuring and revealing, and allowing the movement of shadows and light patterns to animate a room, a wall, or a courtyard'. In contrast, 'Springstar', 2004, is a completely independent gateway sculpture isolated on a traffic island at the entrance to a large office and warehouse complex in Santa Fe Springs, California. Made of aluminum masts, laminated dichroic glass, stainless steel cables, concrete, copper, internal and external flood lighting, the sculpture references images of a large unfolding desert flower, a fountain or a falling star.

'Springstar', Golden Springs Industrial Park, Los Angeles County, California, 2004, by Ed Carpenter. Photographed by Ed Carpenter

Opposite Page:
'Lightstream', Dallas Convention Center Expansion, Dallas, Texas, 2003, by Ed Carpenter. Photographed by Ed Carpenter & John Rogers

Although the artist David Wilson (b.1941) also embraces the grid, he treats the window like a two-dimensional surface through which the third dimension can break through. He uses transparency, colour and texture to alternately open up, transform or block the view. Born in Britain, he trained at the Central School of Arts and Crafts before immigrating to the United States in 1963 and becoming the head of a major stained glass studio in New York City. During his time there he befriended Robert Sowers and also saw an exhibition of stained glass windows by Frank Lloyd Wright, which he described as 'an eyeopener'. In Wilson's glass screens for a private house in Peapack, New Jersey, the influence of Wright is apparent in the choice of motifs similar to the Native American arrow motifs and rectilinear flowers of Wright's Prairie School period. In his recent work, Wilson applies an austere Minimalist sensibility to the time-honoured techniques of leaded glass. At first glance his 'Wavewall', made for the Corning Corporation in New York in 2000, could be misperceived as a simple undulating grid reflected in a mirror along its length. Close observation reveals that every lead and bar of colour has been placed as precisely as in a composition by Mondrian. Subtle shifts of colour, texture and line engage the eye almost indefinitely. On a smaller, domestic scale, a similar design creates a elegant entry for a private apartment.

Vagelos House, Peapack, New Jersey, 1992, by David Wilson. Photographed by Richard Walker

Window, Nations Bank Building, Atlanta, Georgia, 1992, by David Wilson. Photographed by Richard Walker

'Wavewall', Corning Incorporated,
New York, 2000, by David Wilson.
Photograph © David Sundberg/Esto

'Wavewall' (detail), Corning Incorporated,
New York, 2000, by David Wilson.
Photograph © David Sundberg/Esto

Hallway, Hampshire House apartment,
New York, 2000, by David Wilson.
Photographed by David Wilson

Wilson's monumental projects are equally effective. For the North East Corridor Monorail Station at Newark's Liberty International Airport, he designed great slashing diagonals of colored and textured glass that accelerate the sensation of forward movement. These are framed by grids of clear bevelled cubes that scatter the light from their prismatic surfaces, while bars and tiny squares of colour create a counterpoint of syncopated pattern. His rich vocabulary of materials also includes mouth-blown antique German and French glass, as well as small accent pieces of dichroic glass. Like the stained glass in a medieval cathedral, the densely packed, complex design of his window wall for the Stamford Courthouse, Stamford, Connecticut, bathes the interior spaces and surfaces with patterns and colours that move slowly throughout the day. 'I see the art and craft of stained glass capable of endless reinvention', Wilson has written. 'In fact, this reinvention of an ancient and traditional process along with the manipulation of light is the root of my love for this medium.'

North East Corridor Monorail Station, Newark Liberty International Airport, Port Authority of New York and New Jersey, Newark, New Jersey, 2002, by David Wilson. Photographed by David Wilson

Stamford Courthouse, Stamford, Connecticut, 2002, by David Wilson, a project of the State of Connecticut Commission on the Arts. Photographed by Richard Walker

A Passion For Paint

In contrast to geometric forms of abstraction, Linda Lichtman (b.1941) takes a painterly approach to architectural glass. She initially trained as a social worker before turning to art, and in the early 1970s she earned a B.F.A. in painting from the Massachusetts College of Art and studied with Patrick Reyntiens at Burleighfield House in England. Her work combines vivid luminosity of colour, achieved through painting, staining and laminating, with the eloquent human gesture. She often paints directly on the surface without preparation or design sketches, treating the glass as a transparent canvas upon which strongly expressive marks are recorded. Although she prefers vigour and simplicity over exquisite refinement, she adds delicacy and sometimes representative imagery through a variety of subtractive techniques like acid etching and engraving. For her 1991 window, 'Tree of Knowledge, Tree of Light', for a branch library in Brookline, Massachusetts, she used acid-etched stained glass and float glass, leaded and laminated, along with vitreous paints, enamels and silver stain to create blocks of colour patterned with abstract vegetative forms.

In 'Images of the Charter Oak (Quercus Alba)', a stained glass installation surrounding the front entrance of Charter Oak State College in New Britain, Connecticut, Lichtman incorporated the symbolic oak leaf at the client's request. The coloured glass is translucent, allowing light to filter into the space, and the rich jewel-toned hues have been washed onto the glass like watercolour paints onto wet paper. The areas of clear glass integrate the artwork with the clear glass doors and windows above and allow light to enter the lobby. 'Changes and Variations on the Theme of Growth', located at the headquarters of Connecticut State University in West Hartford, treats similar themes of evolution and transformation in the realm of the intellect as well as the natural world. It is a two-part installation – on the ground floor painted glass panels flank the entranceway, while the second site is a ribbon of windows on the first floor. Vigorous black brush strokes outlining shapes of leafy growth are scribbled on top of mottled colours that suggest the cycle of the seasons.

'Images of the Charter Oak (Quercus Alba)', Charter Oak State College, New Britain, Connecticut, 1999, by Linda Lichtman. Supplied by the artist

'Tree of Knowledge, Tree of Light', Coolidge Corner Branch, Brookline Public Library, Brookline, Massachusetts, 1991, by Linda Lichtman. Supplied by the artist

'Images of the Charter Oak (Quercus Alba)' (detail), Charter Oak State College, New Britain, Connecticut, 1999, by Linda Lichtman. Supplied by the artist

'Changes and Variations on the Theme of Growth', Connecticut State University Headquarters, West Hartford, Connecticut, 2001, by Linda Lichtman. Supplied by the artist

'Changes and Variations on the Theme of Growth' (detail), Connecticut State University Headquarters, West Hartford, Connecticut, 2001, by Linda Lichtman. Supplied by the artist

When an old music hall was renovated into a new courthouse in Lewiston, Maine, Lichtman was commissioned to create 'The City on the River', an eight-part installation that appears in various locations throughout the building. The theme of the work is the state's distinctive natural environment. The deep blues of the background, sandblasted to create texture, represent the sky, ocean and the Androscoggin River while the dynamic green brushstrokes suggest the needles of the state tree, the White Pine. 'A Kind of Blue-Green', created in 2002 for the Hitchner Hall Biology Building at the University of Maine in Orono, plays with the various associations the colours evoke – from blue-green algae to 'Kind of Blue', the jazz album by Miles Davis. Inscribed along the borders of the panels are names of famous biologists from Maine and the Latin names of plants and animals that are native to the state. One of Lichtman's recent projects is 'Totems of Light', 2004, for the Airport Station of Boston's subway system that serves both Logan Airport and the neighbourhood of East Boston. The installation is in two parts. The east window faces the sea as well as the airport; here the imagery evokes the ocean, the sky and the marshlands now covered by the asphalt runways of the airport. The west window faces densely settled East Boston and uses bright colours and playful shapes to evoke the liveliness of this multi-cultural community. In addition to her site-specific public art, Lichtman also creates glass paintings of brilliant luminosity.

'The City on River' (detail), Lewiston District Courthouse, Lewiston, Maine, 2002, by Linda Lichtman. Supplied by the artist

'The City on River', Lewiston District Courthouse, Lewiston, Maine, 2002, by Linda Lichtman. Supplied by the artist

'A Kind of Blue-Green', Hitchner Hall
Biology Building, University of Maine,
Orono, 2002, by Linda Lichtman.
Supplied by the artist

'A Kind of Blue-Green' (detail), Hitchner
Hall Biology Building, University of
Maine, Orono, 2002, by Linda Lichtman.
Supplied by the artist

Top-Left:
*'Totems of Light' (East Window), Logan
Airport MBTA Station, Boston,
Massachusetts, 2004, by Linda Lichtman.
Supplied by the artist*

Above:
*'Totems of Light' (East Window – Close
View), Logan Airport MBTA Station, Boston,
Massachusetts, 2004, by Linda Lichtman.
Supplied by the artist*

Left:
*'Totems of Light' (West Window), Logan
Airport MBTA Station, Boston,
Massachusetts, 2004, by Linda Lichtman.
Supplied by the artist*

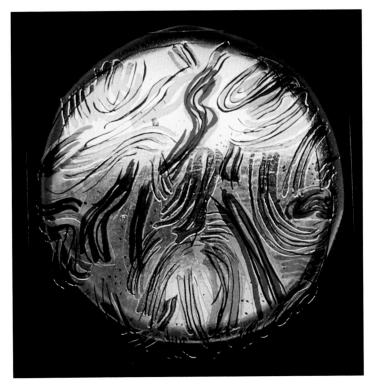

Above:

*'Totems of Light' (West Window - detail),
Logan Airport MBTA Station, Boston,
Massachusetts, 2004, by Linda Lichtman.
Supplied by the artist*

Top-Right:

*'Color Landscape', 2004, glass painting
by Linda Lichtman. Supplied by the artist*

Right:

*'Laguna Dream', 2004, glass painting by
Linda Lichtman. Supplied by the artist*

The abstract style of artist Narcissus Quagliata (b.1942) can best be described as explosively intense and colourful. Born in Rome, Quagliata studied painting first with the Italian Surrealist Giorgio de Chirico and later, at the San Francisco Art Institute, with the Abstract Expressionist Richard Diebenkorn. He now resides in Mexico, but also works in the United States and in Europe. He recently installed a stained glass dome in the rotunda of the Basilica of Santa Maria degli Angeli in Rome, a building adapted by Michelangelo in the 1560s from the Baths of the Emperor Diocletian. For a new mixed-use office building in the heart of Mexico City, Quagliata designed the vivid 'Retorno al Cosmos'. Ignoring the grid of lead lines, this vast explosion of flowing colours evokes the 'Big Bang' of cosmic creation or destruction.

The artist Peter Mollica (b.1941) practices a different form of painterly abstraction. Born in Newton, Massachusetts, he served a four-year apprenticeship to the stained glass artist Christy Rufo during the late 1960s and travelled throughout England, France, Germany and Denmark to examine ancient and modern stained glass windows. In 1971 he published *Stained Glass Primer: a handbook of stained glass technique* (reprinted 1987), followed in 1977 with Stained Glass Primer, *Vol. 2: Advanced Skills and Annotated Bibliography* (reprinted 1982). He spent the summer of 1975 working with Ludwig Schaffrath in Germany and England. He and his family now live in California.

Retorno al Cosmos', Reforma 115,
Mexico City, 2005, by Narcissus Quagliata.
Supplied by the artist

'Retorno al Cosmos', Reforma 115, Mexico
City, 2005, by Narcissus Quagliata.
Supplied by the artist

In Mollica's work, amorphous shapes of streaky glass framed with wavering lead lines often seem to float ambiguously in space. In his architectural installations, this floating effect is intensified when his work is surrounded by the clear glass required for interior illumination. The influence of his German mentor can be felt in the irregular contours of the long crimson forms in his window in the Hollywood Branch Library in Portland, Oregon. While these nebulous shapes may reference a row of books on a shelf, they also suggest the hovering forms of such abstract expressionist painters of the 1970s as Adolph Gottlieb or Robert Motherwell. In his windows elsewhere in the same building, whimsical triangular shapes supported by 'columns' play off the gables and porches of the houses seen through the glass.

'Self-Portrait #7', 1987, by Peter Mollica.
Supplied by the artist

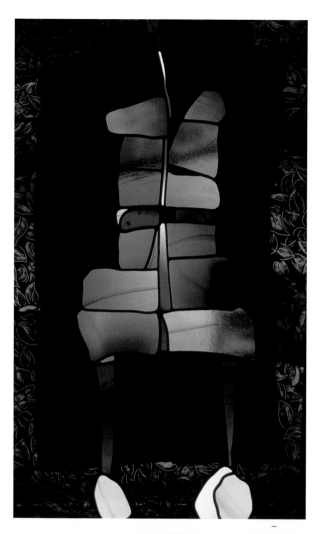

'Self-Portrait #9', 1987, by Peter Mollica. Supplied by the artist

Window, Hollywood Branch Library, Portland, Oregon, 2002, by Peter Mollica. Supplied by the artist

*Reading Room and Meeting Room
windows, Hollywood Branch Library,
Portland, Oregon, 2002, by Peter
Mollica. Supplied by the artist*

In 2004, for the Northside Community Center in San José, California, Mollica created windows flanking the entry and other small windows in various parts of the building. The Center serves the Filipino community and the architects wished to incorporate distinctly Philippine cultural elements into the structure. Mollica's stained glass represents the colourful sails of a 'vinta', a boat used by Muslims, and the background is made of translucent capiz shells, reminiscent of windows found in many older Philippine homes. For the Millbrae Public Library in 2004, Mollica created stained glass 'spandrels' for the windows above the stacks. In daylight, the irregular squares appear turquoise against the daylight outside. At night, the same squares are transformed into gold under artificial illumination.

Entranceway, Northside Community Center,
San José, California, 2004, by Peter Mollica.
Supplied by the artist

Entranceway (detail), Northside Community Center, San José, California, 2004, by Peter Mollica. Supplied by the artist

Above:

Window (daylight), Millbrae Public Library, Millbrae, California, 2004, by Peter Mollica. Supplied by the artist

Left:

Window (night), Millbrae Public Library, Millbrae, California, 2004, by Peter Mollica. Supplied by the artist

Figures and Stories

Although abstraction might seem a natural partner for modern architecture, the figural tradition of stained glass painting is also alive and well, if somewhat on the edge of the mainstream. The glass paintings of Cappy Thompson (b.1952) tell magical stories through completely pictorial means; she does not engage in such issues as, for example, the exploration of the lead line as an expressive design element. Thompson came to glass from a background as a painter and printmaker and became fascinated by the medium during an internship at a stained glass studio while attending Evergreen State College. She calls her paintings 'picture poems', equating them with the fairy tales she heard as a child, and strives to create the same emotional resonance for the viewer. 'My emotions are stirred by such things as naïve, symbolic drawings, flat perspectives, and dream-like qualities found in primitive painting and in outsider and folk art', Thompson has said. 'Magic is in the wildly imaginative mythic figures, jewel-toned landscapes, and anthropomorphised animals of Persian miniatures and Indian painting.'

Thompson's early panels were based on European mythology, fables and folktales. Her 1992 paintings of 'Aesop's Fables' are alive with colour and wit, completely filling the allotted space with anecdote in the stylised manner of a medieval artist. A large interior partition for a private residence, completed in 2002, is called 'Muses Bestowing Blessings on the Pacific Northwest'. Made up of twelve panels, the composition depicts the Muses as crowned flying angels, dropping blessings on a fortunate couple below who drink wine in a gazebo by the ocean, accompanied by a musician plucking a cello. The painting is largely in *grisaille*, or tones of grey, a medieval technique that is a favourite of the artist.

'Aesop's Fables', 1992, by Cappy Thompson.
Photograph by Dick Busher

Top-Left:
'The Fox and the Grapes' from 'Aesop's Fables', 1992,
by Cappy Thompson. Photograph by Michael Seidl

Bottom-Left:
'The Lion and the Mouse' from 'Aesop's Fables', 1992,
by Cappy Thompson. Photograph by Michael Seidl

Top-Right:
'The North Wind and the Sun' from 'Aesop's Fables', 1992,
by Cappy Thompson. Photograph by Michael Seidl

Bottom-Right:
'The Milkmaid and her Pail' from 'Aesop's Fables', 1992,
by Cappy Thompson. Photograph by Michael Seidl

'Muses Bestowing Blessings on the Pacific Northwest',
private residence, Medina, Washington, 2003, by
Cappy Thompson. Photograph by Spike Mafford

In 2003, Thompson was commissioned by the Museum of Glass in Tacoma, Washington, to create 'Gathering the Light', a mural of reverse-painted vitreous enamels on mouth-blown glass, laminated to stainless steel panels. The subject is an allegory of the museum and the glass world, with muses showering inspiration upon a mythical land of glassmakers. From an island populated by glass artists, craftsmen, arriving visitors, and even a glass-collecting mermaid, a footbridge leads to a Temple of the Muses, an allusion to the Museum of Glass. By far her most monumental work to date is 'I was Dreaming of Spirit Animals…', a glass window wall 33 feet long and 90 feet tall completed in 2003 for the new south terminal of the Seattle-Tacoma International Airport. The mural, commissioned by the Port of Seattle, consists of 63 approximately 5 by 9 foot units painted with vitreous enamels. It depicts a couple asleep in a tower, while behind them the animals in the constellations of the Northern Hemisphere glow in the arc of the night sky. The mythical horses Pegasus and Equilius draw a chariot bearing the Sun and the Moon, who sprinkle stars upon the dreamers and travellers below.

'Gathering the Light', Museum of Glass, Tacoma, Washington, 2003, by Cappy Thompson. Photograph by Spike Mafford

'Gathering the Light' (detail: 'Temple of the Muses'), by Cappy Thompson. Photograph by Spike Mafford

'Gathering the Light' (detail: self-portrait of Thompson painting a vessel), by Cappy Thompson. Photograph by Spike Mafford

'Gathering the Light' (detail: glass blower), by Cappy Thompson. Photograph by Spike Mafford

'Gathering the Light' (detail: mermaid), by Cappy Thompson. Photograph by Spike Mafford

'I was Dreaming of Spirit Animals…', Seattle-Tacoma International Airport, 2003, by Cappy Thompson. Photograph by Russell Johnson

'I was Dreaming of Spirit Animals…' (detail), by Cappy Thompson. Photograph by Russell Johnson

'I was Dreaming of Spirit Animals…' (detail), by Cappy Thompson. Photograph by Russell Johnson

Although not, strictly speaking, an artist in architectural glass, Judith Schaechter (b.1961) is impossible to overlook in the evolution of figural stained glass. Schaechter draws on many of the same sources as Cappy Thompson, including imagery from the middle ages, from folk art and from the natural world. But there any similarity ends, for her work is as unsettling in its content as it is exquisite in execution. During her training as a painter at the Rhode Island School of Design, Schaechter took an elective course on stained glass with Ursula Huth. Overwhelmed by anxiety when confronted by the blank canvas in the painting studio, she felt liberated by the craft demands of the new medium and less pressure to produce 'High Art'. She now lives and works in Philadelphia, creating about ten to twelve panels a year, most of which portray images of sex, death, violence, panic, despair and terror that resonate with contemporary life. In 'Haemophelia' for example, a female figure in quasi-ecclesiastical dress (a self-portrait) stands in a niche within a stained glass window. Her hands clutch at the blood that drains from her body while she peers up in dread at the hand of a doctor feeling for a dying pulse.

'Dream of the Fisherman's Wife', 2004,
by Judith Schaechter. Supplied by the artist

'Haemophilia', 2004, by Judith Schaechter.
Supplied by the artist

Opposite Page:
*Pale Oval', 1999, by Judith Schaechter.
Supplied by the artist*

'Wreck of the Isabelle A',
2004, by Judith Schaechter.
Supplied by the artist

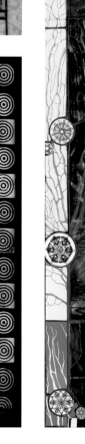

'Bigtop Flophouse Bedspin',
2001, by Judith Schaechter.
Supplied by the artist

Schaechter's themes are painstakingly rendered in flash glass, usually in tones of warm red, orange and flesh with blue and yellow. The glass is cut, sandblasted, engraved and filed, then painted with enamels and cold paint and assembled copper foil. Although many find it disconcerting and uncomfortable, her work is unquestionably stunning in its visual appeal. 'Beauty', according to the artist, 'is considered the most horrible crime you can commit in the modern art world. People are suspicious of anything that makes them feel as though they may lose control. Beauty forces you to confront your helplessness as well as your dark side. My work is not intended to make comfortable people unhappy, although it may make unhappy people comfortable'. She is the only stained glass artist whose work has been selected for inclusion in a prestigious Whitney Biennial, a survey of American art in 2002. This was seen by many as a significant, long-overdue mark of recognition of stained glass by the 'establishment' as equal in value to other forms of contemporary art.

'Rejects', 2000, by Judith Schaechter.
Supplied by the artist

Creative Technologies

The work of some artists defies categorisation as it encompasses many different forms of expression, including abstraction and representation, depending on the context. One example is Stephen Knapp (b.1947), who exploits glass in a number of innovative ways made possible by new techniques. His lightpaintings and floating light sculptures are completely abstract, while his kiln-formed and mixed-media pieces can be abstract or representational, depending upon the client's wishes. Born in Worcester, Massachusetts, Knapp received a Liberal Arts degree from Hamilton College in 1969. For ten years he worked as a fine art photographer, working increasingly with designers and architects to create large site-specific photo installations in etched metal or porcelain enamel applied to steel. Through these complex experiments he became interested in creating images in glass and developed industrial techniques for creating large-scale kiln-formed glass – sheets of glass that, when heated, would 'slump' or mould themselves to a form below. He began to create tempered kiln-formed art glass walls and doors that were strong enough for use in architectural settings.

Kiln-formed Glass Walls, Harnischfeger Industries, Milwaukee, Wisconsin, 1996, by Stephen Knapp. Supplied by the artist

Opposite Page:

'Chicago's Treasures', CNA Insurance Companies, Chicago, 1998, by Stephen Knapp. Supplied by the artist

'Fragments of Time', Splendour of the Seas ship, Royal Caribbean Cruise Lines, 1996, by Stephen Knapp. Supplied by the artist

In 1996 Knapp created a series of kiln-formed tempered-glass walls for Harnischfeger Industries, a corporation located on the edge of Lake Michigan in Milwaukee, Wisconsin, that produces heavy equipment for mining and material handling. The translucent walls interpret this industry with abstract images of gears, mechanical elements and movement, while the dramatic light of Lake Michigan is captured by the irregular textures and patterns created by the process. Completely different is 'Fragments of Time', a 1996 mixed-media installation of black kiln-formed glass and marble commissioned for a Royal Caribbean Cruise ship. Working with a theme of Greek and Roman exploration, he created a series of 'ruined' columns and steles with hieroglyphs and faces, that support large overlapping sheets of kiln-formed glass. Greek and Roman temples, ships, and relics of antiquity appear in relief on the glass. In 1998 he authored *The Art of Glass*, about glass in public places (reprinted 2000), and the same year completed 'Chicago's Treasures', an art glass wall for CNA Insurance Companies that represents images from the city – landmarks, public buildings, sculpture – that viewers can touch and identify.

Knapp's work quickly gained international renown and he has received numerous architectural commissions. These include 'The Crystal Quilt' for Love Library at the University of Nebraska, which houses an original Shakespeare Folio, a curving wall of kiln-formed glass for the Congregation of St. Agnes in Fond du Lac, Wisconsin and 'The Christ Doors' for the Solanus Casey Center, a pilgrimage site and museum for the Capuchin religious order in Detroit, Michigan. In addition to pioneering kiln forming, Knapp has also created a series of kinetic light sculptures that add the dimension of movement and shadow to his work. 'Stories from Light – Told and Untold – A Continuous Journey', for the Women and Babies Hospital of Lancaster, Pennsylvania, creates a rainbow ceiling in the central rotunda. In the centre, a group of sculptural images of women, made from stainless steel and dichroic glass, revolve slowly in space, casting ever-changing shadows of intense colour.

'The Crystal Quilt' (3 of 18 panels), Love Library, University of Nebraska, Lincoln, 2001, by Stephen Knapp. Supplied by the artist

Kiln-formed Glass Walls, Congregation of St. Agnes, Fond du Lac, Wisconsin, 2002, by Stephen Knapp. Supplied by the artist

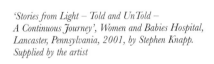

'Stories from Light – Told and UnTold – A Continuous Journey', Women and Babies Hospital, Lancaster, Pennsylvania, 2001, by Stephen Knapp. Supplied by the artist

'The Christ Doors', Solanus Casey Center, Detroit, 2002, by Stephen Knapp. Supplied by the artist

Another glass artist of astonishing versatility is the Canadian Lutz Haufschild (b.1943). Although he moved to Canada in the 1970s, he was born in Germany and trained at the Advanced Institute of Art and Technology in Hanover, where he was a student of Johannes Schreiter and a teaching assistant to Jochem Poensgen. As a result, Haufschild's work is steeped in the modern German tradition. His panel of 1986 with outsized letters spelling 'GLASS' is a tribute to Schreiter and a celebration of the sensuous beauty of mouth-blown 'antique' glass.

His architectural commissions are often monumental in scale, such as his best known work, 'The Wave' of 1996 for the departure lounge of Vancouver International Airport. This installation is 35 feet high and 135 feet in length, consists of thousands of tiny pieces of glass set on edge between sheets of clear glass so that they sparkle in the sun. The effect is of a massive seascape crested above the viewer's head and poised to engulf him.

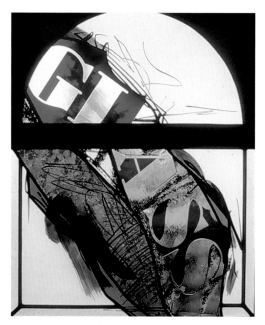

Panel, 1986, by Lutz Haufschild, Museum of Contemporary Glass Art, Langen, Germany. Supplied by the artist

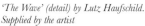

'The Wave' (detail) by Lutz Haufschild. Supplied by the artist

'The Wave', departure lounge, Vancouver International Airport, 1996, by Lutz Haufschild. Supplied by the artist

Haufschild's work is always a response to the architectural context, rather than a statement of an individual style. In his work for the Bata Shoe Museum in Toronto he created a shimmering veil of delicate pattern that backgrounds itself to the structure and clarity of the architecture. Called 'Spectra Veil', the huge screens of bevelled glass dissolve in light, with only a thin diagonal line of colour to indicate the location of the plane. In a similar vein, his transparent bevelled screens called 'Light in Equipoise', for a private residence in Ottawa, separate the sky-lit foyer from the private areas of the house, sliding open when guests are entertained. In a completely different vein, 'Taunus Sail' for the City Hall in Taunusstein, Germany, is a commanding work of painterly abstraction in bright primary colours, suspended overhead with steel cables. Yet another mode is expressed in Haufschild's autonomous panels, 'Blue Heart' and 'Questions of the Heart'. These seem to draw inspiration from the work of Pop Art figures like Robert Indiana, while rendering a simple image in a more ambiguous and complex way.

What's next for architectural glass? The possibilities have just begun to be explored.

'Spectra Veil' (detail), by Lutz Haufschild.
Supplied by the artist

'Spectra Veil', Bata Shoe Museum,
Toronto, 1995, by Lutz Haufschild.
Supplied by the artist

'Light in Equipoise', Potter residence,
Ottawa, by Lutz Haufschild.
Supplied by the artist

'Taunus Sail', City Hall, Taunusstein, Germany, 1998, by Lutz Haufschild. Supplied by the artist

'Blue Heart', private collection, New Delhi, India, by Lutz Haufschild. Supplied by the artist

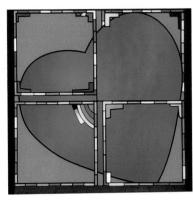

'Questions of the Heart', Canadian Museum of Civilization, Ottawa, by Lutz Haufschild. Supplied by the artist

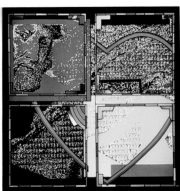

XV
The Czech Connection

The Czech Connection

Because of an abundance of raw materials, the region of central Europe known historically as Bohemia has been a major centre of glassmaking since the Middle Ages. Many of the basic decorative techniques of the craft, such as cutting, engraving, enamelling and gilding, were developed there by the area's renowned artisans, who were often lured away to factories in other countries. In the mid-19th century glass schools and apprenticeship programs were established and a thriving cottage industry grew up for hand-working small batches of glass for jewellery and other uses. From the 1890s, the production of shimmering iridescent glass in the Art Nouveau style was pioneered by the firm of Loetz Witwe in Klöstermuhle (see Chapter 2). The independent republic of Czechoslovakia was founded in 1918 and its capital, Prague, became a sophisticated urban centre where artists explored the major European art movements, including Expressionism, Symbolism, and Surrealism. Cubism, especially, had a strong impact on architecture, sculpture and the applied arts, including glass.

Czechoslovakia's artistic connections with Europe were ruptured by the Second World War. With the establishment of a new socialist government the glass industry was nationalised, and the country's tradition of excellence in glass was recognised as an important symbol of national cultural achievement. The government established Arts and Crafts centres where experimental artistic work in glass could be fostered, while at the same time restricting the practice of other arts – painting, sculpture, graphics and film – to the limitations of Soviet-style Social Realism.

Among the pioneers of artistic glass in Czechoslovakia, Stanislav Libenský (1921-2004) and Jaroslava Brychtová (b.1924) are internationally revered both as gifted artists and inspiring teachers. Born in Sezemice, Libenský studied for four years at the School of Decorative Arts in Prague (re-named the Academy of Applied Arts in 1945). He then settled in Nový Bor where he worked as a designer in a government glass factory and as a painting instructor at the local Secondary School for Glassmaking. In 1963, he became the director of the glass studio at the Academy of Applied Arts in Prague, remaining there until 1987. The daughter of a distinguished sculptor, Jaroslava Brychtová grew up in Zelezný Brod before moving to Prague to study sculpture at the Academy of Fine Arts, where she chose glass as her medium. From 1950 until 1984 she was head of the Department of Architectural Glass in the glass factory in her home town. The couple met in the mid-1950s and married in 1962. The work produced during their long careers, as individual practitioners and as collaborating partners, was both ground-breaking in its significance and reflective of the country's shifting political forces.

Libenský's early glass was in the vessel tradition, enriched with figural and religious imagery enamelled in pale colours and delicately etched with a technique similar to dry-point printmaking. For his blown-glass bowl, 'Expulsion from Paradise' of 1948, texture and shading were created with etched lines of extraordinary delicacy, with highlights added in transparent enamels. For an artist still in his twenties, the expressive elegance of this technique is astonishing in its refinement. But by the late 1940s, such scriptural subjects were prohibited by the Communist regime and these lyrical religious pieces could not be shown and were packed away.

After meeting and deciding to work together, the two artists evolved a complimentary working relationship and began to explore glass casting on an intimate scale. Libenský, who considered himself to be fundamentally a painter, created designs and detailed drawings, while Brychtová, the sculptor, translated these into three dimensions. For their first collaborative piece, a shallow bowl of green glass with a human face called 'Miska', Libenský's drawing is a graceful suggestion of form. Brychtová added the luminosity of diffused light in her final sculpted and cast interpretation.

Detail, 'Expulsion from Paradise', 1948, by Stanislav Libenský, Source: ArtForum, www.gallery.cz. With permission Mr. Zahradnik, son of S.Libenský

'Expulsion from Paradise', 1948, by Stanislav Libenský, Source: ArtForum, www.gallery.cz. With permission Mr. Zahradnik, son of S.Libenský

Drawing for 'Miska' (Head Bowl),
1953-54, by Stanislav Libenský.
From the Collection of The Corning
Glass Museum, NY

'Miska' (Head Bowl), 1955-56, by Stanislav Libenský and Jaroslava
Brychtová. Museum of Decorative Arts, Prague. Source: ArtForum,
www.gallery.cz. With permission Mr. Zahradnik, son of Libenský

SF314

During the later 1950s and early 1960s, their work moved away from figural imagery towards greater abstraction. They experimented with slabs of coloured glass set into concrete *dalle de verre* and began to explore abstract cast glass on a larger and larger scale. Although in part this direction was determined by government pressure as abstraction was considered safely 'apolitical', they also drew on the strong tradition of Czech Cubism as well as other movements in contemporary art. During a period of liberalisation artists were able to learn about Abstract Expressionism, Conceptualism, Minimalism, Neo-Constructivism, Op-Art, and even performance art, although they were still isolated from the west.

For 'Lap' of 1965, Libenský and Brychtová abandoned the vessel form for a complete integration of painting and sculpture, resulting in a thinly cast but robust relief over a meter in height. Determined to make an impressive showing at the 1967 Montreal World Exposition (Expo '67), the government commissioned three relief sculptures for the Czech pavilion. One of these, 'Blue Concretion', was made of 24 sections of back-to-back reliefs in blue glass, mounted in a metal frame about two meters square. The varying thicknesses of the glass modulated the depth of hue, creating a sculptural form that the artists called 'colour in space'. The result was a revelation to North American glass artists, including Dale Chihuly, then a graduate student. At a time when Harvey Littleton and other pioneers of the studio glass movement were making their first tentative steps towards hot-working, Libenský and Brychtová were casting glass on a monumental scale.

'Lap', 1965, by Stanislav Libenský and Jaroslava Brychtová. Source: ArtForum, www.gallery.cz. With permission Mr. Zahradnik, son of S. Libenský

'Blue Concretion', 1966-67, by Stanislav Libenský and Jaroslava Brychtová. Source: ArtForum, www.gallery.cz. With permission Mr. Zahradnik, son of S.Libenský

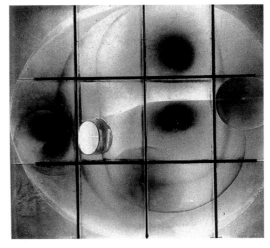

'Lap Study', 1953-54, by Stanislav Libenský, From the Collection of The Corning Glass Museum, NY

The political leniency of 'Prague Spring' ended in August, 1968, with the Soviet invasion, after which life became more difficult for many artists in Czechoslovakia. The Libenskýs stayed busy with numerous large public projects, such as 'Heart/Red Flower', cast in red glass for the Czech embassy in New Delhi, India, in 1976. But the exploration of geometric forms in clear 'optical' glass, such as 'Sphere in a Cube' and 'Cube in a Cube' was more characteristic of their work during the 1970s and early 1980s. The prismatic planes comprising these simple shapes, one enclosed inside another, channel light into and through the small sculptures, changing the view within as the surroundings change.

In addition to their sculptural glass, the Libenskýs carried out numerous architectural projects as well. As early as the mid-1960s, the couple created two windows for the Chapel of Saint Wenceslas, the nation's patron saint, in the 14th Century cathedral of Saint Vitus, within the walls of Prague Castle. For this important public commission they created abstract windows of cast glass in pale colours that created the effect of light filtering through the original stained glass windows of the Gothic period. They returned to the challenge of placing new glass in historic buildings in the early 1990s by creating a series of windows for the Gothic chapel at Libenský Horsovský Týn with bladelike shapes in pastel glass. In clear glass, the window wall of Prague's Old Town Hall is composed of cast half-cylinders, across which a flower-like form emerges and the 'Crystal Window' in Kyoto, Japan, is a triumph of controlled optical distortion.

'Sphere in a Cube', 1970, by Stanislav Libenský and Jaroslava Brychtová. Source: ArtForum, www.gallery.cz. With permission Mr. Zahradnik, son of S.Libenský

'Cube in a Cube', 1983-86, by Stanislav Libenský and Jaroslava Brychtová. Source: ArtForum, www.gallery.cz. With permission Mr. Zahradnik, son of S.Libenský

'Heart/Red Flower', 1976, for the Czech Embassy, New Delhi, India, by Stanislav Libenský and Jaroslava Brychtová. Source: ArtForum, www.gallery.cz. With permission Mr. Zahradnik, son of S.Libenský

Two Windows, St. Vitus Cathedral, Prague Castle, 1964-69, by Stanislav Libenský and Jaroslava Brychtová. Source: ArtForum, www.gallery.cz. With permission Mr. Zahradnik, son of S.Libenský

Chapel Windows, gothic chapel, Horsovský Týn, 1990-99, by Stanislav Libenský and Jaroslava Brychtová. Source: ArtForum, www.gallery.cz. With permission Mr. Zahradnik, son of S.Libenský

Crystal Wall/Window, Prague Old Town Hall, 1983, installed 1990, by Stanislav Libenský and Jaroslava Brychtová. Source: ArtForum, www.gallery.cz. With permission Mr. Zahradnik, son of S.Libenský

Crystal Window, Glass Wall, Kyoto, Japan, 1998, by Stanislav Libenský and Jaroslava Brychtová. Source: ArtForum, www.gallery.cz. With permission Mr. Zahradnik, son of S.Libenský

With retirement in the mid-1980s, Libenský and Brychtová were able to devote themselves to work that was more completely their own. They had their first American exhibit at Habatat Galleries in New York City in 1984. The 'Velvet Revolution' of 1989 brought liberation from Communist rule and new challenges for artists in a privatised economy. With the relaxation of previous restrictions, the Libenskýs returned to depictions of the iconic human figure in such sculptures as 'The Last Emperor'. In abstract works like 'The Green Pyramid', the irregular surfaces are transformed into translucent veils of colour that diffuse the sculpture with inner light. With liberation also came a flood of international commissions and in the last years before Stanislav Libenský's death in 2004 the couple produced approximately 12 new pedestal sculptures a year.

As teachers, Libenský and Brychtová have influenced three international generations of artists working in glass over their 45-year partnership. In 1982 Libenský was invited to teach at Pilchuk at Dale Chihuly's invitation. Among those they influenced at home are Pavel Trnka (b.1948), Marian Karel (b.1944), Ilja Bilek (b.1948), Oldrich Pliva (b.1946), Dana Vachtová (b.1937) and Gizela Sabóková (b.1952).

'The Last Emperor', 1989, by Stanislav Libenský and Jaroslava Brychtová.
Source: ArtForum, www.gallery.cz.
With permission Mr. Zahradnik, son of S.Libenský

'Green Eye of the Pyramid' 1993, by Stanislav Libenský and Jaroslava Brychtová.
Source: ArtForum, www.gallery.cz.
With permission Mr. Zahradnik, son of S.Libenský

'Three Columns' by Stanislav Libenský and Jaroslava Brychtová, Mayo Clinic, Rochester, Minnesota, 2002 Mayo Foundation Commission

'Zyklus Spectrum', 1984, by Pavel Trnka,
with the assistance of Jan Frydrych. From the
Collection of The Corning Glass Museum, NY

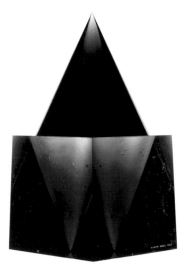

'Blue Cone', 1989, Marian Karel. From the
Collection of The Corning Glass Museum, NY

'Silent Understanding', 1998, Ilja Bílek.
From the Collection of The Corning Glass Museum, NY

'Come to Me', 2002-2004, Gizela Sabóková. From
the Collection of The Corning Glass Museum, NY

'The Elements I', 1980, Dana Vachtová.
From the Collection of The Corning Glass Museum, NY

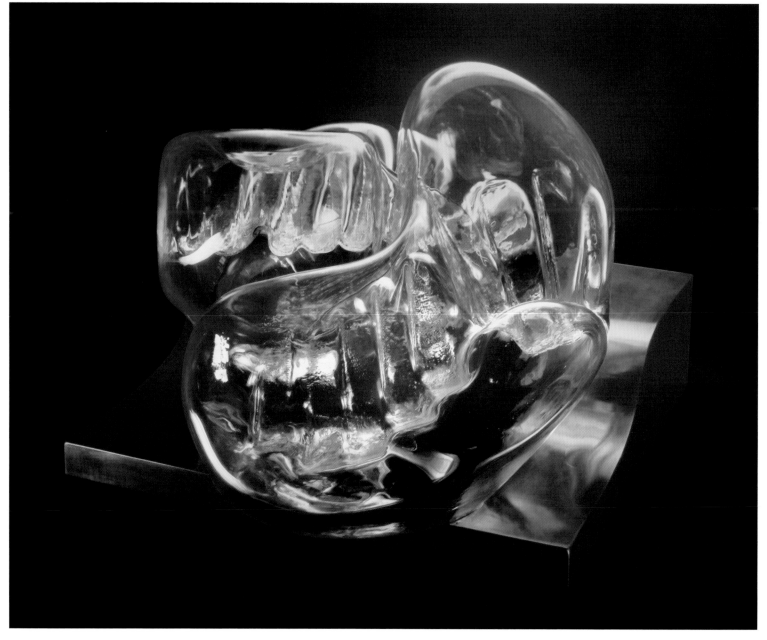

'Column', 1977, Oldrich Pliva.
From the Collection of The
Corning Glass Museum, NY

XVI

New Ideas in Australia

Advertisement by the Australian firm of Brooks, Robinson and Co.,
Melbourne in 1914 for the magazine 'Building'. Henry Brooks and
Edward Robinson founded the company in 1869 and were highly successful
importers of stained glass windows for homes and churches from the UK.
Supplied by The Caroline Simpson Library and Research Collection,
Historic Houses Trust of New South Wales, Australia

Stained Glass Windows

THE production of the combined skill of the cleverest designers and of craftsmen long experienced in leaded glazing, Brooks Robinson's Stained Glass Windows never fail to realize the highest ideals of Art and Workmanship. Water Colour sketches free on request.

Electrical Goods, Gas Fittings, Wall Papers, Mantelpieces, Fireplaces, Paints, Varnishes, etc.

Brooks, Robinson & Co.

59=65 Elizabeth Street,   =   =   =   Melbourne

New Ideas in Australia

The relationship between the settlers in Australia and the world they left behind materially affected the practice and purchase of stained and studio glass. A few stained glass workshops had been set up by enterprising emigrants, but most of Australia's domestic glass arrived as ballast along with cast iron items such as gates and railings on the return run for ships trading in wool. Offloaded, the stained glass panels would be cut down and rearranged to fit whatever door or window the customer wanted. Comfortable homes might be embellished with stained glass windows featuring landscapes and flowering branches skillfully painted and surrounded by an ornamental frame. Windows in this format can still be seen in Edwardian Villas in London suburbs. The attractive bird roundel, for example, was a popular feature in many houses. Other motifs such as vignettes of the countryside provided a central feature for more ornate door panels which might include bullions and textured glass. These decorative schemes in England and Australia were generally taken from pattern books supplied by the stained glass firms. Customers would order the design that appealed to them while the art of the craftsman lay in skillfully cutting and painting the glass.

Detail of a stained glass roundel featuring a bird on a branch in a London house, circa 1905. Supplied by Caroline Swash

Alan Sumner (1911-1994) was an important influence in the development of the direction taken by Australian glass. He learnt the craft of making stained glass windows at E.L.Yencken and Co., a commercial studio in Melbourne with whom he worked for most of his life. However, he was also a skilled and thoughtful independent artist, studying life drawing and composition in the evenings at George Bell's school of 'creative art' after his day spent at the glass studio. Later he passed on these high standards of work to students at the National Gallery School in Victoria, becoming its Director in 1953. The attractive seascape 'Point Cook' exemplifies the clear imagery and freshness of colour that made Sumner's paintings and prints so popular. Indeed he used the process of lithography as a way of bringing his landscapes to a wider and less affluent public. He once described his pictures as places where 'something is always just about to happen'. His stained glass windows were always opposite and well crafted. A complex window 'The Four Seasons' made in 1977 for Kew City Library shows how well he could combine rich and inventive imagery within a suitably linear composition. By working in print and paint as well as stained glass, Sumner provided an important example for others to follow.

The conclusion of World War II was celebrated with a number of new commissions for educational and civic buildings. The most adventurous architects used the talents of Australian artists in new and remarkable ways. One of the most impressive additions in glass was the magnificent new ceiling for the Great Hall of the National Gallery of Victoria commissioned from the artist Leonard French.

Leonard French (b.1928) was born in Melbourne and learnt engraving with his father. He earned his living as a sign writer for several years before working his passage to study art and artists in Europe. He returned to Melbourne in 1951 and exhibited his 'Iliad' series of pictures at the Peter Bray Gallery. Other shows followed to considerable acclaim, but the paintings that established his career were created as a group entitled 'Genesis' in preparation for an application for a Rubenstein Scholarship. In the painting 'Man in the Garden', the primeval figure of Adam, surrounded by flowers, stands four square in the Garden of Eden. This powerful and original picture reveals French's absolute command of his own painterly language. Having absorbed the lessons of post-cubist constructivism that he had learned in Europe, French found his own authoritative way of presenting images. The high quality of his work was noted by the influential Sydney art dealer Rudy Komon who took an interest in the artist and promoted his career.

In 1963, French was asked to create a glass ceiling for the Great Hall of the National Gallery of Victoria. French had never cut glass in his life, but in 1965 he was awarded a Harkness Fellowship to travel to the USA. There he learnt the techniques needed to realize the commission. He imported 10,000 glass bricks, known as dalle de verre, needed for the work from Belgium. These had to be cut into shape, chipped along the outer edges to bring sparkle to the composition then fitted into wooden frames for casting in cement. French completed this lengthy and arduous process in 1968.

'Point Cook' by Alan Sumner, 1959.
© Christie's Images Limited

'Man in his Garden' by Leonard French.
© Christie's Images Limited
© DACS 2005

Opposite Page:
Glass ceiling for the Great Hall of the National Gallery
of Victoria, Melbourne by Leonard French, 1963-68.
With permission National Gallery of Victoria

Glass ceiling for the Great Hall of the
National Gallery of Victoria, Melbourne
by Leonard French, 1963-68.
With permission National Gallery of Victoria

'From the Fire' by Leonard French, 1974-76.
© *Christie's Images Limited*
© *DACS 2005*

Meanwhile, French continued to paint. He had exhibitions at roughly two-year intervals that explored the themes which interested him regardless of trends in aesthetic fashion. The enigmatic painting 'From the Fire' with its references to death and resurrection shows the artist at the height of his powers. A lithograph made in 1970 is one of a set based on the theme of 'The Journey'. The next decades saw French involved in several important commissions. In 1971, he was invited to make a glass 'Mandala' called the Lindesay Clarke window for the Robert Blackwood Concert Hall in Monash University, near Melbourne. The simple mandala form, the age old symbol of life, has been given authority by the solid framing of the external wall of the building. At the Australian National Library in Canberra, French's massive and brilliantly coloured windows dramatise the interior spaces. Concrete glass tended to be used by architects for buildings such as this Library with its precious manuscripts for which a secure environment was needed.

'The Ship' a lithograph made by Leonard French in 1970. One of a series of ten entitled 'The Journey'.
© Christie's Images Limited
© DACS 2005

Leonard French continued to combine painting with glass commissions. In 1978, he made panels for La Trobe University in Melbourne and ten years later, 47 windows and paintings for Haileybury College, Keysborough in Victoria. The renown of these daring architectural features had the effect of reinforcing the concept of stained glass as a fine art.

In 1961, Bill Gleeson added the medium of glass to the curriculum at the Royal Melbourne Institute of Technology alongside metalwork, ceramics, jewellery and print, painting and sculpture. Gleeson had trained as a stained glass craftsman, working at the Melbourne studios of Brooks, Robinson and Co. from 1946 until 1955. However, he was able to see possibilities for the medium beyond the architectural context. He added basic kiln forming to traditional stained glass studies and encouraged one of his tutors, the young German immigrant Klaus Zimmer, to develop his ideas from print into glass.

Klaus Zimmer (b.1928) has become an important figure in the Australian glass scene, partly through years of teaching on the Glass Studies course at the Chisholm Institute of Technology (now Monash University) but mainly through the example of his work. Zimmer's route to fame was typically Australian. He was born in Berlin and endured the Second World War as a teenage soldier in the Wehrmacht. He returned to education with the peace, studying design in the Bauhaus tradition in Berlin. He then took an assisted passage to Australia – one of the few countries to welcome young Germans – and worked for the Snowy Mountains Hydro Electric Authority.

Zimmer's ability as a designer got him the job of senior Lecturer in charge of Preliminary Art and Design studies at Chisholm Institute of Technology. When Bill Gleeson decided to expand the glass course, Zimmer was sent to Europe to study technique at the Glass School at Hadamar in Germany. Further travels included contact with the

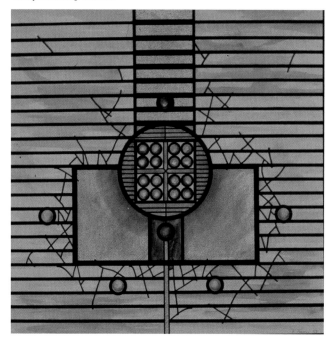

Designs for two stairwell windows by Klaus Zimmer for New Parliament House, Canberra. With permission of the artist

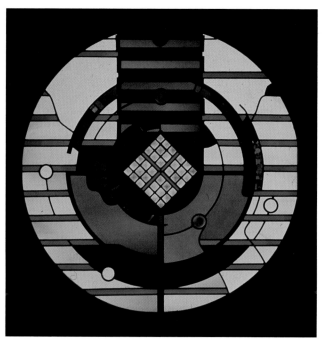

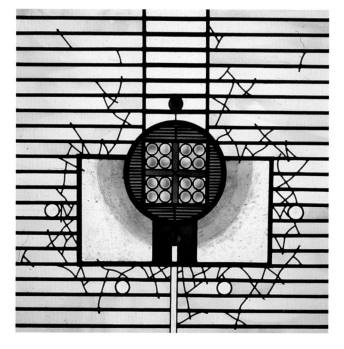

Completed windows by Klaus Zimmer for the stairwell in New Parliament House, Canberra. With permission of the artist

German studios and their most important artists, Ludwig Schaffrath and Johannes Schreiter. He also spent several months assisting Patrick Reyntiens at his studio at Burleighfield.

Returning to Australia, Zimmer set about developing the course at Chisholm. Building on his recent connections in Europe, he inaugurated a series of seminars/workshops with help from the Goethe Institute and the newly formed Crafts Council of Australia. By these means Schreiter and Schaffrath brought a measure of German expertise to Australia. In 1983, Zimmer founded Australia Studios in Box Hill, Victoria, designing and making panels and windows. In 1986, Zimmer was invited to make stairwell windows for the Parliament House at Canberra, his designs convey his admiration for the achievements of the German masters as well as his own developing vision in glass. This commission was followed by two more windows for Parliament House, this time for the Prime Minister's Dining Room. The two panels, 'The

Europeans' and 'The Aborigines', reveal a considerable development in the artist's mode of expression. The linear abstraction of Zimmer's early work has disappeared to be replaced by something far more dynamic and idiosyncratic.

Zimmer's major architectural achievement at this time were the nineteen stained glass windows and thirty miniatures made in 1988 for St Michael's Uniting Church, Collins Street, Melbourne. These carefully balanced windows transform the interior with a warm colour scheme and well designed iconography.

'The Europeans (Blue)', by Klaus Zimmer.
With permission of the artist

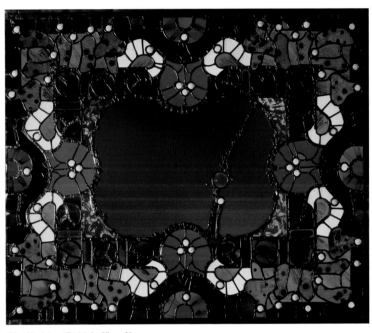

The Aborigines (Red)', by Klaus Zimmer.
With permission of the artist

*'To See Through The Winds of the Storm'.
Stained glass window in St Michael's Uniting
Church, Melbourne by Klaus Zimmer, 1988.
With permission of the artist*

*'Be Not Afraid'. Stained glass window in
St Michael's Uniting Church, Melbourne by Klaus
Zimmer, 1988. With permission of the artist*

*'Discovering the Gift and Power of a New
Creation'. Stained glass window in St Michael's
Uniting Church, Melbourne by Klaus Zimmer,
1988. With permission of the artist*

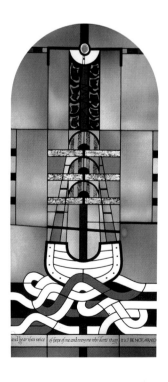

However, Zimmer's intimate, carefully crafted panels are the works that have endeared him to so many people. These unique pieces are not produced as samples for some future commission but are intended to be placed in the home where they must continue to 'speak' in natural and artificial light. With this in mind, Zimmer has used gold and silver lustres as well as enamels to enrich the surface of the glass. His method of binding the glass pieces together is particularly startling. Zimmer uses lead like a jeweller, melting, cutting, rasping, sanding and polishing the dark surface of the base metal to set off the coloured glass. Looking back over the evolution of these autonomous works he observed 'I have made extravagant decoration a form of artistic expression for the post-modern era. Over five decades I have developed a language of abstract curvilinear images and calligraphic marks and invented the studio techniques needed to express them in lead and glass'. Although these panels have sprung from the history of a European past, they are indisputably new. There is an absence of 'tradition' about them and a resolute confidence of expression which is entirely Australian.

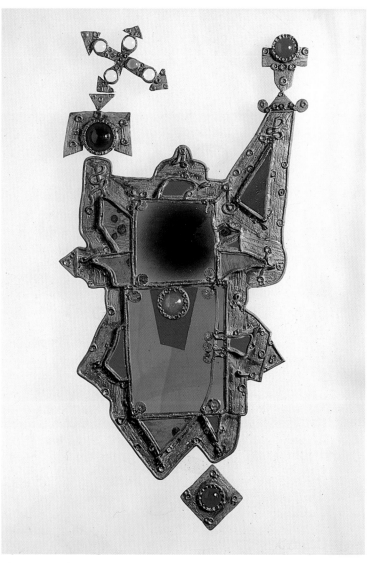

'Dance under the Southern Cross'. Glass and lead panel by Klaus Zimmer, 1990. Provided by Julia Dunn. With permission of the artist Klaus Zimmer

Detail of 'Journey' by Klaus Zimmer showing ornamental quality of the lead work. Provided by Julia Dunn. With permission of the artist Klaus Zimmer

Opposite Page:
'The last Changsha' glass and lead panel by Klaus Zimmer in the National Gallery, Victoria, 1983-85. Provided by Julia Dunn. With permission of the artist Klaus Zimmer

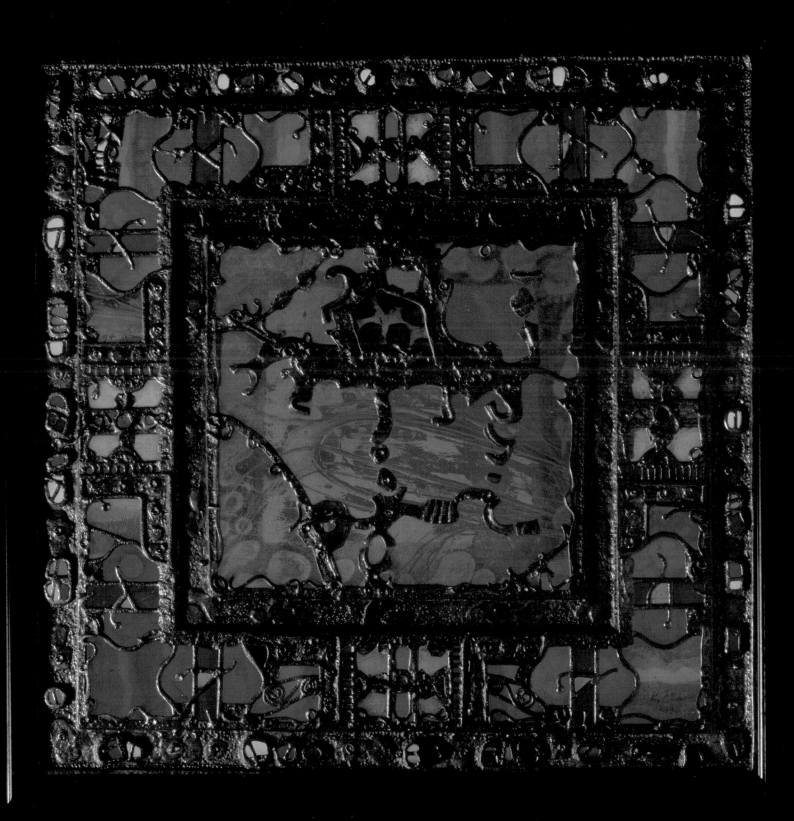

The effort to develop a fresh Australian language in glass has been tackled in a very different way by Cedar Prest (b.1940). She studied first at Melbourne University then moved to London for a post graduate course in glass at Hornsey College of Art. Like Zimmer she worked in Patrick Reyntien's studio at Burleighfield and later visited Germany (on a Crafts Board study grant) to see the magnificent windows still being made during the 1970s as part of post-war reconstruction. In Adelaide she learnt glass blowing with the studio glass artist, Sam Herman, a former student of Lipofsky and a pioneer of the British glass movement.

One of Cedar Prest's recent works was a wall of Australian made glass for the arrivals foyer of Sydney International at the Freedom Glass Studio, WA in a particularly expressive way. Inevitably her talents were enlisted by the church and she made many windows including Pilgrim Church, Guildford Grammar, St Michael's Ukranian Church, Croydon, St John's Church, Maitland and the clerestory for St Peter's Cathedral in Adelaide. However, Cedar Prest's interpretation of her role in glass was very different from the 'high ego' approach of the German masters. She became increasingly convinced not only of the importance of relating decoration to the place in which the building was situated but of including the people who would use the building in the creation of the work of art itself.

Prest's first community glass project was for five big windows in the Parks Community Centre in a tough area of Mansfield Park, a suburb of Adelaide. She succeeded in enthusing 80 volunteers in the creation of 5 new stained glass windows for the centre's cafeteria, library, children's library, sports lounge and swimming pool. Not only did the volunteers help design the work but they learnt to make the windows themselves. Prest observed 'The work takes time. The community becomes bonded, share their life stories. Problems often get healing and always there's pride in their collective achievements. Together they have learned, thought about local content, researched and chosen themes for the design. Finally they have all fabricated'. Prest found that some of the volunteers discovered a new direction for their lives through this activity. Indeed Prest has continued to explore ways in which the practice of working with glass could heal. With this in mind in 1995 she ran experimental workshops with patients at the Memorial Hospital Pain Clinic in North Adelaide to explore the pain blocking effects of art activities.

'High Tide, East Coast'. Glass construction made for the arrivals Foyer of Sydney International Airport by Cedar Prest, 1993-95. Supplied by Cedar Prest

Wall of glass with ribbons in Parks Community Centre, Mansfield Park, Adelaide made by Cedar Prest and volunteers. Supplied by Cedar Prest

Top:
*Wall of glass with Australian plants in Parks
Community Centre, Mansfield Park, Adelaide made by
Cedar Prest and volunteers. Supplied by Cedar Prest*

Above:
*Wall of glass for the Children's Library in Parks
Community Centre, Mansfield Park, Adelaide made by
Cedar Prest and volunteers. Supplied by Cedar Prest*

Following the success of her first community project, Prest was invited to work with volunteers on the creation of stained glass panels for Araluen in Alice Springs and the Chaffey Theatre, Renmark, South Australia. A year later she worked with students to make a paved courtyard and fountain for Yirrara College, Alice Springs. She mobilized large groups of volunteers for three further projects – windows for the entrance foyer of the Middleback Theatre, Whyalla, door surrounds for the Uringa Hostel, Tumby Bay and 48 panels of glass on the theme of the local landscape for the Kalamunda Library in Perth (with Judy Kotai). In 1987, Prest travelled to Alice Springs to work with Aboriginal volunteers from the local Larapinta Town camp in the making of a large foyer Bicentennial window for the Araluen Arts Centre. The designs were based on stories which crossed that piece of land in a Dreaming painting commissioned from the Aboriginal statesman and artist Wenten Rubuntja. Commenting on the experience, Prest observed 'We city-born and bred Australians are very self conscious about our National identity. We recognise that the Aboriginals express a true culture and we wonder about the validity of our own. If we had a dreamtime would it have to be European? The Aboriginals have taken 40,000 years to evolve theirs! But the land has already proved for us a rich source of myth, story and song'.

Sam Herman who introduced Cedar Prest to hot glass, arrived in Australia in 1974, loved the place and decided to stay, opening a Glass Workshop at the Jam Factory in Adelaide. His lively approach to kiln forming and glass blowing encouraged a number of artists to make glass their material of choice. However, the man responsible for bringing new ways of working with hot glass to Australia was the German artist Klaus Moje (b.1936).

A volunteer leading up a panel for the Araluen project, Alice Springs, 1983. Supplied by the artist

Cedar Priest working on the cartoon for the stained glass window in Australia Place, Perth, 1982. Supplied by the artist

Stained Glass window by Cedar Priest for Australia Place, Perth, 1982. Supplied by the artist

Moje grew up in Hamburg, cutting and grinding glass at an early age for the Moje family business. He then studied at the two famous glass schools of Rheinbach and Hadamar before setting up his own studio in partnership with his wife Isgard Moje-Wohlgemuth. For the next four years he made and restored stained glass windows. Almost by accident, Moje found the technique for which he is now so famous. Visiting his suppliers, he saw a variety of coloured glass rods for sale, decided to buy them and started to try various ways of working with them. He succeeded very rapidly in creating interesting pieces for he had his first exhibition of mosaic glass in 1975 and within four years was invited to share his expertise as guest lecturer at colleges all over the world including Pilchuck in the United States, the Royal College of Art in London and the Rietveld Academy in Amsterdam. A 'Mosaic' piece by Moje will have been made of fused glass rods slumped (melted) over a mould in the kiln, then ground and polished to give clarity to the shape and colour of the vessel.

In 1982 Moje accepted an invitation to start a new Glass Workshop at the Canberra School of Art. He stayed there for ten years, training an entire generation of young Australian enthusiasts to the highest standards. The new methods used at the Glass Workshop, combining hot-glass working with a furnace as well as kiln forming, would not have been possible without the research conducted in Portland, Oregon by the Bullseye Glass Company. In 1980 Bullseye developed 'Tested Compatible' glass designed specifically for fusing, giving artists the raw material to create brilliantly coloured vessels and sculptural forms.

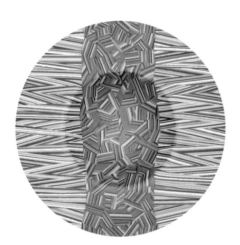

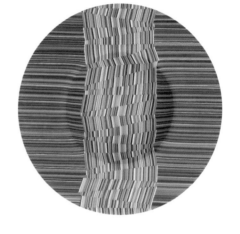

Impact series by Klaus Moje, 2004.
Supplied by the artist

Floating Red, wall piece by Klaus Moje.
Supplied by the artist

It is fascinating to consider how different Moje's work might have been if he had never left Germany. Like Zimmer, it would appear that he has been deeply affected not only by the extraordinary landscape of Australia but by the version created in art by those who have lived in it. 'Landscape, 1959' by Sir Sidney Nolan, for example, presents a strongly coloured and richly textured rendition of cliffs and the sea, far removed from the European artistic tradition. However, the Aboriginal vision of Australia seems to have made a deep impression on the imagination of young Australians searching for a unique personal and national language in art. The evocative works by Pedro Wonaeamirri, Nita Kaniyangka and Millie Skeen Nampitjin combine absorbing pattern with satisfying colour in the presentation of deeply held images.

'Untitled' by Millie Skeen Nampitjin, 1988.
© Christie's Images Limited

'Landscape, 1959' by Sir Sidney Nolan.
© Christie's Images Limited

Opposite Page:
'Untitled' by Pedro Wonaeamirri, 1992.
© Christie's Images Limited

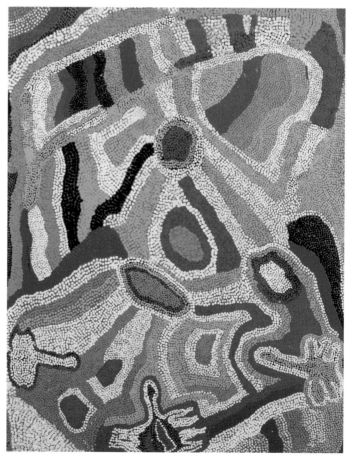
'Tjitirr, South of Lake Gregory'
by Nita Kaniyangka, 1990.
© Christie's Images Limited

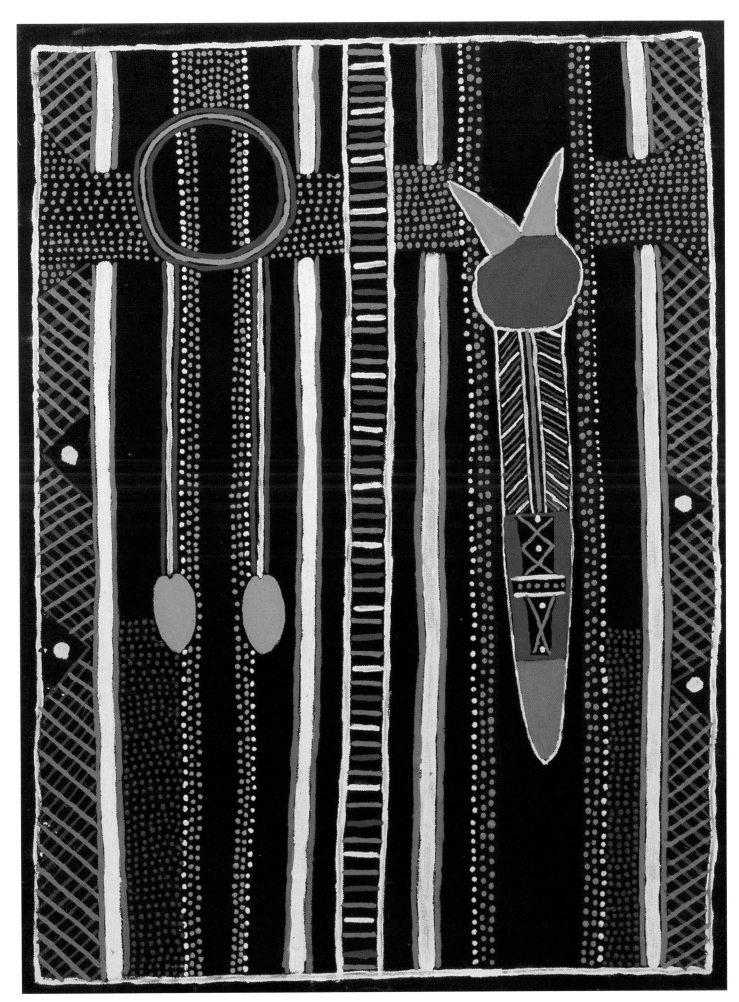

Giles Bettison (b.1966) has been successful in his search for a visual identity. He studied with Klaus Moje at the Canberra School of Art and since graduating has developed his own way with glass and acquired an international clientele. Bettison has studios in America and Australia, indeed his aerial traverse from one to the other has inspired his 'Vista' range of vessels. The imagery for this series clearly relate to the Australian landscape and also have a strong affinity with Aboriginal ways of seeing.

Bettison's method of making the patterned glass consists of cutting thin strips of coloured sheet and fusing them in a kiln. When cold, the strips are taken out, cut up, rearranged and refired. This twice fired mix of glass provides a subtle and complex colour batch for blowing into beautiful forms. Unlike the pioneers who were full of wild and expressive enthusiasms, Bettison is one of a group of highly professional artists obsessive about perfection and detail.

'Vista NOLA', by Giles Bettison, 2004. With permission Giles Bettison

'Cell 7', by Giles Bettison, 2001. With permission Giles Bettison

'Vista NOLA', by Giles Bettison, 2004. With permission Giles Bettison

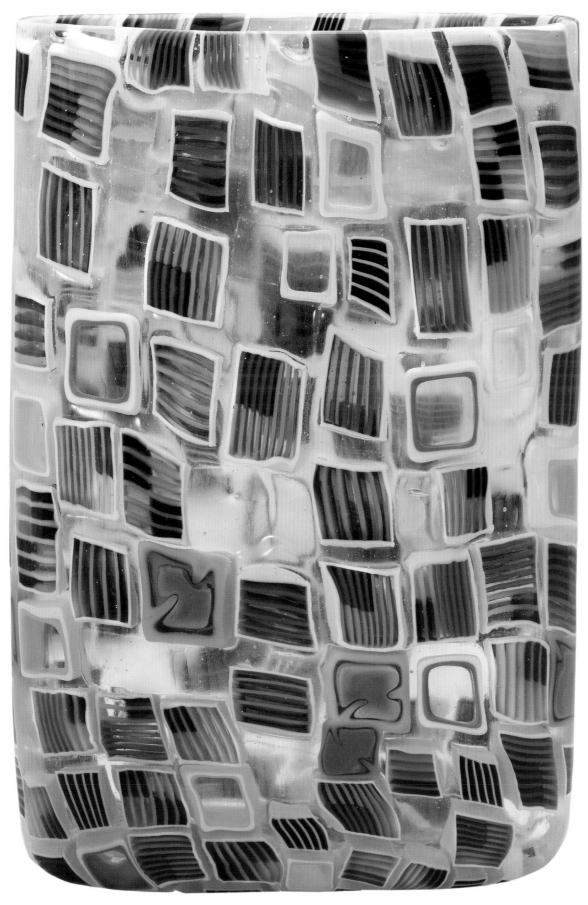

The American connection has been crucial to the development of Australian glass. Through the Crafts Council of Australia, support has been given not only for Australians to visit Europe and the United States, but for American artists to tour Australia. In 1974, the Californian glass artist, Richard Marquis, toured Australian art colleges with a small furnace demonstrating glass making. Nick Mount (b.1952) travelled with him as his assistant. From this friendship grew a lifelong dialogue in glass. The photograph with its title 'a thousand light beers from home' was taken in California with Marquis on the left and Nick Mount on the right. After America, Mount traveled to Venice where he saw for himself the teams of skilled craftsmen making glass of astonishing clarity of form. On returning to Australia, he set up his own studio 'Budgeree Glass' in Budgeree, Victoria and began to blow table pieces as well as one off items which he sold at local galleries. While working on multiple orders, Mount gradually became a remarkably skilled glass blower. A series of cleverly made glass funnels are Mount's tribute to the unsung competence of the early artisans. He also made some exquisite small sculptural pieces inspired by fishing floats. Mount continues to find inspiration from objects such as these which are beautiful in themselves and also entirely practical.

In 1984 Mount moved back to Adelaide, setting up a workshop in the run down industrial area near the docks. This was a short lived enterprise but the experience helped in his next appointment, the running of the Jam Factory Contemporary Craft and Design Centre from 1994-1997. Here he encouraged commissioned work, promoting trainee skills through the repetition needed to maintain standards. He was also responsible for bringing Lino Tagliapietra to the Jam factory in 1996 to demonstrate the skills of Venetian glass blowing.

'A thousand light beers from home' Richard Marquis and Nick Mount in California,USA, 1975. Supplied by Nick Mount. Photograph by Raffi Delbourgo

Family group at Budgeree, Budgeree Glass in Norwood, South Australia, 1986. L to R: Greg Price, Mike Shaw, Nick Mount, Peta Mount, Sue Maschio, Hugo Mount, Pauline Mount. Front: Pippy Mount. Cat: Mrs Dawkins. Photography by Imaginaction

Glass Funnels by Nick Mount.
Supplied by Nick Mount

Pink and Grey Fishing Floats,
by Nick Mount, 1982. In private collection.
Supplied by Nick Mount

Mount's own work has taken new directions and perhaps his most exciting recent creations are a series of 'scent bottles'. Of these he says 'They are part of an evolving series of pieces I have been working on for the past three years. They refer in form and scale to the tradition of creating large, highly decorated glass vessels used for display purposes in apothecaries and perfumeries'. Some of the most engaging have details drawn in graphite and coloured enamel. 'With the first ones, I was using them to demonstrate my craft skills, to allow me to use new processes, to develop new skills, to open up new horizons. Soon, an endless series of possibilities were laid out before me.'

A closer relationship with fine art has been opened up by Warren Langley (b.1950) and Brian Hirst (b.1945). Although both have been influenced by the example of American glass artists, their work is inspired less by the sensuous beauty of glass than the desire to embed their own ideas in an historical matrix relevant to today's Australia. Brian Hirst trained in sculpture and print as well as glass, first at Monash University then Sydney College of Art followed by a year as senior lecturer at Canberra College of Art. His work in glass reflects the insight he has gained from his study of the graphic as well as the three dimensional arts. Indeed Hirst's references spring from a continuing fascination with history and civilization. He has mentioned the personal importance of a small cycladic sculpture at his local museum but he has also suggested that the objects made during the classical era and the ornamental arts of Japan have influenced his views on decoration, especially the decorative possibilities of precious metals.

'Scent Bottles' by Nick Mount.
Supplied by Nick Mount

*Decorated glass vessels by Nick Mount,
2003. Supplied by Nick Mount*

Brian Hirst uses gold and silver as an integral part of his vessels, picking up the precious metal while the glass is still a molten ball then working into the surface when the glass is cold. These vessels reveal Hirst's background in graphic art, while his use of textures in combination with the sheen of silver give the glass an almost metallic air. Hirst's fame as a glass artist was greatly enhanced when he won the 'World Glass Now' prize awarded by the Hokkaido Museum of Modern Art in Japan in 1994. The winning piece was a black three legged cauldron displayed within a dark metal frame inscribed with the same image. Several versions of this concept were made by Hirst including the 2002 votive bowl and panel which relate to the winning piece in subject and colour. Other pieces in his recent exhibition 'Relationships in Form' take the same votive object as starting point. They show the method of exploration conducted by the artist. Some resemble drinking vessels, others are sculptural objects in their own right and a few are almost pictorial in their approach, presenting the three legged cauldron as a flat bright shadow. Indeed, there is great reassurance gained from awaiting the evolution of such an artist's work. Just as the forms of glass in ancient days emerged slowly under the influence of worshipper and priest, so these contemporary tributes have been permitted their own gradual development.

'Votive Bowl' by Brian Hirst.
With permission Brian Hirst

Left & Opposite Page:
Votive Bowl sequence from the
'Relationships in Form' exhibition, 2002.
With permission Brian Hirst

Warren Langley has a background in science and his interest in glass only began after a visit to the workshops in Pilchuck. He opened his own studio in Sydney in 1978. The imagery that he includes in his kiln cast sculptural work is mysterious and poetic. Here in 'Spirit of Earth' Langley has added brightly coloured details to a roughened free standing triangular form. When he used similar imagery for a glass picture to highlight an end wall in the offices of ANA House in Sydney, Langley stretched his ideas to include neon lighting. Indeed, Langley has been an active participant in the effort to bring light and glass together in the creation of new and interesting ways of decorating and even perceiving the built and natural environment. He has been involved in several municipal festivals including the 'Floating Land Festival' at Noosa, Queensland to which he submitted a piece 'Mapping the Tide' using fibre optics. His most important work to date is The Australian Nurses War Memorial in the capital, Canberra made in 1999. Weighing 32 tonnes, the kiln formed glass monument represents the epitome of the technology Langley had been working on since the early 1980s.

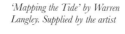

'Mapping the Tide' by Warren Langley. Supplied by the artist

Photograph of Warren Langley. Supplied by the artist

Australian Nurses War Memorial, Canberra by Warren Langley. Supplied by the artist

Opposite Page:
'Spirit of Earth' by Warren Langley. Supplied by the artist

In 1990 he started the Ozone Glass Company with John Clapin and his brother Michael, with the aim of bringing new ideas in glass design to a wider audience. The company produces such utilitarian items as bowls, stairs and counter tops as well as carefully designed large scale work for architecture. With this support, Langley has been able to take on commissions for a number of sites, such as new glass for the ANZAC War Memorial and the Manly Library in Sydney, the Commonwealth Law Court in Adelaide and recently the Mosman Swim Centre. Langley's company also works with other designers. Tony Masters, for example, designed impressive glass walls on themes of marine life for the United Airlines building in Singapore.

Australian studio glass seems to be in a state of vigorous health. There are numerous opportunities for practitioners to meet and show their work. Museums now take the subject of glass seriously and are in the process of accumulating collections covering a wonderfully wide range of international work. Galleries world wide are acquiring works for sale and selling new glass to a growing band of enthusiastic collectors. The artists themselves take enormous care over their own training, studying for many years to develop the difficult skills required to handle this most subtle, brilliant though fragile of materials. It is certainly impossible to select individuals from the young artists currently practicing. The husband and wife team of Ben Edols and Kathy Elliott are making exquisite vessels in the Italian tradition. Scott Chasling who recently won the Ranamack Prize (2004) in Adelaide has a glorious palette and plenty to say in glass. Others making fine glass and exhibiting in Australia and oveseas include Catherine Aldrete-Morris, David Hay, Deb Cocks, Simon Butler, Jane Bruce, Maureen Cahill, Kevin Garden, Rob Knottenbelt, and Sam Jupurilla.

Mosman Swim Centre by Ozone Glass.
Supplied by Warren Langley

Wall of glass for United Airlines, Singapore designed by Tony Masters, fabricated by Ozone Glass. Supplied by Warren Langley

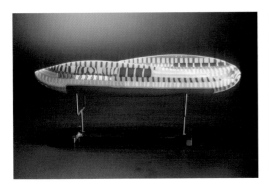

Glass vessel by Scott Chasling.
Supplied by the artist

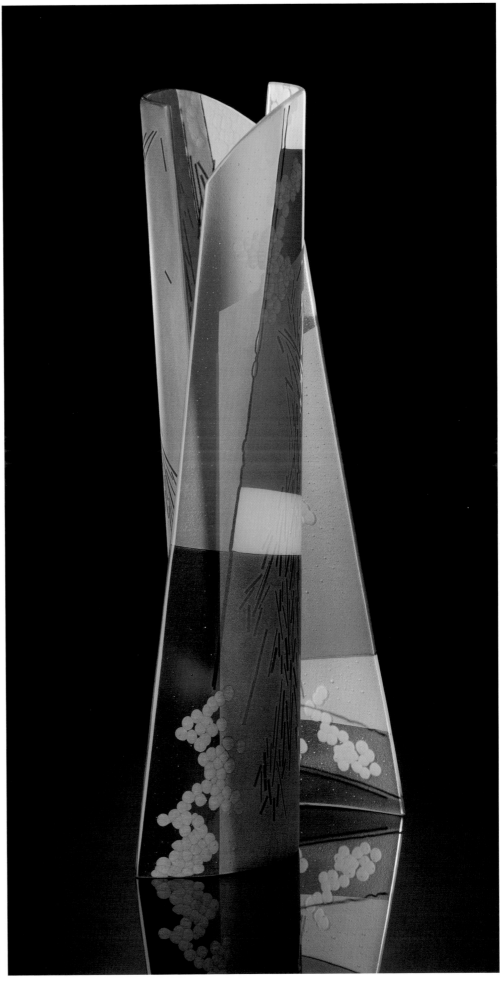

Kiln formed glass, wheelcut and polished by
Catherine Aldrete-Morris, exhibited at the
Sabbia Gallery, Sydney, 2005

XVII
Japanese Glass Today

A two-panel tea ceremony screen depicting a bull headed shrike perched on a vine, late 19th/early 20th century. © Christies Images Limited

17th century 'Rimpa School' folding screen depicting Autumn and Winter flowers and grasses. © Christies Images Limited

XVII

Japanese Glass Today

Japan's prestigious craft traditions have been practiced for centuries, but stained glass as an artistic medium has appeared relatively recently. Traditionally, the 'windows' of Japanese houses were sliding partitions of translucent rice paper that allowed only filtered light into the interior. With the expansion of overseas trade during the 19th century Meiji period, glass began to be used in architecture for its transparent and protective qualities. Stained glass was occasionally imported by Christian missionaries for domestic or religious buildings, but it was not produced in Japan itself until the 1890s.

When stained glass did 'come of age', however, the traditional style of Japanese ornament was easily adapted to the new medium. In a two-panel 'tea ceremony' screen made in the late 19th century, for example, the contrast between the bravura brushwork of the elegant vine and the formal structure of the frame displays a sophisticated balance of disparate elements. This refined design sophistication is also characteristic of the best contemporary Japanese work in architectural and studio glass. A 17th century screen by the Rimpa School reveals yet another aspect of the Japanese control of ornament. Here, flowers have been arranged in balanced clusters against a sumptuous gold-leaf background. The plants have been selected to symbolise the time of year: bush clover, miscanthus grass, thistle, Chinese lantern, chrysanthemum and bamboo all suggest the seasons of autumn and winter. When glass was added to the means available for artistic expression, this sense of poetry, elegance and clarity of observation was carried over into the new material.

The first stained glass studio was opened in Tabata, Tokyo, in 1913 by Sanchi Ogawa. He trained in Japanese painting at the Tokyo Fine Art School and then travelled to America to learn the craft at a commercial studio in Chicago. The expressive panel, 'Watonai,' in the collection of the Tokyo National University of Fine Arts and Music, shows Ogawa's mastery of technique and his competent integration of Japanese subject matter into the new language of glass and lead. Although stained glass occasionally appeared in decorative schemes, primarily in a Western style, Japan's love affair with glass did not truly begin to flourish until the last quarter of the 20th century. During a period of industrial expansion in the 1970s and 80s, enthusiasm for glass as an architectural medium was encouraged by the perceptive commissioning of landmark works from European artists.

The German stained glass artist Ludwig Schaffrath designed a dramatic glass wall for the Omiya Railway Station in Kyoto between 1981 and 1982. The subject is speed itself, presented in a series of orderly, vigorous wave-like movements in light-coloured glass held in place by a rich, dark red grid. This is one of Schaffrath's finest works in which he exploits the linear possibilities of the lead line (see Chapter 9). The subtle range of opal glasses used in the window have been invigorated with clusters of clear and coloured bullions (small shaped pieces of thick glass). This combination of clarity, verve and attention to detail is very much in tune with the Japanese aesthetic. Another magnificent import was the 69-foot 'Tower of Joy for Children' created by the renowned French artist Gabriel Loire for the open-air Museum of Modern Art at Hakone, south of Tokyo. Clambering up the central stairway, children of all ages can enjoy the brilliant colour of the glass set into the dark matrix of the structural concrete walls. Loire has filled the glowing space created by the 480 panels of glass with a mixture of images imaginatively linked to childhood.

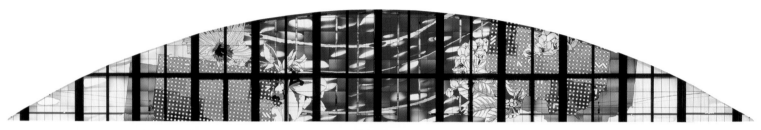

'Flowers on a sunny coast', Glass Decoration in Miyasaki Airport by Toshio Takami, 1995. Supplied by the artist

Detail of 'Flowers on a sunny coast', Glass Decoration in Miyasaki Airport by Toshio Takami, 1995. Supplied by the artist

Today, while Japanese artists have fully absorbed the western tradition of stained glass, they have created a manner of expression that is uniquely their own. The influence of the German aesthetic is apparent in an attractive window entitled 'Flowers on a Sunny Coast' made by Toshio Takami for Miyazaki Airport in 1995. However, the mix of motifs is entirely Japanese and the design contains surprising contrasts. The central blue passage presents a flower-filled view of the sea, yet the blocks of green and grey glass, pierced with glittering oeils de verre (literally, 'eyes of glass'), hint at the mechanised world we live in. Another lively artist working within the German idiom is Shimpei Sato (b.1953). He came to the medium from a background in graphic design and only discovered glass while studying at San Francisco Academy of Art in the late 1970s.

While fascinated by colour, Sato admits that drawing is what interests him most. For this reason he was particularly attracted to the work of the German artist Johannes Schreiter (See Chapter 9). His own windows reflect this passion. In the panel 'Red Beam-1', now in the Glass Museum at Langen in Germany, Sato has used line and colour to create an art work filled with subtle ambiguities. 'With lines I create an expanding three-dimensional space with the material planes of stained glass. The most important source of my stained glass work is drawing, drawings that go through various changes as the lines continue to move until they are finally completed.' A coloured glass decoration made in 1989 for the Tateshina Art Land Hotel shows how well Sato has understood the possibilities of the screen ornamented in contemporary terms. The restless composition extending across a slightly obscured light background gives visual interest to a potentially dull interior. Related to this is Sato's comment that he creates in the same way for a building as he does for his independent panels and drawings. His debt to Schreiter is freely admitted, yet his creations have an excitable, restless quality that is entirely his own.

Shimpei Sato and his dog. Supplied by Shimpei Sato

Glass room divider 'Being 5, Moon Reflection' in the Tateshina Art Land Hotel by Shimpei Sato, 1989. Supplied by Shimpei Sato

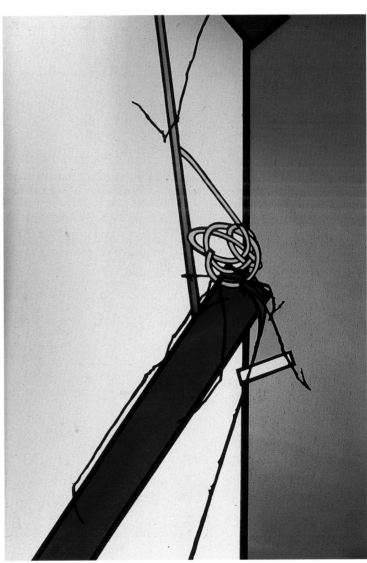

Detail of 'Red Beam-1' in the Glass Museum at Langen in Germany by Shimpei Sato, 1996. Supplied by Shimpei Sato

While Sato and Takami were influenced by the German masters, Hiroko Nakamura was fascinated by the work of the English artist John Piper. In the course of her studies in the history of western crafts, she toured Italy, France and England. She was particularly inspired by the superb baptistery window at Coventry Cathedral by John Piper and Patrick Reyntiens. On her return to Japan, she enrolled in the only course in Tokyo that included glass as one of several decorative media. She set up her own studio in 1990 and one of her early commissions was for a window in the Chapel of the Missionary Sisters of the Immaculate Conception. Her colour scheme and sense of spacing clearly owe something to the soft shapes evolved by Reyntiens to express Piper's particular way with paint. Allowed to choose her own subject, Nakamura selected 'the idea of life as an unfolding journey with many twists and difficulties on the way'. In the Juroku Bank Building at Gifu, she made a confident and dramatic wall of glass for an important passage way. The strong scaffolding of rectangles recalls the proportions of traditional Japanese window openings, while the brilliantly coloured flowers are the symbol of Gifu City. The nearby Nagara River flows symbolically through the composition. The image of a river continues to interest Nakamura. A glass mural made in 1997 for Tokyo's Mitsui Urban Hotel features her favourite blue colour, broken by fan-shaped arcs in brown and gold. Nikken Sekkei, the architectural firm involved in the construction of the Seki Country Club, asked for a ceiling decoration with the theme of nature. Nakamura produced a warm, abstract window filled with interlocking forms that suggest growth.

Wall of glass in the Juroku Bank Building, Gifu by Hiroko Nakamura. Supplied by Caroline Swash

Window for the Missionary Sisters of the Immaculate Conception by Hiroko Nakamura, 1990. Supplied by Caroline Swash

*Glass mural for the Mitsui Urban Hotel,
Tokyo by Hiroko Nakamura, 1997.
Supplied by Caroline Swash*

*Ceiling decoration, 'Terra' for Seki Country
Club by Hiroko Nakamura, 1995.
Supplied by Caroline Swash*

Sachiko Yamamoto (b.1948) not only visited Europe, she stayed for several years. An architect by training, she travelled to Wales in 1990 to learn about glass under Tim Lewis at the prestigious Swansea College of Art. She received a number of awards for her work and stayed on as Lewis's assistant at his Glantawe Studio in Morriston, Wales. Armed with excellent craft skills, she returned to Japan and set up her own studio, making windows in the unique system that she had developed during her long apprenticeship. As a member of the Women's International Stained Glass Workshop group, Yamamoto has exhibited all over the world. To create the sparkling appearance she desires, she places glass on edge at different angles, creating a low relief of glinting surfaces. When completed, her compositions are sandwiched between layers of strengthened glass. This manner of working with glass has developed from a personal sensitivity towards the material's light-transmitting qualities. A panel made for the exhibition '30cm squared', organised by the British Society of Master Glass Painters at the Cochrane Gallery in 2004, gives some idea of the sparkle and liveliness of Yamamoto's work.

In Japan, Yamamoto has completed a number of commissions for homes, churches and public buildings. A subtle version of the 'Tree of Life' motif was made for the west window of St Andrew's Church in Tokyo in 1996. Here she used gold leaf to pick up reflected light. Her concern is always for the role that glass can play in the interior spaces of a building. Writing about her work in the foreword to the 'Traces of Travel' exhibition held in Ireland in 1997, Yamamoto observed that 'one of my clients told me that she was enjoying the sight of my glass window, my creation, brought to life by the sunlight dancing through

it. This was the most pleasing expression of appreciation I have ever had. One of the pleasures of working with architectural glass is that the glass brings the space around it alive for always'. Recently Yamamoto has taken her work into new areas of experience. With wonderful generosity she now shares the fabrication of the glass with the communities who will enjoy the window. 'Glass shows thousands of different characteristics depending on the light. My theme is to make the best use of the given space and to define the beauty of the glass. At the same time, my wish is for everyone to know the enjoyment of glass-making by experiencing the process together. Therefore I have tried to simplify the creation process'.

As the artist in charge, Yamamoto creates the overall concept and designs the layout of the proposed window. She also prepares the coloured glass. Cut into strips, the glass is then chopped into squares ready for her volunteers to work with. The secret of this process is the use of VHB tape with which the glass strips are attached to a backing sheet. A wall of edge-bonded glass was made for the Nagoya Wild Flower Garden in 2002. First, volunteers fit the taped glass into position and the artist checked the density of the coloured zones, adding more glass where needed. Yamamoto has found that people of all ages can work with glass in this way without any diminution of standards. She has, however, had some difficulty in persuading clients, apprehensive about glass being made by non-professionals, to allow her to use this fabrication method. Yamamoto counters this with the observation that 'the work becomes something very special, personal and to be proud of for the participants. I consider this as a very important aspect of an art work in a public space.'

'Play with Gold'. Exhibition panel by Sachiko Yamamoto made for the Exhibition '30cm squared' held by The British Society of Master Glass Painters at The Cochrane Gallery, Holborn, London in 2004. Supplied by Caroline Swash

Completed glass wall 'Nagoya Wild
Flower Garden' by Sashiko Yamamoto and
volunteers, 2002. Supplied by the artist

'Tree of Life '. West window in St
Andrew's Church, Tokyo by Sachiko
Yamamoto, 1966. Supplied by the artist

Checking the position of the glass on the completed
glass wall 'Nagoya Wild Flower Garden', 2002.
Supplied by the artist Sachiko Yamamoto

Volunteers working on the glass for the
'Nagoya Wild Flower Garden', 2002.
Supplied by the artist Sachiko Yamamoto

Another member of the International Women's Group is Yoshi Yamauchi (b.1939). She trained as a painter at the Musashino Art University and then studied in Venice before joining the Hein Derix Studio at Kevelaer in Germany. Since 1974 she has been a full-time glass painter working on numerous important commissions for the firm. Despite her long years in Germany, her own work retains the accuracy and verve associated with Japanese decoration.

Public Art has become a lively part of the city scene in Japan and a cool and stylish low relief by the Korean artist Kyong Hee Cho includes optical glass as well as areas of colour. The sequence of simple but scintillating recessed glass pictures entirely suits the clean lines of the Kuramae Station of the Ohedo Subway Line in Tokyo, which opened in 2000. The artist works as a product designer and regrets the loss of the physical manipulation of glass in her projects. 'It is sometimes irritating to be working on something which I am not able to create by myself because there are fewer opportunities for me to use my hands

and skills and be inspired by raw materials', she says. In her case, the purity and clarity of the finished piece can only be achieved in a commercial studio.

France has also exerted a considerable influence on Japanese glass. Two young artists, Kenichi Kikuchi and Yoshitomo Tsurumi have both studied in the glass department of the famous School of Applied Arts in Paris. They have learnt the subtle and contemplative art of glass painting where it is taught along traditional lines. Kenichi Kikuchi was there between 1978 and 1982. His 'Column of Statue' is an exquisitely realised and enigmatic window that includes references to the Virgin Martyrs of medieval fame, carved to stand forever against the pillars of the cathedrals of France. Yoshitomo Tsurumi completed his studies in Paris in 1991. A charming panel made in 2004 is a portrait of his Korean wife and their baby in national dress. In this work he has succeeded in his stated aim, the harmonisation of the technique of western decorative art with eastern sensibility.

'Path 1' 2004 by Yoshi Yamauchi.
Supplied by the artist

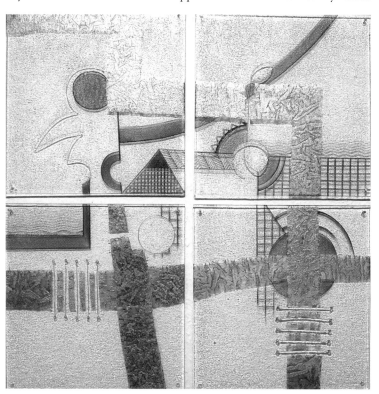

Below-Left:
'Transparent Light and Shadow', Glass relief in Kita-Shinyokohama Station of the Yokohama Municipal Subway Line by Kyong Hee Cho, 1993. Supplied by the artist

Below:
'Form of Light' recessed glass panels for Kuramae Station of the Ohedo Subway Line by Kyong Hee Cho, 2000. Supplied by the artist

Keiko Mikaide has acquired as much fame in the United Kingdom as in Japan. She was one of the first artists to see the possibility of glass as an art form in conjunction with nature. Her forest of glass plants caused a sensation when it was first shown. The interaction between a fragile, sensuous yet strong material such as glass and the living plant has inspired a number of installations. Mikaide's most recent adventure has been the creation of a glass plantation in Edinburgh's Royal Botanic Garden.

London was the starting off point for the young Kyoto artist, Yoko Machi. She trained first at art school in Chelsea and then at Central Saint Martin's School of Art, where she was awarded a two-year fellowship. Her response to the alien land of England led to several interesting works in glass which brought her participation in the 'Japan 2001' exhibition at the Birmingham Museum and Art Gallery as well as a solo show in London. Among her exhibits was 'The Bridge', a subtle screen-printed and multi-layered panel of moveable glass pieces that forms a bridge to another world.

A single glass 'plant' by Keiko Mikaide. Supplied by the artist

'Hydrosphere' site-specific installation by Keiko Mikaide at the 'Elemental Traces' exhibition at the Royal Botanic Garden, Edinburgh. Supplied by the artist

'Hydrosphere solo Exhbition' by Keiko Mikaide at Aberdeen Art Gallery which included 1800 lampworked borosilicate glass plants. Supplied by the artist

'Lanterns 2005' by Keiko Mikaide. Supplied by The Scottish Gallery

'The Bridge' by Yoko Machi made for the exhibition Japan '2001' held at the Birmingham Museum and Art Gallery. Supplied by Caroline Swash

Japanese Cut Glass

The technique of cutting lead crystal glass originally developed in Japan during the 300 years of the Edo period (1603-1867). During the industrial reforms of the Meiji in the 19th century, however, the traditional workshops became run down and were finally closed. New factories, built with technology imported from Germany and England, caused a revolution in glass-making. For the first time glass tableware, bottles and window glass became available to ordinary people. Cut glass retained its prestige and still attracts artists sensitive to the physical purity of the material and responsive to its sculptural possibilities. Cut-glass vessels continue to be prized in Japan as ornaments for the home and as attractive gifts.

Kagami Kozo (1896-1985) was the pioneer of truly original cut glass in Japan. He had studied pottery and industrial design before travelling to Germany to learn from the renowned master Wilhelm von Eiff at the Art College in Stuttgart. Returning to Japan he founded the Kagami Crystal Company. Not only did Kozo run an extremely efficient factory but he trained a number of superb artists, including Wataru Hayashi, Genichi Egashiroa, Mitsuru Kagami, Fumio Sasa, Junshiro Sato and Takeo Yoshida. A subtle vase by Takeo Yoshida has been moulded and cut to give a liquid effect to the glass. The deliberately roughened planes of a vase made by Mitsuru Kagami in 1988 form a striking contrast to the silky surface of the crystal. A cleverly cut vase by Fumio Sasa allows the artistic flower arranger new possibilities. Junshiro Sato is a particularly interesting artist. He worked with Kagami Crystal from 1939 and stayed with the company until 1972. In 1956 he founded the Japan Designer Craftsman Association. In old age he produced a strangely dramatic glass block inscribed with the footprint of Buddha for the Zenryu-Ji Temple.

Today, designing for a company remains one of the ways to learn about glass and make a living. In the recent (2005) exhibition of glass held at The University Art Museum at the Tokyo National University of Fine Arts and Music, no fewer than 17 of the 41 exhibitors were either working for or had trained with one of the glass firms. Mariko Sato, who created a surprising group of glass pillows, is one example. From 1963 until 1967 she worked in the design department of the Sasaki Glass Co., but now explores the possibilities of glass in her own way in the studio she started in 1982. Her approach is in tune with that of many young Europeans who view glass as a fine art medium for exploring contemporary ideas and attitudes.

The Studio Glass
Movement in Japan

This combination of commercial skill and inventive vision is also a feature of the Japanese studio glass movement. The first artists to break the brilliant but restrictive formulae of crystal work were Toshichi Iwata and Kyohei Fujita. Toshichi Iwata (1895-1980) came to glass after twelve years' study. He trained first in Japanese painting, then metalwork and sculpture, and finally oil painting with the artist Saburosuke Okada (1869-1939). Okada had worked in France and knew how hard the life of a painter could be, so he encouraged Iwata to consider glass as a career. He is alleged to have said 'You have experience in various arts, why don't you have a go at glass?' Iwata bought a shut-down glass factory in 1931, reopening it as the Iwata Glass Company. In 1935 his first collection of vases, pots and mugs, all made of blown glass, were shown at the Matsuzakaya Department Store in Tokyo. Iwata was unusual in both practising and promoting blown glass at a time when cut glass was still very fashionable. However, his glass was reasonably priced and sold well. An unusual vase made by Iwata in 1935 has an attractive wavy pattern and attached loops of glass along each side.

Gradually Iwata's technique improved and he was able to make plates and wine glasses as well as vases and pots. He held regular exhibitions of his yearly production in the same department store gallery. These shows were enormously popular and even inspired appreciative poetry. The lines below by the poet Akiko Yosano are part of a sequence of seven 'tanka' (poems of 31 syllables) written in praise of Iwata's wares.

During the 1950s, Iwata responded positively to the suggestion that he mass produce art glass. He decided to create a series that would be designated 'similar to the original'. These vessels would have an attractive appearance, be similar in design and yet unique. The flower shaped vase with expressive black and green patterning is similar to those made at that time. Indeed, this series was created in the spirit of Mingei, the early 20th century Japanese equivalent of the Arts and Crafts movement, which celebrated traditional folk crafts and promoted the production of beautiful things at affordable prices for ordinary people to enjoy. Another aspect of this philosophy is reflected in Iwata's interest in the art of Japanese boxes. The form of these moulded glass containers was derived from traditional lacquered boxes used in the tea ceremony, a 16th century ritual that underwent a nationalistic revival in the 1920s.

Surrounded by the whiteness of
The blizzard-patterned glass
I feel as if
I am nestled
In the bosom of nature

Supplied by Mitsumura Suijo Shion Publishers, Tokyo

*Appearing more elegant
And evanescent
Than the flower
The novel glass vase awaits
Its eternal appraisal*

Supplied by Mitsumura Suijo Shion Publishers, Tokyo

In later years, Iwata became interested in the possibilities of adapting his ideas in glass for architecture. During the 1960s he created a range of coloured flat-glass sheets that he called 'Colorato'. These were shown at his 25th one man show at the Takashimaya Department Store. Although Iwata was invited to make a few commissions using this new glass, including the front wall of the Nissei Theatre in Tokyo and a 'light cascade' for the entrance hall of the Royal Hotel, Osaka, he failed to find a viable regular market. Although often in financial difficulties, Iwata was entirely happy when working with glass and continued to experiment with new glass forms all his life. The shell motif in particular fascinated him; from the 1970s onwards, he tried out different combinations of colour and form in the search for new versions of this classic shape.

Osaka Roay Hotel, 'Kobaku'
1965 by Toshichi Iwata.
Supplied by Mitsumura Suijo
Shion Publishers, Tokyo

Kyohei Fujita (1921-2004) was distantly related to Toshichi Iwata and through this connection joined the Iwata Glass Company in 1947 after training in metal craft at the Tokyo Academy of Arts. He left the company after two years, determined to work in glass in an independent way. His early works were simple vessels not dissimilar to Iwata's own productions. These were exhibited in 1957 in the gallery of the Matsuzakaya Department Store in Tokyo. The glass sold and a few years later he was offered another solo show, this time at the Tokyo Takashimaya gallery with which he has been associated ever since. Even at this early stage Fujita was interested in two very different ways of expressing his ideas in glass. His disciplined vessels, such as his individually gilded plates, are superb examples of controlled craftsmanship. However, he also made wildly expressive pieces in which the liquid glass appears to have bewitched its maker. Fujita promoted this 'flow glass' at a solo show at the Takashimaya Department store. His interest in working the material in this way never entirely left him.

Blown glass vase by Toshichi Iwata in the Museum of Modern art, Hokkaido, 1935. Supplied by Mitsumura Suijo Shion Publishers, Tokyo

'Shell Scent', 1976 by Toshichi Iwata. Supplied by Mitsumura Suijo Shion Publishers, Tokyo

However, the vessels that would bring him lasting fame were very different. Fujita had always admired the lacquer work of the 17th and 18th centuries in Japan, particularly the decorated boxes made to hold ink, poems or seals. He was especially impressed with the work of Ogata Korin (1658-1716). During his lifetime, Korin's popularity was such that an entire school of decoration came to be known as 'Rimpa', after the second character of Korin's name.

An exquisite two-tiered writing box of a later date is based on the type made famous by Ogata Korin. The surround to the ink stone has been decorated with stylised snow flakes painted in gold against a silver background. On the lid is a winter-flowering plum blossom with the name 'uguisu' (bush warbler) inlaid in mother-of-pearl. The 'Inro' is a layered purse for carrying either seals or money and is worn attached to the belt. An example made in the 19th century in the Rimpa style has been decorated with gold and silver foil. The autumnal scene depicts three deer by a stream with scattered maple leaves.

These three examples of Rimpa decoration give some idea of what inspired Fujita when he came to make his own versions of these beautiful things in glass. Fujita's first attempts at creating new work true to the Rimpa style were quite modest. However, even a box from the 1970s reveals considerable skill in its fabrication. From the moment when the glass boxes, which he called 'kazaribako,' were exhibited in 1974 at the 'Glass in Japan' exhibition at the Kanagawa Museum of Modern Art, Fujita was in demand for lectures, workshops and exhibitions in Japan, Europe and America.

A two tiered Suzuribako (writing box), Meiji period (late19th/20th century). The form of this box is loosely based on a type associated with Ogata Korin. © Christies Images Limited

A four case 'Inro', a purse attached to the belt for carrying seals or money in 19th century Rimpa style. © Christies Images Limited

'Heian' by Kyohei Fujita, 1979.
© Christies Images Limited

A lacquer tea container, Edo period.
© Christies Images Limited

Fujita spent a considerable amount of time in Venice working with the glass blowers at Murano. This enabled him to carry out the complex processes needed to make his boxes. Separate moulds had to be made for the top and base and hot glass blown into them. Afterwards the gold and silver foil would be applied and another layer of clear glass added. When the glass had cooled, the shapes were sandblasted and polished for maximum effect. Metal mounts outlining the rim complete the vessel. The most attractive and luxurious of the 'kazaribako' are those designated 'Rimpa'. They were made in the 1990's when Fujita was at the height of his powers.

Fujita was always keen to experiment and very reluctant to be type cast. While receiving so much interest for his Rimpa boxes, he continued to make vessels in a more limpid, fluid way, mixing the Venetian tradition of pure form and exquisite colouring with a more random and organic 'feel' of his own. He once said that he wanted to make 'not Venetian glass but Fujita glass made in Venice'.

With such a well-developed tradition behind them it is difficult to see how Japan's glass artists can go wrong. The adventurous dialogue with Europe and the United States will surely continue to prove beneficial to everyone. It is to be hoped that architects will commission exciting new work from their gifted glass designers. Glass in the built environment always adventurous projects to which artists can respond. Certainly there are no lack of new ideas among young artists. The lively installation 'Play the Glass', created for the 2003 Venice Biennale by Hiromi Masuda, shows a cheerful lack of pretension. She says 'the process of blowing is like feeling the rhythm with both the glass and my body, the wind through the blowpipe creating the shapes or the music of the glass...as a plastic material, glass inspires my imagination.'

'Genji-tale' by Kyohei Fujita, 1992. Courtesy of The Heller Gallery

'Water Vessel-Old City' by Kyohei Fujita, 1992. Courtesy of The Heller Gallery

'Genji-tale' by Kyohei Fujita, 1995.
Courtesy of The Heller Gallery

'Red and White Plum Blossom' by Kyohei Fujita,
1999. Courtesy of The Heller Gallery

XVIII
The Way Ahead

XVIII

The Way Ahead

Glass is an extraordinary medium. It breaks easily, requires expensive equipment to change its shape and needs complex, time-consuming systems to attach it safely to a building. When the 'idea made glass' is finished, the light plays with it in so varied a way that its appearance can never be predicted. Why would anyone want to get involved with a material so illusive and so capricious? For those who work with glass the reasons surely lie in the very problems that the material presents. Glass transmits light, reflects light, conjures with light. The sculptural possibilities of its molten form make marble and bronze look dull. The associative power of its saturated colour toys with our sensations as happily as any fashionista could wish. Glass has novelty and glass has history – it is a wonderful language to work in.

'Silent Yet Deadly', installation of cast glass sculptures on Winchelsea beach, East-Sussex, by Emily Bellhouse. Supplied by the artist

Glass in the Built Environment

Architectural glass has the capacity to transform the mood and spirit of a building. Colour can be thrown across space, sparkling passages of pattern can illumine a dark area, and movement can be suggested to enliven a static interior, often with the simplest means. The spell of stained glass has cast its light across thousands of years, yet today exciting new technologies are waiting to be exploited. So much is available to make our built environment healthier, livelier and more satisfying. Glass can do this. While some architects are still reluctant to use the possibilities that glass can give them, the added value of richly coloured or sparkling glass is attracting ever more attention. So what might the future hold?

Contemporary architecture needs contemporary art. In many countries a 'Percent for Art' scheme requires construction budgets for a new public building to include a set percentage for art. This has brought opportunities for architects and artists alike. Examples range from a small but telling addition such as Kate Maestri's coloured canopy above the entrance to a renovated London office to a major statement, such as the balustrade she designed for The Sage, Gateshead. This curved structural wall consists of 51 toughened glass panels, screen printed with ceramic enamel to bring the right note of colour to the interior of Foster and Partners superb building. Elsewhere in Europe, Sweden's National Public Art Council (NPAC) has been supporting projects that allow artists and craftspeople to work in tandem with architects in the enrichment of the whole building. The NPAC provides roughly half the cost of the artist's contributions. Other projects encourage the active participation of those who use the space. In Wales, the artist Chris Bird-Jones has recently been commissioned by Cywaith Cymru (Art Work Wales) to improve the appearance of the entrance to offices recently built for Denbighshire County Council with a pavement based on the subject of the local rock formation, the 'Clwydian Range'. With volunteers from the council workforce, Bird-Jones selected quarry samples then supervised the sandcasting process needed to form 34 glass cores, each representing a town or village in the county. Once completed, the glittering cores form points of interest along the route towards the new building. The success of these ventures depends upon the happy combination of artistic expertise and local involvement. The continuation and extension of these initiatives will certainly encourage the innovative use of glass in years to come.

Volunteers searching for quarry samples in preparation for designing glass cores for the new paved access area for Denbighshire County Council, 2004. Photograph by Chris Bird-Jones

Detail of a glass core showing dichroic glass inclusions designed by Chris Bird-Jones with volunteers from Denbighshire County Council, 2005. Photograph by Chris Bird-Jones

Volunteers from Denbighshire County Council watching sand casting by glassblower Simon Eccles at Wolverhampton University, 2005. Photograph by Chris Bird-Jones

View of the partially completed access area, showing the placing of the glass cores designed by Chris Bird-Jones with volunteers from Denbighshire County Council, 2005. Photograph by Chris Bird-Jones

Coloured canopy above the entrance to a
London office by Kate Maestri, 2000.
Supplied by the artist.

Building booms do not always favour sophisticated decoration. In China, however, artists from all over the world have contributed to the enrichment of the country's swiftly growing cities. The Korean artist Ahn Pil-Yun has made an outdoor sculpture for the International Finance Centre (IFC) luxury shopping mall on Hong Kong's central waterfront. The concept was based on the four seasons with the sun rising over Victoria Harbour. At night, lit with internal halide lights, the sculpture glows like a ship in the dark. By day the tiled structure forms part of an open air garden. At the same mall, the Shanghai-born artist, Shan Shan-Sheng, has created one of the largest suspended glass sculptures in the world. Her 'Dancing Ribbons' spans the main entrance. These projects have been sponsored by Henderson Land Development Co. Ltd. whose Chairman, Dr. Lee Shau Kee, sees Public Art as 'supporting and expressing cultural and community aspirations and promoting a city as a creative and vibrant place. For Hong Kong to be truly Asia's world city, we must also be Asia's cultural city'.

'A state of Flux' (daytime) by Ahn Pil-Yun for the IFC, Hong Kong, China, 2004 (Arena Aug 2004). Supplied by Harry Cardross

'A state of Flux' (Nighttime) by Ahn Pil-Yun for the IFC, Hong Kong, China, 2004 (Arena Aug 2004). Supplied by Harry Cardross

'Dancing Ribbons', by Shan Shan-Sheng for the main entrance of the IFC, 2004 (Arena, Aug 2004). Supplied by Harry Cardross

Detail of 'Dancing Ribbons', by Shan Shan-Sheng for the main entrance of the IFC, 2004 (Arena, Aug 2004). Supplied by Harry Cardross

Detail of 'Dancing Ribbons' by Shan Shan-Sheng for the main entrance of the IFC, 2004 (Arena, Aug 2004). Supplied by Harry Cardross

Today the range of possibilites are as wide as man's imagination. Gardens, cruise ships, night clubs, hospitals, concert halls and gardens can all gain from the judicious use of glass. The time honoured tradition of a fountain or formal sculpture has been updated by several artists including the American sculptor Howard Ben Tré, Peter Layton, Simon Moss and Neil Wilkin in the UK and Jean Marie Geron in Belgium, while the challenge of using glass for oudoor seating, subject to the elements, has been explored by the Swedish artist Bertil Vallien.

The liveliest exponent of the use of glass in landscape is undoubtedly Dale Chihuly (see Chapter 12). His Millennium installation at the Citadel in Jerusalem involved 42 tons of glass worked into 10,000 separately blown parts. These were fabricated at studios in USA, Norway, Finland, The Czech Republic and Japan. Dr Wolfgang Schmölders, one of the foremost authorities on contemporary glass wrote of the intensity of the experience of visiting this exhibition in his magazine 'Glashaus'. He observed that 'the visitor is taken by surprise and cannot get enough of the intense colours and refraction of the glass. He discovers and appreciates the lively contrast between the glass sculptures and the brightness of the light reflecting stone. An invasion from a different world seems to be taking place, peaceful and different to the many conquests the city has had to endure'. His comments are a reminder of the importance of place in the choice of contexts for glass.

While Chihuly's travelling exhibitions are hugely popular, it is vitally important that other new ideas in glass reach the audience they deserve and that young artists have opportunities to show what they can do. Because of their link with changing styles and fashions, the 'applied' or 'decorative' arts have always welcomed new ideas. Fine art, too, has changed. Mixed media, installation art and arranged interventions have become accepted parts of the public's art experience. There appears to be a generational shift in these reactions too, as young people are often receptive to non-traditional forms of art, which bodes well for the future. Museums and Government organisations have been sensitive to these shifts and have supported activities that might otherwise have languished for lack of occasion.

'Crystal Stream', water sculpture by Peter Layton and Simon Moss for Celebrity Cruises, 2002 (daytime view). Supplied by the artist

'The Crystal Tower' designed by Dale Chihuly and made in the United States, shown in Jerusalem, 2000. Supplied by Glashaus-Verlag. Photograph by Doris Kürbis

'The White Tower' designed by Dale Chihuly and made in the Czech Republic, shown in Jerusalem, 2000. Supplied by Glashaus-Verlag. Photograph by Doris Kürbis

'The Red Speers' designed by Dale Chihuly and made in Finland, shown in Jerusalem, 2000. Supplied by Glashaus-Verlag. Photograph by Doris Kürbis

For the Coastal Currents Arts Festival held in September, 2003 on the south coast, the young British artist Emily Bellhouse chose the sea itself for her installation of imaginative glass objects placed at the edge of the tidewater. 'Washed Ashore' took place on three beaches, Bexhill, Hastings and Winchelsea in East Sussex and drew many visitors who confessed that they felt comfortable looking at art on a beach, whereas they might not in a gallery. She found that comments made by people 'wandering down from the promenade' were particularly useful. Bellhouse actively encourages audience participation and was pleased when the vicissitudes of weather meant that her audience had to help move the glass in a hurry, thus handling and touching the work. Trained in product design, Bellhouse worked for a pharmaceutical company before turning to glass.

Helen Maurer also encourages interaction with her work. Her installations tell stories through shapes and colours transmitted in light. Pieces of glass are positioned beneath an overhead projector, creating magical tableaux when projected by angled light into space to be caught up on another surface, a wall or screen. The audience can thus pass around and through the image mysteriously formed by the items on the projector surface. The contrast between the glass model and the quiet drama of the coherent image is both breathtaking and deeply moving. Through her choice of subjects, Maurer plumbs the elusive realm of memory, an important aspect of all our lives and a fascinating area of exploration.

'Washed Ashore', solid blown glass sculptures on Winchelsea Beach, East Sussex, 2003, by Emily Bellhouse. Supplied by the artist. Glass blown by Tom Atherton. Photograph by Roger Bamber

Light construction, 'In the Green Room' by Helen Maurer, 2003. Supplied by the artist

Light construction, 'Set for Battle' by Helen Maurer. Supplied by the artist

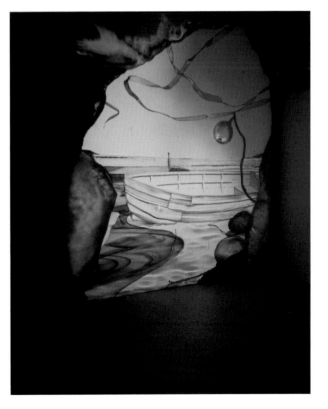

Light construction, 'Cave Painting' by Helen Maurer, 2003. Supplied by the artist

The idea of glass as a 'precious' material remains an important aspect of its appreciation, today as in the past. Certainly this way of thinking is encouraged by galleries and salesrooms where the language employed to describe glass refers repeatedly to the vigour and physical dexterity required to work with it. Evidence of these abilities is nowhere seen more clearly than in the areas of glass blowing, lampworking and glass engraving. Lino Tagliapietra trained in the demanding world of the Venetian glass blowers and his fame overseas rests with the example of his practise and his inspirational teaching. As the foremost exemplar of the exacting art of glass blowing, he has challenged his students, such as the American Dante Marioni, to achieve ever higher levels of skill. In perfection of form and clarity of thought their work ranks with the best of any age.

The American, Paul Stankard has rescued the traditional Venetian art of lampworking from the banality of the seaside souvenir. Lampworking, the art of assembling and manipulating fragments of glass with heat from a small flame, has been used for centuries to create whimsical glass figurines or applied decoration, such as handles, for blown vessels. The charm of Stankard's work lies in its intricacy and in his inventive selection of the fruit, flowers, insects and tiny human figures suspended in the transparent matrix of glass.

Lamp or flame working has also been used by artists in the fabrication of glass jewellery. The great Venetian glass makers of the Renaissance prized bead making among their many skills. Now a wonderful range of compatible colours allow artists to create beautiful and wearable things. Glass jewellery has long been popular in Germany where exhibitions of new work are shown alongside fine art pieces. The renowned glass artist Isgard Moje-Wohlgemuth, for example, makes glass jewellery while Sylvia Kirsch showed her glass necklaces, alongside fused and sandblasted bowls and goblets by Gabriele Köstner and installations by Helga Reay-Young at the State Museum in Gottingen as early as 1998. The first German glass bead congress was held in 2003 at the Glass

Snowdrop glass vessel by Jackie Allwood. Supplied by the artist

Museum Wertheim attended by 150 people with 25 exhibitors. In the United States, the Bead Museum in Prescott, Arizona sponsored an exhibition of modern glass beads in 1993. Enthusiasts who gathered there formed the Society of Glass Beadmakers (SGB) which later became the International Society of Glass Beadmakers (ISGB) Beads and glass jewels have become much more than accessories and may be seen as a wonderful new art form. Beads can be made from blown and kiln formed glass and decorated in all the ways to which glass responds – engraving, sandblast and etch.

Glass engraving lacks the colour of lampworked glass, but the generally small scale of the engraved object rewards close attention. By engraving on the inner and outer surfaces of clear glass vessels, the British artist Laurence Whistler revived many of the exacting techniques lost through mass production and helped to make glass engraving a precious and valuable art (see Chapters 10 and 13). Engraving requires a focused vision and the patience to acquire the skills needed to become proficient. At present there is a dearth of glass engravers,

yet demand is such that those who practice the art have never been busier.

The sheer polished vessels used by artists for engraving and lampwork decoration are made at glass factories all over the world. The continued existence of these glassworks has always been precarious, dependent on market forces and driven by fashion. To engage the interest of the buying public, glass works must continue to make items for everyday use as well as collectables. The Royal Dutch Crystal factory at Leerdam in Holland held an exhibition in 2003 that featured 'contemporary' designs for tableware and other useful products created by leading architects, artists and designers from 1915 onwards. Today, Siem van der Marel (b.1944), the factory's house designer since 1966, uses the latest technology in the making of wine glasses, clocks and paperweights. His 'four seasons' set of vessels combines clarity of form with glowing colour. Van der Marel sees himself as a designer rather than an artist: 'Production is the most important thing. I'd rather make a good design – accessible for a lot of people – than make one-of-a-kind objects'.

Engraved decanter with pattern of grasses and mouse stopper, by Jackie Allwood. Supplied by the artist

The consistent demand by the glass factories for expertise in glass design and manipulation is vital for the future of glass workers everywhere. For example, the glass artist Ann Wolff (b.1937) learned her craft first at the Pukebergs Glasbruk in Sweden and subsequently at Kosta Boda, where she worked as a designer from 1964-1970. Her 'Snowball' candle holder continues to be popular for festive winter table settings. Independently, Wolff has made remarkable things using glass in her own inimitable way. Her architectural glass contains images that stimulate the imagination of the viewer while retaining an authoritative presence within the building. Besides working in flat glass, Wolff has created complex images that explore the female experience on vessels of varying shapes and sizes and on freeform pieces. Recently she has experimented with cast glass, first in the Czech Republic and later in her own studio in Transjö, Sweden. Wolff's engagement with issues that all women encounter has brought her work a responsive audience.

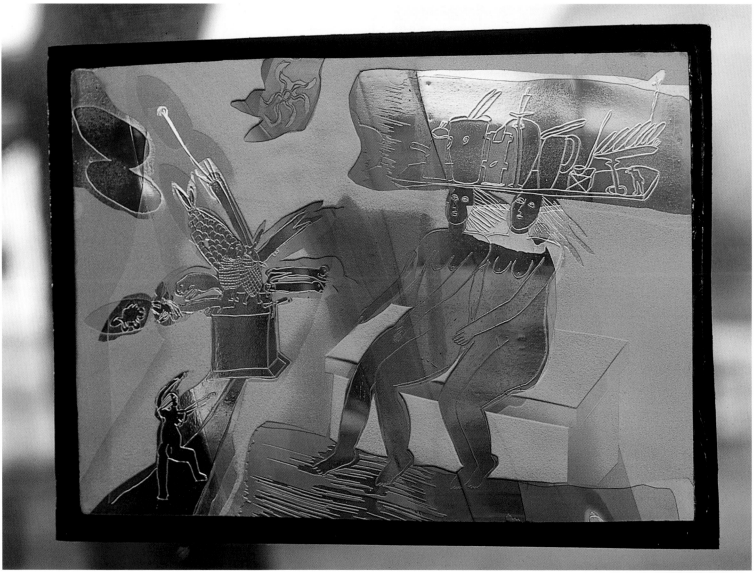

Details of etched and sandblasted work by Ann Wolff showing the strength and delicacy of her unique imagery, 1979. Supplied by Caroline Swash

Collaboration and Support

The practise of almost all the arts tends to be an introspective process. Ideas emerge in solitude; so much must be done by the artist's hand alone. So it is encouraging to encounter groups of artists who have joined together voluntarily to work on similar themes. One such organization is the International Women's Stained Glass Workshop. The group was founded by the German artist Helga Reay-Young who organised an exhibition in 1988 entitled '36 women from 12 countries'. The show travelled in Germany and France and was bought in its entirety for the Nishida Museum in Toyama, Japan.

From this first show emerged the idea of a bi-annual workshop and exhibition, each one being held in a different country. The first was hosted in 1989 by Sigrídur Ausgeirsdóttir in Iceland, the second in Wales, the third in Austria then Japan, Ireland, America, New Zealand and Canada. Each exhibition relates to the previous gathering so that every show has a theme, yet the artists' responses are different. The joy of these events is the lack of rivalry and commercial pressure. Here art is made in glass in a very pure and cheerful fashion, a delight to see.

Women's International Glass Workshop, Colarado 1999
L-R Holly Sandford, Mary Mackey, Cornelia König, Marie Foucault-Phipps, Helga Reay-Young, Waltraud Hackenberg, Linda Lichtman, Ginger Ferrell. Supplied by Caroline Swash

'Memories', glass and wire by
Helga Reay-Young, 1996.
Supplied by the artist

The women themselves have benefited greatly from these experiences. Reay-Young has established a reputation as one of Europe's most interesting artists and has evolved her own methods of helping her audience to see ordinary things in a new way. Influenced by the ideas of the Arte Povera movement in Italy, she works in the simplest materials, glass and wire exploring what she describes as the 'always felt and rarely seen relationship between nature and an artistic concept'. The Irish painter, Mary Mackey has found a parallel universe in the possibilities of coloured glass. She seeks to pin down the fleeting moment of 'Sudden clarity sensed in a special place, a particular time ... the impression and feeling stored and enriched by the treasuring of it until it becomes expressed'. The American artist Ginger Ferrell combines a background in photography and design with glass. An intrepid explorer of new techniques, she is intrigued by the possibilities of the story. The fine New Zealand artist Holly Sandford uses recognisable images in a painterly style. She has achieved fame in her country as an architectural glass artist. Deborah Coombs is currently making superb painterly windows in the United States while British artists Chris Bird-Jones and Chinks Vere Grylls use glass to make light work in interesting ways on different surfaces.

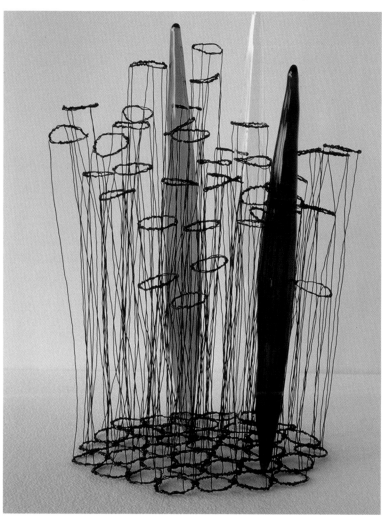

'Breaking the spell II', glass and wire by Helga Reay-Young, 2000. Supplied by the artist

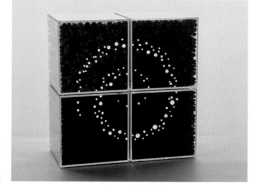

'Continuity', 4 glass cubes, glass rods and tree branches by Helga Reay-Young, 2002. Supplied by the artist

'One Tree Hill', layered glass and tree branch by Helga Reay-Young, 2004. Supplied by the artist

'Serendipity', mixed media piece by Helga Reay-Young, 2004/5. Supplied by the artist

'The importance of light', timber and glass rods by Helga Reay-Young, 2000. Supplied by the artist

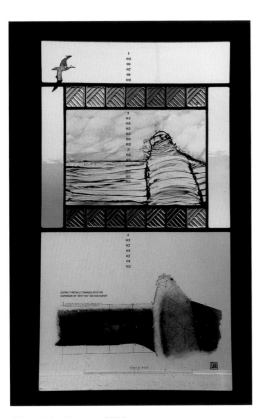

*'Tears of the albatross', exhibition
panel by Ginger Ferrell, 2004.
Supplied by the artist*

*'Beautiful Bjork', exhibition
panel by Ginger Ferrell, 2005.
Supplied by the artist*

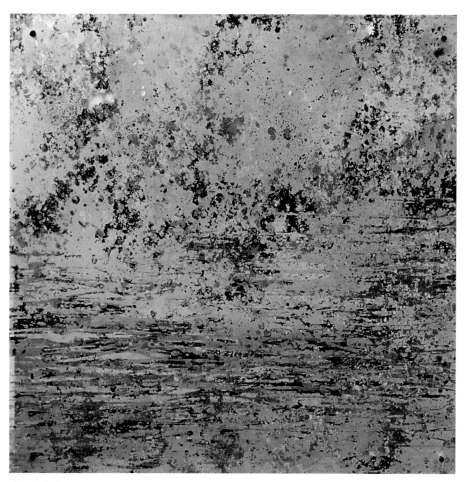

'The sky behind', exhibition panel by
Mary Mackey shown at the Lavitt Gallery,
Cork and the Catherine Hammond Gallery,
Glen Garrif, 2005. Supplied by the artist

'Stone windows', Ireland by Holly
Sandford, 2000. Supplied by the artist

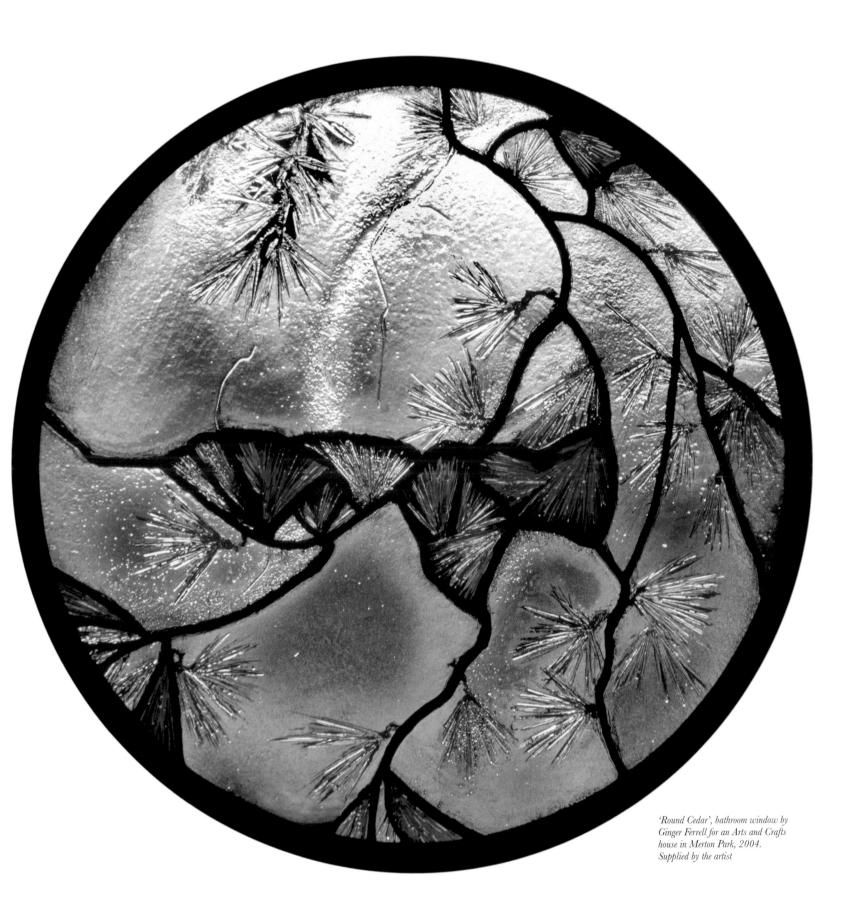

'Round Cedar', bathroom window by
Ginger Ferrell for an Arts and Crafts
house in Merton Park, 2004.
Supplied by the artist

'Residential', window by Holly Sandford, 2003. Supplied by the artist

'From dark places', enameled and fused glass with wood by Chris Bird-Jones, 2004. Supplied by the artist

Detail of installation using dichroic glasss at Y Capel, Llangollen by Chris Bird-Jones, 2003. Supplied by the artist

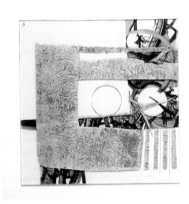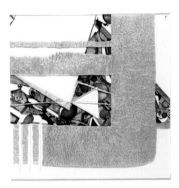

'Untitled 2003', fused glass with metal foil and asphalt lacquer paint by Yoshi Yamauchi. Supplied by the artist

'Untitled 2004', glass panel by Yoshi Yamauchi. Supplied by the artist

'Untitled 2004', glass panel by Yoshi Yamauchi. Supplied by the artist

The Women's Workshop group organise events themselves, finding suitable exhbition spaces in the selected countries, producing their own publicity material and sharing expenses. This pattern of voluntary effort exists in many other, more formal groups. Tutors on glass courses, for example, arrange master classes and exhibitions for their students that provide essential contact with professionals in the field. Unfortunately this activity is threatened in the European Union, as the concern on the part of managers of art institutions about new health and safety regulations has caused the closure of many glass courses. It is hoped that new centres will be built to take their place in the future.

Societies for the advancement of glass art have existed for some time in the English-speaking world. These too, are run by volunteers whose out of pocket expenses are supported by membership fees with occasional assistance from grant-giving bodies. The British Society of Master Glass Painters, Contemporary Glass Society and the Canadian Artists in Stained Glass fall into this category. The Stained Glass Association of America supports individuals and firms designing and conserving architectural glass – mostly for churches. At Wheaton Village, Millville,

New Jersey a hot glass workshop, galleries and craft studios have been established to preserve and celebrate the glass making tradition established there in 1806. Glass artists Paul Stankard and Thomas Patti initiated a fellowship scheme which has been running since 1983 to enable artists to work at Wheaton Village with technical support.

The European Studio Glass Association (ESGA) was founded in 2003 by a group of studio glass lovers and collectors who had noticed the lack of European support for the medium. Their first action was to create a web site to inform enthusiasts of current events and to display new works. Acting as a pressure group, they encourage museums to acquire historic pieces of studio glass and promote the presentation of new work. Programmes organised by groups such as these support the art and craft of glass in valuable ways and it is vital that they continue to do so.

Within the last 20 years, museums have begun to take an interest in glass, particularly studio pieces. In 2003 there were already over 300 museums worldwide with glass in their permanent collections and most

Interior of Icelandic artist Sigrún Einarsdóttir's shop. Supplied by the artist

'Whisper' suspended glass curtain made of interlinked rings by Chiho Hitomi winner of the Bombay Sapphire prize, 2002. Supplied by the artist

large museums have significant holdings. In the United States, The Corning Museum in Corning, New York, has the most internationally comprehensive archive of images and objects, but several smaller museums are devoted to focused collections, such as the Museum of American glass in Millville, New Jersey and the Museum of Glass in Tacoma, Washington, for contemporary glass. In Britain, national museums such as the Victoria and Albert in London have recently added contemporary studio glass to their permanent collection of stained glass panels in the permanent collections and arranged related exhibitions and lectures. Specialist centres devoted exclusively to glass exist at Ebeltoft Glasmuseet in Denmark, Broadfield House Glass Museum in the West Midlands and the Pilkington 'World of Glass' Museum at St Helens outside Liverpool. There are three important glass museums in Germany at Frauenau, Immenhausen and Linnich. There is a glass museum at Romont in Switzerland, one at Charleroi in Belgium and two glass museums in France at Sars Poteries, Charleroi and Liége. In Japan, glass has an enthusiastic following and museums can be found at Koganezaki, Niijima, Notojima and Kitazawa.

Located on the west coast of the United States, Pilchuck stands apart. Here legendary courses are run every year, taught by experts from all over the world. Examples of contemporary glass are held in the Prescott collection of Pilchuck Glass in Seattle and the Pilchuck Glass Collection at Stanwood. Workshops such as those held at Pilchuck form an important part of any artist's development. The Canadian artist Lutz Haufschild studied there in 1983 when Johannes Schreiter was tutor. He felt that the schools success had to do with its philosophy expressed in the sentence 'you don't really teach art but expose students to practising artists'. From the beginning hot glass and architectural glass were taught or rather experienced at Pilchuck, allowing young artists the opportunity to try out new ideas away from their own studios in a spectacular forest setting. The success of this venture has inspired others. The most recent glass school to open in Europe has been North Lands Creative Glass in Lybster, a small fishing village situated on the northeast coast of Scotland. Founded in the 1990s. North Lands offers courses and master classes every summer with emphasis on new materials and working methods in hot glass of all kinds.

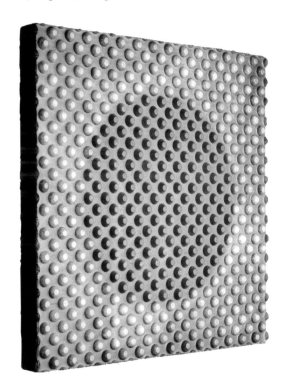

Examples of Sigrún Einarsdóttir's work in glass. Supplied by the artist

Prizes have certainly played an important part in promoting studio glass as part of the wider intellectual community. The annual Bombay Sapphire prize for glass attracts a wide variety of entries including architectural schemes and studio pieces. Short listed entries are displayed at the firm's London show room, bringing the most exciting ideas in glass to a wide audience. An exquisite glass chandelier by the Japanese artist Chiho Hitomi won the Bombay Sapphire prize in 2002. Another London based prize, The Jerwood, is awarded to a contemporary artist working in a medium chosen by the Jerwood committee. Glass was the medium for 2003, metal for 2004 and wood for 2005. The Jutta Cuny Franz prize for glass is an annual award established in memory of this exceptionally talented young German artist. In 2003 there were 172 entrants from 31 countries from as far afield as Chile and Brazil. Another important prize for studio glass was inaugurated by the Hokkaido Museum in Sapporo Japan.

Often an artist's reputation will be established by the attention received as a result of winning a prize and even small sums can make a difference. For many years the City livery company, The Worshipful Company of Glaziers, has organised a modest student and young artist prize for the best design and sample panel for an architectural commission. Even preparation for submission involves students in the correct procedure for a commission, a learning process that will help the young artist in the future.

'Sure enough, the duck', panel by Peter Young in the collection of the Stained Glass Museum, Ely, 1998. Supplied by Caroline Swash

'Paraxis II', 2005, by Anthony Scala, winner of the Glass Sellers award in 2005. Supplied by the artist

Glass table lamps by students at the National College of Art and Design, Dublin, 1995. Supplied by Caroline Swash

'Queen Esther – Mask for a Purimspiel', by Ruth Taylor Jacobson. Supplied by Caroline Swash

Commissions in both studio and architectural glass remain subject to the ebb and flow of the economy. Studio glass needs a captivating environment for display in a place where an audience can be lured into a buying mood. Many studio glass artists show several different kinds of vessels, an affordable range of candle holders and wine glasses, for example, while the more complex exhibition pieces are in the process of gestation. Sigrún Einarsdóttir, for example, makes beautiful ornamental vessels of different kinds at her studio in Kjalarnes, Iceland. She and her sister also create wall pieces and exhibit their new work in Galleries in mainland Europe. Ironically, the commercial glass firms do the reverse, holding exhibitions of dramatic new, sculptural work in order to attract attention to their commercial designs.

For some mysterious reason glass has become an important medium, simply through the possibility of its expressive powers. The whole question of commissioning work is fraught with wonder and excitement. It is important that as many people as possible indulge in this pleasure! Coloured glass for a new door panel can add to the personality of the home, while a glass panel changes imperceptibly with the light throughout the day, becoming an intriguing presence in the room. A commissioned blown or engraved piece can mark a special occasion in a unique way. Private patronage is vital; so too is public support. The memorial window need not be trivial or mediocre but adventurous and beautiful. The dark library need not be plain glazed but could be enhanced with sparkling glass that will pick up light from every part of the room and multiply it a thousand-fold.

East Window for Hemsby Parish Church, Norfolk, by Caroline Swash, 1985. Supplied by Caroline Swash

Detail of the glass wall panel with programmed lighting by Julian Ewart, 2000. Supplied by Caroline Swash

Glass mural using printed photo collage by Deborah Sundersky. Supplied by Caroline Swash

Glass wall with panel with programmed lighting by Julian Ewart, 2000. Supplied by Caroline Swash

The ancient skills need not be abandoned but instead given new life. Eccentricity is a vital element. Indeed, we need new glass that refuses to 'fit in' to traditional approaches. We need work that is personal and serious and consistent, that takes no notice of fashion or what is popular. The antithesis of this approach is equally important. For we also require a subtle responsive dialogue with architecture, for the use of glass as an element within a building – part of the orchestration of space. It is to be hoped that the future will bring more stained glass of real profundity of thought for our churches and also more sparkling, shifting, light transforming projects for our offices and public buildings and new ideas being shown all over the world using glass.

'Karakia – Maori Prayer' by Kathy Shaw 2004. Selected for the New Glass Revue 26 organised by Corning Glass Museum, New York. Supplied by Caroline Swash

'El's Tree' etched and painted panel by Kathy Shaw, 2002. Supplied by Caroline Swash

A room divider between the Hotel lobby and the reception seating area of the Sheraton Hotel, Frankfurt Airport, Germany designed by Hildegard Pax, 2001. The multilayered glass composition is constructed of sandblasted and etched glass panels with coloured rods. Supplied by Hildegard Pax

Part of the room divider at the Sheraton Hotel, Frankfurt Airport, Germany. Supplied by Hildegard Pax

Detail of the room divider at the Sheraton Hotel, Frankfurt Airport, Germany. Supplied by Hildegard Pax

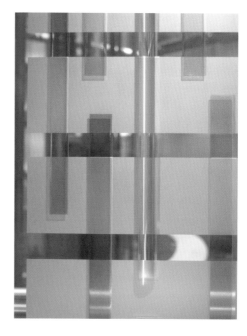

Detail of one of the panels for the White & Case reception area by Hildegard Pax showing the effect of the layered glass. Pax describes her architectural glass as having 'shadows and projections which are captured within the work creating new visual experiences'. Supplied by Hildegard Pax

Three panels from the White & Case reception area. Supplied by Hildegard Pax

Glass panels in the reception area of offices of White & Case, London designed by Hildegard Pax, 2004. The float glass panels have sandblasted, dichroic and bonded elements including glass rods. Supplied by Hildegard Pax

Glass wall with linear decoration for the upper corridor in the Wales Millenium Centre by Rodney Bender, 2000. Supplied by the artist

Structural glass blocks between slate wall surfaces in the Wales Millenium Centre by Rodney Bender, 2000. Supplied by the artist

Glass plates made to the designs of the Danish architect Jorn Utzon by Rodney Bender, 2002

Interior of Neubiberg Church with coloured glass designed by Thierry Boissel. Supplied by the artist

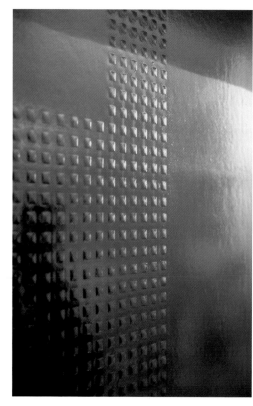

Far Left:
Coloured and textured glass in Neubiberg Church designed by Thierry Boissel. Supplied by the artist

Left:
Detail showing the textured glass in Neubiberg Church designed by Thierry Boissel. Supplied by the artist

'Birds' window for St Francis Church at Villengen-Schweningen by Thierry Boissel. Supplied by the artist

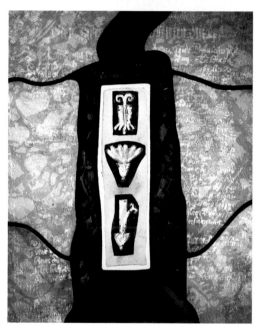

*'Traveller's Flowers'. A series of three exhibition
panels by Caroline Swash based on Icelandic
iconography, shown at the Kopavogur Art Museum
and the Cochrane Gallery, London, 2005.
Supplied by Caroline Swash*

'Carved Spoons' A series of three exhibition panels by Caroline Swash based on Icelandic iconography, shown at the Kopavogur Art Museum and the Cochrane Gallery, London, 2005. Supplied by Caroline Swash

Glossary

Acid-etching
A process that involves corroding all or part of a glass surface with hydrofluoric acid. If used with cased glass, the process exposes the layer beneath, which is usually in a contrasting colour. The process is also used to create texture or a matt appearance.

Annealing
The process of cooling hot glass very gradually to eliminate internal stresses that produce cracks and breakage.

Antique glass
Glass made using traditional, non-industrial methods; mouth-blown hand made glass.

Appliqué
A technique in which pieces of glass are bonded onto a clear glass sheet to create a collage of colours.

Bevelled glass
Flat glass where the edges, which usually meet at right angles, are cut away, producing a chamfered edge. This can be done for decorative effect and also to prevent chipping.

Blown glass (mouth-blown glass)
Glass made by blowing air through a hollow blow-pipe into a gather of molten glass and then shaping it using manual techniques, without the use of moulds. Considered to be the highest level of glassmaking requiring talent, artistry, skill and strength.

Bullions
Technically, the thickened point at which the blow pipe was attached to a piece of blown glass. Usually used interchangeably with 'pebbles'.

Came (or calme)
A strip of lead that in cross-section is formed like an H, used to hold pieces of glass together in a panel or window.

Cameo glass
An object formed of two or more layers of coloured glass (see 'cased' or 'flashed' glass), in which the surface has been cut through by carving or acid etching to reveal the layers beneath, leaving the design in relief.

Cane
A thin rod of glass. These are sometimes fused together in decorative patterns and sliced to make millefiori or mosaic glassware.

Cartoon
The full-scale drawing from which a stained glass window is made.

Cased glass
Glass made of several layers fused together, made by blowing one layer inside another.

Casting
The process of pouring molten glass into a mould and allowing it to harden

Cire perdue
Literally, 'lost wax' – a technique that involves pouring molten glass into a mould formed from a wax original. Since the wax is destroyed during the process each piece is unique.

Cold paint
Paint that is applied after the glass has cooled; it lies on the surface and is not fired into the glass.

Combed decoration
Threads of opaque glass applied to a molten glass surface of a different colour. The threads are then combed or dragged with a tool to produce a feathered or zigzag pattern before the glass hardens.

Confetti glass
Clear or lightly tinted glass embedded with fragments of deeper colour.

Copper foil
Used instead of lead to bind pieces of glass together in a window or panel. Individual pieces of glass are surrounded by copper tape, laid edge to edge and soldered along the join.

Coupe
A shallow glass bowl.

Crystal
Colourless transparent glass made with lead oxide.

Cut glass
Glass decorated with facets and grooves made by cutting into the surface with a rotating wheel of iron or stone. Cut glass has a high degree of light refraction.

Dalle de verre
Thick chunks or slabs of coloured glass fractured with a hammer and set into concrete or epoxy; used in stained glass windows.

Diamond point engraving
The use of a needle with a diamond point to lightly scratch the surface of glass.

Dichroic glass
Glass made with a thin layer of a metal oxide such as chromium, silicon, titanium, aluminium or zirconium depending on the colour wanted. Dichroic glass changes colour depending on whether it transmits or reflects light.

Drapery glass
Glass pulled or twisted into folds while still in a molten state.

Enamel
A pigment composed of one or more metal oxides and powered glass that is fused onto the surface of glass when fired at a low temperature. The resulting colour, which is only discernible after firing, is not as susceptible to wear as cold colours.

Engraving
The process of cutting a design into the surface of glass. This can be done using a wheel (see 'wheel-carving'), a diamond point (see 'diamond point engraving') or by stippling (see 'stippling').

Etching
The process of decorating glass by using hydrofluoric acid to eat away portions of the surface. The glass is covered with an acid resistant wax which is scratched with a tool to produce the design. The object is then dipped in acid to etch the exposed areas into the surface.

Faceted glass
Glass in which the rounded surface has been flattened in small areas, often to resemble cut gems.

Favrile glass
The trade name registered by Tiffany in 1894 for glass that was sprayed while hot with metallic salts to produce an iridescent lustre. The colours, often bluish green or golden, depended on the colour and density of the metal. It was initially intended to reproduce the appearance of ancient Roman glass, excavated after being buried for centuries in damp soil. The name is derived from the German word Faber, meaning colour and/or fabrile, which in Old English means handmade.

Flashed glass
Glass made by coating a base of clear or lightly tinted glass with a thin layer of coloured or opaque glass. Often shortened to 'Flash glass'.

Flat glass
Glass made in a thin sheet with parallel sides. The term 'flat glass' is often used to encompass the entire craft of stained glass, to differentiate it from 'hot glass' or 'studio' glass that is blown, moulded or cold-worked using a variety of techniques.

Float Glass
The primary industrial method for making flat glass, introduced by Pilkington Brothers in 1959. A continuous ribbon of molten glass from the furnace floats across a bath of molten tin under strictly controlled conditions and is then polished and annealed.

Flocking
Pulverized wool or felt applied to glass to produce a texture or pattern.

Fluogravure
A process developed by Muller Fréres in which enamel is bonded to the surface of a single or double layer glass vessel, then etched with acid so that it appears painted.

Frosted glass
Glass with a matt or clouded surface created by hydrofluoric acid and ammonia, a technique used extensively by René Lalique. Also, a network of fine cracks across the surface of a vessel produced by immersing hot glass briefly in cold water.

Fused glass
Two or more pieces of stained glass placed either side by side or in layers, which are melted together.

Gaffer
The lead glass blower of a team; the master blower.

Gather
A mass of molten glass attached to the end of a blowpipe.

Glass paste
A material made by grinding glass into a powder, adding a flux to facilitate melting, then heating and pouring into a mould. More commonly called 'pâte de verre'.

Internal decoration
Various types of embellishment applied on the inside surface of a glass vessel and therefore seen through the glass body.

Jewels
Small pieces of thick glass moulded with facets on one or both sides to resemble cut gems.

Kiln
A furnace or oven for melting glass or fusing enamels

Kiln-formed
Glass shaped by heating in a kiln until it 'slumps', or melts, into or over a mould beneath it.

Lampworking
A technique for assembling and manipulating fragments of glass with heat from a small flame. Lampworking is often used to create tiny glass figurines or applied decoration, such as handles, for blown vessels.

Lead
A heavy, soft, bluish-grey metal used to bind pieces of stained glass together into a window or panel (see 'came').

Lustre
An iridescent effect produced by spraying metallic salts onto the hot surface of a glass vessel.

Marquetrie de verre
A technique in which fragments of hot glass are embedded into a molten glass surface.

Martelé glass
Literally, 'hammered'. Glass with a multi-faceted surface in imitation of hand-hammered silver.

Moulded glass
Glassware made by blowing or pressing molten glass into a mould, which determines its shape. The glass was originally mouth blown, but by the end of the 19th century the process had been adapted to machines.

Mounts
Decorative metal attachments placed on a glass vessel that is generally of good quality. These may be functional (i.e., handles) or ornamental.

Mullions
The vertical bars separating the openings of a multi-light stained glass window, especially in Gothic architecture, or placed between glass panes.

Murrine glass
Modern glassware in which inserts of contrasting glass have been embedded as large pieces or long streaks.

Opal/Opalescent glass
Iridescent glass (see 'Lustre' and 'Favrile' glass).

Overlay
The outer layer of cased glass.

Pâte de cristal
A transparent form of pâte de verre.

Pâte de verre
Literally, 'paste of glass'. See 'glass paste'.

Patination
A technique similar to electro-plating for covering a glass surface with a thin layer of metal.

Pebbles
Irregular rounded bits of stained glass resembling cabochon gems, sometimes used in windows or panels to give depth and texture.

Plated glass
An American term for 'cased' glass.

Plating
Two or more pieces of stained glass laid one behind the other and leaded together to produce a special effect.

Press-moulding
Glassware shaped by placing molten glass in a mould and pressing it with a metal plunger to form the interior surface. In the resulting piece the interior shape is independent of the exterior shape.

Quarries
Small panes of clear or lightly tinted glass shaped as a diamonds, squares or rectangles and leaded together to make whole windows or surrounds for stained glass.

Rolled glass
Sheet glass made by passing the hot glass between rollers, often imprinted with a pattern.

Roundel
A small panel of stained glass, often circular, upon which a detailed religious or secular subject is depicted in enamels and, sometimes, silver stain.

Sand-blasting
Subjecting the surface of glass, often partly covered by a template, to a jet of air containing sand, crushed flint or powdered iron in order to etch a design or texture.

Silver stain
A mixture of silver salts and neutral yellow ochre that, when fired at a low temperature, produces a yellow colour on clear or white glass. Used to decorate stained glass windows from about 1300 onward, silver stain is applied to the exterior of the glass, while the inside surface is painted in the normal way.

Slab glass
Antique glass blown into a square bottle and then cut into flat sections. Made from around 1890 until the 1940s, slab glass is irregular in thickness and intensity of colour.

Slumping
A technique of slowly heating glass until gravity forces it to conform to the contours of the form on which it rests.

Stippling
Striking glass with a diamond or hardened steel point to produce an image or design made up of many shallow dots or tiny scratches called 'stipples'. Different densities of stipples are used to create highlights or details.

Tempered glass
Glass that is made stronger or more durable through a physical or chemical process.

Tracery
The network or interlace of mullions in the upper part of a Gothic stained glass window.

Turtleback tiles
Irregular slabs of blown glass, often iridescent.

Verre eglomise
Glass painted on the back.

Vitreous enamel
A pigment that is transformed into glass when fired (see 'enamel').

Vitrification
The process of changing materials into glass by heat and fusion.

Wheel-carving (wheel engraving)
The process of embellishing a glass surface by grinding with a rotating wheel, using abrasive discs of various sizes and materials. Also, with cased glass, creating a design in relief by carving away the surface to reveal a contrasting layer of glass beneath.

White glass
A term used to describe glass that is either clear and transparent or milky and translucent in appearance.

Index

INTRODUCTION I-IV

ARCHITECTURAL & STUDIO GLASS IN THE UK 336-399

Beleschenko, Alex (b.1951) 344-349
glass for atrium St John's College, Oxford 344,345
Herz Jesu Church, Munich 'Gospel of Nails' 347-9
screen St John's College, Oxford 344
Southwark Station 346, 347
The Lighthouse, Glasgow 346, 348
Cardross, Harry 340-343
Clarke, Brian 350-358
Stansted Airport:
100 New Bridge Street: Prudential Group
New Synagogue, Darnstadt: Country Club, Yuzurihara, Japan
Conference & Leisure Centre, Bari, Italy: Gagosin Gallery
Jones, Graham (1958) 359-363
Swansea College of Art: 'Poet's Corner', Westminster Abbey: Minster Court, City of London: Freiburg Church, Germany: Melancthon Church, Dortmund
Layton, Peter 338
Lawson, John 340-343
Ramada Hotel, Dubai
Younger, Alan 340
Laylayty Wedding Hall, Jeddah

Glass and the Community 364-373

Coin Street Cooperative, South Bank, London 364
Donlin, Martin 366-369
Oracle Centre, Raading: 'Urban Splash' Tibb Street Bridge Link, Manchester
Hiscott, Amber 366, 367
Swansea College of Art: panel for Great welling Hospital: Wales Millenium Centre
Jones, Catrin 364, 365
City Library & Club centre, Sunderland: 'The Wind that Blows me is called light': 'The Laboratory of the Spirit'
Lewis, Tim 370, 371
with students: Memorial window to Lifeboat men lost in the Samtampa disaster: All Saints Church, Rhinwbina, Cardiff
Littleton, Harvey 374
Smyth, Ann 372, 373
Glass walls for the Public Records, Kew 1995
Michael Tippett Centre, Bath Spa, University

College: Royal College of Art - 3 day Conference 1998 'The Search for Meaning' at Victoria & Albert Museum

Studio Glass 374-387

Brocklehurst, Keith 378
Handscape 2005: Inquisition 2004
Bruce, Jane 375
glassblowing - Glasshouse
Cook, John 374-378
Head of Ceramics & Glass, Leicester Polytechnic; Conference 'Working with Hot Glass': British Artists In Glass (society)
Cummings, Keith 379, 380
'Pools': 'Lilac Time'
Fladgate, Deborah 380
'Pod 1' module
Flavell, Dr Ray 379
Edinburgh: Greenpiece: Interface: Shoal
Herman, Sam 374, 375, 378
Fulbright Scholar, Edinburgh: Department of Glass & Ceramics, Royal College of Art: The Glasshouse, Neal Street
Lane, Danny 386-387
studied Central St Martin's with Patrick Reyntiens: 'Etruscan Chair': Miss Wiggle
Layton, Peter (b.1934) 382-385
energized the glass movement in Britain: British Artists in Glass: The Contemporay Glass Society: Workshop in Rotherhithe 1970: London Glass Blowing Workshop: Vessels 386-387
Leckie, Audrey 388, 389
Libenský, Stanislav 374
Meech, Annette 375
Gourd Vase Bulbes Ranges
Newell, Steven 376
Courtesan Series: 'Devils Conspire': 'My Omi's': 'The Thing that he desires': 'Moon Dance'
Solucn, Pauline 375
Vessels
Tooley, Stan 375
Williams, Christopher 375

Engraved Glass 388-399

Ainslie, Chris 388, 389
Coleman, Katharine 392-393
Dreiser, Peter 392, 388
The Techniques of Glass Engraving

Denison-Pender & James 388, 399
stippled engraved goblets 399
Gilliam, Tony 388
Harris, Josephine 388
engraved bowl and Roundel
Kinnaird, Alison 393-396
'Psalmsong': 'Streetwise' 395, 396
Leckie, Audrey 388
Malejam, Julian 392
Newell, Steven 376
Pennell, Ronald 394, 396
Hon. Professor, Academy of Arts, Prague: Hon. Professor The University of Wolverhampton
Reekie, David (b.1947) 396
Stourbridge College of Art: North Staffordshire Polytechnic
Reid, Colin 396-398
Cotswolds 1981 - New Mills, Stroud: Spiral Form; 'Bamboo Scroll' 398

ARTS & CRAFTS MOVEMENT IN ENGLAND AND AMERICA (THE) 1-19

Burne-Jones, Edward 4-6
Morris, William 2-7
Church of Jesus, Troutbeck-East Window: 'David Poeta': All Saints, Cambridge
Webb, Philip 6

British Glass from 1890-1930 9-11

Morris, William 9, 14
Newill, Mary 10, 11
Parsons, Karl 10, 11
St Cecilia: 'Hammer & Tongs'
Whall, Christopher 9, 10, 12
Windows 15th century Lady Chapel, Gloucester: St Chad

The Stained-Glass Revival in Ireland 12-13

Child, Alfred E. 12
Clarke, Harry 13
9 panels, 'Queens': 'Rape of the Lock'
Geddes, Wilhelmina 12
Healym Michael 12
Hone, Evie 12
influenced by Gleizes: panel St John; Gouache
Purser, Sarah 12
'The Tower of Glass'

The Arts & Crafts Movement in America 14-19

Elmslie, George Grant 18, 19
Babson, Henry B. House windows 19

Greene, Charles Sumner & Green Henry, Mather 18
  Adelaide M. Tichenor House inspired by
  Japanese garden: window for Tichenor House 19
Hubbard, Elbert 14
  Boycroft Arts & Crafts Community in East
  Aurora: Prairie School
Hunter, Dard 14
  Rycroft Inn
Lloyd Wright, Frank 14-18
  window Auditorum Building 15: Skylight 15:
  Casement & Transom,
  Bradley House 16: Lamp & Vase 18

ART NOUVEAU IN AMERICA 38-63

La Farge, John (1835-1910) 41, 42, 43

Tiffany Stained Glass Windows 44-51

  'Snowball' panel 44, 45
  Exposition Universelle in Paris 1900 44
  'Chansons de Printemps' (1895) Colonial Club
  New York 46, 47
  Allegorical subjects 48
  'Swan Fountain' 1905 49
  'River of Light' 50
  Danner Memorial Window 1913 51

Tiffany Blown Glass 52-57

  influenced by archealogical sites: Roman
  Empire; Egypt; Cyprus Cameo glass 55
  Blue 'Favrile' glass 52
  vessels and lamps 52-57

Tiffany Lamps 58-63

  Geometric designs: Islamic & American
  Indian motifs 58
  Cone shades 1906 60
  Irregular Border shades 62-63

ART NOUVEAU IN EUROPE 20-37

  Scientific breakthroughs in chemistry
  & technology 23

Glass Making in France 24-31

Berge, Henri 28
  pate de verre
Clos, Henri 1880's 28
Daum Fréres 28
Despret, Georges 28
Gallé, Emile (1846-1904) 22-29
  L'Eternal Debat 23: new colours and forms:
  Marqueterie de verre: Cameo glass: overlay
  glazes: predominance of natural forms for
  decoration 24-27
  Exhibition Universelle in Paris 1900 awarded
  Grand Prix & Legion d'Honneur 28
  Martelé glass 28
Majorelle, Louis 28
Muller Fréres 29
  Lamps and Vessels 24-31, 32-37

Germany and Austria 32-35

  Jugenstil 32
  Darmstadt glasswork
Bing, Siegfried 32
Christian, Désiré 32
Hoffmann, Josef 35
Koepping, Karl 32
Koloman, Moser 35

Schneckendorf, Josef Emil 32
Witwe, Loetz 34
Werlstalle, Wiener 35

Art Noueau in Britain 36-37

Dresser, Dr Christopher (1834-1904) 36
  'Clutha' glass ancient influence 36
MacDonald, Margaret 37
Rennie Mackintosh, Charles 37

CZECH CONNECTION (THE) 448-461

  Bohemia centre of glass making since
  the Middle Ages
Bilek, Ilja 460
  'Silent Understanding', Corning Glass Museum
Brychtová, Jaroslava 452, 453, 455-458
Karel, Marian 460
  'Blue Cone', Corning Glass Museum
Piva, Oldrich 461
  'Column', Corning Glass Museum
Libenský, Stanislav 451-458
  studied-School of Decoraative Arts in Prague:
  director of the Glass Studio-Academy of
  Applied in Prague: 'Expulsion from Paradise'
  and detail: drawing for 'Miska' (Head Bowl):
  'Miska' Head Bowl with Jaroslava Brychtová:
  'Lap Study': 'Lap' with Brychtová: 'Blue
  Connection' with Brychtová: 'Heart/Red
  Flower' with Brychtová-Czechoslovak Embassy,
  New Delhi, India: 'Sphere in a Cube' with
  Brychtová: 'Cube in a Cube' with Brychtová:
  Two windows, St Vitus Cathedral, Prague
  Castle: windows Gothic Chapel Horowsky,
  Tyn with Brychtová: 'Crystal Wall'/'Window',
  Prague Town Hall with Brychtová: Crystal
  Window, Glass Wall, Kyoto, Japan with
  Brychtová: 'The Last Emperor' with Brychtová:
  'Green Eye of the Pyramid' with Brychtová:
  'Three Columns' with Brychtová
Sabóková, Gizela 460
  'Come to Me', Corning Glass Museum
Trnka, Pavel 459
  'Zyklus Spectrum'
Vachtová, Dana 460
  'The Elements 1', Corning Glass Museum
Witwe Loetz 451

COVENTRY AND BEYOND 234-295

Spence, Basil 237-286
Church of St Mary-le-Bow, London 238-239
Clarke, Geoffrey & New, Keith 238
Hayward, John 238-239
Hutton, John 238
Léger Fernand 238
Traherne Margaret 238
Thomas, Brian (1912-1990) 242, 245-247
Shakespeare's 'Bottom & Puck': Hamlet & Lady
Macbeth 244-5
Webb, Christopher (1886-1966)
  St Lawrence Jury 244-245

**The Stained Glass Artists of Coventry
Cathedral 248**

**The Baptistery Window: John Piper & Patrick
Reyntiens 249-265**

Piper, John & Reyntiens Patrick 249-256
  The Baptistry Window 249

Piper, John 249-257
  'Venice Fantasy' 249-250: 'Abstract' 251
  'The Way the Truth and the Life' with
  Reyntiens, Oundle School 252: George VI,
  Memorial Chapel, Windsor: East window St
  Bartholomew's Church, Nettlebed: 253:
  'Nativity', Iffley Church, Oxford 254: Benjamin
  Britten Memorial Window, 255: Foliate Heads
  'The Green Man' 256
Piper, John & Reyntiens, Patrick 258
  Liverpool Metropolitian Cathedral 258:
  St Margaret's, Westminster, 258-9: Chapel,
  Robinson College, Cambridge 258
Reyntiens, Patrick 260
  Head of Fine Art, Central & St Martin's College
  of Art 'Sister's of Mercy', The Nunnery,
  Whitechapel: 'Apollo & Slaying of the daughters
  of Niobe' 260-2: 'Hercules and the Cretan
  Bull' 264: Commedia del Arte' 1990

**The Nave Windows of Coventry Cathedral:
Lawrence Lee, Keith New, Geoffrey Clarke
266-285**

Clarke, Geoffrey 270
  panel High Altar Cross 270
Lee, Lawrence 267
  Plants and Flowers: Tradescant (father & son),
  St Mary Lambeth: 'Adam & Eve': Persian
  Garden 267: Church of St Mary the Virgin,
  Cuddington, Surrey 268
New, Keith (b.1924) 267, 272-275
  Windows Highgate School Chapel; St John's
  Church Farm Street, London: St John's Church,
  Ermine, Suffolk: Painting gardens at Penhurst:
  Commonwealth House, Holland Park, London
Bradley, Ray 282-285
  Post House Hotel, Hampstead: Vanwall Racing
  Car Works: Bar Hill Shared Church,
  Cambridge: windows Harley Library,
  Southampton University: Upper Perrin Gallery,
  Leighton House Museum & Art Gallery
Fisher, Alfred 276-277
  Pierre Fourmantrau Metz set up dalle de verre
  studio: Church of the Latter Day Saints, London
Fairs, Tom 282
  Holborn College of Law, Language &
  Commerce, Red Lion Square, London
Ghosh, Amal (b.1933) 274
  Central School of Art & St Martin's: Eastman
  Dental Institute, London
Traherne, Margaret 276-278
  Glass Unity Chapel, Coventry: 'Pictures for
  Schools': Memorial window St Peter's Church
  Wootton Wawen: glass in Liverpool and
  Manchester Cathedrals
Younger, Alan 269
  'Rose' for St Alban's Cathedral: glass Henry VII
  Chapel, Westminster Abbey

The Engraver's Art 286-291

Dodson, Marigold 288, 289-291
  'King Lear' 290: Dunkirk Memorial 291:
  Screens Mercury House, London:
  Plymouth Civic Centre panels
Hutton, John 286-291
  'Zodiac', Cinema, Christchurch, New Zealand:
  Screen, Royal Scottish Museum: 'Angel'

lunette, Guildford Cathedral: Air Force Memorial at Runnymede: 'Angels' glass wall Coventry Cathedral

The Engraving Revival 292-295

Peace, David 292-293
Church of St Botolph, Aldgate, London: Roundels 'Images of Rajastan': 'Icarus': St Mary's Church, Newick, Sussex
Whistler, Lawrence 293-295
Window St Nicholas Church, Moreton, Devon: 'The Grass Cathedral' St Hugh's College, Oxford: 'Come Hither' Museum & Art Gallery, Birmingham

FORM AND FUNCTION 88-103

Albers, Joseph (1888-1976) 98, 100, 101, 102, 103
Director Black Mountain College 102
'Factory' 101
Bauhaus 92, 94-98, 100
'Homage to the Square' 102, 103
Brandt, Marianne (1893-1983) 96, 98
tableware, cutlery, lamps; ceiling light 96, 97
Cézanne, Paul, 90
van Doesberg, Theo (1883-1931) 92, 93, 98
Feininger, Lyonel (1871-1956) 93
Bauhaus Manifesto 93
Chicago Bauhaus 92
Gropius, Walter 92, 94, 145
Itten, Johannes (1888-1967) 94
Adolf Hotel, Stuttgart 94
Klee, Paul and Felix 94
Mondrian, Piet (1872-1944) 92
Picasso, Pablo 90
van de Velde, Henry 92
Wagenfeld, Wilhelm, (1900-1990) 95
Weimar School of Art
Braque, Georges 90, 91
Cubism 91

GLASS BETWEEN THE WARS 64-87

Influences, Skyscrapers & Jazz Clubs in New York; Europe Cubism, Vorticism & Futurism; Exotic Mesoamerican, African, Egypt artefacts and Art Deco

Art Deco Glass in France 68-79

Bouraine, Marcel (Sculptor) 74, 77
Brandt, Edgar 68
Delatte, André 74, 79
Gallé, Emile 68
Goupy, Marcel 74, 78
Argy-Rousseau, Joseph-Gabriel 74-76
Lalique, René 70-77, 84
Luce, Jean 74, 77
Majorelle, Louis 68
Marinot, Maurice 74, 77, 79

Art Deco Glass in England & America 80-83

Stuart Glass and Brierley Crystal
Farquharson, W. Clyne (1906-1977) 80, 81
Forsyth, Moira & Gordon 80
Knight, Dame Laura 80
Murray, Keith (1892-1928) 80-81
Ravilous, Eric 80
Sutherland, Graham 80
Waugh, Sidney (1904-1968) 82, 83

Architectural Glass 84-87

Bernard, Oliver 85, 87
Strand Palace Hotel 85, 87
Ingrand, Paula & Max 85
restaurants & apartments in France
Jouve, Paul (Sculptor) & Jeanin, Gaetan 85, 87
Lalique, René 84, 85
Dining car panels, Côte D'Azur Pullman 84: St Matthew's Church, Milbrook, Isle of Jersey: Aztec motif Ziggarat 85

GLASS DESIGN IN SCANDINAVIA AND ITALY 140-159

Finland 145-147
Aalto, Alvar (1898-1976) 145
'Orkidea' 1953
Sarpaneva, Timo (b.1926) 145
Milan Triennial Exhibition 1951
'Finlandia' & 'Marcel' vases
Sterns, Thomas 142
Wirkkala, Tapio (1915-1976) 145
Milan Triennial Exhibition 1951

Sweden 148-153

Orrefors Glasbruk 1898
Cyrin, Gunnar 153
'Cycle Touring'
Gate, Simon (1883-1945) 148
'Bacchus Bowl' - Paris Exhibition 1925
Hald, Edward (1883-1980) 149, 151
'Fireworks': engraved panel 149
Graal Technique used by Gate & Hadd 150
Lundin, Ingeborg 150
'Apple' glass
Öhrström, Edvin (1906-1994) 150
'Ariel' glass: 'Red Panther'
Palmquist, Sven 150, 151
'Ravenna' technique
Rytkönen, Martii 152
'Ravenna' bowl
Vallien, Bertil 153
'Journey'

Italy 154-159

Venice
Barovier, Ercole (1889-1974) 155, 156
Buzzi, Tomaso 154
'Coppa delle Mani'
Brancomi, Fulvio 155, 156, 157, 158
'Pezzato' & Scozzese vases
Brancomi & Venini 155-157
'Fazzoletto'
Fuga, Anzolo 156, 158
'Murrine' vase
Martens, Dino (1894-1979) 155
Poli, Flavio, (1900-1984) 156, 158
Sequso Vitre d'Arte
'Corroso' vase
Scarpa, Carlo 155
'Macchie' stained bowl 155
Sterns, Thomas 156, 159
'Focciate de Venezia'

INNOVATION IN GERMANY 198-233

The problem was to develop a visual language for the post war era. Would Medieval be appropriate?

Benner, Walther 202
'Madonna and Child' Stiftskirche, Herdecke
Derix Studios Taumustein, Kevelaer, Wiesbaden and Rottweil 202
Klos, Joachim 224, 225, 226
'Mystical Rose' St Kosmos and Damian, Bienen: Mid Glamorgan Crematorium, Brigend
Poensgen, Jochem 219-223, 226
Police Academy, Münster-Hildrup: Church of St Martin, Bad-Orb:Chapel, Senior Citizens Complex, Heiden, Borken: Telecom Regional Headquarters, Osnabrück 224
Reyntiens, Patrick & Schreiter, Johannes Swansea 211, 232
Schaffrath, Ludwig 206-210
Aachen Cathedral 206: Hesszsches Landesmuseum 207: Labyrinth Window, Aachen 205: Liotas School, Bad Neuheim; Pool at Ubach-Palmburg 209, 210: St Antonius Hospital: Training Centre, Aachen 209, 210
Schreiter, Johannes, 211-220, 226
Professor School of Decorative Arts, Frankfurt 212: Bremen Academy of Arts 212; Brotherhood of St John, Leutesdorff 212: Dedication Room, EKD, Berlin 216: Franciscan Church, Rothenburg 216: Juvenile Centre 216: Library, Medical College of St Bartholomew, Royal London Hospitals 217, 218: Limburgh Cathdral 215: Church of the Holy Ghost 217

The Painter in Glass 226-233

Buschulte, Wilhelm 226-227
Chapel of St Katharine's Hospital, Unna: Protestant Church, Worms: St Peter's Church, Aachen
Meistermann, Georg 228-232
Church of St Mary, Kôln-Kalk 232: Cupol of Church of St Gereon, Kôln: Glass wall West German Broadcasting House, Kôon 229: Horsemen of the Apocalypse, Old Town Hall, Wittlich 230, 231
von Stockhausen, Hans Gottfried 232, 233
Stuttgart Academy; taught in Pilchuck and Edinburgh 232: Liebfraneu Church, Koblenz: Church of St Maria zur Wiese, Soest - Tree of Jesse 233

JAPANESE GLASS TODAY 496-517

Tea Ceremony Screen: Rimpa Screen 498
First Stained Glass School; Tabata, Toyko 1913 500
Cho Kyong Hee, Korean artist 506
Kuramae Station on Obeda Subway Line, Tokyo 506
Kikuchi, Kenichi 506
School of Applied Arts in Paris: 'Column of Statue' 506
Loire, Gabriel 500
'Tower of Joy for Children' 48 panels, Museum of Modern Art, Hakone
Machi, Yoko 508, 509
Central St Martin's School of Art: 'The Bridge' Japan 2001 Exhibition Birmingham Art Gallery 509
Mikaide, Keiko 508
British influence: Royal Botanic Garden,

Edinburgh: 'Hydrosphere Solo' Aberdeen
Art Gallery
Nakamura, Hiroko 502, 503
Influenced by John Piper & Patrick Reyntiens
in Coventry: Chapel of the Missionary Sisters
of the Immaculate Conception: Juroku Bank
Building, Gifu: Mitsui Urban Hotel, Tokyo -
glass mural: Seki Country Club
Ogawa, Sanchi 500
Tokyo School of Fine Art: 'Watanai' Tokyo
National University of fine Arts & Music
Sato, Shimpei 501
San Francisco Academy of Art: 'Being 5,
Moon Reflection', Tateshima
Art Land Hotel: 'Red Beam-1' Glass Museum,
Langen, Germany
Schaffrath, Ludwig 500
Omija Railway Station, Kyoto
Takami, Toshio 500
'Flowers on a Sunny Coast'
Tsurumi, Yoshitomo 506, 507
Studied in Paris: 'Les Deux'
Yamamoto, Sachiko 504, 505
Studied Swansea College of Art: Women's
International Stained Glass Workshop: panel
'Play with Gold' Exhibition British Society
of Master Glass Painters; 'Tree of Life',
St Andrew's Church, Tokyo: 'Traces of Travel'
exhibited in Ireland: 'Nagayo wild Flower
Garden' 504, 505

Japanese Cut Glass 509

The Studio Glass Movement in Japan 510-517

Fujita, Kyohei 513-516
Worked in Venice and Murano 516
'Heian': 'Genji-tale': 'Water Vessel Old City':
'Genji-tale': 'Red and White Plum Blossom'
Iwata, Toshichi 510, 512, 513
'Shell Scent': vessel Museum of Modern Art,
Hokkaido
'Kobaka' Osaka Roay Hotel
Korin, Ogata 514
Two tiered Suzuribako

NEW IDEAS IN AUSTRALIA 462-495

The original source of stained glass was
offloaded from trading ships, and cut down
to suit the doors or windows.
Aldrete-Morris, Catherine 495
Glas Form
Bettison, Giles 482-485
Studied at the Canberra School of Art: 'Visia'
Vessels: 'Blue': 'Billet 13': 'Billet 24'
French, Leonard 466-472
Studied in Europe: 'Man in the Garden': 'Great
Hall' the National Gallery of Victoria 467, 468:
'From the Fire': 'The Ship': panels La Trobe
University; 47 windows Haileybury College,
Keyborough, Victoria 472
Gleeson, Bill 472
Introduced glass to the syllabus at the Royal
Melbourne Institute of Technology
Hirst, Brian 488, 490, 491
Mohash University, Sydney College of Art,
Canberra College of Art: 'Glass Now' Hakkado
Prize: Bowls

Langley, Warren 492-494
Australian Nurses War Memorial: 'Spirit of
Earth'; Mosman Swim Centre
Moje, Klaus 479, 481, 482
Studied and travelled widely, Royal College of
Art, London, Pilchuck in USA, & Rietveld
Academy, Amsterdam: 'Impact' Series:
'Floating Red'
Mount, Nick 486-489
Glass Funnels: Fishing Floats: 'Scent Bottle':
Group of 'Scent Bottles': 'Scent Bottles':
Decorated Glass Vessels
Nolan, Sir Sidney 480
'Landscape'
Prest, Cedar 476-478
Studied at Hornsey College of Art, London
with Patrick Reyntiens, and visited Germany:
Children's Library 477: Memorial Hospital Pain
Clinic, North Adelaide: Parks Community
Centre, Mansfield Park, Adelaide: St Peter's
Cathedral: St John's Church, Maitland:
Guildford Grammar School: St Michael's
Ukrainian Church
Zimmer, Klaus 472-475
Chisholm Institute of Technology now Monash
Univesity: Glass School Hadamer: inaugurated
seminar Workshops Craft Council of Australia:
influenced by Schaffrath and Schreiter:
window Luther's College, Croydon 'I saw Him':
Parliament House, Canberra: Dining Room the
Prime Minister's House: 'European Blue': 'The
Aborigines Red': St Michael's Uniting Church,
Melbourne: 'Southern Cross': 'The last
Changsha'

**NORTH AMERICAN ARCHITECTURAL
GLASS 400-447**

Chagall, Marc 402
rediscovery of early stained glass windows 404
dalle de verre 405
Elskus, Albinas 404, 405
taught at Parson's School of Design, New York
& Pilchuck: 'Metamorphosis'
Loire, Gabriel 403
First Presyterian Church, Stamford,
Connecticut
Loos, Adolf 403
'Ornament is Crime': 'Less is more' philosophy
'Percent for Art' programmes 404

Divine Geometry 406-415

Carpenter, Ed 406-411
University of California: studied with Patrick
Reyntiens: Justice Centre, Portland, Oregon
407: Transom windows Rockfeller Centre,
New York 408-9: 'Skygrass' 409: 'Light
Stream' 410: 'Springstar' Golden Springs
Industrial Park Los Angeles County 411
Sowers, Robert 404
Wilson, David 412-415
Central School of Arts & Crafts: To USA 1963:
Nations Road building, Atlanta, Georgia: 412:
Vagelos House, Peapack, New Jersey:
'Wavewall' Corning Corporation, New York
413: Hallway Hampshire House, New York
416: North East Corridor, Monorail Station

Newark Liberty Airport, New York & New Jersey
415: Stamford Court House 415

Passion for Paint 416-427

Lichtman, Linda 416-419
Massachusetts College of Art: studied with
Patrick Reytiens: 'Tree of Knowledge, Tree of
Light', Brookline Public Library, Massachusetts
416: 'Changes and Variations on the Theme
of Growth' 416: 'The City on River' 416:
'A Kind of blue-Green' 417: 'Totems of Light'
418-9:
Mollica, Peter 422-425
Travelled in Europe: published Stained Glass:
'Self Portrait's': Reading Room & Meeting
Room, Hollywood Branch Library, Portland,
Oregon 423: Northside Community Center,
San José,California: Window (daylight),
Millbrae Public Library, California 425
Quagliata, Narcissus 420
'Retorno al Cosmos', Mexico City:

Figures and Stories 428-439

Schaechter, Judith 434-437
'Haemophilia': 'Pale Oval': 'Wreck of the
Isabelle A': 'Bigtop Flophouse Bedspin':
'Speech Balloon': 'Rejects'
Thompson, Cappy 426-433
European Mythology and Fables: 'Aesop's
Fables': 'The Fox and the Grapes':
'The Lion and the Mouse'; 'The North Wind
and the Sun': 'The Milkmaid and her Pail'
427: 'Muses Bestowing Blessings on the
Pacific Northwest' Medina, Washington:
'Gathering Light' Tacoma, Washington 429,
430, 431: 'I was dreaming of Spirit Animals...'
433: 'Dream of the Fisherman's Wife' 434

Creative Technologies 440-447

Haufschild, Lutz 444-447
Panel, Museum of Contemporary Glass Art,
Langen, Germany: 'The Wave': 'The Wave',
departure lounge, Vancouver International
Airport 445: 'Spectra Veil', Bata Shoe
Museum, Toronto: 'Light in Equipoise',
Potter Residence, Ottawa 446: 'Tauanus Sail',
Tauanustein, Germany: 'Blue Heart', private
collection, New Delhi, India: 'Question of the
Heart', Canadian Museum of Civilization,
Ottawa: 447
Knapp, Stephen 438-443
Kiln formed Glass Walls, Harmischfeger
Industries, Milwaukee, Wisconsin: 'Fragments
of Time', Splendour of the Seas ship, Royal
Caribbean Cruise Lines: 'Chicago's Treasures',
CNA Insurance Company, Chicago 438-439:
'Crystal Quilt', Love Library, University of
Nebraska, Lincoln: Kiln formed Glass Walls,
Congregation of St Agnes, Fond du Lac,
Wisconsin: 'Stories from Light - Told and
Untold - A Continous Journey', Women and
Babies Hospital, Lancaster, Pennsylvania: 'The
Christ Door', Solanus, Casey Center, Detroit

**PIONEERS OF STUDIO GLASS: THE
GREAT LEAP FORWARD 296-309**

Chihuly, Dale 305

Eisch, Erwin 300, 305
  glassmaking in Zweinsel: set up programme
  at Rhode Island School of Design
Gallé & Tiffany 300
Herman, Sam 308, 309
  Vase 1977: Vase 1978: Glass and Metal Lamp
Labino, Dominick 304
  Sculpture from 'Emergence' Series
Liposký, Marvin 306, 307
  Californian Loop Series #30: 'Soviet Series':
  'Four Seasons - Summer, Autumn, Winter,
  Spring'
Littleton, Harvey 300-303
  'Four Seasons': 'Rose Opal Combination C
  Form': 'Red-Blue Sliced Descending Form':
  'Opalescent Red Crown'
Leafgreen, Harvey 300
Wittmann, Otto 300

POST IMPRESSIONISTS IN GLASS 104-139

Bazaine, Jean 119, 120,121
  L'Gare Maritime': Baptistery at Audin-court:
  'Untitled': 'Finistère':
Braque, Georges 110, 112, 114-115
  'Ocean': 'L'Oiseau' window Foundation
  Maeght, St Paul-de-Vence:
Chagall, Marc 110, 124-127
  Chichester Cathedral window; detail of the
  window; 'Mother and Child': 'Crucifixion':
  'Horse and Rider' Tudesley Church in Kent:
  'David and the Angel': 'detail King David
  playing the harp', and East Window,
  Fraumünster Church, Zurich
Couturier, Father Marie-Alain 110
  helped Matisse with windows in the Chapel of
  the Rosary in Vence: invited Léger, Rouault, and
  Chagall - windows for 'Notre-Dame-de-Toute-
  Grace' 1937-43
Denis, Maurice 107, 108, 135
  Exhibition - paintings, sculpture & metal work
  for 'Village Français': window, Church of Notre
  Dame, Le Raincy, Ile de France
Le Corbusier, Charles-Edwouard Jeanneret 136-139
  Chapel Notre Dame de Haut, Ronchamp,
  Interior of Chapel 138: 'Poémes L'Angle droit':
  detail of recessed window 139
Léger, Fernand 110, 111, 115, 116
  'Nature morte au parapluie': Untitled window
  Audincourt Church, Besançon 115: exterior
  views of the Church of Notre-Dame-de-Toute-
  Grace 111
Malraux, André 107
  Ministry of Culture: International Exhibition of
  Decorative & Industrial Arts' Paris 1923 107
Manessier, Alfred 116, 117, 118, 120
  'Le Port': 'Les Champs au bord de Mer': 'La
  Passion': 'Pentecost', Church of St Sépulchre
  118: windows in Cathedral of St Nicholas,
  Friburg, Switzerland: 6 windows in Parish
  Church of Les Bréseux, Doubs
Matisse, Henri 128-134
  'Still Life with Fruit': Chapel of The Rosary,
  designs & exterior detail: 'Composition La
  Croix Rouge': 'la Dance': 'River of Life': 'River
  of Life' inteior of nursery school at Le Cateau:
  Chapelle de Rosaire, Vence, France; interior of

the Chapelle du Rosaire
Perret, Auguste 134
  built Church in Paris Notre Dame de Raincy
Ronault, Georges, 112, 113
  'Amazon': 'Christ'; 'Christ of the Passion',
  Church of Notre-Dame-de-Toute-Grace, Assy
Simon, Brigitte 116
  'The Empty Tomb'
Ubac, Raoul 122, 123
  'La Lampe': 'Ardoise': windows for Nevers
  Cathedral
Villon, Jacques 108, 109
  'Londres', 'Paysage',, 'L'arrivée des Nageurs',
  windows in Metz Cathedral

'ROCK-STAR' OF GLASS (THE) 310-335

Chihuly, Dale 310-335
  Born in Tacoma, Washington, attended the
  University of Washington; Rhode Island School
  of Design, Providence, Rhode Island; visited
  Murano:
  'Cadmium Yellow Venetian with Flower':
  'Niijimia Floats': 'Crimson Lake Venetian':
  'Navajo Blanket Cylinders': cylinder with Horse
  drawing: Pink Basket Set with Blue Lip Wrap:
  'Tabac Basket with Oxblood Spots': Seaforms
  318-319: Macchia Range bowls 320-321:
  soft cylinders 322, 323: Opalian Venetian:
  Cadmium Yellow Venetian with Flowers 324:
  'Emerald Green Ikebana with Stem' and Plum
  Ikebana with single Stem 326-7: Chandeliers:
  Coppe della Salute, Venice - Mercato del
  Pesce di Rialto, Venice 327-329: Palm House
  installation, Chicago: Niijama Floats, Franklin
  Park Conservatory, Columbus
Marioni, Dante 324 325
  'Red Trio with Yellow': 'Coloured Vessel
  Display' 325
Tagliapietra, Lino 324

Chihuly's Students: 332-335

Dailey, Dan 332
  Started the Glass Department, Massachusetts
  College of Art: 'every object tells a story':
  'Statuesque' (lamp): 'Le Vent': 'Anguish'
Glancy, Michael 334
  Studied jewellery at RISD: 'Beta Pictoris':
  'Arete-the-Virtue' (glass sculptures)
Toots, Mary Ann 335
  'Bushfire' from Fierra, del Fuego Series
Tré, Howard Ben 332-333
  Large scale casting and patinating glass with
  a layer of metal: 'First Vase', Washington DC,
  Smithsonian American Museum: 'Two'

SCANDIVIAN ARCHITECTURAL GLASS 160-197

Scandanavian glass became recognised after
World War II, with a 'hunger' for new forms of
expression. Norway organised a competition
for new glass for Stavangar Cathedral, the
winner was Victor Sparre, one of the largest
dalle de verre glass for Tromsdalan Church -
The Arctic Cathedral, Tromso.
Beskow, Bo 166-168, 170-177
  Art Academy in Stcokholm travelled to Rome,

Paris and Portugal and USA: glass in Studio:
The 'Creation' window, Skara Cathedral: Noah
and his Ark: 'Passion' window: The 'Apocalypse'
window in Skara Cathdral: detail of 'Death'
and 'Horseman' and 'the parable of the wise
and foolish virgins' in 'Apocalypse' window:
'Minotaur' and one of the 'Musicians Series':
Forseth, Einar 166-168
  Gotherburg Art School: glass mosaics - The
  Banqueting Hall, Stockhausen: 'Queen of the
  Mälaren': design in his studio: windows for
  Halmstad Church: Mosaics in the Golden Hall,
  Stockhausen Radhuset: glass & concrete
  windows for the Columbarium

Iceland

Breidfjord, Leifur 188-197
  Robert Burns Memorial Window, St Giles
  Cathdral, Edinburgh: 'Yearning for Flight',
  Keflavik Airport, Iceland: Life Drawings:
  Window for The National Library, Reykjavik:
  Exterior of Hallgrims Church at night: glass
  windows for Hallgrims Church: Interiors of the
  Supreme Court of Iceland: Glass Walls for the
  Engineer Savings Bank: detail of one of the
  glass walls for the Engineer Savings Bank:
  interior of Fetla and Hola Church: Cartoons
  and colour designs for Fetla and Hola Church
Helgadóttir, Gerdur 178-187
  Reykjavik and Florence: Moved to Paris and
  studied with the Russian Ossip Zadkine: Work
  exhibited in Paris: 'Firmament': windows
  Skalholt Church: design for windows and glass
  windows and detail of window Kopavogur
  Church: 'Untitled' 184: 'Composition' and
  'Untitled' 185: 'Meeting 1' 186: View of
  Exhibition:
Rodhe, Lennart 164, 165
  'Realities Nouvelles' Exhibition: detail of
  'Skogen': mural at the Elementary School,
  Angby:

WAY AHEAD (THE) 518-553

Colour in the Built Environment 522-532

Architectural Glass, 'Percent for Art' scheme 522
Allwood, Jackie 530, 531
  'Snowdrop glass vessel': Decanter, pattern
  of grasse, mouse stopper:
Bellhouse, Emily 520, 522, 528
  South Coast of England: 'Silent Yet Deadly'
  520: 'Washed Ashore': Coastal Currents Arts
  Festival 2003 528:
Bird-Jones, Chris 522,
  Cywaith Cymru (Art Work Wales): 'Clwydian
  Range':
Chihuly, Dale 526, 527
  'The Crystal Tower': 'The White Tower':
  'The Red Speers'
Layton, Peter & Moss, Simon 526
  'Crystal Stream'
Maestri, Kate 522
  Canopy above entrance to a London Office
Marioni, Dante 530
Maurer, Helen 530, 531
  Light Constructions - 'In the Green Room':
  'Set for Battle': Cave Painting

Pil-Yun, Ahn 524
    'A State of Flux' (daytime): 'A State of Flux'
    (nightime)
Reay-Young, Helga 530, 531, 533
    Installation at State Museum Gottingen: Glass
    Museum Werthwim: Bead Museum, Prescott,
    Arizona: Society of Glass Bead Makers (SGB):
    'Breaking the Spell': 'Continuity': 'one Tree
    Hill', 'Serendipity': 'The importance of light':
    'Memories'
Shan-Sheng, Shan 525
    Dancing Ribbons, the Main Entrance of the
    International Finance Centre, with details
Tagliapietra, Lino 530
Tré, Howard Ben 526
Whistler, Lawrence 531
Wolff, Ann 532
    Details of her etched and sandblasted work 532

Collaboration & Support 533-553

Bird-Jones, Chris 534, 538, 539, 540
    'From dark places': Detail installation -
    dichroic glass at Y Capel, Llangollen
Baden-Fuller, Kate 544
    Etched circular window
Bender, Rodney 549, 550
    Upper corridor - Wales Millenium Centre:
    structured glass blocks - Wales Millenium
    Centre: glass from Uzan's design
Boissel, Thierry 550, 551
    Interior of Neubiberg Church: Glass Neubiberg
    Church: detail textured glass, Neubiberg
    Church: 'Birds window', St Francis Church,
    Villengen Schweningen
Einarsdóttir, Sigrún 540, 541
    Shop: examples of her work
Ewart, Julian 544
    'Queen Esther' panel with programmed lighting
Ferrell, Ginger 555
    'Tears of the albatross': 'Beautiful Bjork':
    'Round Cedar'- Arts & Crafts House, Merton
Finn, Ben 545,
    'Olympian Birth'
Glass lamps-students National College
of Art & Design, Dublin 542
Hitomi, Chiho 540
    'Whisper': Bombay Sapphire Prize - Glass
    Chandelier:
Mackey, Mary 534, 536
    'The sky behind'
Moje-Wohlgemuth, Isgard 530
    glass jewellery
Pax, Hildegard 547
    Room divider, Hotel Lobby, Sheraton Hotel,
    Frankfurt Airport and details: Panels for White
    & Case reception area
Sandersky, Deborah 544
    Glass mural using printed photo collage
Sandford, Holly 535, 536, 538
    'Stone Windows': 'Residential'
Shaw, Kathy 546
    'Karakia - Maori Prayer': 'Eli's Tree'
Swash, Caroline 552, 553
    'Traveller's Flowers': 'Carved Spoons' images
    based on Icelandic iconography:

'Green Arbour' Library window - The Multiple
    Sclerosis Headquarters, Kilburn, London
Yamauchi, Yoshi 539
    'Untitled 2004': 'Untitled 2004'
Young, Peter, 542
    'Sure enough, the duck'
Whistler, Lawrence 531
Uzan, Jorn 550
    design glass made by Rodney Bender

Glass Artists

A

Aalto, Alvar 116, 144, 145
Ainslie, Chris 388-339
Albers, Joseph 100-103
Aldrete-Morris, Catherine 494, 495
Allwood, Jackie 530-531
Ardel, Atle 163
Argy-Rousseau, Joseph-Gabriel 74-77

B

Barovier, Ercole 155-156
Bazaine, Jean 106, 116, 118-21
Beleschenko, Alex 344-349, 370
Bellhouse, Emily 520, 522, 528
Bender, Rodney 370, 549
Bernard, Oliver 85, 87
Beanner, Walther 202
Ben Tré, Howard 332-333, 526
Beskow, Bo 164, 169-177
Bettison, Giles 482-485
Bianconi, Fulvio 155-156, 158
Bilek, Ilja 460
Bird-Jones, Chris 379, 522, 534, 538-540
Boissel, Thierry 350-351
Bouraine, Marcel 74, 77
Bradley, Ray 282-285
Brancomi, Fulvio 155-158
Brandt, Edgar 68
Brandt, Marianne 96, 98
Braque, Georges 90, 91, 110, 114
Breidfjord, Leifur 188-197
Brocklehurst, Keith 378
Bruce, Jane 375
Burne-Jones, Edward 4-6
Buschulte, Wilhelm 226-227
Buzzi, Tomaso 154
Brychtová, Jaroslava 452, 456, 455-458

C

Carpenter, Ed 406-411
Cardross, Harry 340, 343
Cézanne, Paul 91, 96
Chagall, Marc 110, 124-127, 402, 403
Chasling, Scott 494, 495
Chihuly, Dale 156, 305, 312-332, 526-527
Child, Alfred E. 12
Cho, Kyong Hee 506
Christian, Désiré 32
Clarke, Brian 350-358
Clarke, Geoffrey 238, 270
Clarke, Harry 13

Clos, Henri 28
Coleman, Katharine 392-393
Cook, John 374-378
Coombs, Deborah 534
Couturier, Father Marie-Alain 110, 126, 132, 134, 136
Cowdy, Harry 375
Cummings, Keith 379-380, 381, 396
Cyrén, Gunnar 150, 153

D

Dailey, Dan 332-333
Daum Fréres 28-29, 68-69
Delatte, André 74, 79
Denis, Maurice 107-108, 134, 135
Denison-Pender, James 388, 399
Dodson, Marigold 288-289
Donlin, Martin 366-369, 370
Dresser, Dr. Christopher 36
Dreiser, Peter 388-392

E

Eisch, Erwin 300, 305, 313
Einarsdóttir, Sigrún 540-541, 544
Eiske, George Grant 118-119
Elskus, Albinas 404, 405
Ewart, Julian 544-545

F

Fairs, Tom 277, 280, 281
Farquharson, W. Clyne 80-81
Feininger, Lyonel 92, 93, 94
Ferrell, Ginger 534-535, 537
Fisher, Alfred, E. 276-277
Fladgate, Deborah 378, 380
Flavell Dr. Ray 379
Forseth, Einar 164, 166-168
Forsyth, Moira & Gordon 80
French, Leonard 466-472
Fuga, Anzolo 156, 159
Fujita, Kyohei 510, 513-517

G

Gallé, Emile 22-29, 32, 53, 68, 300
Gate, Simon 148, 150
Geddes, Wilhelmina 12
Geron, Jean Marie 526
Ghosh, Amal 274
Gilliam, Tony 388
Glancy, Michael 334
Goupy, Marcel 74, 78
Gleeson, Bill 472

Greene, Charles Sumner 18
Greene, Henry Mather 18
Gropius, Walter 92, 94, 145

H

Hald, Edward 148, 149, 150
Harris, Josephine 388
Haufschild, Lutz 444-447, 541
Hayashi,Wataru 509
Hayward, John 238-241
Helgadóttir, Gerdur 162, 178-187
Herman, Sam 308-309, 374, 375, 378, 416, 478
Hirst, Brian 488, 490-491
Hiscott, Amber 366-67, 370
Hitomi, Chiho 540, 542
Hoffmann, Josef 35
Hollaway, Anthony 281
Hone, Evie 12
Huré, Marguerite 134
Hubbard, Elbert 14
Hunter, Dard 14
Hutton, John 238, 286-293, 388

I

Ingrand Paula and Max 85, 87
Itten, Johannes 94
Iwata, Toshichi 510-513

J

Jones, Catrin 364-365, 370
Jones, Graham 359-363, 370
Jouve, Paul 85, 87

K

Kagami, Mitsuru 509
Kaniyangka, Nita 480
Karel, Marian 458, 460
Kikuchi, Kenichi 506
Kinnaird, Alison 392, 394-395, 396
Klos, Joachim 224-226
Knox, Archibald 6-7
Koloman, Moser 35
Korin, Ogata 514
Kozo, Kagami 509
Klee, Paul & Felix 94
Knapp, Stephen 440-443
Knight, Dame Laura 80
Koepping, Karl 32-33

L

Labino, Dominick 300, 304
La Farge, John 41-43

Lalique, René 66, 70-74, 76, 84, 85
Lane, Danny 386-387
Langley, Warren 488, 492-494
Layton, Peter 338, 378, 379, 382-385, 526
Lawson, John 340-343
Le Corbusier, Charles-Edouard-Jeanneret 136-139
Lee, Lawrence 238, 266-268, 370
Leafgreen, Harvey 300
Leckie, Audrey 388, 389
Léger, Fernand 110, 111, 115-116, 238
Lewis, Tim 209, 370, 371, 504
Lichtman, Linda 416-421
Libenský, Stanislav 374, 452-458
Lindstrand, Vicke 148
Lipofsky, Marrin 298, 305, 306-307
Littleton, Harvey 299, 300-303, 313, 324, 374
Lloyd Wright, Frank 14-18, 406
Loire, Gabriel 403, 500
Loos, Adolf 403
Luce, Jean 74, 77
Lundin, Ingeborg 150, 151

M

MacDonald, Margaret, 37, 57
Machi, Yoko 508, 509
Mackey, Mary 534, 536
Maestri, Kate 522, 523
Majorelle, Louis 68
Malraux, André 107
Manessier, Alfred 116-118, 120, 230
Marinot, Maurice 74, 78-79, 334
Marioni, Dante 324-325, 530
Martins, Dino 155, 158
Matisse, Henri 110, 128-134
Maurer, Helen 528-529
Meech, Annette 375
Meistermann, Georg 228-231, 370
Mikaick, Keiko 508
Moholy-Nagy, Laszlo 96, 98, 99
Moje, Klaus 478, 479, 480, 482
Mollica, Peter 422-427
Mondrian, Piet 92, 412
Morris, William 2-7, 9, 14, 94, 334
Mount, Nick 486-489
Muller Fréres 29-31
Murray, Keith 80-81

N

Nakamura, Hiroko 502, 503
Nampitjin, Millie Skeen 480
Nash, Paul 80
New, Keith 238, 271-275
Newell, Steven 375, 376, 377
Newill, Mary 10-11
Nolan, Sir Sidney 480

O

Ogawa, Sanchi 500
Öhrström, Edvin 150
Okada, Saburosuke 510

P

Palmquist, Sven 150-151
Parsons, Karl 10, 11
Pax, Hildegard 547, 548
Peace, David 292-293, 388
Pennell, Ronald 394, 396
Perret, Auguste 134

Pil-Yun, Ahn 524-525
Piper, John 236, 249-256, 258, 359, 502
Pliva, Oldrich 458, 461
Poensgen, Jochem 218-223, 226, 228, 370, 444
Poli, Flavio 156, 158
Powell, Harry 6-7
Purser, Sarah 12
Prest, Cedar 476-478

Q

Quagliata, Narcissus 422

R

Rainey, Clifford 387
Ravilious, Eric 80
Reay-Young, Helga 530, 531, 533, 534
Reekie, David 396
Reid, Colin 378, 396-398
Rennie Mackintosh, Charles 34, 37
Reyntiens, Patrick 128, 188, 208, 211, 232, 236, 238, 258, 259, 260, 265, 359, 406, 416, 473, 502
Rodhe, Lennart 164, 165
Rouault, Georges 110, 112-113
Rushbrooke, Karlin 378, 380
Rytkönen, Martii 150, 152

S

Sabóková, Gizela 458, 460
Sasa, Fumio 509
Sandersky, Deborah 544
Sandford, Holly 535-536, 538
Sarpaneva, Timo 145, 146
Sato, Junshiro 509
Sato, Mariko 509
Sato, Shimpei 501
Scala, Anthony 542
Scarpa, Carlo 154, 155
Schaechter, Judith 435-439
Schneckendorf, Josef Emil 32
Schreiter, Johannes 203, 209, 210-218, 226, 228, 350, 370, 405, 444, 473, 501, 541
Schaffrath, Ludwig 204-208, 226, 228, 350, 370, 405, 406, 422, 473, 500
Scott, Sally 292-293, 388
Shan-Sheng, Shan 524, 525
Shaw, Kathy 546
Simon, Brigitte 134
Skarre, Jorgen 163
Smyth, Ann 372, 373
Solven, Pauline 374, 375
Sowers, Robert 404
Sparre, Victor 163
Spence, Basil 168, 237-286
Stankard, Paul 530-531, 540
Sterns, Thomas 142, 159
Sumner, Alan 466
Sundberg, Per B. 150, 152
Sutherland, Graham 80
Swash, Caroline 552-553, 544

T

Tagliopietra, Lino 324, 486, 530
Takami, Toshio 500, 501, 502
Tiffany, Louis Comfort 41-42
Tiffany Blown Glass 52-57
Tiffany Lamps 58-63

Tiffany Stained Glass Windows 44-51
Thomas, Brian 245-247
Thompson, Cappy 428-434
Thorn-Prikker, Jan 202
Traherne, Margaret 238, 276-278
Trnka, Pavel 458, 459
Tsurumi, Yoshitomo 506, 507
Tookey, Fleur 375
Tooley, Stan 375

U

Ubac, Raoul 122-123

V

Vachtová, Dana 458, 460
Vallien, Bertil 150, 153, 526
Venini 154, 155-157
Villon, Jacques 108, 109
van der Velde, Henry 92
van Doesberg, Theo 92, 93, 98
von Stockhausen, Hans Gottfried 232, 233

W

Wagenfeld, Wilhelm 95-96
Waugh, Sidney 82, 83, 299
Webb, Christopher 242-244, 245
Webb, Philip 6
Wendling, Anton 204, 206
Whall, Christopher 8-10, 12
Williams, Christopher 375
Whistler, Simon 388, 390-391
Wilson, David 412-415
Wirkkala, Tapio 145
Wittman, Otto 300
Witwe, Johann Loetz 34-35, 53, 451
Whistler, Lawrence 293-295, 531
Wolff, Ann 532
Wonaeamirri, Pedro 480

Y

Yamauchi, Yoshi 506, 539
Yamamoto, Sachiko 370, 504-505
Yoshida, Takeo 509
Young, Peter 542
Younger, Alan 268-269, 340

Z

Zimmer, Klaus 472-475, 480
Zynsky, Mary Ann (Toots) 334, 335